After Modernity?

After Modernity?

*Secularity, Globalization, and the
Re-enchantment of the World*

JAMES K. A. SMITH
editor

BAYLOR UNIVERSITY PRESS

Cover Design: Andrew Brozyna, ajbdesign

Library of Congress Cataloging-in-Publication Data

After modernity? : secularity, globalization, and the re-enchantment of the world / edited by James K.A. Smith.
    p. cm.
  Includes bibliographical references and index.
  ISBN 978-1-60258-068-8 (pbk. : alk. paper)
  1. Globalization--Religious aspects--Christianity--Congresses. 2. Secularization--Congresses. I. Smith, James K. A., 1970-

  BR115.G59W43 2008
  261--dc22
                          2008010624

Table of Contents

❖

Acknowledgments

This book represents some of the fruit of a national research conference that was generously funded by the Lilly Fellows Program in Humanities and the Arts at Valparaiso University in 2005. Staged as the fifth annual national research conference sponsored by the Lilly Fellows Program, their support provided a unique opportunity to bring together an international and interdisciplinary team of scholars to engage complex and challenging phenomena at the intersection of globalization and secularization in a post-9/11 context. I would like to thank the board of the Lilly Fellows Program for providing the grant that made the conference possible. The conference was, for me, a unique intellectual experience of rich, honest interdisciplinary conversation—bringing together folks (theologian and economists, art historians and geographers) who don't often talk to each other, and more often than not, tend to talk past one another. While conversation at the conference was at times animated, it was also conducted in a spirit of charity and humble listening. Overall, I think the conference was a singular opportunity for scholars from a wide array of disciplines to be together in the same room, in a charitable environment that encouraged openness, and to explore differences and disagreements in a positive way (some of the exchanges between economists and theologians were the most memorable!). I would like to thank the many presenters at the conference for their contributions and for taking part in lively discussions that will bear fruit beyond this book. (For the complete conference program, visit http://www.calvin.edu/scs/lfp.) Special thanks to our plenary speakers—Peter Berger, Graham Ward, and Iain Wallace—for setting the stage for our conversation.

The conference, which took place November 10–12, 2005, was managed by the Seminars in Christian Scholarship at Calvin College, of which I was then director. I am especially grateful to the outstanding staff of the Seminars program, Alysha Chadderdon and Marilyn Rottman, for consistently conjoining professional expertise in logistics with the warmth of Christian hospitality, providing just the right space for intellectual conversation.

I am grateful to John Steven Paul, program director, for his support of both the conference and this ensuing book project. I have also appreciated working with the authors whose work is collected here. I am grateful for their persistence, promptness—and patience! Thanks, too, to those presenters whose work is not collected here but has already begun to appear in other venues. This book is just a slice of the fruit of the conference.

I would like to say a special thank you to the cadre of economists who participated in the conference, both as presenters and participants. Given some of the theoretical frameworks hovering in the background of many papers, the economists sometimes found themselves swimming against the current. But I was impressed by their exemplary engagement with opposing viewpoints and their patient but unapologetic replies to criticisms. In an era when, even in the academy, conversations tend to take place only in the safe and isolated environs of like-minded choirs and cabals, the economists modeled a kind of risky engagement that our toughest questions require. In particular, I would like to thank Dave Richardson not only for his unparalleled scholarly contributions to these issues, but for modeling this spirit, and for his constant encouragement both during conference planning and while pulling together this book. May his tribe increase.

An earlier version of chapter 2 was published in *New Blackfriars* 85 (2004): 212–38. My thanks to Fergus Kerr for permission to reprint it here. Portions of chapter 5 also appear in Lambert Zuidervaart, *Thinking Otherwise: Social Philosophy after Adorno* (Cambridge University Press, 2007). We are grateful to Cambridge University Press for permission to reprint that material here. An earlier version of chapter 7 appeared in *Studies in Christian Ethics* 19 (2006): 39–61. Thanks to editor Susan Parsons for permission to reprint a version of the article in this volume.

Part I

INTRODUCTION

Chapter 1

Secularity, Globalization, and the Re-enchantment of the World

James K. A. Smith

Religion in a Globalized World: Paradigms and Problems

Despite the confident prognostications of social scientists in the late nineteenth and twentieth centuries regarding the "withering" of religion and the inevitable secularization of the world, at the turn of the millennium talk of globalization and the march of modernity is inextricably linked with the phenomenon of religion.[1] In our *début de siecle* climate—in an "age of terror" and in the wake of September 11, 2001—much popular and journalistic attention has been given to the relationship and tension between globalization and religion. Much of this has focused on links between religion and violence, and especially the role of Islamic extremism or fundamentalism as its own kind of globalizing force, operating under the banner of antiglobalization.[2] But the "globalization and religion" conversation does not concern only certain forms of Islamic extremism. As the work of Philip Jenkins and others has pointed out, Christianity itself has been globalized in new ways. No longer a "Western" religion, the center of gravity of global Christianity has shifted to the southern hemisphere.[3]

This book, however, is not primarily interested in the globalization *of* religion, whether it be the explosive growth of Christianity in the global South or the creeping expansion of Islamic extremism in the majority world as well as the thriving metropolises of the West.[4] Rather, this collection takes up a third cluster of questions and issues found at the nexus of globalization and religion. In particular, we are interested in the links between globalization, capitalism, and secularization—and the valuations and permutations of "religion" (by no means monolithic) that attend this constellation. In addition, and conversely, this volume explores different religious—particularly Christian—evaluations of and responses to globalization.

It is important to note at the outset the slipperiness and polyvalence of a buzzword like "globalization." Its lexical plasticity is notorious. In its most benign sense, globalization simply refers to an integration of global networks across national borders—economic networks, primarily, but also networks of labor, information, and so on.[5] In more suspicious and critical formulations, globalization is simply the term of art for the oppression and exploitation that attend global capitalism.[6] To avoid any kind of simplification, we might extrapolate from a maxim of Edmund Husserl's phenomenology: just as Husserl points out that consciousness is always "consciousness *of* . . . ," so too globalization is always globalization *of . . . .*[7] The building of transnational networks of commerce, interaction and exchange is not an inherently negative phenomenon. Indeed, one could argue that the church's vision of catholicity is precisely a vision of a globalized community. The church was transnational before markets were. At issue, then, is not the phenomena of globalization as such, but rather what is being globalized and the forms that this globalization takes.

Here religious voices and questions take on a new significance when brought into conversation with globalization. In particular, two sets of questions are generated at the nexus of religion and globalization. The first set concerns how religion is positioned by the discourses and project of globalization. If globalization is tantamount to the globalization *of* capitalist and free-market organizations of commerce and exchange, and if this is the outworking of a logic of modernity, and modernity is driven by the logic of Enlightenment, then the creeping expansion of globalization should be tantamount to a globalization of the Enlightenment—and thus of the Enlightenment's account of religion's withering and shriveling. The distinctly modern pedigree of capitalism, and thus its affiliation with the Enlightenment, entails an expectation regarding the place and value of religion in a globalized world. In this way, the discourse of globalization is often attended by expectations regarding global *secularization*, yielding what has come to be known as the "secularization thesis."[8] According to this sociological predictive thesis, the gradual but steady growth of modern Enlightenment will roll back the superstition and mythology associated with religion. Agents who participate in the market that yields iPods and jet aircraft couldn't possibly cling to the magical world of religious belief. Progress in modernity would be the progress of rationalization, Weber suggested, which would mean a radical "dis-enchantment of the world" and thus a secularization of society.[9]

The secularization thesis, however, has fallen on hard times.[10] The prophetic prognostications of Weber and his ilk proved to be only the predictions of false prophets—with the interesting exception of Europe (though even that exception is contested).[11] The reevaluation and reassessment of the confidence placed in the secularization thesis has yielded a need to revise accounts of the relationship between the globalization of capitalism and technology, on the one hand, and religion on the other. What was expected to be the triumphant march of demythologizing modernity—exporting the mechanism of scientific rationality, technological progress, and economic growth—rolling back the superstition of religious belief has not come to pass.[12] Instead, we have seen the mechanisms of religious belief appropriating and taking up the fruit of modernity (televangelist global TV networks, Al-Qaeda Web sites, industries of religious marketing) for un- and antimodern ends.[13] But in this respect, one could wonder just who is appropriating whom: is it that the forces of religious belief are beating modernity with its own tool—akin to David slaying Goliath with Goliath's own sword? Or is it the case that the market and modernity are subtly winning this contest, transforming "religion" into a commodity that is commensurate with globalized capitalism?[14] Has the "religion" that has perdured into late modernity become merely the chaplain of the forces of globalization, marshaled for exercises in foreign policy that are primarily interested in the expansion of freedom in the form of free markets?[15] If the only religion that survives modernity is a religion wholly commensurate with and subservient to the market, might we—for the sake of religion—hope for a little *more* secularization? If these are the only gods left to us, might we not—even as the faithful—hope for another Nietzschean announcement of the death of such gods?[16]

So the first cluster of questions revolves around the theoretical expectations and descriptive evaluations of religion generated by the modern social sciences—particularly sociology, economics, anthropology, and political science—as well as historical accounts of modernity and the Enlightenment which spawn capitalism and hence globalization. In this first cluster we are interested in the connections between modernity, science, rationality, democracy, technology, and their expansion—and what that means, meant, or was expected to mean for the fate of religious identities and communities. As discussed further below, a core aspect of this book is an interrogation of globalization and secularization along these lines.

At the nexus of religion and globalization, there is also a second set of questions, which concern the shape of religious responses to and evaluations of globalization *as* the globalization of capitalist organization of commerce and exchange. If we take globalization to be largely synonymous with the expansion of global markets; increased deregulation; the deterritorialization of capital, enabling increased flow across and above the limits; and regulation of the nation-state, then just how do (or should) religious communities evaluate and respond to such phenomena? What concerns of justice are engendered by the phenomena related to globalization?[17] In what ways might globalization and global capitalism be its own "religion"?[18] In what ways might global, catholic religious traditions be alternatives to globalization, or alternative globalizations?[19]

The religious response to globalization is by no means monolithic. Some are largely positive, though not without critique.[20] Others are more cautious.[21] Still others are trenchantly critical.[22] Behind these responses to and evaluations of globalization are elemental questions about the commensurability of catholic Christian faith (or, for that matter, Islamic faith) with the philosophical anthropology operative behind capitalist organizations of commerce and exchange.[23] So the phenomena of globalization generate not only complex theoretical questions, but also on-the-ground questions of formation and discipleship. And given the pervasive presence and effects of globalization, it is imperative that religious communities and religious scholars engage both clusters of questions and problems related to globalization.

Religious Engagements with Globalization and Secularization: A Multidisciplinary Strategy

This book brings together an interdisciplinary team of scholars to engage both of these clusters of questions at the intersection of globalization and religion—growing out of a conference devoted to these questions held at Calvin College in Grand Rapids, Michigan, November 10–12, 2005.[24] At the heart of the project for the conference and ensuing book was a desire to bring together a multidisciplinary team necessary for engaging such a complex topic. If a fantastic analogy can be permitted, the diversity of our gathering called to mind the Council of Elrond. Just as at that strategic gathering in Rivendell, the pressing questions of secularity and globalization brought together, not a motley crew, but a wide spectrum of scholars who approach these questions from very different angles and with different interests: some came to these questions through the discourse of empire, others from social science discussions about the secularization thesis. Some approached the topic from ongoing discussions in global economics or economic geography, others from theological and philosophical challenges to the epistemology that undergirds the notion of the secular, still others as proponents of a secular theology. Some were interested in challenges and opportunities for the arts in a globalized world, others were concerned about matters of justice and considered the realities of globalization with suspicion.

In sum, this book brings together a constellation of scholars who would not normally cross paths. (I'll not press the analogy by suggesting which constituencies represent the elves, dwarves, and hobbits!) This presented an unprecedented opportunity for a conversation across a number of different boundaries and divisions. Now, like the Council of Elrond, we didn't expect all would be rosy: we all came with our suspicions and concerns. But a common quest was an occasion for charitable conversations so that, at the end, we came to value even those we might have perceived with suspicion as a Boromir.

In this book we are trying to hook together two themes which are not all that often engaged in tandem, but which I think ought to be: secularity and globalization. It is their conjunction that generates a unique set of questions. (In other words, the most important term in our title might be the "and.")

The Politics of Knowledge: Epistemology and Secularity

As noted above, for a century or more some version of the secularization thesis held sway: a distinctly modern, Enlightenment confidence that superstitions and self-incurred tutelage of religious tradition would gradually wither away, or at least have the good sense to stay out of the public sphere and only show itself on weekends. This would leave us with public spaces—especially universities and politics—where policy and debate were governed only by the sober wisdom of a Reason tethered to naturalistic science. And insofar as this steady march of secularity was supposed to be integrally linked to the growth and expansion of technology, industry, and commerce, we can identify the point of the "and" in our title: if globalization is the global expansion of a mode of life, production, and commerce that grew out of the machinations of modernity, then the global spread of market forces would also entail the global expansion of secularity. The market itself would become a force of secularization outside the West.

This book, as we've suggested, is a sign that this story didn't quite play itself out as expected. All kinds of evidence could be marshaled here, but for just a few examples one could point to the explosion of Christianity in the global South, the continued expansion of Islam (including militant forms of Islam, which attracts followers from the West as well), and the significant role played by evangelical Christianity in American politics. These phenomena, and more, represent on-the-ground counterevidence to the secularization thesis.

But it is also important to recognize that the secularization thesis suffered from serious theoretical challenges as well. In fact, as early as 1969, Peter Berger was already pointing out the chinks in its armor.[25] "Secularization consciousness," he pointed out in *Rumor of Angels*, "is not the absolute it presents itself as."[26] While at that time he still projected the process of secularization as "a cultural concomitant of modern industrial societies,"[27] he nevertheless called into question a totalitarian conception of the secular, noting that "there is scattered evidence that secularization may not be as all-embracing as some have thought, that the supernatural, banished from cognitive respectability by the intellectual authorities, may survive in hidden nooks and crannies of the culture."[28] In fact, already in 1969, Berger turned the tables on the triumphant purveyors by "relativizing the relativizers," as he put it: "the contemporary situation is not immune to relativizing analysis. . . . We may agree, say, that contemporary consciousness is incapable of conceiving of either angels or demons. We are still left with the question of whether, possibly, both angels and demons go on existing despite this incapacity of our contemporaries to conceive of them."[29]

Calling into question what we might call a secular fundamental-ism[30]—a secular*ism* that would shut down the confessional plurality of the public sphere—Berger turned the critical tools of sociology upon sociology itself, opening the space for a critique of prescriptive notions of secularization.[31]

Over the next several decades, such a principal critique of secu-larism and the secularization thesis would gain steam, such that today we have a number of very different schools of thought advo-cating a postsecular standpoint. Consider, for example:

- Jürgen Habermas' call for space for religion in public discourse as part of a "post-secular" paradigm.[32]
- George Weigel's similar critique of the poverty of secularism in Europe and a rejection of the secular thesis regarding the alleged "neutrality of worldviews."[33]
- Graham Ward and John Milbank's unveiling of secularity as a kind of quasi-theology, carving out space of confessional dis-course as its own critical theory.[34]
- Slavoj Žižek's retrieval of Paul and G. K. Chesterton as resources for a postsecular politics.[35]
- Jeffrey Stout's unhooking of liberalism and democracy from the wagon of secularism in *Democracy and Tradition*, reopen-ing the public sphere, as it were, to religious voices and iden-tities.[36]
- William Connolly's contestation of both theocracy and secular fundamentalism, calling for a pluralistic "asecular" or "post-secular" refashioning of the public sphere.[37]

If secularity or secularism as matters of policy and political doc-trine[38] itself has still survived these criticisms (as curious relics of a no-longer-sustainable epistemology), the secularization thesis has not, and one of the questions we might ask is whether there will be a trickle-down effect from this. A number of the contributions to this book can be located along this axis of questioning. If both secular-ism as a matter of policy and political doctrine and secularization as a sociological expectation are undergirded by a distinctly mod-ern, Enlightenment account of rationality as neutral, unbiased, and pristinely objective, then the postmodern critique of such modern notions of knowledge should entail criticisms of the sociological and political projects that grew out of this Enlightenment soil.[39] In other words, one effect of a postmodern critique of knowledge should be a postsecular construction of the public sphere (whether the sphere of the university, political discourse, etc.).

But here we can already identify a new worry: if there is such a trenchant critique of secularism, might we not worry that some sort of postmodern feudalism would like to rear its head? Wouldn't the collapse of secularity open the door for all sorts of theocracies and new Constantinian arrangements? As Graham Ward aptly remarks, "Even today it might be remarked that in certain countries of the world a good dose of secularism would break the repressive holds certain state-ratified religions have over people's lives."[40] A critique of modernity, secularity, and their globalization does not entail a romantic return to parochial medieval theocracy.

And so we are left to ask: is there a third way? My question is perhaps best articulated by William Connolly: "Is it . . . possible to refashion [or reject] secularism as a model of thinking, discourse, and public life without lapsing into the 'opposite' view that 'Christianity' or 'the Judeo-Christian tradition' [or Islam] must set the authoritative matrix of public life?"[41] What would a postsecular world look like? How would it impact the way we think about political discourse, policy formation, the production of art, and global exchange of resources? These are central questions taken up in the essays collected here.

The Re-enchantment of the World: Ontology and Secularity

This epistemological implication of the postmodern critique of Enlightenment notions of rationality—breaking open the spaces of the public and political sphere for religious voices and identities— finds an ontological analogue in the reenchantment of the world. Thus in a recent book, Graham Ward suggests that if we can speak about something like "postmodernity," one of its features is "the re-enchantment of the world."[42] This theme of reenchantment is invoked by many as a way of getting at the postsecular challenge to the flattened world bequeathed to us by a reductionistic secularism—a theme already broached by Peter Berger.[43] Such invocations of enchantment are not only coming from theological quarters. Even William Connolly calls on us to "cultivate those fugitive spaces of enchantment lodged between theistic faith and secular abstinence. For secular stories of disenchantment and theological nostalgia for a past when enchantment is alone thought to have been possible combine to squeeze out these alternative spaces of possibility."[44] In this respect, both theologian and atheist would be united in a postsecular resistance to the secular disenchantment of the world.

In fact, on this notion of reenchantment as an aspect of postsecularity, we can find a (perhaps) surprising convergence between a 1969 remark by Peter Berger and a 2005 claim made by Graham Ward. In *Rumor of Angels*, Berger noted, "It was only with the onset of secularization that the divine fullness began to recede, until the point was reached when the empirical sphere became both all-encompassing and perfectly closed in upon itself."[45] But Berger goes on to note that while secularism might tell this story about this world, *this does not make it so*. We might say that Ward, in his recent book, *Cultural Transformation and Religious Practice*, extends this critical point by noting that "secularity does not ontologically secure the world as independent of God."[46] And indeed, the burden of Ward's earlier book, *Cities of God*, was to unveil the secular disenchantment of the world *as a story*, and to offer an alternative narration of a "sacramental worldview."[47] Despite its over-reaching claims to be the "value-free" description of "the way things are," the secularist disenchantment of the world is a particular narration of the world that is contestable. In other words, the secular story about the world—and human beings, and our relationships—is just that: a story. To resist it, then, requires the imagination to think the world otherwise. It might require, in other words, that even our theorizing be "fantastic." Reenchantment requires a kind of theorizing that is imaginative—which is not constrained by the rules and regulations imposed by the "plausibility structures" of secular modernity (which are themselves relative).

Here, Tolkien's little essay "On Fairy-Stories" seems instructive not only for the writer, but for the theorist. (It was Žižek who remarked that "only a devout Christian [like Tolkien] could have imagined such a magnificent pagan universe."[48]) Fantasy, Tolkien remarked, aspires to the "elvish craft" of "Enchantment."[49] Indeed, he suggests that this enchantment is that to which "all forms of human art" aspires. For "at the heart of many man-made stories of the elves lies," he says, "open or concealed, pure or unalloyed, the desire for a living, realized subcreative art which is inwardly wholly different from the great desire for self-centered power which is the mark of the mere Magician." And rather than being a gnostic means of escape, Tolkien asserts, "Fantasy is a natural human activity. It certainly does not destroy or even insult Reason; and it does not either blunt the appetite for, nor obscure the perception of, scientific verity. On the contrary, the keener and the clearer is the reason, the better fantasy will it make." Even social scientists, we might suggest, can be fantastic theorists. The work collected in this volume seeks to embody this kind of fantastic theory, resisting the flattened reductionism of "secular" theory and articulating an account of the world that is enchanted but not magical—in short, the world as creation.

The Re-enchantment of Place: The Geography of Globalization

Concerns of knowledge and metaphysics, epistemology and ontology, come together in a third core thread of this collection: the importance of geography as the "between" of culture and nature, of human construction and the givenness of "reality." Indeed, it has always seemed curious to me that, in many conversations of globalization, we don't often hear the voices of geographers.[50] How strange that discussions about the globe and the earth's resources would tend to ignore the disciplinary voice of geography. For as Janel Curry has written, geography focuses on the "life layer" of the earth and asks two essential questions that seem crucial to considerations of globalization: "Where are things located? and Why are they located where they are?"[51] Geography, she notes, "is unique among the social sciences in that it views humans and nature as an irreducible whole."[52] Geography recognizes the material conditions of culture in the fullest sense; it is also one of the quintessential "interdisciplinary" disciplines, what Iain Wallace describes as a "radically integrative discipline."[53]

Tolkien, inventing races of beings and imagining societies and communities, recognized that social beings are essentially geographical beings. Thus, the invention of hobbits also required the invention of Middle Earth—and where would we have been as children without those wonderful maps in *Lord of the Rings*? If geography is essential to this fantastic world, it must also be essential for a "fantastic" theoretical account of global realities. So the core geographical questions—Where are things located? and Why are they located where they are?—are elemental questions for any thinking about globalization, to be supplemented perhaps by one other question that recognizes the movement of things: Where do things go and why? Geography often seems to always embody a critical, almost prophetic edge in its answers to these questions. Geographers, for instance, can bring real weight to claims made in other quarters (I'm thinking of Deleuze and Guattari) that, despite a certain worldliness, the global expansion of market economies has in fact deterritorialized economy—unhooking it from the particularities of place and letting it float in quite unrestricted ways, such that all that is solid melts into the thin air of online shopping. In contrast, geography reminds us of the incarnational ontology of place. Geographers also speak to us of the texture and finitude of the globe upon which globalization takes place, reminding us that our dreams of production and consumption run up against issues of resources and sustainability. Despite the naturalism that nourishes secularization and the expansion of globalization, there is a strange paradox whereby global capitalism treats the globe's resources as if they were infinite and ethereal. In this respect, it is the enchanted sense of the world as creation that points out the imploding paradox of naturalism's disenchantment.

The chapters that follow bring together multidisciplinary voices grappling with a complex phenomenon, with a particular interest not in the globalization *of* religion, but more critically concerned with globalization *as* religion—and the Christian response to such phenomenon. Rather than being unified by a party line, the studies here find coherence in their common concern: to think Christianly—which is to say, somewhat fantastically—about the related phenomena of globalization and secularization. While the diagnoses and prescriptions differ, together the essays constitute an imaginative vision of reenchantment.

Part II

RETHINKING SECULARITY, SECULARIZATION, AND GLOBALIZATION

Chapter 2

The Gift of Ruling
Secularization and Political Authority

John Milbank

Today, it seems, all the ancient global realities have fallen under a kind of secular last judgment, heralded by the onset of a secular Armageddon. What is Islam, and is it violent and intolerant? What is Catholicism, and is it sexually hypocritical and sadistic? What is Christianity, and is it an irrational sect? What is Europe, and is it inherently bureaucratic and decadent? What is America, and is it inherently violent and expansionist? What is the West, and is it inherently greedy and imperialist?

In the midst of all this questioning, though, rather strangely, we do not seem to question the abstract ideas carried by the Western instances among these ancient realities. We still seem to believe in what we have transported, if not very much in the modes of transport. Thus, we do not often question the ideas of liberal democracy or of human rights, but assume rather that the actual collective realities that we have inherited may now be, in various ways, threatening the instantiation and further extension of these ideals. In the United States, many people lament the apparent start of a transformation of republic into empire and of democracy into the rule of manipulative elites. Less often do they ask whether the American modes of republic and democracy have of their very nature always nurtured both imperialism and oligarchy.

Rather, the story we tell ourselves is that since 1945 and even more since 1990, the dark demons of the past have been put to rout. Now, however, they are returning in the form of fundamentalist religion, which is producing both a dangerous mutation in Islam and a dangerous mutation in American conservatism. Once more, irrationalism is asserting itself. We should not be surprised: humans have always been massively prone to superstition, and enlightenment is history's late and most fragile bloom. Once again we must be vigilant—although the rationally illumined divide as they have done ever since the eighteenth century between advocacy of a vigilance through intensified deployment of regulatory economic and legal institutions (the Franco-German way) or else a military heroism whose ancient spirit liberalism must somehow keep alive against its own deepest inclinations (the new American way, much inspired by Leo Strauss and Carl Schmitt).

I do not believe this relatively comforting story. I do not want to deny that all our major inherited collective realities deserve to come up for judgment. They do. But I want to argue that that which seems above reproach—namely, liberal democracy—should now most of all come under our judging scrutiny.

Let us ask, first of all, why the West gave birth to liberalism? Not why the West and nowhere else, because this assumes that it was likely to arrive everywhere sooner or later. Rather we should ask why the West gave birth to anything so fantastically peculiar and unlikely. Liberalism is peculiar and unlikely because it proceeds by inventing a wholly artificial human being who has never really existed, and then pretending that we are all instances of such a species. This is the pure individual, thought of in abstraction from his or her gender, birth, associations, beliefs, and also, crucially, in equal abstraction from the religious or philosophical beliefs of the observer of this individual as to whether he is a creature made by God, or only material, or naturally evolved and so forth. Such an individual is not only asocial, he is also apsychological; his soul is in every way unspecified. To this blank entity one attaches "rights," which may be rights to freedom from fear or from material want. However, real historical individuals include heroes and ascetics, so even these attributions seem too substantive. The pure liberal individual, as Rousseau and Kant finally concluded, is rather the possessor of a free will—not a will determined to a good or even open to choosing this or that, but a will to will. The pure "nature" of this individual is his or her capacity to break with any given nature, even to will against oneself. Liberalism then imagines all social order to be either an artifice, the result of various contracts made between such individuals considered in the abstract (Hobbes and Locke) or else as the effect of the way such individuals through their imaginations fantastically project themselves into each other's lives (roughly the view of the Scottish Enlightenment).

Why did thinkers in the West, from Machiavelli, through Hobbes and Locke to Montesquieu, embark on such a seemingly unreal approach to human association? According to Pierre Manent, the French Catholic liberal political thinker, this was because of the so-called theologico-political problem bequeathed to it by Christianity.[1] The western Middle Ages inherited from Plato, Aristotle, and Cicero the idea that political life is natural, and that a civilized political life most of all fulfills human practical nature when we participate in the political process, make friends among the like-minded, and achieve a balanced economic independence exercised by magnanimity toward others. The highborn man in the city is a respected owner, only in so far as he is a judicious and generous giver. Christianity, however, posited above this natural political goal for human beings a supernatural end: for the righteous the life of heaven and the vision of God face-to-face. According to Manent these two goals, natural and supernatural, came into conflict in three different ways. First of all, Christianity was relatively indifferent to the mode of secular political order and its dignity: its job was simply the disciplining of sin and the ordering of things destined to pass away. Second, however, in a countervailing tendency, the superiority of the supernatural order could be used to justify interventions of the church in secular rule, and indeed the doctrine of the plenitudo potestatis of the pope legitimated a final overruling of kings in all matters and in all circumstances. Even if before 1300 or so, this overruling was not deemed to be coercive and was not founded on a papal claim to eminent dominium even over material things, after 1300 even these claims were made by some.[2]

Third, in Manent's opinion magnanimity and humility could not sit easily together: Western Christendom was divided in its admiration both for the prideful hero and the self-abnegating saint.[3]

On this view, then, there was nothing stable about medieval order. Kingdoms and city states, the realms of feudal warfare and trade, were always chomping at the bit, searching for more secular pasturage. However, nearly everyone remained Christian; they accepted the superiority of the supernatural, and therefore could not simply reassert the autonomy of politics from theological considerations and ecclesiastical control, without seeming to revert to paganism. Although pagan political participation, heroism, friendship, and magnanimity were still affirmed, they were considered, following Augustine, but "glittering vices" if not informed by supernatural humility, patience, forbearance, forgiveness, faith, hope, and charity.

This appears to leave the secular nowhere to go if it wishes to expand its breathing space: neither the order of nature, nor the order of grace. For just this reason, according to Manent, the secular was therefore forced to invent a third, artificial realm, built on a consideration not of humanity as it really is, nor as it might ideally become, but rather as it most generally and abstractedly and minimally might be considered. In this way no rival *ideal* to Christianity was proposed, even if an amoral nonevaluative rival to traditional theological reflection was nonetheless put forward. Henceforward the realm of politics was thought of not as the realization of a natural *telos*, nor as the abetting of a supernatural one, but simply as the most efficient coordination of competing wills, and their summation into one common, powerful collective will. From a theological point of view, the human individual was thus not here thought of as a creature, as a divine gift, as defined by his sharing-in and reflection-of, divine qualities of intellect, goodness, and glory, but rather as a bare being, existing univocally no more and no less than God taken as an abstract possibility and not as the creator. The only thing that now distinguished this bare existence from a blade of grass or an asteroid was its reflexive capacity for self-moving: its will, which might be equally for good or for evil.

Such a choice was now politically irrelevant. Or rather, as Manent says, if anything, there was, from Machiavelli through Hobbes to Montesquieu and Hegel, a bias toward the primacy of evil.[4] Respect for the good was now seen as the everyday unexceptional reality, but no longer as the normative defining one: that rather belonged to the exceptional suspension of normality in the moment of crisis that reveals a deeper truth and on that basis makes founding civil gestures. This truth emerges in circumstances of pure anarchy and of threat to the city or its rulers: then evil assumes priority precisely in the face of violence. All lies, subterfuges, and resorts to counterviolence then become justified. Manent is the only liberal I have read who admits that liberalism is at bottom Sadeian and Satanic. (This

seems strange for a Catholic, but then sometimes in French Catholicism a Catharist streak still lurks....)

What is impressive in Manent's genealogy is his insistence on
the contingency of Western liberalism. Even though he is a liberal, liberalism is not for him the sane, commonsense residue that
remains once one has sloughed off Gothic superstitions. Instead it is
rather shaped by the Christian Gothic crisis, and therefore remains
perpetually haunted by it.

Nonetheless, I believe that he does not push this approach far
enough. The odd thing about all his writings is that though his central theses revolve around religion and theology, he says very little about either. In particular, his treatment of the Middle Ages is
cursory, and I would argue in some crucial ways inaccurate. Let us
examine the three aspects of his theologico-political crisis.

The first two concern tensions between the natural and supernatural ends. Here Manent associates attempts to merge the two
with the Baroque, whereas to the contrary, if certainly the Baroque
sometimes attempted this, it was only trying to heal its own, not a
medieval wound. Overwhelmingly the research of historical theology in the twentieth century showed that the Middle Ages did not
tend to recognize a natural end that was actually, as opposed to formally, independent of the supernatural one. In political terms this
means that Manent wholly overstates ecclesiastical indifference to
the modes of secular rule: if political forms permitted within Christendom might be either aristocratic or monarchic with a certain
indifference according to relatively democratic circumstance, then
this was true of pagan thought also. But there was no indifference
to the substantive exercise of justice, or a "Lutheran" tolerance of
any enforced peace so long as it was formally peace. Manent is on
far surer ground when he stresses the perpetual interference of the
supernatural claims in those of the natural: from Augustine onward,
the church showed a desire to infuse secular practices of warfare,
punishment, trade, and feudal tenure with the exercise of mercy
and forbearance. Even in relation to the function of doing justice,
it is arguable that Christianity had an innovative impact: Oliver
O'Donovan plausibly contends that Paul for the first time made *judgment* (the provision of equity) the sole legitimating ground of government and no longer also the guarding of a terrain, which paganism
had always included. This renders rule purely active and donative

rather than reactive and defensive (another way in which Paul is more Nietzschean than Nietzsche). And if Christianity asked the state to attend more closely to mercy and justice, inversely its own household communities from the outset took over in part from the *polis* the political function of *paideia*: training in ultimate virtues.[5]

Moreover, salvation itself was not simply an individual matter in the patristic and medieval period: redemptive charity, for example, was a state pertaining between people, not simply a virtue exercised by an individual. The church itself was a complex multiple society and not simply the administrative machinery for the saving of souls into which it later tended to evolve. Hence to speak of secular and sacred concerns in this period can be to overlook the fact that monasteries were also farms, that the church saw to the upkeep of bridges which were at once crossing places and shrines to the Virgin, and that the laity often exercised economic, charitable, and festive functions in confraternities that were themselves units of the church as much as parishes, and therefore occupied no unambiguously secular space. Indeed the first freely shaped voluntary associations in the Christian West tended to be religious ones: the various religious and lay orders did not see constitution making (any more than canon law itself) as at variance with the idea that the constituted body was itself a divinely instituted gift and event of grace. Hence while indeed it is true that Christianity, unlike Judaism and Islam, enforces no detailed religious law, and even instills a law of charity beyond legality as command and restriction, this did not so clearly open up the space of the secular as is often thought. For the greater free play given to human social inventiveness opened by the displacing of the notion of divine law from the center of religious consciousness applied also or more within the religious sphere than within the sphere of worldly rule. In the latter case, Christianity more positioned what it regarded as the regrettably necessary use of coercion outside the redemptive sphere, yet even this was relative and qualified by degrees; the church also directly exercised some coercion, while the theological warrant for its just exercise even in secular instances was finally assistance to redemptive processes. Moreover, if the *sacerdotium* could also be coercive, the *regnum* could also exercise a positive pastoral concern in the material sphere, for the regnum fell at least half within the *ecclesia*.[6]

One should remember too that the supreme laymen, namely kings, were anointed, and assumed that they had thereby received a

Christic office in another aspect to that received by the priesthood: Christ being understood following the New Testament as fulfilling the offices of prophet, priest, and king.[7]

So to speak of the secular in the Middle Ages can be problematic. For this period the *Saeculum* was not a space but the time before the eschaton: certainly some concerns that were more worldly belonged more to this time, but this did not imply quite our sense of sheer indifference and neutrality as concerns religious matters when we speak of the secular. Indeed one can go further: temporal concerns existed in ontological contrast to eternal ones, but both were religious as falling under divine judgment. Manent writes too much as if the secular *in our sense* was frustrated during the Middle Ages, perpetually struggling to express itself, just waiting for the right language. But surely his own insights show that there is no secular in our sense outside liberalism, and that therefore before the invention of this discourse, there was nothing waiting to be articulated.[8] (The same point applies to the question of religious tolerance. Again this was not something frustrated in the Middle Ages, since it was as yet inconceivable as compatible with social and political order. Apart from Judaism—in which Christendom, like Islam, saw a complex and unique case—there were no other religious points of view seeking expression. Heresies were the work of minorities themselves seeking hegemony, and the forms they took often—as with Catharism—appeared to threaten not simply the church's authority, but the sanctity of the body, the significance of our compromised life in time, the offer of salvation to all, and the general mediation of the sacred in nature, image, word, and event.)

A direct way to instance this issue is Manent's example of the Italian city republic. He simply takes it for granted that they were always somewhat secular, neopagan realities, trying to escape church control because of an overwhelmingly preoccupation with the secular business of manufacture, trade, politics, and warfare. However, recent research (for example, by Augustine Thompson, OP) utterly belies this: the earlier Italian republics were not founded on pagan models, but were more like "confraternities of confraternities"; citizenship was liturgically linked to baptism (as the free-standing baptisteries of Italian cities still attest today) and participation in local church and civic life (often astonishingly and directly democratic in character) were so complexly interwoven as to be inseparable. Suspicion of the pope and even of the clergy does not here amount to secularity as Manent's modern conservative French piety appears to assume. Moreover, the emergence of a more pagan republicanism with Machiavelli coincided with an evolution of the city-states toward princedoms and local imperialism.[9]

We are starting then to see that liberalism is yet *more* contingent than Manent allows. It is not so clear after all that the Middle Ages contained an entirely irresolvable tension. If that were the case, one must then ask: why should *not* it have been possible to reassert the independence of pagan virtue? Manent's claim that this was impossible seems actually to concede that there was no real notion at this time of an entirely independent natural end. Besides, it is clear that some thinkers, notably Dante, did try to make this assertion. One can say perhaps that the attempt failed, but if it did then again this was because the notion of a substantive natural end valid in its own right could not yet easily find favor. (And one should also add that, as Dante's case shows, even such a purely natural end remained "religious").[10]

Finally, Manent can only insist on the incompatibility between magnanimity and humility by explicitly denying Aquinas' own opinion to the contrary.[11] In effect, Manent says that Christian virtue is the abject reception of divine gift; Aquinas, by contrast, says that we should recognize greatness of soul as the crucial divine gift—our sharing in God's generous rule. In possession of magnanimity, a man may even "deem himself worthy of great things," but only "in consideration of the gifts he holds from God." For ourselves, nevertheless, in humble consideration of our weakness we should not boast, because we are deluded if we think we are sure of the range of our powers or their stability. We should rather more strongly acknowledge magnanimity in others and its source in God, since we are its beneficiaries—since it helps to mediate divine grace to us. Aquinas therefore sees no problem in the Christianization of the notion of a governing and generous dispersal. If he does qualify the goodness of magnanimity, it is more in terms of charity than of humility: supreme ethical virtue is now not to be independent of the help and assistance of others (as Manent, to be fair, also notes, yet strangely fails to link to charity as friendship), and so friendship no longer ornaments magnanimity. Rather magnanimity promotes friendship.[12] So it is less that supernatural humility and natural magnanimity are in tension for Aquinas as that supernatural charity elevates and perfects natural (Aristotelian) friendship, stressing more its mutuality and its scope—downward beneath humanity and upward beyond him to God. (It is clear from the example of St. Francis and others that a new stress on "befriending creatures" was itself allied to transformed social practices.)

Within these perspectives, the invention of liberalism appears still more of a mystery. What can one suggest instead of Manent's thesis, or rather in modification of it? First of all, one should take more seriously Charles Péguy's view, which Manent mentions, that despite the bridges and the confraternities, the orders of chivalry and the at times semibaptized cults of erotic love, the medieval church did not adequately incarnate Christianity in the lay and material orders. Lay paths to salvation were seen as more perilous than clerical ones; increasingly the laity were removed (often understandably in the name of anticorruption, yet still with exclusive effect) from influence over specifically clerical and sacramental matters. It never quite worked out how, if contemplation is the highest end of human life, then leisure could be the basis of culture for every individual as well as for the whole of society. Nor did it question a theory/practice duality or come to the realization that work also can be contemplative. This was also a failure to grasp adequately its own reality; it took Chateaubriand, Hugo, Pugin, and Ruskin in the nineteenth century to point out that medieval contemplation was also the work of the church masons, the composers, and the poets. One can sum this up by saying that the Middle Ages never quite understood that if liturgy stands at the summit, then this is at once a humanly crafted work (involving in the end all of society, lay and clerical) and a divinely received gift; here we both shape and see.

Thus Christianity, one could argue beyond Manent, was thus not inherently prone to duality; rather its contingent modes of clerical development encouraged such duality.

A second point is linked to the first one. The more the clergy tended to see themselves as specialists in salvation and sacramental mediation, then the more the mediation of the transcendent by symbols, by nature, by society, and by reason was played down. Instead, the resources of scripture, tradition, hierarchy, sign, and sacrament started to be viewed as so many positive, given, revealed facts. In this perspective the clergy became like shadows of the wielders of physical force; they were now the quasi-literal exponents of quasi-literal circumstances.[13] This attitude went along with a new theology that stressed the inscrutability of the divine will. This was still a giving, generous will, but the gifts of material well-being or of salvation now tended less to be seen as disclosing to us the very inner life of the Trinity. In consequence, life on earth and the process of salvation started less to be seen as entering into this Trinitarian life.[14]

I think that in our current circumstances, it is here important not to overlook the fact that these new developments involved certain echoings of medieval Islam—even when paradoxically the aim was to escape just this influence. First of all, the tension between revealed word and Greek reason was far greater in Islam, which never arrived at the kind of synthesis achieved by Aquinas: indeed, the latter, like most thinkers in the Latin West, never saw himself as a philosopher in the way the great Arabic developers of Aristotle and neoplatonism did. Second, the Islamic world tended to resolve this tension in the political world by minimizing the role of natural equity: the Caliph's inscrutable word was law because he had been appointed by the inscrutable command of Allah. This voluntarist approach to political rule later became dominant in the West also, wherein it encouraged first papal and later royal absolutism.

It may seem to us that absolutism and liberalism are opposites, but in fact they spring from the same root, since they both have to do with the primacy of the will. In the early modern West, the competition of individual wills was only resolved by investing all political rule for the first time in a single sovereign will. This applies whether or not this will was seen as ruling by divine right or by contract or both, and whether it was seen as the will of the king or as the democratic will of the people. If this entire tendency both echoes Islam and foreshadows enlightenment, then that is less surprising when one remembers that Islam saw itself as a more final religion than Christianity, since it is more manifestly a universal monotheism, purged of the mysterious, mystical, and unfathomable (Trinity and Incarnation) and reinstating the practical order of law beyond the anarchy of love. A rational as well as pious stress on unity paradoxically promoted the arbitrariness of a willing source— since this is one of the strongest paradigms of unity—all the way from Mohammed to Montesquieu. Hence the whole line of thought that goes "Islam needs the enlightenment which Christendom has passed through" is somewhat shallow. In a certain sense one can say that, while Islam failed to engage with the Christian other and went into a decline, Christianity did engage with the Islamic other with multiple consequences and even the enlightenment (think of deism) is in some degree an upshot of a subtle "Islamification." (Certain *philosophes* spasmodically admired Islamic despots, just as they did the greater "rationality" of both Islam and Judaism.)[15]

So although Manent is right to stress the importance for liberalism of Machiavelli's neopagan cult of heroic virtue and the free but mortally doomed republic, he is wrong to ignore additional ecclesiastical and theological roots of liberalism. Even though the latter eventually enshrines secularity, the invention of an autonomous secular realm is perhaps mainly the paradoxical work of a certain kind of theology. This theology tends to lose sight of the fact that created being is only a gift, only exists as sharing in divine existence and as perpetually borrowing this existence. Instead, God is now idolatrously regarded as a kind of very big literal fact, who established other facts alongside himself and grants to these facts certain autonomies, certain areas of purely free decision—like a government decreeing that "normally" police cannot enter a private house or say what should go on there (the qualifier "normally" being also relevant to the nature of that kind of theology). The same norms of noninterference now pertain between individuals: already Duns Scotus substituted for the "common good" contractually agreed-upon conventions as sufficiently guaranteeing the civil peace.[16]

So liberalism is not witness to a kind of tragic truth or fanta-sized Manichean Christianity. Instead it witnesses the failure of the church regarding the laity and the growth of a somewhat positivist and formalist theology of divine power which itself helped to invent liberalism. Manent significantly ignores the echo of this theology in Hobbes and Locke, who were by no means yet purely secular thinkers, but more like Christian heresiarchs.[17]

But what is wrong with the liberalism that this theology engendered? Here I have nothing to add to the profundity of Manent, the chastened liberal.[18] With Manent let us note the following: Liberalism assumes the greater reality of evil over good; liberalism begins by suppressing the soul, or rather by assuming a gross psychology largely for the sake of administrative convenience. Liberalism, as the liberals Rousseau, Constant, and Tocqueville further diagnosed, in practice bifurcates the soul, by ensuring that it must submit to a tyranny of mere opinion, given that no opinion is for liberalism inherently right or wrong. As a result, it is perpetually swayed away from its own opinion, which remains elusive. Furthermore, as Montesquieu gleefully pointed out, under liberalism, since only what is generally represented is publicly valid, the spectacle of representing always dominates the supposedly represented people, ensuring that what they think is always already just what they are represented as thinking. Thus Tocqueville noted that in America, the freest society on earth, there is least of all public debate, and most of all tyranny of general mass opinion.[19] Instead of debate, as Manent also points out, one has competition, not just in the economic realm, but also in the cultural realm. In the absence of collective standards, or even a collective search for standards, the only standard is a regulated *agon* according to formalized procedures.

Beneath all of these woes of liberalism lurks one fundamental point: it lacks any extrahuman or any extranatural norm, which ensures that it revolves in an empty circle. As Manent says, for liberalism it is nature alone that gives, although she cannot command, cannot authorize, before the arrival of the state. Inversely, the sovereign state, or the effectively sovereign free market, can alone command, but it does not give: it only lays down boundaries or offers products or opportunities. Apparently it does not force us, but equally by the same token it provides us with nothing. The state legislates, the market exchanges on behalf of human nature which it represents. Yet without the state or market this human nature is not really entitled to be represented—therefore, representing and represented compose an empty hall of mirrors: in the middle, the soul of humanity is no longer there where we suppose it to be. And since there are no more souls with intrinsic destinies and purposes, no projects can be allowed: opinions cannot be permitted any influence. In theory, the church can offer to people its rule of charity and reconciliation; in practice, its scope for doing so is limited by the sovereign state. If, for example, the citizens of New York chose to run their city according to that liturgical order which its Gothic sky-scrapers so strangely intimate (indeed Manhattan constitutes one gigantic cathedral-castle), with a third of the days off per year for worship and feasting, neither state nor market would permit this. Liberalism allows apparent total diversity of choice; at the same time it is really a formal conspiracy to ensure that no choice can ever be significantly effective. Already Tocqueville noted that in the United States nothing really happens; its apparent dynamism conceals an extraordinary stasis. (And if change does occur, Americans tend quickly to deny that anything was ever any different; today, for example, if shops in the United States cease to stock a product, they will often deny that they ever have stocked it.)

Without souls or purposes, equally victim to mass manipulation, there is no longer anything for people to share. Under liberalism we no longer really meet each other; establish connections, yes, but truly make friends, almost never. There is no longer anyone to be friends with, as a hundred novelists have told us. Removed from society and friendship, liberal man focuses like Locke's Adam on dominating nature. But even here he does not escape empty circularity. His business with nature is to be guided by nature, by an accurate science of nature; this, however, is always incomplete, so he fantasizes complete stories of evolutionary genetics whose real truth is the undergirding of unlimited programs for self-alteration and the commodification of the biosphere. But even were the full story apparently known, how would the fact of evolutionary drift tell him how to modify himself, and how would he be sure this was a pure goalless drift unless a legitimation of random modification, obedient only to choice, was just what he secretly sought?

Manent, like many others, contrasts these phenomena with the antique pursuit of natural virtue, but he also contrasts them with the Augustinian idea of the rule of grace. Grace itself, for Augustine in the *Confessions*, was at once gift and rule: it "orders what it gives, gives what it orders." But just as the market divides purely contracted exchange from the realm of the free-giving that expects no return, so also the liberal state sunders ruling which gives nothing, but formally and disinterestedly mediates, from a free giving that can no longer command the other. Thereby though, both rule and gift are, from a Christian point of view, denatured. "Rule" for theology means "provide good order," and so to give something. Indeed for Augustine and Aquinas it means to give ruling itself—to give a share in ruling. When my mind rules my body, my body acquires the habit of self-control, so body also commands body. Similarly, political rule is for Aquinas communication, an imparting of power that must take place if it can, or else power falsely reserved will fester.[20] This means that every time one rules, one loses ruling in part, except in the sense of fully retaining the capacity for ruling, or even increasing it through its very exercise. Even in the case of God, God loses no rule because in utterly sharing it, God is sharing ruling, which is in itself a mode of sharing. Thus God the supreme ruler is within himself an imparting of the *Verbum* and *Donum*. But liberal sovereignty is not like this: because it gives nothing, it entirely reserves all power to itself as a sinister stagnant pond of pointless possibilities.

One can see the contrast by a brief illustration. Prior to 1548, the kings of France gave privileges of trade and manufacture to the city of Lyon after visiting it and first receiving tributes of presents and pageants from the city. The king, though superior, thereby acknowledged Lyon's share in his ruling; hence, when he delegated ruling power to the city he appropriately received something back from it. The rule of the traditional anointed king was therefore not just a giving. It could even be exercised as a mode of gift-exchange, in which to some extent the city obligated the monarch. But in the year 1548, Henry II decided that the partying had to stop: he stayed in Paris, received nothing, and merely issued the privileges as written documents. Lyon understood that what it had received it might also not have received, that it was no longer ruled, but commanded—that what it had received were no longer gifts but devices of state policy, manipulated by murderous *politiques*.[21]

In such modes the traditional ruler shared his sovereignty and thereby ruled. His sovereignty—whether that of medieval kings or Roman senators—was not just a lone impotent word prior to action; it was also already an action: the king really went to Lyon. In this way the sovereign was always already an executive. The executive forces that existed apart from him were multiple and beneath him, mediating his crowned rule. But under fully developed liberalism, starting with Montesquieu, the sovereign is apparently qualified at the center by the independent executive.[22] Is this really wise and benign? Not entirely; in some ways it is highly sinister. For the fact that the executive is now at the center confirms and does not qualify the monopoly of sovereign power at the center. For it confirms and further reveals that this sovereign commands and does not truly rule or give. Just because the sovereign word is absolute and empty, speaking only the freedom of the individual and its own freedom, none of its words ever mean anything, and therefore never devolve in action. For precisely this reason, the very sovereignty of the sovereign needs the supplementation of the executive. The latter must both interpret and act, although both aspects are bound in the circumstances to involve a certain individual arbitrariness. The modern executive does not share in ordering, and therefore what he or she gives is blind, banal, and empty, like a fact or a bare univocal existence.

From the outset—despite the protestations from different political wings of John Adams and Thomas Jefferson—the American division of powers was intended to balance out oligarchic forces and limit the power of the masses. The federalists, like Machiavelli, envisaged a republic sustaining its strength and freedom by the muted encouragement of internal agonisms. (For this reason Leo Strauss was wrong in ostensibly regarding the American principle as the opposite of the Machiavellian one, although the current actions of his many students now in power suggests that they may have had direct access to one of those opposite esoteric meanings of which he was so fond.)[23] It is not surprising then, that the republic defined as regulatively free should go on needing external enemies, nor that the sustaining of the internal agonism should seek out endless new frontiers. As with ancient Rome, as Augustine in effect diagnosed, the empire may have corrupted the republic, but it was still the republic, with its agonistic and defensive understanding of virtue, that generated the empire. (In any case talk of a specifically "republican empire" has a long pedigree in the United States—for example, in some writings of Walt Whitman.[24])

I am of course hinting at reasons that liberal democracy, with and not against its own nature, can turn internally oppressive and externally expansionist. But surely I am missing out on a whole dimension here regarding our present global troubles: the renewed role of religion. What has that to do with the historical course of liberalism?

Well, here again Manent is of considerable help. He argues, as we have seen, that liberals themselves have sooner or later become aware of the empty hall-of-mirrors factor that I have invoked. He gives the crucial example of the period in French thought after the French Revolution and before 1848. Suddenly, in that period, all political thought—conservative, liberal, and now socialist—became obsessively religious in one way or another.[25] Why this break with eighteenth-century norms? Manent argues that once Rousseau had defined the liberal individual as pure will, it became clear that this will is in excess either of the economic market (civil society) or the sovereign political state, precisely because these two will nothing, or else will each other in a futile circle. Suddenly what Rousseau's "general will" willed became the nation, history, society or culture. Because there was a certain new realization (especially in Tocqueville, and there are British and German parallels to this) that politics could not be about anything without the recognition of superhuman norms, the nation, history, and so forth started to be imbued with quasi-religious values. These were brutally deconstructed much later by Charles Péguy—who showed, for example, that the historical point of view suppresses the inexplicability (beyond a certain point) of every historical event by fantasizing an exhaustive circumstantial or causal account (one thinks of those admirable one-thousand-page *Annales* volumes ultimately inspired by Michelet whom Péguy partially had in mind) that idolatrously seems to mimic the mind of God. Likewise, Péguy saw that the very idea of sociology supposed that one had fantasized a kind of eternal normative society that displaced the function of God himself.[26]

Manent follows Péguy in dismissing the 'quasi-religions' of historicism, sociology, *Bildung*, and national development. However, his assumptions regarding the supposed Christian dilemma means that like Leo Strauss (who is a strong influence) but for somewhat different reasons, he continues to espouse both political liberalism and political economy as better than any possible alternative, even though, again as with Strauss, the antique *polis* with an élite in charge remains for him the irreplaceable guide to genuine human nature. To both Strauss and Manent one can here validly pose the question: does not this mean that one requires slavery (at least in some form) to reveal true human nature and sustain the pursuit of real excellence, not negative freedom alone? (And this may well be another esoteric view covertly entertained by the scions of the neo-Roman empire, north as well as south of the Potomac.) And why is a more widely dispersed pursuit of excellence not in principle possible? Why outside the sheltered bubble of the American campus is resignation to the mass pursuit of only negative freedom inevitable?

In addition, one can point out that, while Manent is refusing the quasi-religions of sociology and historicism, he is still embracing the quasi-religions of the Machiavellian Hobbesian republic and the Hobbesian-Lockean translation of theological voluntarism. By contrast, the new early nineteenth-century attention to society, history, and culture sometimes—as with Coleridge, the Oxford Movement, the Catholic Tübingen School, Chateaubriand, Lamennais, and Ballanche in France, and the French and English Christian socialists (Pierre Buchez, Ludlow, Ruskin, Thomas Hancock) involved a genuine recovery of Christianity that newly stressed both its links to poetic, not literal language, and the patristic idea of the church as a new kind of society.[27] These efforts were taken up again by Péguy, and setting to one side his often unjustifiable nationalism, it is hard to agree with Manent that he is confusing the mystical with the political. To the contrary, Manent is here misled by his own failure to see how grace in the Middle Ages already sought to sanctify the material realm; hence, he also fails to see that much nineteenth-century neo-Gothicism tried to take this process further. Christianity has gradually redefined virtue as existing primarily in the charitable exchange of gift throughout the cosmos and human society and between the creation and its maker. In this way the invocation of grace has democratized virtue and suggested a deepening embodiment of this virtue in the social order as a truly Christian project. Indeed without such an embodying, how can day-to-day life perpetually raise us up into the supernatural?

Already in the Middle Ages John Wyclif had said that, since God is One, whenever he gives his natural gifts, he also gives us his supernatural gift.[28] Wyclif, building on the more valid aspects of the Franciscan vision, thereby suggested that all ownership and rule is by grace (by borrowing from God) and that the justification of both property and government is communicative distribution: just as the priest receives the gift of dispensing the sacrament in order to induct others into the common life of grace, so also the property owner owns in order to induct others into the common material life and the ruler rules in order to induct others into the shared life of society.[29] This was a valid radicalization of Augustine, and it was a pity that Wyclif's Franciscan separation of "spiritual" ownership of the life of interior grace from material *dominium* reinstituted a duality that his theory of *dominium* by grace tended to negate. Because of this duality he was led into a doubtful Erastianism that disallowed any actual material ownership to the church.

The same duality sets in motion again the voluntarist logic of the other English Franciscan legacy that Wyclif in general resisted: if the church is too pure to own things, then owning is thereby downgraded and a drastically secular domain is encouraged.[30] By contrast, if owning is by grace, then a just appropriation ought to permit genuine private property, which is thereby not impure and can be ascribed (as by Aquinas) to Adam in paradise.[31] The same consideration applies also to a noncoercive ruling linked to a natural hierarchy of talents: such a rule also could be exercised by the unfallen Adam.

However, the later English thinkers John Fortescue (in the fifteenth century) and Richard Hooker (in the early seventeenth century) tended creatively to blend somewhat Wyclif-like notions of owning and ruling by grace and gift-giving, with Thomist notions of natural possession and natural hierarchy. This allowed them further to elaborate Aquinas' own synthesis of Aristotle and Augustine: there is a natural "ownership" based on use and a "political government" that existed before the fall, founded in sociability, differential endowments of ability and consensual association (the Whig element that Aquinas already adds to Aristotle). On the other hand, somewhat arbitrary property ownership and royal government are necessities consequent upon the Fall. Nevertheless they are both, for Fortescue and Hooker, founded in natural law, not the *ius gentium*, since they both perpetuate, in straitened circumstances, the prelapsarian goals of communication of material goods and the benefits of peaceful order. Likewise, the natural principle of tacit consent is perpetuated in the importance given by both thinkers to "parliaments, councils, and the like assemblies" (Hooker). Here then, a certain line of English political theory linked Germanic common-law principles of free association with a Latin and realist sense of intrinsic equity— avoiding the rationalist barbarism of nominalism and voluntarism. This same synthesis (with Thomist input) avoided also the ambiguity of Wyclif's Franciscan-derived spiritualism, along with his drift (albeit less marked than with Ockham) to a notion of subjective, not objective right. (This notion in Wyclif is linked to the idea both of a sheerly material pure possession and to a certain Pelagian independently human reception of grace. It is also completely linked to his very extreme, almost Platonic, mode of realism. Here the shared essence is so common and hypostasized that it leaves the individual *external* to the essence: so radically free and singular.)[32]

Wyclif's notions had politically radical consequences: the heir of a king *not* ruling by giving should be deposed; the heir of a property not dispensing its bounty should be ousted. In this scheme then, there was nothing merely otherworldly about the impact of grace, but these worldly consequences were a logical elaboration of Augustinian principles.

In many ways the nineteenth-century Christian socialists took up again the spirit of Wyclif; but whereas he had spoken of ruling and owning by receiving the divine gift and passing it on, they now spoke also of the worker as receiving the gift of craft and passing it on, and furthermore argued that all human ruling, owning, agriculture, and trading is a kind of working—not only a receiving of the gift of creation, but an extension of the divine creative process itself.[33] These thematics are in fact supremely well summed up by Péguy.[34]

But in all this, Manent seems only to discern a contamination of religion with an attempt to fill the empty heart of liberalism with the pseudo-religion of society, history, and culture. It is exactly here though that Christian socialism can contest his (very subtle and chastened) Christian liberalism. For if one argues that the Middle Ages already practiced and promoted a political rule by giving, a mode of freedom in which one gives what one commands, and commands what one gives, then there was no inherent Christian problem that needed the liberal invention of the empty negative freedom of a mythical individual. Grace *can* validly be incarnated as the exchange of gifts according to a mutual and continuous discovery of what should be given and what should be received. In shaping and constructing new gifts, we constantly rediscern our human teleology; here Manent also fails to see that Christianity had already historicized nature, since the fullness of human nature only arrived with the event of the God-man and is further unfolded in the life of the church. Christianity does not inevitably encourage liberal democracy, yet it always should encourage another mode of democracy, linked to the idea of the infallible presence of the Holy Spirit in the whole body of the church and by extension humanity across all times and places (since all human society in some degree foreshadows *ecclesia* and in this way always mediates some supernatural grace). Unlike liberal democracy, this Christian democracy has a hierarchic dimension: the transmission of the gift of truth across time, and the reservation of a nondemocratic educative sphere concerned with finding the truth, not ascertaining majority opinion. Without this sphere, democracy will not be able to debate about the truth, but will always be swayed by propaganda: mass representation will represent only itself, not the represented. Christian democracy, though, should also be Christian socialism—not the somewhat limited Christian democracy of so-called Christian-Democratic parties. (Or, one can say, it should be "Christian social democracy," and one should add that there can be Jewish and Islamic democracy also, and that in many parts of the world—France perhaps imminently—we shall need hybrids. I believe that within the more metaphysically realistic Platonic-Aristotelian and mystical versions of these three monotheisms, a large shared social ground can emerge.) It should not be resigned to the existence of poverty as a field for the reactive exercise of personal charity; instead it should see the eradication of poverty as the chance for the fuller arrival of a festive charitable exchange.

I have been writing intermittently about the nature of the nineteenth-century revival of religion and its links with the dilemmas of liberalism. In the later nineteenth century, though, the quasireligious nature of this tendency became more marked, and one had the paradox of secular religions: notably positivism and Marxist socialism. In the latter case, Marx perpetuated Rousseau's attempt to discover something substantive within the immanent terms of liberalism itself: the gap between individual and state could be closed, because the general productive will of all was to be identified with the productive will of each. This, however, elevates the emptiness and purposelessness and illusory transparency of production as such: this general pursuit of production is bound to result in tyranny and is only a variant, after all, of liberal political economy. Positivism was both more honest and more sinister: it promoted at once liberal science and the formal inescapability of the rule of the will, with indifference as to content. Inevitably, positivism mutated into fascism, Nazism, and Stalinism (which had a strong component of Georgian fascism: the Georgian *Khvost* carried out a purge of Jews and Leninists, and it was Hitler who broke his pact with Stalin, not vice versa). These phenomena were bizarrely both ultramodern and atavistically mystical. But this contradiction is only the extreme and most telling variant of the attempt to fill the empty heart of liberalism with society, culture, history, and so on. It is now an attempt made in strictly immanent terms consistent with liberalism itself: thus the new dark heart espoused is patently arbitrary, even to many of its espousers. If it is a myth to supplement formal emptiness, it is also itself a myth of apocalyptic emptiness—a myth of will, of the will to power, which reaches back into our animality under the banner of race.

Since 1945 and 1990, however, liberal democracy has been restored. So what has happened to the great endeavor from 1800 to 1865 to infuse psychic and bodily content into liberalism's hall of mirrors? The attempt seemed discredited by totalitarianism.

This is partly why, since 1970, we have seen the reinstatement of eighteenth-century modes of liberalism, of the pure, empty echo chamber—though it is also in part because the forced submission of capital to the demands of labor was creating a crisis of profitability. But is there any stability here, any Hegelian end of history in liberal mutual recognition of human rights? The answer is no, for several reasons. First of all, between 1945 and 1990 communism still existed. The stability of liberal democracy in the West partly depended upon its existence. Why? The answer is that fear of the communist alternative helped to keep capitalism reasonable; it tended to protect trade union rights and the welfare state. Also communism gave to the West a binding purpose: oppose the gigantomachy of totalitarian regimes.

After the collapse of communism we had exactly twelve short years of liberal democratic stability. It seems then that it cannot really bear its own hegemony. Without the external state socialist alternative to modify and negatively define it, the central *aporia* of liberalism tends to reappear: which is primary, the representing state or the represented market? In Europe, once again, the middle of society and history has been reinterpreted, this time as the project of Europe itself, whose nature and fate remain very uncertain. But once more we note a certain neo-Gothicism: already Europe has become a bewildering maze of interlocking and overlapping jurisdictions, in some ways once again like Christendom, with a relative disregard for nation-state sovereignty, although the question definitely remains of its submission to a sovereignty writ large.

Meanwhile, the United States, which was only ever a nation-state through racist attempts to invent a white nation, finds its statehood and economic hegemony in dire crisis: undercut by other rising nations or transnational political realities, by international corporations, and by those using the free market and freedom of information only to subvert the market and the trade in knowledge. (For example, the United States recently stemmed the decline of its manufacturing base by encouraging the inflow of foreign capital; this, however, has generated a massive and unprecedented national debt. At the same time, a long-term response to overproduction in the face of rival producers overseas has been the diversion of capital into finance, which in turn has caused a "realization" crisis: there is too little in which one can viably invest. Both the resisting of creditors and search for new investment fields tends to dictate an imperial solution.)[35] The U.S. response, perhaps inevitable given its history and the nature of its polity, is to seek to safeguard itself by exporting itself and rendering itself a globally pervasive reality. Here economic, political, and symbolic dominance are inseparable. If the increasingly free market is potentially vulnerable to those increasingly disadvantaged by it, then it must be extended everywhere; as it is vulnerable and porous it must also be politically imposed everywhere and relentlessly policed. Finally, since neither the market nor policing can suppress opinion and acting on opinion, the American market way of life, the spectacle of its capitalist order, must be ceaselessly displayed with every product, every police maneuver. This is the more possible because, increasingly, America is less an actual place with roots and history than it is a virtual microcosm of the globe. By one set of statistics, it is the most powerful nation on the earth; by another—for example, infant mortality—it is just another third-world country. Within the United States, a mass of dispossessed are kept in thrall by the image of America—by the idea of aspiration, by the notion that failure is their fault and yet contradictorily that tomorrow may still bring a golden dawn.

However, the myth of America, the myth of the market, is not enough. America and the market must stand for something; otherwise one would have once again fascism. It is clear that we do not have this, but something new and different. State socialism, positivism, fascism and Nazism all embraced, but severely qualified, the values of the market and of abstract production. Since 1970, though, we have had a revived and purified liberalism, a neo-capitalism. This neo-capitalism, in postmodern style, openly exults in the liberal hall of mirrors. However, the pure empty reflection is always in some sense impossible; not necessarily the real, but at least more positive symbolic values always cast their shadow, even in the fairground. So neo-liberalism does not seek, like fascism, to fill liberalism's empty heart with darkness; rather it rejoices in this emptiness and yet still at some level seeks to escape it—not to fill the middle, but at once to celebrate and yet exit the vicious circle of representing and representation.

This, in my view, is just the role of fundamentalist or extreme evangelical Protestantism. Everywhere a revival of the latter has accompanied the emergence of neocapitalism, or else Jewish, Islamic, and even Buddhist and Hindu parodies of Protestant evangelicalism have performed the same job.[36] Fundamentalism has its roots partially in theological voluntarism, so here we see a certain return to the religious roots of liberalism itself. God has given us the creation for our free use; he handed over a material and social world to private ownership without gift and to merely formal and contractual regulation, yet this regulation itself echoes the arbitrary covenants God has established for our salvation. A contract is literal and unambiguous, supposedly. So is God's word to us, supposedly. Here the freedom of the state and of the individual remain, and remain unbridged, yet they are sacralized as echoing the sovereign freedom of God. This is not classical fascism, but if one wants to speak of a new "religious market fascism," then I would not demur.

It is not an accident that this tendency is most marked in the United States and has its headquarters there. In a sense the United States never had a nineteenth century—never had historicism and the cult of society and culture and socialist populism. In a way it remains up to the present eighteenth century in character, but a specific, different eighteenth century noted by Tocqueville. Moreover, this difference has itself always bifurcated: on the one hand, Tocqueville noted that the most liberal country was in fact *not* liberal at all—not most essentially driven by the market, by the state, nor even by the trade in polite civility that he also recorded.[37] At bottom, because Americans were the real settlers of Eden, they had given the lie to liberalism, by showing that at the outset lay not the lone individual but rather the art of association—always for concrete, and so religious purposes. The United States was first of all a bizarrely plural neo-Gothic multitude of churches and sects. Here was the source of a genuine Christian republicanism and of the exchange of real gifts, and this source remains today. However, Tocqueville also noted the tendency of American religion towards the ersatz: people embraced religion in the United States, he suggested, often for half-admitted pragmatic reasons—the American version of filling up the empty heart of liberalism.[38] Religion in the United States, he observed, tends to be simplified and nonintellectual, popular rather than learned (in Europe today it is just the opposite), acting as a safety valve to ensure that Americans, unlike Frenchmen and women, do not use their freedom to question bourgeois ethical values, which indeed became in America further banalized. Religion in the United States had already decided on all the big questions, which tended (and tends) to shore up the bizarre notion that the American Constitution has decided forever on all the big political questions.

As I have already indicated, there are today Islamic and Jewish partial parallels to this quintessentially Protestant fundamentalism. Islamic fundamentalism tends to be urban and middle class—opposed to material and sacramental mediation of the sacred, pro-capitalist, and textually literalist. Conservative Zionism likewise qualifies Judaism to embrace a modern race-based state, the unrestricted market economy, and a relentlessly literal reading of the Hebrew Bible, which ties prophecy to land in perpetuity.

All these fundamentalisms are modern. Modern science insists on literalism as regards facts, and Protestant fundamentalism was born (around 1900) in a construal of the Bible as presenting a parallel universe of revealed facts alongside the realm of natural facts.[39] Catholic, orthodox Christianity, by contrast, insists that the abiding truth of the Old Testament is allegorical: literal violence points figuratively to a future revelation of embodied peace in Christ.[40] In science, the literal, observable thing tends to incite dissection, vivisection, stasis, and death; this alone permits control and regularity. Likewise in religion, a revealed word that is both arbitrary and literal can only be ascertained in its instance when it is not the communication of gift, but rather the imposition of violence, of an ending and a death-dealing. Science and fundamentalism can then readily collude with each other.

Hence today the world is increasingly governed and fought over by a fearful combination of literal readers of the Hebrew scriptures together with out-and-out postmodern liberal scientific nihilists who shamelessly rejoice in the ceaseless destruction of every rooted and ancient tradition and even the roots and long habits of nature herself.

So if today there is a problem of the recrudescence of intolerant religion, this is not a problem that liberalism can resolve, but rather a problem that liberalism tends to engender. We cannot oppose it in the name of liberal human rights, because this notion also revolves in a futile circle: these rights are supposedly natural, yet inert uncreated nature has never heard of them. They only exist when the state proclaims them, yet the state alone cannot legitimate them, else they cease to be natural and so general and objective.

A person's right is only a reality when recognized by another. But in that case, the duty of the other is the inner reality of right. Why should a person not be tortured? Because he owns his body by right? But in that case the liberal state will always exert its right of eminent domain in an emergency when the rights of the majority can be said to justify this, as today in the case of the pursuit of terrorists and "terrorists." Talal Asad has pointed out that the liberal idea that torture "transgresses human rights" has in no way prevented nearly all liberal states from resorting to torture. The real difference from nonliberal states is that *they torture in secret*. Asad explains this in terms of the history of the West's attitude to evidence and pain: once, direct confession was regarded—quite reasonably, since circumstances and witnesses may always mislead—as the crucial factor in truth, in a period when neither the inflicting nor the suffering of measured pain (witness asceticism) was regarded so negatively as it is today. From the Enlightenment onward, though, increased horror at pain and its exhibition in an era now more confined to notions of imminent and palpable happiness was conjoined with a greater trust (linked to an empiricist sensibility) in circumstantial evidence: a trust that then and ever since has, in fact, led to horrendous miscarriages of justice. This betrays the fact that, at bottom, liberalism cares more about ravages to the body than violations of the spirit. The former nevertheless, as Asad so precisely notes, are still admitted, and in fact on an unparalleled scale where they can be quantified and made part of a utilitarian calculus: reasons of state in modernity have thus permitted massive civilian casualties in war, and continue to permit for the same reason torture in secret (and now in the open)—in fact an augmentation of pain's intensity where the circumstances are deemed to warrant this.[41]

A person should not be tortured rather because of one's intrinsic value, because he or she resides in the image of God or something like that. Such a view recognizes that spiritual and bodily integrity are inseparable, and that the body is more than a possessed domain which may be troubling to its mental owner. For the former view the body confesses as much as the mind, and therefore must not be violated—for the sake of truth as well as mercy. Torture may be often carried out by religions, but only genuine religion, not liberalism, can promise a rationale to stop torture.

Likewise, there is no right to freedom of religious opinion or expression, as if truth were something one could own and develop at random; rather, truth requires free consent, else it is not understood, and a freely consented-to partial error displays more truth than an obviously or subtly coerced, or even a mechanically habitual opinion. But this principle that truth requires free consent, that profound truth is irreducibly subjective, is itself entirely religious: indeed fully at home only, one could argue, in Judaism, Christianity, and Islam. As with the prohibition of torture, only the religious notions of these traditions which insist on "consent of the heart to truth" fully safeguard free consent, since if this is only a "property we have in our person" a government will always appropriate this private property for general use in an emergency—suspending religious liberties along with other freedoms. Indeed, Asad also argues that in a situation where biotechnical companies "own" human genetic material, the question of when the human is in the subjective "owning" position, including owning rights, and when he or she is in the object-position of a thing possessed, becomes itself something that only the market decides. Hence it becomes clear that the entrepreneurial capitalist's rights, which international human rights agreements also underwrite, are the only real serious rights of rights discourse.[42]

What really guarantees human dignity and freedom, I have just argued, is something like the idea that the individual is in the image of God. This image is for Christians restored to luster by baptism and chrism. Christic anointing renders us all kings, all rulers. As kings we are not impotently free with no necessary influence, but more realistically we are dangerously free with inevitable influence. We are free as givers: to give a gift is to run the risk of violence; it is always something of an imposition. But if every free act proceeds outward it is itself both always a gift and something of an imposition. Nobody ever asked me "to say just that," "do just that," and it may hurt, indeed it may rankle forever. Inversely, though, we cannot be free only by trying to dominate: every time I act and give, I am somewhat bound to the people who suffer my actions, receive my gifts.

For this reason, Pope John Paul II has stressed in his political thinking, as Russell Hittenger has pointed out, that while Christian kings have mostly vanished, the kingship of all remains the key to Christian politics. For Christianity the human being is a *Basilikon Zoon* (Eusebius of Caesarea) before he or she is a *Zoon Politikon*. Each Christian occupies a *munus*, which is an office linked to gift in the sense of talent. This talent exists for others as well as oneself; it must be communicated. Thus the pope points out, in a way that seems commensurate with Wyclif, that human political rule commences not just in Adam's dominion over nature, but also in the mutual bestowing on each other of Adam and Eve. After the fall, this mutuality and bestowing were contaminated, and women especially were subordinated and degraded. But Christ the King restores to us the idea that to rule is to serve: he gives to us again the *munus regale* itself.[43]

Today, then, we need to surpass liberal democracy and search again for the common good in ceaseless circulation and creative development, a search that may involve laws, but more fundamentally involves charity beyond the law. Our poles of reference should not be the fantasized pure individual nor the pure sovereign state (natural or globalized) nor the pure free market. Instead we should locate and form real groups pursuing real goods and exchanging real gifts among themselves and with each other according to measures judged to be intrinsically fair. We need to acknowledge the place and point of families, schools, localities, towns, associations for genuine production and trade (not the mere pursuit of profit), and transnational bodies.[44] However, if we conceive this within immanence or theological voluntarism (as with Calvinist versions of corporatism: Kuyper, etc.), then these groups will themselves be reduced to quasi-individual mutually contracting entities and we will be back in the empty liberal echo chamber.

Instead, all these groups can communicate and exchange with each other only if all are conceived as operating under grace. Only if we can come to regard corporate bodies as receiving the objective and subjective gifts of created realities that are already imbued with prehuman meaning. Only if we can conceive the work of these bodies as further realizing the natural order in order to offer the gift of Creation back to a God who is no arbitrary sovereign but a giver who can order what he gives because it is intrinsically true, good, and beautiful.

Only a global liturgical polity can save us now from literal violence.

Chapter 3

The Time Between
Redefining the "Secular" in Contemporary Debate

Michael S. Horton

As one surveys the ecclesiastical landscape in the United States, it is difficult to resist the impression that the body of Christ is more a constellation of political action committees than a communion founded, sustained, and expanded through the ministry of word and sacrament. As the Protestant left and right are rival siblings of an American revivalism that regarded the church as a society of moral transformers, it may be wildly optimistic to imagine a scenario in which these bodies might become churches again while allowing for a broad-ranging diversity on public policy questions. Instead, the priorities seem to be reversed, with "Christian capitalism" and "Christian socialism" offered as alternative fundamentalisms between which one must choose.

Carrying its brief for Christian Americanism, "Christianity and Democracy: A Statement of the Institute on Religion and Democracy" begins with the words, "Jesus Christ is Lord," and asserts, "We believe that America has a peculiar place in God's promises and purposes." The confessors seem compelled to add, "This is not a statement of national hubris." Capitalism is also included in this general divine approbation.[1] Although the policies vary considerably, American potestantism (conservative and liberal) has a long history of identifying the church wih cultural, moral, economic, and political agendas of a particular party. In part due to the confusion of America with Israel, this tendency has been deepened through the emphasis of nineteenth-century revivalism on the church as a society-transforming institution. Frederic Jameson is justified in concluding, "This is less to deny that there is a religious revival in course today all over the world than it is to suggest that what is called religion today (in a variety of forms, from left to right) is really politics under a different name."[2]

While the Christian left and right differ on the details, they both embrace what we might call a correlationist approach, closely identifying American values—variously defined—with Christian faith and practice—variously defined. Add to this mix the more academic polemics of secularists like John Rawls and Richard Rorty on one hand and a rising tide of what has been called the "new traditionalism" on the other, represented by such notable Christian thinkers as Alasdair MacIntyre, Stanley Hauerwas, and the working group known as Radical Orthodoxy, led by John Milbank and Graham Ward. I refer here to this latter position as ecclesiastical communitarianism. Whatever the enormous differences between these approaches to the public square, they all fail to do justice to the secular as the "time between the times." At least, that is my contention in this chapter.

Suggesting ways in which we might affirm a theology of the secular that nevertheless refuses to surrender to a secularist account, this chapter especially highlights the significance of Christian eschatology in order to relocate the debate from spatial metaphors to temporal ones. I argue that from a theological perspective, secularity is defined not by an imaginary territory of creaturely autonomy, but by God's different covenantal relationships in different epochs of redemptive history. Inscribing the moral law on the human conscience, the covenant of creation provides an adequate norm for the temporal city even when it is not explicitly acknowledged. Nevertheless, the covenant of grace, corresponding to the Jerusalem that is coming down from heaven, makes the church a "creature of the Word" (*creatura verbi*), specifically, the announced Word of the gospel.

Christendom and Its Critics

Much of the current debate over the relation of Christ and culture turns on one's evaluation of "Christendom," simply understood as the fusion of cult and culture that typically entails the identification of the kingdoms of this world (or a specific geopolitical regime) with the kingdom of Christ in this present age. I take Christendom to be an imaginative construct funded at least in large measure by an allegorical interpretation of Israel's story, a hermeneutic that arises out of a Platonist metaphysics (a connection that is celebrated by John Milbank).[3] By "typological," I mean a hermeneutic of promise and fulfillment that integrates vertical divine intrusions (eschatology) and the unfolding of redemption in successive stages of covenant-making events (history). "Allegorical" interpretation, on the other hand, represents the ascent of mind from history as such (since it is conceived as the realm of transitory shadows) to spiritual and eternal truths. While typological interpretation is attentive to the "once and for all" character of transitional events, allegorical interpretation tends to spiritualize historical narratives as illustrations of higher truths. Typological interpretation is not to be confused with literalism, however, since the "ordinary sense" (*sensus literalis*) requires sensitivity to the genre in which promise and fulfillment are expressed. Protestant fundamentalism, for example, with its reading of apocalyptic literature as if it were a newspaper, represents a parody of this ordinary sense. In Byzantine and Western medieval allegorical practice, the new holy land (as in Holy Roman Empire) could invoke the category of holy war to drive out the new Canaanites. There were medieval debates, of course, over who ultimately was the temporal head of this body of Christ, but everyone agreed that the empire and Christ's kingdom were one. Milbank evokes nostalgia for the Gothic age when "citizenship was liturgically linked to baptism . . . and participation in local church and civic life . . . were so complexly interwoven as to be inseparable."[4] Apparently this blending of cult and culture is preferable to liberal democracy despite the history of exclusion and persecution (especially of Jews, but also of dissenting Christians) from Theodosius to early New England. Rather than recognize the heavenly Jerusalem as an eschatological irruption ("coming down from heaven") in the form of Word and sacrament, the "new covenant" according to Christendom was simply a revival of the Sinai covenant with its theocratic polity. Passages from the old covenant's theocratic code could be invoked for current ecclesial and cultural operations because they were not regarded as having become obsolete signs with the arrival of the heavenly reality. (At this point, ironic similarities between Christendom's hermeneutic and that of Protestant fundamentalism seem greater than Milbank allows.) In other words, the dominance of the allegorical over the typological (*sensus literalis*) interpretation of scripture surrendered historical sensitivity to timeless principles that were always true and applicable in any phase of covenantal history. As the New Israel, Christendom could justify its claims over both cult and culture, whether the Davidic leader of the Lord's armies was pope or emperor.

Even more than in Augustine's defense of the two cities, the Reformation provided rich resources for opposing what Calvin called the "contrived empire" of Christendom, but squandered this opportunity by reviving the ideal of a "holy commonwealth"—nation-states covenanting with God to be ruled according to biblical law. This also represented an allegorized meganarrative of the old covenant. Now secularized in American mythology as a metanarrative of manifest destiny, presidential speeches on both sides of the aisle continue to draw on Christendom's legacy.[5] Neither the church nor the secular polis seems content with its own divinely ordained jurisdiction and commission: the church craves worldly power, and the state is only too happy to reciprocate in exchange for political endorsements.

Unlike correlationists who see a strong connection between the American story and the story of Israel, ecclesial communitarians see these in sharp conflict. Yet they still share the fundamental confusion of cult and culture, the kingdom of God and the kingdoms of this age, redemptive grace and common grace, that keep the myth of Christendom alive even as at least some of them (like Hauerwas) are sharply critical of that legacy. According to William T. Cavanaugh, a representative of radical orthodoxy, "The modern state is best understood . . . as a source of an alternative soteriology to that of the Church. . . . The body of the state is a simulacrum, a false copy, of the Body of Christ. The Eucharist, which makes the Body of Christ, is therefore a key practice for a Christian anarchism."[6] In terms reminiscent of the radical Anabaptists of the sixteenth century, Cavanaugh assures us that eucharistic praxis "challenges the false order of the state."[7] It would seem that if a state is not explicitly suspended in "being" (i.e., the church), it is at least on the last rung of the ontological ladder, perhaps even already succumbing to the nihil (nonexistence).

In radical orthodoxy (hereafter RO), such criticisms coalesce with a nostalgia for Christendom. Milbank tells us, "Once there was no 'secular.' . . . Instead, there was the single community of Christendom, with its dual aspects of sacerdotium [priesthood] and regnum [kingship]."[8] According to a typological hermeneutic, these two orders that defined Israel's theocracy converge in Christ and his spiritual reign in the church through Word and sacrament. However, in an allegorical reading advocated by Milbank, Christendom replaces Christ as the fulfillment of prophecy. As Milbank continues his narrative, this unity was sundered first by nominalism, then by the Reformation, which mediated nominalism to modern political theory, reaching its apogee in Hobbes. In part, this came about "by abandoning participation in Being and Unity for a 'covenantal bond' between God and men," which in turn "provided a model for human interrelationships as 'contractual' ones."[9] Furthermore, in a dazzling historiographical feat, Milbank asserts that the absolutist hermeneutics of Spinoza and Hobbes "is really rooted in the Lutheran sola scriptura . . ."[10] Concerning civil laws and punishments, "The Church . . . must have done forever with Luther's two kingdoms, and the notion that a State that does not implicitly concern itself with the soul's salvation can be in any way legitimate."[11]

More recently, Milbank has applied this narrative to the "war on terror." Once united by neoplatonism, the cultures of Judaism, Christianity, and Islam were driven apart, in the direction of nominalism (the Christian West) and "a doctrinally orthodox, scriptural, and legalistic civilization" (Islam).[12] "There is now a terrible symbiosis arising between Zionism and the American Protestant and un-Christian literalistic reading of the Old Testament in the Puritan tradition, which equates Anglo-Saxondom with Israel." This reading, says Milbank, is "idolatrously nontypological and non-eschatological."[13]

Yet while Milbank puts his finger on the problem of equating "Anglo-Saxondom with Israel," he fails to realize that the underlying hermeneutic—far from "literal"—is really allegorical—Milbank's own preferred method, with quite different effects than a typological and eschatological reading. Israel's history serves as an allegory—a meganarrative—of our nation's or civilization's history: this is the allegorical method that inspired the Christendom of the crusades and its subsequent versions. As a critique of the secular metanarrative, Milbank's work is especially illuminating, but an adequate theology of the secular will have to be more radical, challenging the allegorized meganarrative that helped found it.

For Milbank, it seems, the problem with the "Puritan" reading is simply its identification of modern nation-states with Israel's covenant. He does not challenge the principle that such a state can or should attempt to transcend its secular vocation. One may not favor

Islam's "sacral state" based on "sacred laws." "But on what basis can one decide that an Islamic sacral state, especially if it took a more sophisticated form than that envisaged by the Taliban, is not permissible?"[14] The upshot seems to be that if we return to the neo-platonism that was shared by Judaism, Christianity, and Islam, recovering an allegorical hermeneutic, a mystical hierarchy calibrated to the ladder of being, and thus a sacred polis, we could attain greater global harmony. If theurgic neoplatonism is the common thread, then the notion of a sacral state seems acceptable to Milbank, as long as it is more sophisticated than the versions currently on offer. Neoplatonism operates as the natural theology for Milbank's universalist ecclesiology in which Christian socialism will replace, among others, the U.S. Constitution.[15] The trouble "is not 'totalitarianism' pure and simple, but the emptiness of the secular as such, and its consequent disguised sacralization of violence."[16] Milbank advocates a recovery of "the Biblical and Platonico-Aristotelian metaphysical legacy common to Christianity, Judaism, and Islam," according to which it is held that "human wisdom can intimate, imperfectly but truly, something of an eternal order of justice."[17] This human wisdom is grounded, according to Milbank, in mimesis and methexis—a participation in the heavenly city, whereas I will argue that it derives from a distinct covenant with its own means and ends in God's purposes for history.

Graham Ward is less nostalgic for Christendom than Milbank: We cannot "defend the walls of some medieval notion of Christendom. Christendom is over; and with it Christian hegemony."

> But, we are also beyond pluralism. Pluralism, that is, that recognized different faiths as species of the one generic religion or even different symbolic world-views that were all ultimately grounded in and expressive of the one simply, existential reality. We have moved beyond pluralism because there is no view from no where, no objective knowledge; the view from no where is itself a cultural ideology—often Western, white, and male.[18]

Nevertheless, conflating religious and political pluralism as Ward does here only further muddies the waters, as does the assumption that the latter necessarily entails "the view from no where." It is the point of a principled pluralism to allow different voices from different locations to address our common life in the secular city. Political pluralism allows individuals and groups freely to argue claims even to universally binding truth. What it proscribes is the use of coercion to defend those claims. Conflating political and metaphysical or religious pluralism, most citizens of liberal democracies seem to think that truth is a private, subjective affair. Ecclesial communitarians and secularists seem to accept this conflation, resulting in either the rejection or celebration of liberal democracy.

Chastened by Karl Barth and John Howard Yoder, Hauerwas is more suspicious of natural theologies than Milbank, yet Yoder's Anabaptist perspective and radical orthodoxy converge in the suggestion that the church represents an alternative to the secular state. Yoder insisted, "The meaning of history—and therefore the significance of the state—lies in the creation and work of the church."[19] In my view, however, this requires either the Christian's abandonment of the common (the Anabaptist tendency) or the sacralization of the common by assimilating it to a "higher" ontological register (Christendom).

According to Hauerwas, the capitulation of American Catholicism to the First Amendment represents a fateful moment. "Does that mean I do not support 'democracy'?" asks Hauerwas. "I have to confess I have not got the slightest idea, since I do not know what it means to call this society 'democratic.' Indeed, one of the troubling aspects about such a question is the assumption that how Christians answer it might matter."[20] Although he offers a more sophisticated and nuanced case against the liberal state, Milbank is just as sweeping in his indictments, suggesting that "'liberal democracy' is a mere virtual circus designed to entertain the middle-classes of the privileged world."[21]

Missing from RO is the nuance, paradox, irony, and dialectical tension that we find in Augustine's account. While Augustine trims the sails of the commonwealth's pretensions to absolute and ultimate ends, RO seems to think that if a commonwealth is not somehow grounded or suspended in absolute and ultimate ends coinciding with the City of God, the commonwealth is a charade. Augustine's account seems far more subtle than a simple antithesis between the church as a pure "community of virtue" while the modern liberal state is utterly bankrupt. Given his understanding of the church itself as a communion in which the City of God is still imperfectly realized, the contrast is not so much between the church and the world as between this age and the age to come.[22] Any adequate theology of the secular will have to account for the fact that the relation between the church and the reign of God is a confession of faith more than a visible reality (*simul iustus et peccator*), and for the fact that the fallen kingdoms of this world are not abandoned by God. In my view, as I will argue, Augustine does a better job at this than many of his contemporary interpreters.

In all of these writers, the secular is identified with secularism—liberal democracy with John Rawls' and Richard Rorty's antitheological theology masquerading as a neutral public discourse. Concern for individual rights is treated as concomitant with irreconcilable hostility toward tradition and community. Even a sympathetic interpreter of RO, James K. A. Smith, can note, "Cavanaugh confuses a particular direction the modern state has taken with the structure of the state as such."[23]

Yet if, as both Catholic and Reformed traditions have held, there is such a thing as nature that does not reduce to naturalism, then why can't the secular be a way of talking about the status of certain creaturely entities (persons, places, things) not ontologically but eschatologically—that is, in terms of the use that God makes of them in a particular period of redemptive history? Yet for RO, the participatory ontology tends to elide eschatological differences in specific epochs: instead of two kingdoms in this age, there is, as an eternal truth, a real kingdom of God and its false secular copy. Eschatology—that is, the recognition of the present secularity of cultural activities that will one day be redeemed and reintegrated into the kingdom of God—is barely legible in Milbank's static ontological category of participation.

As I argue below, the secular is a time when that which is other than the church is upheld by God's providential Word in common grace. Grounded in the covenant of creation, secularity characterizes that which God has not (at least yet) brought into the covenant of grace and yet is affirmed and made fruitful by the Spirit at work providentially in all that God has made. Thus, "the secular" is not a nontheological space, but a time in which cult and culture have not yet been reunited. Creation, providence, and common grace are sufficient to generate a Christian theology of the secular without assimilating the covenant of creation into the covenant of grace or requiring "the secular" to be ecclesially suspended. If it is true, as I believe it is, that Christians should resist the totalizing claims of democracy and individualism (especially in the churches, where a different economy upholds community), it does not necessarily follow that such values are demonic in their limited sociopolitical sphere. The church simply cannot offer itself, any more than the state can offer itself, as a be-all and end-all of the common good. The good that Christ's kingdom announces is of a different order: a peace, justice, and harmony that is known only in union with Christ. Yet the church itself enjoys the benefits of relative peace, justice, and liberty that it shares in common with the secular polis.

Cult and Culture: The Genealogy of Profanity

For Augustine, the distinction between the two cities was grounded not in a universalist ecclesiology within a single economy of redemptive grace, but in the two loves, which themselves were ultimately the historical realization of God's eternal predestination of some from Adam's fallen race for salvation, leaving the rest to their just perdition. Thus, despite his Platonist worldview, Augustine does not relate the two cities in terms of the real and the shadow, but in terms of two distinct peoples, one founded in the covenant of creation and the other in the covenant of grace.[24]

Consequently, each city has its own polity, serving distinct ends through distinct means, revealing that each is determined by two different loves and therefore by two different ends and means. These are in sharp conflict, and in emphasizing Augustine's affirmation of the legitimacy of the state in this time between, I do not want to forget his sharp construal of the antithesis. Against any correlationist approach, Augustine says that compared to the City of God, the "virtues" of the commonwealth turn out to be "vices."[25] Yet this is a comparison of things earthly with things heavenly, not a verdict on whether civic virtue in a fallen world is possible. Such comments are always balanced by an affirmation of God's preservation of the secular order under divine providence. Yet the earthly city is always Babylon—it is never converted, as are many of its inhabitants, into the dwelling place of God. The kingdom of God advances through the proclamation of the gospel, not through the properly coercive powers of the state, although the church makes use of the relative peace that is possible in the earthly city.[26] These two cities we find "interwoven, as it were, in this present transitory world, and mingled with one another."[27]

The earthly city is not everlasting and can never bring about true rectitude because even when—indeed, especially when—it apes the everlasting peace, tranquility, order, and justice of the heavenly city, it ends up bringing about greater disasters. Yet in the same breath, Augustine affirms, "However, it would be incorrect to say that the goods which this city desires are not goods, since even that city is better, in its own human way, by their possession."[28] It is of great value and service as far as it goes.[29] A Christian would then approach politics not with the question as to how the world can best be saved, but how it can best be served in this time between the times.

The fact that the earthly city is transitory and dominated by self-love does not lead Augustine to a disavowal of its legitimacy as a divinely ordained institution. Judged by the polity of the age to come, the pax romana is indeed a parody of the City of God.[30] Yet this only means that we should not confuse the relative security, peace, and justice of the temporal city with the consummation; it does not mean that, for the time being, the state is a false copy of the heavenly kingdom. Each has its own distinct and divinely ordained ends and means, determined by its distinct loves.

To be sure, if a commonwealth is defined by "the weal of the people," Rome fails that test.[31] Nevertheless, this is where some admirers of Augustine stop short. Crucially, Augustine adds, "If, on the other hand, another definition than this is found for a 'people,' for example, if one should say, 'A people is the association of the multitude of rational beings united by a common agreement on the objects of their love,' then it follows that to observe the character of a particular people we must examine the objects of its love."[32] "By this definition of ours," says Augustine, "the Roman people is a people and its estate is indubitably a commonwealth"—despite its propensity for violence and internal strife.[33] Christians share in the common curse and common grace of this earthly city. While they do not bring about God's reign in the secular city by their own activity, citizens of the Heavenly City serve in anticipation of that day when "all injustice disappears and all human lordship and power is annihilated and God is all in all."[34] Until then, citizens of the heavenly city execute also their vocation as citizens of the earthly city, contributing toward a relative peace, justice, and harmony of wills that is important if not ultimate.[35] The peace of the earthly city is to be prized, not scorned for falling short of the heavenly peace won by Christ.[36] Thus, the secular is not demonic except when it assumes the pretension of ultimate justice, truth, goodness, love, and peace. In my view, this proper limitation of secular power to penultimate goods is precisely what is at stake both in the so-called war on terror and the war on the modern (secular) state. It is by confusing the penultimate goods and ends of the commonwealth with the ultimate goods and ends of the City of God that Augustine's sharp antithesis between the two orders (or ages) must be invoked. In my view, such confusion is the move that religious correlationists make when they identify the commonwealth (or particular political policies) with the reign of God and that secularists make when they claim the secular as a space of autonomy defined by absolute immanence. Yet ecclesial communitarians seem to offer a negation based in some sense on the secularist's definition of the secular. In my view, Christians must defend the view that the secular is not self-existent even though it does not participate in the covenant of grace.

I would therefore contest Graham Ward's reading, according to which, "This city [of God] makes possible the cities of the everyday; and makes possible their redemption. This is the informing idea in Augustine's theology of the city; an idea lost in Luther's theology of the city."[37] Citing Augustine's definition of a commonwealth taken from Cicero, Ward simply concludes that according to the bishop of Hippo it "was never fulfilled," because this can only happen in Christ.[38] Yet, as we have seen, Augustine is contrasting ultimates, not contesting the relative justice, peace, good, and order of the secular as such.[39] Ward misses the subtlety of the argument: If held to its own pretentious standards (which civic patriotism often bandies whenever it wraps itself in priestly robes), the earthly city is a parody of the City of God, says Augustine. Yet if its wings are clipped, restricting its ambitions and province to temporal community and welfare, a certain kind of commonwealth is indeed possible.

Nevertheless, Ward continues, "But as the 'natural' order," such empires "constitute the condition for the possibility of the parodies which follow. The heavenly city itself must make possible the earthly city, such that in the saeculum 'city' is used figurally, virtually."[40] In other words, on Ward's interpretation, Augustine's *civitas terrena* is not only a shadow of the real City (which Augustine's Platonist leanings might support), but a false one—a parody. But is this consistent with the hardly incidental grounding of the two cities in predestination and the concrete, historical realization of this decree in the equally "real" lines of Cain and Seth to which Augustine's redemptive-historical analysis appeals? Nevertheless, Ward resolutely asserts, "There are not two kingdoms—the civitas terrena, like Augustine's famous understanding of evil itself, is a

privatio bone—it has no real substance; it is virtual."[41] This seems
to be an overreading of Augustine's argument that misses his dialectical nuances. The earthly city is never transformed into anything like the City of God, yet it is not a mere shadow tending toward
nonbeing. In fact, to the extent that the earthly city is treated as a
copy (even a shadowy one) of the City of God, the former is always
tempted to assert its demonic pretensions to a sacred order.

Expecting too much of the earthly city, it is not surprising that
such theologies end in disappointment with its failure to mirror the
City of God. In some ways, the radical reformers of the sixteenth century simply reflected the negative moment of "Christendom," and
perhaps this accounts to some extent for the otherwise odd alliance
of Anabaptist and Anglo-Catholic criticism of the secular state among
ecclesial communitarians. What many contemporary admirers fail
to share with Augustine himself is an acceptance of the eschatologically conditioned paradox of the kingdom's current phase.

While we do not have the space to treat Luther's development
of the "two kingdoms" doctrine, Calvin's elaboration and modification are worth considering in the light of our situation. Despite H.
R. Niebuhr's heavy type-casting in *Christ and Culture*, Calvin distinguished these two kingdoms no less than Luther, yet without surrendering the civil jurisdiction to a realm of pure power. His basis
for this, as we will see, is not the assumption that this civil realm is
sacred or participates somehow in the body of Christ, but because
it is only authorized by God to exercise a limited stewardship of the
commonwealth.

Trained in some of the most distinguished circles of French
humanism, Calvin's first academic treatise was a commentary on
Seneca's *De clementia*. "Whenever we come upon these matters in
secular writers," he pleaded in the *Institutes*, "let that admirable
light of truth shining in them teach us that the mind of man, though
fallen and perverted from its wholeness, is nevertheless clothed and
ornamented with God's excellent gifts." He continues:

> What then? Shall we deny that the truth shone on the ancient
> jurists who established civic order and discipline with such great
> equity? Those whom Scripture calls "natural men" were, indeed,
> sharp and penetrating in their investigation of earthly things. Let
> us, accordingly, learn by their example how many gifts the Lord
> left to human nature even after it was despoiled of its true good.[42]

Opposing what Calvin called the "contrived empire" of Christendom, Calvin says that we must recognize that we are "under a two-fold government, . . . so that we do not (as commonly happens) unwisely mingle these two, which have a completely different nature." Just as the body and soul are distinct without being intrinsically opposed, "Christ's spiritual kingdom and the civil jurisdiction are things completely distinct. . . . Yet this distinction does not lead us to consider the whole nature of government a thing polluted, which has nothing to do with Christian men." These two kingdoms are "distinct," yet "they are not at variance."[43] Like Augustine, Calvin moves dialectically between an affirmation of the natural order and its inability because of sin to generate an ultimate society. The goal of common grace is not to perfect nature, but to restrain sin and animate civic virtues and arts, so that culture may fulfill its own important but limited, temporal, and secular ends, while God simultaneously pursues the redemptive aims of his everlasting city.

Confusing justification before God (the gospel) with moral, social, and political righteousness (the law), the radical reformers undermined both civility between Christian and non-Christian as well as the unique message and ministry of Christ's kingdom. Responding to the radical reformers' insistence that a commonwealth is only legitimate if it is ordered by biblical law, Calvin declares, "How malicious and hateful toward public welfare would a man be who is offended by such diversity, which is perfectly adapted to maintain the observance of God's law! For the statement of some, that the law of God given through Moses is dishonored when it is abrogated and new laws preferred to it, is utterly vain."[44] After all, Calvin says, "It is a fact that the law of God which we call the moral law is nothing else than a testimony of natural law and of that conscience which God has engraved on the minds of men."[45] Even unbelievers can rule justly and prudently, as Paul indicates even under the more pagan circumstances of his day (Rom 13:1-7). In addition to these natural remnants, there is some concept of common grace in Calvin, "not such grace as to cleanse it [nature], but to restrain it inwardly." This grace is tied to providence, to restraint; "but he does not purge it within."[46] Only the gospel can do this.

According to Calvin, natural law can be summarized by the word "equity" (*aequitas*), which generally meant a fairness in human relations that balanced strict justice with charitable moderation. Consequently, "equity alone must be the goal and rule and limit of

all laws."[47] As a natural virtue common to all people, this equity is
"the perpetual rule of love," fountain of all laws. Thus, he considers
"pernicious and hateful of the public order" the requirement that
the laws of nations should be required to follow the judicial laws
of Moses. "Surely every nation is left free to make such laws as it
foresees to be profitable for itself. Yet these must be in conformity to
that perpetual rule of love, so that they indeed vary in form but have
the same purpose."[48] Calvin reflects his debt to patristic and pre-
Scotist natural law traditions as well as a humanist appreciation for
diversity of historical, cultural, and geographical conditions. To be
sure, this is "thin description"; equity does not mandate a particular
form of government (such as democracy, capitalism, or socialism).
Yet this reserve is part of the genius of the concept and its appeal
across a wide range of political regimes.

Love of neighbor—which includes "the most remote person . . .
without distinction"— links justice (duty) and charity (compassion),
"since all should be contemplated in God, not in themselves." This is
what Calvin means by "equity," which requires "mutual servitude"
without tyranny.[49] Calvin does not simply accept the *libido dominandi*
as appropriate to the secular kingdom (Luther's tendency), but he
also does not imagine that the only alternative for civic life is participation in the redemptive grace of Christ and his body. Equity,
engendered by that moral law that is mediated by God through creation to everyone, fills the secular with a rich theological description, centering on the lordship of the risen Christ over what, for the
time being, nevertheless remain distinct "kingdoms."

According to Oliver O'Donovan and Joan Lockwood O'Donovan,
"John Calvin may largely take credit for conceiving and implement-
ing a reintegration of political order and spiritual community that
transformed the historical complexion of Reformation Christianity."
"Even more than the later Luther, he converted the polarizations
of the two-kingdoms model into parallelisms, stressing harmonization of the spiritual and temporal realms as of two communal real-
izations of God's will for fallen mankind, one direct and the other
indirect."[50] Calvin combined "patristic, scholastic, and Lutheran
theological elements with ideas and methods drawn from classical political philosophy, and humanist literary, historical, and legal
scholarship."[51]

Although space does not allow an adequate treatment here, it
is perhaps worth pointing out that neither Calvin nor the Reformed

tradition can be explained away as easily as Ward and Milbank assume in their sweeping genealogy of nihilism. The covenant theology espoused by Reformed thinkers is antithetical to the contractual thinking of nominalism—which is the target of Luther's critique in the Heidelberg Disputation. Whatever the genuine defects of voluntarism, Calvin's relationship to Scotism, much less nominalism, is critical.[52] Its radically voluntaristic concept of God's "absolute power" Calvin called "a diabolical blasphemy" that could only render us balls that God juggles in the air.[53] With respect to the "proper seat of faith," Calvin shows no evidence of being a voluntarist, much less a radical one.[54] While there were "Scotists" amid the Aristotelian Thomists, Augustinian/Franciscan Platonists, and Ramists, all of the major Reformed scholastics explicitly rejected univocity in favor of analogy.

There was no place for an autonomous self to arise in this covenant theology, but different covenants were recognized in scripture, each with its own polity. The covenant of creation was not "pure nature." In fact, it was a fusion of cult and culture. After the fall, however, the two cities are divided until they are reunited in the Sinai theocracy, which has become obsolete with the arrival of the reality (Christ) that it typologically foreshadowed. The covenant of grace, adumbrated after the fall and fulfilled in the new covenant, is therefore not a renewal of the Sinai covenant but a fulfillment of the Abrahamic promise of blessing to Israel and the nations. In this time between Christ's two advents, the holy-common distinction no longer falls along ethnic or geopolitical lines but refers to the body of Christ created by redemptive grace and the political bodies of temporal kingdoms and cultures sustained by common grace. In this view, there is no such thing as a Christian culture. There are Christians pursuing their common vocations with and for their neighbors, gathering regularly in faith, confession, witness, and eucharistic anticipation for the parousia, when cult and culture are reunited in a consummated kingdom beyond any state that has yet been experienced in history. They are scattered throughout the week to fulfill their temporal callings to their neighbors and to receive and witness to their heavenly calling, but have received no commission to transform the kingdoms of this age into the kingdom of Christ.

This distinction between callings, however, did not imply indifference to the common. For one thing, the discipline and fellowship of the ecclesia could have an enormous impact on the society.

Calvin was famously exiled from Geneva for refusing to commune powerful bankers who were exploiting the refugees who had been pouring into the city, illustrating the potential for social good when the church simply exercises its authority within the limits of its jurisdiction granted by Christ. Christians were expected to exercise their secular callings in a manner consistent with Christian teaching, but the church as an institution was not to be regarded as an instrument of cultural cohesion, political ideology, or social justice. This is not because the "secular" was surrendered to a realm of pure power (or pure nature), but because it was understood as the common order of Christians and non-Christians in the intermezzo between Christ's advents.

Thus, there is no need to "sanctify the material realm" or for "day-to-day life perpetually [to] raise us up into the supernatural," as Milbank suggests by appeal to the medieval outlook and nineteenth-century neo-Gothicism.[55] The material realm was sanctified by God in creation; it is fallen, to be sure, but so too is the church. In Milbank's view, the church mediates grace and, according to his universalistic ecclesiology, "All human society in some degree foreshadows ecclesia and in this way always mediates some supernatural grace."[56] By conflating cult and culture in this way, however, Milbank undercuts the integrity both of creation and ecclesia. Created with its own, though entirely dependent, integrity, nature is not in need of elevation into the supernatural, but of liberation from its bondage to sin and death. The church is simply that part of this creation that is being brought into the seminal realities of this liberation, the anteroom of the age to come. Even if culture does not participate in the covenant of grace, it does participate in the covenant of creation and is sustained by divine providence. As for the church, its mediation of grace consists exclusively in its ministry of Word and Sacrament, not in attempts to conform common life in the temporal polis to ecclesial existence in the Spirit.

In Calvin's wake, Reformed thinking moved not only toward greater refinement of its covenant theology, but applied it to the social sphere, where it contributed to the evolution of early modern constitutional theory.[57] It was not by abandoning theology for a supposedly neutral terrain of pure immanence that the Reformers and their heirs spoke in these ways. Unlike some versions of natural law that preceded them and nearly all versions that arose in the Enlightenment, this account was grounded in a history of God's creation and covenant. The seventeenth-century Genevan theologian Francis Turretin, for example, examines the medieval argument for natural law as it reached its apogee in voluntarism. "But the [Reformed] orthodox speak far differently," he says. "They affirm that there is a natural law, not arising from a voluntary contract or law of society, but from a divine obligation being impressed by God upon the conscience of man in his very creation. . . ."[58] The argument is exegetical, in the light of the changing polities in redemptive history. As the Westminster Confession summarized, the judicial laws of Moses are "expired," "not obliging any other [nation] now, further than the general equity thereof may require."[59]

However, the lingering meganarrative of Christendom (allegorized Israel) often kept the Reformation doctrine of the two kingdoms from being worked out in practice even in nominally Reformed lands. Despite Calvin's exegetical defense of the uniqueness of Israel's theocracy, Protestant as well as Catholic nation-states presumed that they too could enter into a national covenant with God with biblical law or canon law as the basis for public policy. Rather than a general equity derived from natural law in creation, which could be realized in a variety of political forms and laws, such nation-states pursued a legalistic application of biblical law that could not fail to end in parliamentary factions and stalemates. Thus, it was not the two-kingdoms doctrine, but its practical rejection, that contributed to a crisis of secular politics whose only solution to the likes of Descartes, Spinoza, Hobbes, and Kant—all the way to Rawls and Rorty—was to be found by appeal to autonomous, universal, and ostensibly neutral foundations that bypassed appeals to revelation.

Despite the persistence of the allegorized meganarrative, the principle of equity remained a dominant theme among Reformed writers, particularly in the realm of civic policy. Thus, a theological justification for human rights could emerge that is nevertheless contrasted sharply with modern foundationalist versions (contractarian, deontological, utilitarian, and pragmatist), yet differs in key respects from the Platonist versions as well.

Interestingly, David Novak argues for a version of natural law from the history of Jewish interpretation of the Noahide laws in a manner strikingly similar to this approach, contrasting a covenantal account with both "new traditionalist" rejection of the concept and medieval as well as modern secularist notions.[60] Similarities between Novak's arguments and Calvin's may be attributed to a shared covenantal paradigm. Novak writes:

> How fundamentally different all this is from seeing natural law as some sort of translation of a higher nature down to the actual affairs of human beings. In that view, there is no primary voice, but only a vision of a polity that might conform to a higher paradigm in the heavens. It is duty without an originating right/claim, for such a right/claim cannot be imagined, but only heard.[61]

Jews develop their theory of rights from their own sources, he insists.[62] Even in Islam, according to Osman bin Bakar, however extremists may conflate categories, shari'ah includes both particular laws governing Muslims and laws that are regarded as universally binding as a result of a common Adamic origin.[63] Augustine spoke of "the everlasting law," as did his heirs.[64] The location of a core of natural law in the concept of equity seems entirely justified even in our common experience, ineradicable even by modernity's pursuit of radical autonomy.[65]

In the same way, I would argue for an account that is grounded in covenant theology rather than in either neoplatonic speculations that are critical of rights-talk or modern theories of rights that lack any transcendent justification for just claims. In terms of our current experience it may be true that "there is no secular in our sense outside liberalism," as Milbank suggests.[66] However, a different conception and affirmation of the secular is possible from the resources of Christian theology, which accounts for the persistence of a valid secular order in spite of attempts to suppress its presuppositions. The very justice that nonbiblical accounts want desperately to secure are only intelligible on biblical grounds. I say "intelligible" rather than "possible" because it is a Christian conviction that non-Christians are able to reflect in their constitutions and legal codes the truth of their covenantal creation even while they refuse to acknowledge the true character of that relationship. They are therefore inconsistent in their rationale, yet capable of reflecting the truth, goodness, and beauty whose sources they nevertheless attempt to suppress. When even secularists accept even a morsel of this natural law (such as the proscription of sexual violence), they are operating on the borrowed capital of this common revelation which they deny in principle. In this account, then, we can speak of a universal knowledge of God's will in creation while grounding it in revelation rather than in universal foundations of autonomous reason and experience.

Reformation theology emphasizes that while the gospel is revealed only in the proclamation of Christ (*verbum externum*), the law is the native property of all human beings (*verbum internum*), the very law of their being which, though suppressed in unrighteousness, cannot entirely be purged from the conscience. The gospel engenders a church founded by a covenant of grace, while the law engenders a secular civitas, founded by a covenant of creation. Not even atheists can suppress everything at the same time. Christians may legitimately pursue a political pluralism on their own theological grounds without surrendering to religious pluralism in the bargain. It is not by resacralizing the secular in the name of Christ and his kingdom, but by resecularizing it—locating it in this time between—that we can preserve the secular or common from both secularist ideology and from Christian triumphalism. Only then can we begin again to recognize the value of equity and "the common" as something more than the war of all against all and yet something far short of the City of God that yet awaits us. In this account, then, the common (or the secular) is defined by revelation, not by secularist autonomy.

Conclusion

Although belonging to the same tradition of pragmatism and Emersonian skepticism as Rorty, in his recent book, *Democracy and Tradition*, Jeffrey Stout challenges both secularists and traditionalists. He takes aim first at the unwarranted secularist criteria Rawls requires for public debate—especially the demand, impossible in a democracy, that religious arguments should be excluded from political discussions.[67] If the strictures of Rawls and Rorty on public discourse were observed, that would have excluded Martin Luther King Jr., who, "writing as a Baptist preacher from a Birmingham jail, claimed than an 'unjust law is no law at all' and defined an unjust law as 'a human law that is not rooted in eternal and natural law.'"[68] At the same time, Stout challenges the ecclesial communitarians (the "new traditionalism," as he calls it) for erroneously equating liberal democracy with this secularist position, offering their own equally untenable ecclesial alternative. In a democracy, we hold each other accountable for the beliefs and practices we all hold as individuals and in our discrete communities. Democracy, like any community, is a "process of reason-exchange."[69] One need not adopt a foundationalist epistemology to recognize the importance of Stout's claim. Christians participate in this process of reason-exchange in various ways through various callings: in their witness on behalf of Christ, as well as in their disparate and sometimes contradictory visions for the civil order.

Stout gets closer to the appropriate Christian response than the ecclesial communitarians, although he remains a religious skeptic:

> But one of the most important findings presented here is that Christian theological orthodoxy is not the source of the new traditionalism's antidemocratic sentiments or tendencies. . . . At a moment when orthodox Judaism in Israel and orthodox Islam around the world are struggling to sort through analogous issues, study of Christian thinkers who have connected theological orthodoxy with democratic practice is an academic topic of global significance. . . . Democracy involves substantial normative commitments, but does not presume to settle in advance the ranking of our highest values. Nor does it claim to save humanity from sin and death. . . . Yet it holds that people who differ on such matters can still exchange reasons with one another intelligibly, cooperate in crafting political arrangements that promote justice and decency in their relations with one another, and do both of these things without compromising their integrity.[70]

Since the churches themselves are divided along cultural, racial, and political lines today, simply identifying with the church over against the world is hardly a panacea.[71]

As for ecclesial communitarians, Stout notes, natural law theorists conspire with modern liberals, in Hauerwas' telling.[72] If the law is written on the conscience, Hauerwas wonders, why so much disagreement, and would it even matter? The church just needs to be the church and "live the gospel."[73] But why must we adopt this false choice? The Christian is obligated to both God and neighbor and is simultaneously called out of the natural bonds of kinship to belong to Christ and called to nourish those natural bonds in a kind of civic piety. Natural law matters because our neighbor, and not merely the church, matters. Whatever lies up ahead, this present age is still of relative importance, however it may pale in comparison to the age to come. It matters that the church continues to remind itself as well as its neighbors of what they already know even when they suppress that truth in unrighteousness.

Here once again, the Emersonian religious skeptic Jeffrey Stout appears more illuminating: "If a personal God exists and chooses to interact with us," he reasons, "then our relationship with God, according to the theory just given, should be capable of giving rise to obligations. If God issues commands to us, these will qualify as a kind of social requirement." This sounds a lot like a divinely revealed covenant rather than the modern social contract. "The theory holds that the goodness of the social bond is essential to giving obligations their force." All of this, says Stout, may still be objectionable to religious skeptics like himself, but at least it isn't mere metaphysical speculation. It makes ontological claims that yield important convictions in favor of human rights.[74]

Of course, Christians will want to talk about more than human rights, and even these will be recognized as deriving from God's covenantal word in creation, providence, and judgment. Equity speaks of responsibilities that exceed the logic of rights, of a civic virtue without which the war of all against all is inevitable, and about the consideration of those on the margins who are often left out of "the process of reason-exchange." Yet while natural equity is more than rights, it cannot be less. The story that the new traditionalism tells is simply false, says Stout, just as false as the secularist tale against which it reacts.[75] While "prophets of excess" like Hauerwas can raise our consciousness of acute problems, Stout suggests,

> The theological antidote for this rhetoric of excess, at least from a mainstream Augustinian perspective, has always been to stress that God not only created this world, but also declared it good, and remains its gracious ruler despite the temporary triumphs of sin. If the world is essentially good, but thrown out of whack by sin, the fitting response to it is not rejection, but an ambivalent mixture of affirmation and condemnation. . . . You are still making a difference when you are engaged in a successful holding action against forces that are conspiring to make things worse than they are.[76]

To be sure, even a theological narrative of the civitas terrena will yield a thin description in comparison to Zion's story, but if the Augustinian interpretation is accurate, what the transitory city of Cain needs most right now are better thin descriptions.

Chapter 4

Probing the Links between Security and Secularization

Ronald A. Kuipers and Mebs Kanji

The Secularization Thesis Then and Now

The "secularization thesis" has become a dominant theme in the academic study of religion over the course of the modern period. Those holding to this thesis credit that heady period of intellectual foment and ferment known as the Enlightenment with inaugurating historical processes of rationalization that would ultimately spell the end of religion as a publicly significant cultural phenomenon. José Casanova provides an effective description of the way in which those who hold to this thesis would come to regard the prospects of religion after Enlightenment: "Reduced to a pre-scientific and prelogical primitive form of thought and knowledge, religion necessarily had to disappear with the ever-progressive advancement of knowledge, education, and scientific worldviews. The 'darkness' of religious ignorance and superstition would fade away when exposed to the 'lights' of reason."[1]

In the early twentieth century, several contours of this secularization thesis would receive confirmation and consolidation through the influential work of the sociologist Max Weber. Foremost among these is the support his work provides for the idea that the modern world is chiefly the product of historical processes of rationalization. In an essay entitled "Science as a Vocation," Weber argues that "the fate of our times is characterized by rationalization and intellectualization and, above all, by the 'disenchantment of the world.'" Weber finds the latter phrase, which he borrows from Friedrich Schiller, so felicitous because it concisely distinguishes modern thought in its freedom *from* primitive, prescientific thought patterns, and thus in its freedom *for* the pursuit of scientific discovery. For Weber, modern processes of rationalization give us a world that is fundamentally "knowable." Rationalization, for him, implies that "principally there are no mysterious incalculable forces that come into play, but rather that one can, in principle, master all things by calculation. This means that the world is disenchanted. One need no longer have recourse to magical means in order to master or implore the spirits, as did the savage, for whom such mysterious powers existed. Technical means and calculations perform the service."[2]

Weber's work also highlights another, related product of historical processes of rationalization, namely, societal differentiation. In "Religious Rejections of the World and Their Directions," he argues that the same processes of rationalization that have enabled ancient tribal religions to evolve from local cults into such monotheistic religious expressions as the Western "prophetic religions of redemption" (with their universalistic "religious ethic of brotherliness") have also served to differentiate separate human value spheres—such as the political, economic, aesthetic, erotic, and scientific or intellectual—and to set them upon autonomous developmental courses. For Weber, this development introduces a growing tension between the "religious" and the "secular," one that grows stronger "the further the rationalization and sublimation of the external and internal possession of—in the widest sense—'things worldly' has progressed." Societal differentiation, then, describes for Weber a process that not only differentiates religion from other spheres of human value, but also one through which the historical axis of cultural power can be seen to shift:

> For the rationalization and the conscious sublimation of man's relations to the various spheres of values, external and internal, as well as religious and secular, have then pressed towards making conscious the *internal and lawful autonomy* of the individual spheres; thereby letting them drift into those tensions which remain hidden to the originally naïve relation with the external world. This results quite generally from the development of inner- and other-worldly values towards rationality, towards conscious endeavor, and towards sublimation by *knowledge*. This consequence is very important for the history of religion.[3]

In explaining Weber's understanding of societal differentiation, Casanova finds it helpful to distinguish between "the secular" as a concept, and "secularization" as a modernizing historical process. As a concept, the term "secular" has pre-Enlightenment origins. The medieval church used it to set up a dichotomous classification of reality into transcendent and worldly realms. Before the onset of modernity, however, "the Medieval dichotomous classification of reality into religious and secular realms was to a large extent dictated by the church." Officially, this meant that medieval societies still viewed themselves in largely religious terms, thus leaving everything within the *saeculum* as "an undifferentiated whole." According to Casanova, this undifferentiated realm could be differentiated into separate value spheres only after the dichotomous way of thinking characteristic of medieval Christian Europe came to an end: "The fall of the religious walls opened up a whole new space for processes of internal differentiation of the various secular spheres. Now, for the first time, the various secular spheres could come fully into their own, become differentiated from each other, and follow what Weber called their 'internal and lawful autonomy.'"[4]

A major result of setting such processes of societal differentiation in motion, according to Casanova, is that the spheres of the economy and the state, emerging from out of the secular sphere, would develop to become the two main axes of modern, post-Enlightenment societies. These two spheres would come to exert the largest gravitational pull of all the newly differentiated value spheres, including the religious. Because they have received such "steering authority" in modern society, religion has found itself relegated to a subsphere with much less cultural gravitas than it formerly enjoyed:

> In spatial-structural terms we may say that if reality before was structured around one main axis, now a multiaxial space was created with two main axes structuring the whole. In the language of functionalist systems theory, each subsystem became the environment for the others but two subsystems became the primary environment for all. In the new spatial structure, therefore, the religious sphere became just another sphere, structured around its own autonomous internal axis but falling under the gravitational force of the two main axes. . . . The religious sphere now became a less central and spatially diminished sphere within the new secular system.[5]

According to the secularization thesis, then, religion in the modern period becomes threatened from two sides, that is, from the historical pressures of both rationalization and societal differentiation.

Today, however, sociologists and other scholars of religion are coming to terms with the fact that such predictions of religion's demise as those put forward in the secularization thesis have been premature. Religious traditions and life patterns have not gone quietly into the private sphere, and various measures of demographic trends, such as the World Values Survey (WVS), show that, if anything, the global population is becoming more rather than less religious.[6] The secularization thesis has nevertheless remained resilient and influential in the face of such countervailing historical trends—in the sociology of religion as well as other intellectual disciplines. Such resilience has led contemporary sociologists of religion like Casanova, David Martin, and Peter Berger to suspect the operation of ideological factors in a thesis that claims to be merely descriptive of historical developments. As early as the 1960s, in fact, Martin began to suspect that perhaps the secularization thesis was "an ideological and philosophical imposition *on* history rather than an inference *from* history."[7]

In the face of such criticism of the secularization thesis, political scientists Pippa Norris and Ronald Inglehart mount what some scholars might view as a rearguard action in its defense. In their book *Sacred and Secular: Religion and Politics Worldwide*, they suggest that "talk of burying the secularization theory is premature."[8] In spite of the fact that WVS data show that, when viewed on a global scale, historical levels of religious participation not only persist but are increasing, they maintain that a qualified version of the secularization thesis can still be maintained and defended. According to their analysis, WVS data show that "the importance of religiosity persists most strongly among vulnerable populations, especially those living in poorer nations, facing personal survival-threatening risks." This aspect of global religiosity suggests to them that "feelings of vulnerability to physical, societal and personal risks" are a key factor driving its increasing levels (4; cf. 14). In advancing this thesis, the authors posit a direct relationship of dependence between the tendency to identify with a particular religion and differing levels of global economic development.

The flip side of this coin, of course, and a primary assumption of Norris and Inglehart's qualified defense of the secularization thesis, is that this key factor of existential vulnerability does not play a salient role in economically developed advanced industrial societies whose citizens are, by and large, not exposed to such threats. When we restrict our focus to such prosperous advanced industrial societies, Norris and Inglehart suggest, we find that the predictions of religious decline put forward by such thinkers as Auguste Comte, Emile Durkheim, Karl Marx, and Weber have been to a certain extent vindicated. Given relatively high levels of economic prosperity and existential security, the authors predict that the importance of religion in people's lives will dramatically wane: "In the long term and in global perspective . . . our theory predicts that the importance of religion in people's lives will gradually diminish with the process of human development" (54). The WVS data supporting this latter prediction provide the primary rationale for the authors' claim that "the concept of secularization captures an important part of what is going on" (4).[9]

Yet have citizens of advanced industrial societies in fact turned away from traditional religion to the extent that Norris and Inglehart claim? And, to the extent that they have, is relative affluence as powerful an explanatory factor as the authors claim it is? In what follows, we challenge both positions. In so doing, however, we in no way wish to contest the claim that, on the whole, identification with and participation in traditional religion is significantly lower in advanced industrial societies than it is in developing ones. All the same, our analysis paints a more complicated picture than the one Norris and Inglehart portray. To this picture we now turn.

Supply or Demand? Questioning Norris and Inglehart on Security and Secularization

Our analysis suggests that the difference between levels of religiosity in advanced industrial and developing societies, while real, is not as dramatic as Norris and Inglehart suggest. What is more, we believe other factors besides just affluence and existential security must be taken into account to explain this difference. In particular, people's confidence in traditional religious institutions seems to differ significantly between these two types of societies. To us, this suggests the possibility that there might be an issue concerning the "supply" of religious services in affluent advanced industrial societies that explains the lower levels of identification with traditional religion they exhibit, as opposed to a decrease in "demand" for these services as a direct result of affluence and existential security.

As the language of "supply" and "demand" suggests, Norris and Inglehart continue to employ a market model of religious trend analysis in their mitigated defense of the secularization thesis. This model, introduced by Rodney Stark and others,[10] claims that "the most influential strands of thought shaping the debate over secularization can be broadly subdivided into two perspectives"—demand-side and supply-side theories (7). Supply-side theories, such as those put forward by Stark and his colleagues, hold that the human demand for religion remains constant and stable, and any observed fluctuations in human religious participation or activity can be explained by fluctuations in the supply of religious services by religious institutions. Demand-side theories, on the other hand, "suggest that as societies industrialize, almost regardless of what religious leaders and organizations attempt, religious habits will gradually erode" (7). That is, as industrialization progresses, the actual demand for religion declines in the affected population. Employing the same language, Norris and Inglehart maintain that "although the original theory of secularization was flawed in certain regards, it was correct in the demand-side perspective" (7).

Norris and Inglehart here offer one plausible interpretation of the WVS data. However, their easy adoption of the market rhetoric of supply and demand masks a potential conceptual problem which we can here only touch upon, but nevertheless wish to emphasize. This problem has to do with the fact that the plausibility of a demand-side interpretation, such as the one Norris and Inglehart offer, relies upon a rather narrow conceptualization of religion. For their purposes, Norris and Inglehart define religious faith as "faith in the supernatural, the mysterious, and the magical" (7). Yet all faith commitments need not assume such an otherworldly form or focus. Norris and Inglehart themselves tacitly recognize this when, immediately after their aforementioned defense of demand-side theories of secularization, they move on to a new chapter section entitled, "The Rational *Weltanschauung*: The Loss of Faith." The very use of the word *weltanschauung* here suggests the possibility that, instead of faith simply having been lost through processes of industrialization, these processes themselves might instead signal the ascendance of a different faith or even faiths. Here "faith" or "religion" would not be construed simply as "faith in the supernatural, the mysterious, and the magical," but rather, along the lines of *weltanschauung*, as a fundamental spiritual orientation funded by trust in an ultimate source of meaning.[11]

On this broader conceptualization of faith or religion, the following description that Norris and Inglehart give of the "rational *weltanschauung*" might also be understood as a certain kind of "faith":

> In this perspective, the era of the Enlightenment generated a rational view of the world based on empirical standards of proof, scientific knowledge of natural phenomena, and technological mastery of the universe. Rationalism was thought to have rendered the central claims of the Church implausible in modern societies, blowing away the vestiges of superstitious dogma in Western Europe. The loss of faith was thought to cause religion to unravel, eroding habitual churchgoing practices and observance of ceremonial rituals, eviscerating the social meaning of denominational identities, and undermining active engagement in faith-based organizations and support for religious parties in civic society. (7)

While Norris and Inglehart clearly do not embrace such an understanding of secularization wholeheartedly, they do think it accurately describes what has occurred in some parts of the world, and thus think it would be a mistake to throw it out entirely (13). Aside from their use of the word *weltanschauung* to describe the aforementioned rationalist worldview, however, they seem unable or unwilling to interpret this historical development in terms of a competition between rival spirits (in the broader understanding of that term). Yet the act of placing ultimate confidence in human powers of rational mastery is a fiduciary act, simply because those rational powers it champions are themselves incapable of (rationally) grounding that confidence. This act is the Enlightenment-style rationalist's "leap of faith," as it were.

We think it is important to identify this conceptual issue here because it has a bearing on the alternative interpretation of the WVS data that we will offer below. The picture that emerges in the following analysis is not simply one of the decline of religious participation in advanced industrial societies (for which evidence does in fact exist). Instead, we offer an interpretation of the WVS data that demonstrates the continued, if challenged and troubled, vitality of ancient religious traditions struggling and sometimes failing to find their feet and remain relevant in changed historical circumstances. Such circumstances make it necessary for one to keep the preceding conceptual issue concerning religion in mind, for in order to understand what is happening to religious traditions in advanced industrial societies, one must first come to appreciate a sociocultural context in which a wide array of different "spirits" (both "sacred" and "secular") now compete for the hearts and minds of the members of these societies. Such an appreciation will be won more easily if we avoid a narrow understanding of what is involved in the idea of religious commitment.

Such a broader understanding of religious commitment also lends support to supply-side theories that view human beings as creatures who share basic religious and spiritual needs that can, more or less adequately, be supplied from sacred or secular sources. It might also be useful to point out here the logical leap involved in the assumption that, simply because people in advanced industrial societies tend to turn less frequently to traditional forms of religion, their demand for what these traditional sources once supplied has eroded. Such people, for example, might well continue living their lives in a spiritual vacuum, and, consciously or unconsciously, experience a resulting anomie or meaninglessness that is psychologically damaging—or they may receive spiritual nourishment from and organize their lives around other trusted sources of meaning. The point we would insist upon, and to which Norris and Inglehart's analysis pays insufficient attention, is that human beings, rich or poor, are creatures with spiritual, as well as physical and emotional, needs. We are creatures who need to relate ourselves to a "more-than-human" world in a meaningful way, to make sense of our lives in the context of so much that appears threatening or senseless.

Of course, one might reply that such a reconceptualization of religion as the one we here propose is overly broad, and the price of adopting it would be to dissolve any point of contrast between the sacred and the secular, thus making it impossible to analyze the demise of the one and the ascendance of the other in any given society. We do not consider this a necessary implication of such a reconceptualization, however, for in adopting it one may still speak of "secular" spiritual orientations and compare them to "sacred" ones. Conceptualizing the problem this way, Norris and Inglehart could still argue that, in advanced industrial societies, "sacred" spiritual orientations have declined, while other more "secular" spiritual orientations have gained ascendance. What would be gained from speaking this way is a greater appreciation for the plurality of spiritual sources that vie for the hearts and minds of people living in advanced industrial societies, as well as a heightened sensitivity to a complex historical situation in which issues of religious identification and participation are, from the start, problematic and anything but simple. In complex societies where such differing forces pull people in many directions, religious traditions and communities, as the WVS data show, can no longer assume automatic authority over, or deference from, the people they have attracted or would hope to attract into their folds. But this does not mean that such traditions and communities have ceased to harbor any spiritual resources that a modern person might find meaningful in the face of the vicissitudes they experience in life.

We believe that something like this more nuanced and differentiated picture allows for a more fruitful interpretation of the WVS data concerning issues of secularization and religious participation in advanced industrial societies than the one that Norris and Inglehart offer. For example, it better explains why, after three centuries of supposedly enlightened development, religious traditions and institutions still survive in advanced industrial societies, even as it explains the setbacks such traditions and institutions have also suffered. Instead of interpreting these setbacks as evidence for the general decline of religion and concomitant rise of secularization in advanced industrial societies, as Norris and Inglehart do, we intend to highlight dimensions of the WVS which show that, even under duress, participation and involvement in traditional religious institutions and practices show stronger signs of life in these societies than Norris and Inglehart claim.

Do WVS Data Suggest a More Complicated Picture of Human Religiosity?

As we mentioned in the previous section, a demand-side explanation of secularization such as the one Norris and Inglehart offer appears especially plausible when one brackets the larger conceptual issue and proceeds to understand religion primarily as they have. The rationalist *weltanschauung* of the Enlightenment that Norris and Inglehart describe so well, a *weltanschauung* that has inspired various processes of industrialization, societal differentiation, and technological development, has adversely affected the tenability of these sorts of "sacred" spiritual beliefs. The question remains, of course, whether this adverse effect is as extensive in advanced industrial societies as they say it is. At any rate, it is fair to say that it has become increasingly difficult to maintain such traditional religious life patterns in the face of these secular-tending historical forces.[12] But the point is precisely that these historical forces are not religiously neutral, but that they have instead introduced an increasing number of institutional presences and pressures that, in an important spiritual sense, vie for the hearts and minds of citizens of advanced industrial societies. We see the terrain, then, not as one of inevitable secularization, but as one in which competing spiritual forces contend for allegiance, and in which individuals and groups struggle to discern which sources best lend meaning and integrity to their increasingly fragmented lives.

We suggest that with modernization and human development come the added pressures of, among other things, a fast-paced consumer capitalist lifestyle. Advanced industrial societies also evince higher levels of "cognitive mobilization" (higher levels of education and increased exposure to media and other sources of information via the expansion of information technology), which adds certain cognitive pressures and dissonances to the issue of one's involvement in religious communities and institutions.[13] The days are fading fast when one's "choice" of religious identification was simply a matter of cultural location and inheritance. To such cognitive pressures, finally, one may add declining respect for institutional authority, including religious institutional authority.[14] The WVS data show a significant disjunct between individual orientation with regard to various spiritual beliefs and the confidence people in advanced industrial societies place in traditional religious institutions. In a fast-paced society that leaves little time for pause or reflection, and in which we nevertheless have come to possess more than just a passing acquaintance with the plurality of spiritual alternatives contending for human allegiance, our deference to traditional religious authorities has become anything but automatic. As we hope to show, factors such as these create new challenges for religious traditions and institutions as they attempt to speak in relevant ways to the vexing issues of contemporary life in advanced industrial societies. But does the existence of these pressures in and of themselves reflect the diminishment of the importance of religion or spirituality in the lives of the members of these societies, as Norris and Inglehart suggest? We think there are other plausible ways to interpret the evidence contained in the WVS.

In order to move the analysis in the direction of such an alternative interpretation, we have parsed our examination of the WVS data into five rubrics. We begin by looking at people's own *subjective evaluations* of the relevance that religion has in their lives. From there, we compare the data measuring the level of people's *religious involvement* across various types of society, whether agrarian, industrial, or advanced industrial. We then examine the role that *prayer* plays in people's lives, both in terms of proportion of people in each type of society who engage in such a spiritual discipline, and also, within those varying proportions, the attitudes that such practitioners have toward that practice and religion in general. From here we move on to an analysis of the various religious *beliefs* that people in these various societies hold, with an eye to the differences that emerge across them. Finally, and perhaps most importantly, we assess the *degree of confidence in religious institutions* displayed by members of each society. Here we find a stark contrast between agrarian and advanced industrial societies, a contrast that we think illuminates the challenge that religious institutions in advanced industrial societies must meet if they are to remain viable organizers of religious participation in the future. We believe that these analyses suggest that, while there is reason to expect that the demand for religion (narrowly defined) in advanced industrial societies may be somewhat lower than in agrarian societies, the question of whether this poses a demand-side decline or raises a supply-side concern still remains. Several signs suggest that the demand for religion, even in advanced industrial societies, still remains relatively strong. Consequently, the future of religion in these societies may not necessarily be destined to diminish, but rather may well depend on how the suppliers (i.e., religious institutions) cope with their changing circumstances.

Subjective Evaluations

We begin with people's own subjective evaluations of the relevance that religion plays in their lives. The evidence portrayed in Figure 1 shows that people in advanced industrial societies do attribute less importance to both religion and God in their daily lives than do people in agrarian societies. In agrarian societies, for instance,

FIGURE 1: SUBJECTIVE RELIGIOSITY

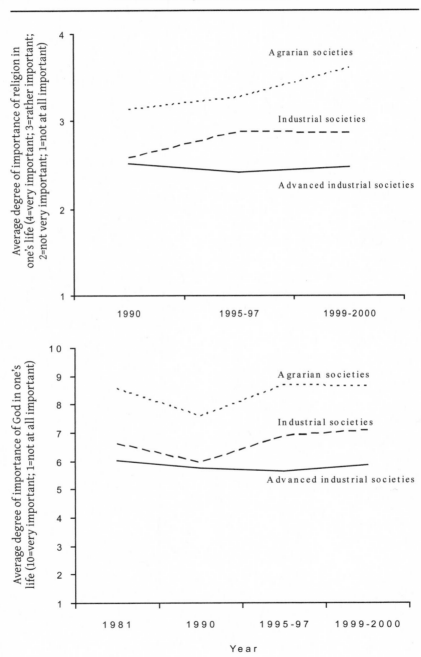

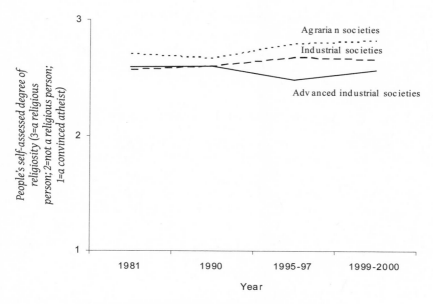

Source: *1981, 1990, 1995-1997, 1999-2000 World Values Surveys.*

religion ranks on average as being between "very important" and "rather important." Moreover, the importance of religion in these societies has increased over the last decade. In advanced industrial societies, however, religion is ranked on average as being between "rather important" and "not very important," with the only cross-time change being a slight decline in importance during the early part of the last decade. Furthermore, on a scale ranging from 1 to 10, where 1 is "not at all important" and 10 is "very important," the average degree of importance attributed to God in agrarian societies ranges between 8 and 9, whereas in advanced industrial societies it hovers around 6.

Do all these measures mean, however, that people in more affluent societies no longer understand themselves as being religious? There is evidence to suggest otherwise. Presumably, if people in more affluent societies no longer considered themselves to be religious, then we might expect them to be more inclined to declare themselves as such in the WVS questionnaire. Yet that is not in fact what we find. In advanced industrial societies, people's self-assessed

Ronald Kuipers and Mebs Kanji

degree of religiosity remains relatively similar to that of their counterparts in agrarian and industrial societies. On average, we find
that most people, regardless of the type of society in which they live
(affluent or poor/secure or vulnerable), consider themselves to be
more religious than not.

Religious Participation and Involvement

Subjective assessment of one's religiosity, however, is not the same
thing as actual involvement in religious institutions and practices.
Are people in advanced industrial societies as involved in religious
life as people in less developed countries? The evidence in Figure
2 suggests a rather ambiguous answer to that question. People in
agrarian societies do attend religious services more frequently
than those in industrial and advanced industrial societies. On average, the frequency of religious attendance in agrarian societies is
between "once a month" and only "on special holy days." In industrial and advanced industrial societies, however, the average frequency of religious attendance ranges from "only on special holy
days" to "once a year."

FIGURE 2: RELIGIOUS INVOLVEMENT

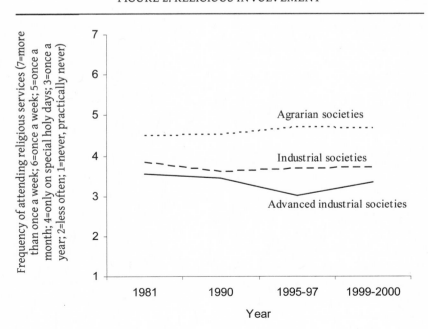

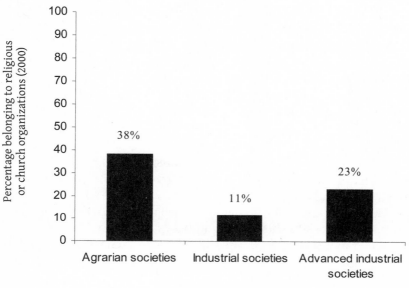

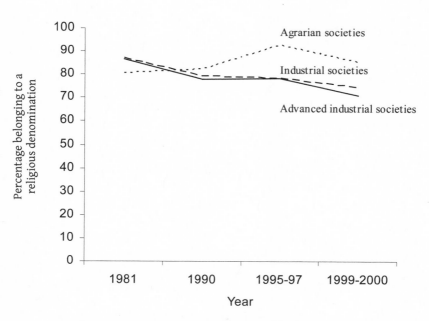

Source: 1981, 1990, 1995–1997, 1999–2000 World Values Surveys.

Should these measurements be interpreted, however, to mean that religious involvement in industrial and advanced industrial societies is destined to decline? Additional evidence presented in Figure 2 suggests that, while people in these societies may place less emphasis on regularly attending religious services, they may be increasingly inclined to join religious or church organizations. The proportion of people indicating that they belong to religious or church organizations declines sharply (–27 percent) as societies shift from being agrarian to industrial societies. However, the percentage of people indicating that they belong to religious or church organizations more than doubles (+12 percent) as societies shift from being industrial to advanced industrial. In agrarian societies, nearly four in ten people claim to belong to religious or church organizations. In industrial societies that number drops to one in ten. And in advanced industrial countries, slightly more than two in every ten people indicate that they belong to such organizations. The difference between the latter two groups problematizes Norris and Inglehart's proposed link between secularization and development.

The results are even more striking when we compare the measures of belonging to a religious denomination across these three types of societies. Do people in more advanced industrial societies show less signs of belonging to a religious denomination than those in agrarian or industrial states? The evidence over the last two decades suggests that although the proportion of citizens in advanced industrial states belonging to a religious denomination has declined, as of 1999/2000 the extent of the differences between developed and less developed countries remains fairly minimal. In agrarian societies, the most recent evidence suggests that eight out of ten people belong to a religious denomination, whereas in advanced industrial societies the number is seven out of ten.

Prayer

People in advanced industrial societies tend to lead faster-paced lives and have different priorities than people in agrarian societies. Such a lifestyle may leave little room for the dedication, pause, and reflection required to seriously engage in religious practices and disciplines. The presence of these and other competing forces may help to account for some of the preceding differences in subjective evaluations of religiosity and involvement in religious practices and institutions. It may also explain why the proportion of people who admit to taking some moments for prayer, meditation, contemplation, and the like is lower in industrial and advanced industrial societies than it is in agrarian ones.

FIGURE 3: PRAYER

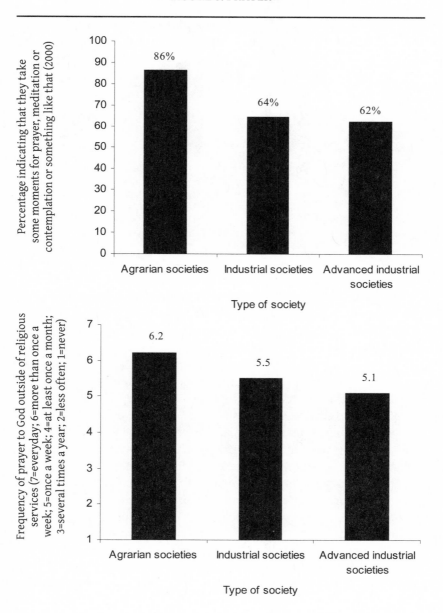

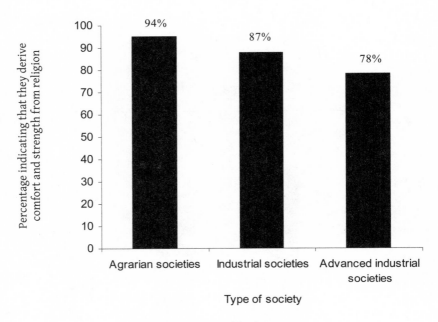

Source: 1999–2000 World Values Surveys.

Figure 3 shows that 86 percent of citizens in agrarian societies take the time to engage in such activities, as compared to 62 percent in advanced industrial societies. However, when we look exclusively at those who do partake in such activities, the evidence shows that the frequency of prayer is not all that different between agrarian societies, on the one hand, and industrial or advanced industrial societies, on the other. The average frequency of prayer in agrarian societies, for instance, amounts to more than once a week, whereas in advanced industrial societies, it is once a week. Moreover, of those who engage in the practice of prayer, the proportion who indicate that they derive benefits from partaking in such activity also does not seem to vary too greatly from one type of society to the next.

In agrarian societies, for example, more than nine in ten people who engage in activities such as prayer, meditation, contemplation, and so on, indicate that they derive a sense of comfort and strength from religion. In advanced industrial states, nearly eight in ten people who participate in such activities indicate that they also derive a sense of comfort and strength. While significantly fewer people may engage in such a spiritual practice in advanced industrial societies, the fact that a high proportion of those who do report a sense of comfort and strength from religion suggests that the existing supply-side of religious culture is still capable of serving as a coherent source of meaning for at least some people in these societies in their attempt to cope with the chaos and flux of modern life.

Beliefs

Is there any evidence to suggest a difference between the particular religious beliefs held by people in more affluent societies from those held by people in agrarian ones? The evidence in Figure 4 again indicates a complex picture that belies any simple answer. In general, people in agrarian societies are more inclined to hold traditional spiritual beliefs (such as belief in God, life after death, the existence of the soul, hell, and heaven) than are people in industrial and advanced industrial societies. Yet certain beliefs, such as the belief in God and the belief that people have a soul, tend to be more widely held across these different types of society than such beliefs as belief in life after death, hell, or heaven.

FIGURE 4: BELIEFS

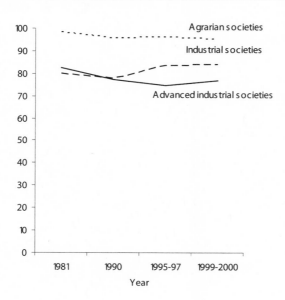

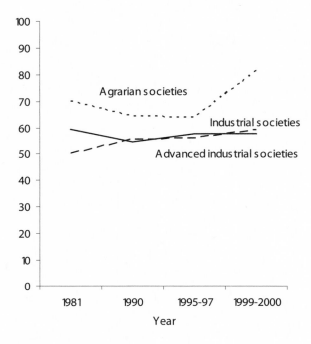

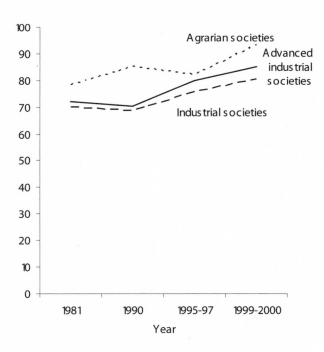

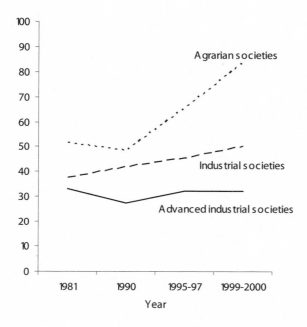

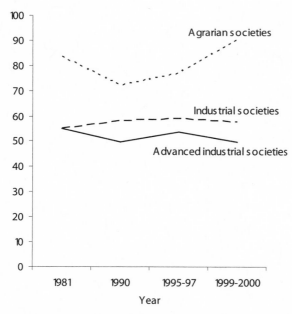

Source: 1981, 1990, 1995–1997, 1999–2000 World Values Surveys.

The most recent evidence indicates that more than seven out of ten citizens in industrial and advanced industrial societies still believe in God. Furthermore, evidence covering the 1980s and 1990s shows that the proportion of people in advanced industrial societies who believe that people have a soul has actually increased (from 72 percent to 85 percent). When it comes to the notion of an afterlife, however, the difference between agrarian and industrial/advanced industrial societies is much greater. Far fewer people in these latter types of society hold such beliefs. Among these populations, approximately six out of every ten people believe in the idea of life after death, five in ten believe in the notion of heaven, and only three in ten believe in the notion of hell.

These findings, however, can be read to pose more of a supply-side concern than to indicate a demand-side decline. At one time, beliefs such as these used to be crucial in sustaining the authority of the church. The promise of salvation made the church a very powerful institution in people's lives. The abuse of this power, in fact, contributed to one of the great historical withdrawals of deference from religious institutional authority, the Protestant Reformation. Even within contemporary religious culture, attitudes toward the ideas of salvation and damnation are changing radically.[15] Here we see the ability of certain segments of religious culture to modify their position with respect to such issues while still remaining recognizably (in this case) Christian. Looking at the supply side of religious culture, then, it is not difficult to imagine certain religious institutions, and perhaps even entire denominations, following such theological trends. In this way, religious institutions may yet prove themselves capable of flexibly adapting to a contemporary context in ways that avoid alienating the citizens of advanced industrial societies who may potentially turn to them for spiritual guidance.

Confidence in Religious Institutions

Further evidence to suggest that secularization trends may pose more of a supply-side concern than a demand-side decline is presented in Figure 5. Evidence from agrarian societies indicates that the average degree of confidence in churches ranges between "a great deal" and "quite a lot." Moreover, the cross-time evidence over the last two decades shows that the average degree of confidence in churches in agrarian societies has in fact increased.

FIGURE 5: CONFIDENCE IN RELIGIOUS INSTITUTIONS

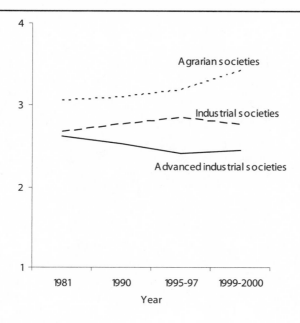

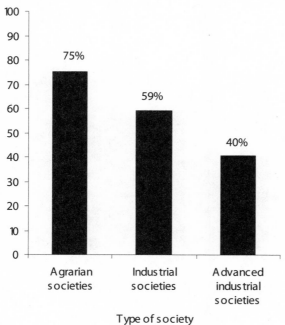

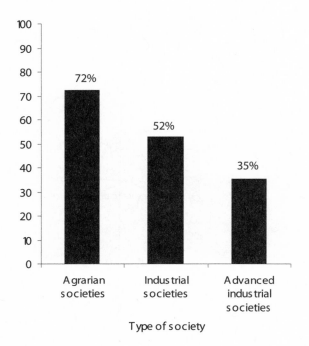

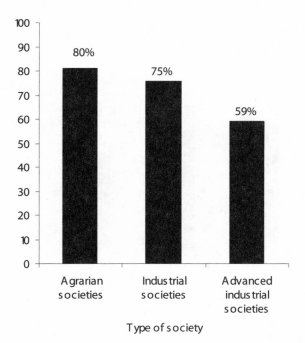

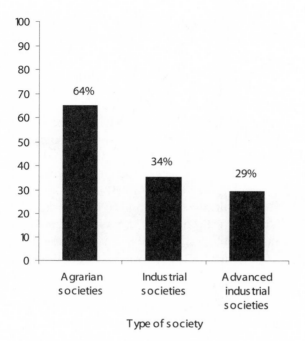

Source: 1981, 1990, 1995–1997, 1999–2000 World Values Surveys.

In advanced industrial societies, however, people's perceptions of religious institutions are not as strong. The average degree of confidence ranges between "quite a lot" and "not very much." Moreover, the average degree of confidence in churches in advanced industrial states has declined over most of the last two decades. What is more, the evidence also shows that people in advanced industrial societies tend to be more skeptical of the church's advice, particularly on issues dealing with morality and the needs of the individual, family life, and social problems. Eight out of ten people in agrarian countries indicate that churches give adequate answers to people's spiritual needs, whereas nearly six in every ten people in advanced industrial states also agree that this is still the case. However, when it comes to giving advice about moral problems and the needs of the individual, 75 percent of people in agrarian societies feel that churches give adequate advice on such matters, while only 40 percent of people in advanced industrial societies feel the same way. Likewise, 72 percent of the members of agrarian societies claim that churches give adequate answers to problems dealing with family life, but only 35 percent of people in advanced industrial societies agree that this is the case. Finally, 64 percent of people in agrarian societies indicate that churches respond adequately to the social problems facing their countries, while only 29 percent of people in advanced industrial societies feel the same way.

On the issue of confidence in religious institutions, we find the starkest difference between agrarian and advanced industrial societies. While other measures indicate the continuing presence of religious vitality and interest in advanced industrial societies, this last indicator reveals a growing gap between that level of vitality and the ability of religious institutions to respond to it or make room for it. The future challenge for religious traditions in advanced industrial societies, then, might well be to address this growing gap in ways that retain continuity with their past, while yet speaking relevantly to the ever-changing present.

Religious Tradition in the Future: Searching for Meaning in Advanced Industrial Society

To their credit, Norris and Inglehart do recognize that the story they tell concerning religion worldwide fails to explain a remaining degree of interest in religion among the citizenry of affluent societies. While they do not consider it to be very significant, they admit that "private or individualized spirituality" has survived the various processes of secularization through which the publics of affluent nations have become "increasingly indifferent to traditional religious values" (74). The authors also duly note a rise in "thinking about the meaning of life" among citizens of affluent advanced industrial nations. From this, they conclude that "while the existing hierarchical religious institutions seem to be losing their ability to dictate to the masses, the publics of most countries showed increasing interest in the meaning and purpose of life. . . . Growing proportions of the public thought about spiritual concerns, broadly defined" (75).

For Norris and Inglehart, however, this increase in thinking about spiritual concerns does not amount to support for supply-side theories that argue for the existence of a steady religious demand in advanced industrial societies. This may be because their notion of demand seems to be linked to *traditional*, hierarchical forms of institutional supply. It is the demand for that particular form of supply that has shown increasing diminishment in affluent societies, and from this they conclude that demand for religion in general does not remain constant. Yet apparently the demand to find meaning in life does: "The need for meaning becomes more salient at high levels of existential security so that, even in rich countries, although church attendance is declining, spiritual concerns more broadly are not disappearing. At the same time, it is clear that these publics are not continuing to support the traditional religious authorities, institutionalized, hierarchical forms of religion, and established religious practices" (75). Norris and Inglehart fail to provide an explanation as to why the need for meaning becomes more salient at high levels of existential security.

This inability to account for the increasing salience of the need for meaning among citizens of advanced industrial societies leads us to wonder what sort of existential security they claim these citizens enjoy. What is the character of a form of security that, even when enjoyed at high levels, fails to provide for one of our most basic human needs, the human need to find meaning in life? Could it be that citizens of advanced industrial societies suffer from an increasing sense of life's meaninglessness, and that this sense in and of itself might constitute a form of existential insecurity that Norris and Inglehart fail to take into account?

In outlining his version of the secularization thesis, Weber himself drew attention to this more problematic side of modern processes of rationalization. In "Religious Rejections of the World and Their Directions," he noticed the existence of a latent tension between the "rational, empirical knowledge" which has "consistently worked through to the disenchantment of the world and its transformation into a causal mechanism" and "the ethical postulate" of religion (including its more "rationalized" forms), according to which "the world is a God-ordained, and hence somehow *meaningfully* and ethically-oriented, cosmos." Weber goes further than simply noting this tension, and proceeds to suggest that the modern path of rationalization in fact stands opposed to any attempt to locate meaning in life: "In principle, the empirical as well as the mathematically oriented view of the world develops refutations of every intellectual approach which in any way asks for a 'meaning' of inner-worldly occurrences."[16] Whether or not this state of affairs constituted a problem for Weber, it is clear from WVS data that it poses a great problem for most citizens of advanced industrial states. If Weber is right, the paradoxical result would be that such people search and long for meaning in a context dominated by a rationalist *weltanschauung* that is precisely incapable of providing it.[17]

In spite of the persistence of the question of life's meaning in affluent advanced industrial societies (among other remaining religious elements), Norris and Inglehart remain confident in the predictive power they believe to have discovered in the association between declining levels of religious involvement and increased levels of human development.[18] In retaining this confidence, they suggest that traditional religion no longer resonates with a growing majority of citizens in advanced industrial societies. Religious culture, they claim, has resonance mainly as a source of comfort to those who suffer from the varying effects of material impoverishment. In societies where such impoverishment has been overcome to a large degree, the demand for religious services drops sharply. Theological or other intellectual attempts to ponder the meaning of life are not to the point here, they say, and such practices were only ever the concern of an intellectual elite anyway: "Under the conditions of existential insecurity that have dominated the lives of most of humanity throughout most of history, the great theological questions concerned a relatively narrow constituency; the vast majority of the population was most strongly concerned with the need for reassurance in the face of a world where survival was uncertain, and this was the dominant factor explaining the grip of traditional religion on mass publics" (20). Fortunately enough for those societies who have reaped the developmental benefits of industrialization, "[t]he modernization process reduces the threats to survival that are common in developing societies, especially among the poorest strata; and this enhanced sense of security lessens the need for the reassurance religion provides" (53).

Our argument here has been that, when we conceive of human religious need otherwise than Norris and Inglehart do, the WVS data can be read to paint a more complicated picture of the shape that this need takes in advanced industrial societies. If we take the importance of locating meaning in life seriously as a basic spiritual need and value, we are able to see a greater spiritual neediness in advanced industrial society than Norris and Inglehart in fact see. Throughout their study, Norris and Inglehart remain remarkably sanguine about the supposed benefits accruing to affluent advanced industrial societies in the wake of the various aforementioned modernization processes, as if these processes themselves introduced no new existential insecurities that were not already there. To cite only a few examples, they give scant mention to the insecurities introduced by such problems as consumerist alienation, economic and infrastructural collapse in an age of post-peak oil production, or widespread ecological destruction. Could not the existence of these looming insecurities provide one explanation of why, in spite of high levels of material comfort and security, the question of life's meaning grows ever more salient for citizens of advanced industrial societies?

Even a thoroughly secular thinker like Jürgen Habermas does not turn a blind eye to the many unintended pathologies that have accompanied the benefits of modernization, and the problem this poses for secularization theories. He thus urges us to "keep in mind that the dialectic of our own occidental process of secularization has as yet not come to a close," and in addressing these pathologies he suggests that a largely secularized society may still have much to learn from traditional religions.[19] In a helpful essay on Weberian disenchantment, Christopher L. Walton suggests that salient possibilities remain for religious culture to make a unique and ameliorating contribution to the problems affecting modern society. Because, as Weber notes repeatedly, the universalistic "ethic of brotherliness" (which, as we have seen, emerges from the rationalized "prophetic religions of redemption") stands increasingly opposed to such rationalized value spheres as a capitalistically driven economy and a bureaucratically managed state, it is able to provide some critical purchase on these problematic forms of social organization.[20] In Walton's words: "Religious people who try to serve the ethic of brotherliness in the various spheres of their lives introduce a form of rationality that is somewhat hostile to the rationalized and intellectualized methods of the modern disciplines. By acting out of an ethic rooted in a perception of ultimate meaning beyond the proper domain of any other discipline, religious people challenge the reigning forms of social organization in ways that may yet prove creative."[21]

Walton's reading of Weber, like Habermas' critique of the current phase of modern processes of secularization and rationalization, suggests that we need not follow David Hume or Friedrich Nietzsche, as Norris and Inglehart implicitly do, and understand religion primarily or only as a product of fear. Perhaps religious traditions are capable of being more than simply placating balms in times of trouble. Perhaps they can also provide resources for critically facing that trouble and overcoming it in a gesture of reconciliation. If so, then religious traditions might well remain relevant spiritual forces in advanced industrial societies, and they might do so in ways that escape the measures for religious participation that Norris and Inglehart's emphasize.[22]

Can traditional religious culture play a new, positive role as affluent advanced industrial societies come to terms with the aforementioned problems of modernization, problems that have now become truly global in scope? At the end of their book, Norris and Inglehart hint at a negative answer, claiming that the growing rift that they see emerging between the sacred and the secular will only become more salient in international political conflicts, even if it need not necessarily enflame those conflicts (216–17). In the face of the challenges that we must meet in the twenty-first century, we suggest to the contrary that the opportunity exists for religious traditions to transform themselves and speak to this broken situation in ways that people may once again find meaningful and helpful. If they would seize this opportunity and demonstrate their relevance on this score, that would perhaps do much to address the alienation that individuals seem to have with respect to the institutional side of religion. Whether or not traditional religious institutions will mount anything like the kind of response we are here suggesting remains speculation on our part, and is not directly supported by our analysis. But our analysis does seem to indicate that the opportunity is there.

Norris and Inglehart offer a fascinating, well-researched portrait of the religious state of affairs across the globe. While we do not think that their analyses and arguments completely fail to capture what is going on, we do think that the picture is more complicated than the one which they present. Affluent advanced industrial societies still show signs of religious life that are more than just vestigial remnants of a bygone age. These indications lead us to believe that a challenging opportunity remains for religious traditions to once again speak meaningfully to a spiritually hungry culture, one that suffers from a loss of meaning.

In an entry in *Culture and Value*, dated 1930, Ludwig Wittgenstein troubles the modernist believer's easy confidence in the processes of intellectualization and rationalization that Weber has described, and which have gone on to become a core component of the secularization thesis. He suggests that people in the grip of this confidence—people who assume, in Norris and Inglehart's words, that "technological mastery of the universe can be achieved"—need once again "to awaken to wonder" and not allow this confidence to send them to sleep again. While many of those who live in affluent advanced industrial societies may be relatively comfortable and fearless now, Wittgenstein warns us that "it cannot be ruled out that *highly* civilized people will succumb to this fear again; and their civilization and scientific knowledge cannot protect them from it." Although, as Wittgenstein also notes, "the *spirit* in which science is transacted today is not compatible with such fear," such incompatibility might simply speak to the poverty of that spirit.[23] Recognizing the problems that various modernization processes have left in their wake, we can slowly begin to see the problematic nature of the spiritual confidence that is evident in the more ideological versions of the secularization thesis. Today we find more than enough cause to search for alternative spiritual sources of meaning, for surely only the most recalcitrant acolyte of the modern progress myth would say that nothing is wrong or that we have nothing to fear. The current challenge for traditional religious institutions in advanced industrial societies, then, will be to mine their traditional resources for spiritual gifts that can resonate with people who continue to search for meaning in life, even and especially under the weight of its modern collapse.

Chapter 5

Alienated Masterpiece
Adorno's Contribution to a Transformative Social Theory

Lambert Zuidervaart

Enlightenment . . . has always aimed at liberating human beings from fear and installing them as masters. Yet the wholly enlightened earth radiates under the sign of disaster triumphant.

—*Max Horkheimer and Theodor W. Adorno*[1]

∞ ∞ ∞

Even in *Dialectic of Enlightenment* the impulse of the Enlightenment is not betrayed.

—*Jürgen Habermas*[2]

Dialectic of Enlightenment deserves the label Theodor Adorno gave the *Missa Solemnis*: "alienated masterpiece." With only one modification, his comments on Beethoven's celebrated and misunderstood composition can express the reception accorded Horkheimer and Adorno's work: "Every now and then . . . it is possible to name a work in which the neutralization of culture has expressed itself most strikingly; a work . . . which occupies an uncontested place in the repertoire even while it remains enigmatically incomprehensible; and one which . . . offers no justification for the [abuse] accorded it."[3] As Adorno observed with respect to the *Missa Solemnis*, "to speak seriously" of *Dialectic of Enlightenment* today "can mean nothing less than . . . to alienate it." Here, however, alienating the work does not require one "to break through the aura of irrelevant worship which protectively surrounds it,"[4] but to disrupt gestures of easy dismissal that prohibit a thoughtful engagement, at a time when debates concerning globalization increase its significance.

This essay considers the contribution of Horkheimer and Adorno's "philosophical fragments" to a transformative social theory. By "transformative social theory," I mean an attempt to evaluate contemporary globalization with respect to the shape of societal evil and the prospects for its removal. The point of such a project is to envision a democratic politics of global transformation.[5] This project calls for scholarly approaches that are normative, comprehensive, and interdisciplinary. But the state of various academic disciplines makes the project very difficult to achieve. While some of the social sciences are open to comprehensive perspectives, they tend to be normatively thin. Although many of the humanities have become more interdisciplinary in recent years, they hesitate to address comprehensive questions. And even disciplines such as philosophy and theology, which tend to be more comprehensive and more attuned to normative issues, have little to offer on questions of societal structure and historical change. So we really do need the sort of normative, comprehensive, and interdisciplinary theorizing that Hegel provided with respect to modernity and that Horkheimer and Adorno famously attempted, albeit in a more fragmentary fashion, for the "dialectic of enlightenment."

Yet their celebrated attempt is frequently misunderstood. Some read *Dialectic of Enlightenment* as darkly rejecting modernity and the secular disenchantment that modernity achieves. Others regard it as desperately affirming a mythical reenchantment of nature and of human life. By contrast, I interpret it as a dialectical disenchanting of disenchantment, as neither rejecting the achievements of modernity nor straightforwardly affirming what modernization sets aside. As I shall explain, the key to Horkheimer and Adorno's delicately calibrated critique of modern secularization, and to a thoughtful engagement with their critique, lies in a Hegelian notion of determinate negation. When interpreted in this way, *Dialectic of Enlightenment* offers crucial insights for evaluating contemporary globalization.[6]

Habermas' Paradigmatic Critique

It is not so much Adorno's opponents as his own successors who make a fresh reception difficult. There is by now a veritable army of "critical theorists" who regard *Dialectic of Enlightenment* as the nadir of the Frankfurt School from whose abyssal aporias all must be rescued. The marching tune of this protective phalanx is familiar. It begins with Jürgen Habermas' muted worries in the late 1960s about an alleged attraction to a mystical "resurrection of fallen nature." As Habermas put it in a public tribute shortly after Adorno's death, "Adorno . . . entertained doubts that the emancipation of humanity is possible without the resurrection of nature. Could humans talk with one another without anxiety and repression unless at the same time they interacted with the nature around them as they would with brothers and sisters?"[7] Over against Adorno as a latter-day St. Francis, Habermas' own stance is firm: "The concept of a categorically different science and technology is as empty as the idea of a universal reconciliation is without basis."[8] Citing Albrecht Wellmer,[9] Habermas links Adorno's ambivalent hope for reconciliation with a tendency to turn Marx' critique of political economy into a philosophy of history that neglects an empirically based theory of late capitalist society.

From these opening strains the battle cry swells into increasingly hostile and hermeneutically astonishing attacks. Albrecht Wellmer, in an otherwise careful and instructive essay, sees in *Dialectic of Enlightenment* an "anthropological and epistemological 'monism'" whose single-minded rejection of "instrumental reason" as "the paradigm of perverted reason" threatens to turn liberation into "an eschatological category."[10] Around the same time, Axel Honneth portrays Adorno's "critical social philosophy" as an exercise in "pessimistic self-clarification" that "cannot commit itself to an idea of historical progress which goes beyond total reification."[11] Relying heavily on the interpretations of Grenz[12] and of Baumeister and Kulenkampff,[13] Honneth claims that Adorno sees "aesthetic theory and negative dialectics" as "the only means whereby a weakened critical social theory can conceptualize capitalist domination."[14] The totalizing of reification begun in *Dialectic of Enlightenment* leaves "an aesthetic cooperation with nature" as the only domain where "the domination-free interpretation of inner nature is possible."[15]

Although Honneth subsequently modifies this portrait of Adorno as gloomy aesthete, the main lines to his critique remain the same: *Dialectic of Enlightenment* reflects Adorno's being "imprisoned to a totalized model of the domination of nature" that renders him unable "to comprehend the 'social' in societies."[16] Indeed, Honneth sees Adorno, not Horkheimer, as masterminding this fatal collapse of critical social theory.[17] It is primarily Adorno who

turns "the interdisciplinary analysis of society" into "the subordi-
nate auxiliary to an aporetic critical theory vacillating between a
negativistic philosophy and philosophical aesthetics."[18] Even Seyla
Benhabib, who sees more potential than Honneth does in Adorno's
concept of "mimetic reconciliation," regards *Dialectic of Enlightenment* as the book that sent critical theory into an aesthetic tailspin.
She claims that Adorno and Horkheimer seek "the alternative to
identity logic and to the domination of internal and external nature
in the aesthetic realm." This "turn to the aesthetic" is "astonishing," she says, because "the aesthetic realm offers no real negation
of identity logic."[19]

The most forceful statements of such objections, however, have
come from Habermas, whom Wellmer, Honneth, and Benhabib
regard as having freed critical theory from cyclopean bondage.[20]
Habermas elaborates his criticisms of *Dialectic of Enlightenment* in two
contexts. First, in the final chapter of volume 1 to *The Theory of Communicative Action*,[21] Habermas tries to show why his own account of
societal rationalization is a worthy and necessary successor to Western Marxist accounts of reification. Here he argues that *Dialectic of
Enlightenment* drives critical theory into a dead end from which only
a *"change of paradigm* within social theory" can deliver it (TCA 1:366).
A paradigm shift is required in order to rescue critical theory from
Horkheimer and Adorno's fatal expansion of Weber's rationalization
thesis, via Lukács' theory of reification, into a totalizing "critique
of instrumental reason": a paradigm shift from the philosophy of
consciousness to a philosophy of communication. According to Habermas, Lukács' theory problematically relied on Hegel's objective
idealism, and it was disconfirmed by the failure of proletarian revolutions. This led Horkheimer and Adorno "to sink the foundations of
reification critique still deeper and to expand instrumental reason
into a category of the world-historical process of civilization as a
whole, that is, to project the process of reification back behind the
capitalist beginnings of the modern age into the very beginnings of
hominization" (TCA 1:366).

Their theoretical totalizing of reification has three consequences, says Habermas, all of which he aims to avoid: (1) it undercuts the normative foundations for critical theory (TCA 1:374–77); (2)
it forces critical theory to appeal to a concept of truth that it cannot
thematize (TCA 1:382–83); and (3) it leads Adorno to renounce social
theory altogether in favor of mimetic "gesticulation" (TCA 1:385).

Indeed, Adorno's sole normative foundation comes "shockingly close" to the archenemy Martin Heidegger: "As opposed as the intentions behind their respective philosophies of history are, Adorno is in the end very similar to Heidegger as regards his position on the theoretical claims of objectivating thought and of reflection: The mindfulness [*Eingedenken*] of nature comes shockingly close to the recollection [*Andenken*] of being" (TCA 1:385).

A similar response to this last theme occurs in *The Philosophical Discourse of Modernity*,[22] the second context where Habermas elaborates his criticisms of Horkheimer and Adorno's alienated masterpiece. Quoting from *Dialectic of Enlightenment*, Habermas says Adorno's *Negative Dialectics* points insistently and relentlessly toward "the prospect of that magically invoked 'mindfulness of nature [*Eingedenken der Natur*] in the subject in whose fulfillment the unacknowledged truth of all culture lies hidden'" (PDM 119–20). Now what was "shockingly close" to Heidegger's "recollection of being" is "magically invoked" as well.

This telling phrase occurs in an essay where Habermas compares *Dialectic of Enlightenment* with Nietzsche's critique of the Enlightenment. The comparison is supposed to "forestall" any confusion between Horkheimer and Adorno's "hope of the hopeless" and postmodern "moods and attitudes" emanating "under the sign of a Nietzsche revitalized by poststructuralism" (PDM 106). By the end of the essay, however, the similarities to Nietzsche, not the differences, stand out. Habermas identifies three similarities. Like Nietzsche, Horkheimer and Adorno (1) do not do justice to "the rational content of cultural modernity" made available in the differentiation of value spheres and expert cultures (PDM 112–14, 121); (2) they undertake a critique of ideology critique that detaches critique from "its own foundations" and regards these foundations "as shattered" (PDM 116–19); and (3) they pursue this totalizing critique from the perspective of "aesthetic modernity," as distinct from scientific or moral modernity (PDM 122–25, 128–29). Consequently, and again like Nietzsche, Horkheimer and Adorno fall into a "performative contradiction": they use reason to critique the ideological corruption of all reason. Unlike Nietzsche, however, they do not seek refuge in a theory of power, refusing instead to develop any theory to overcome "the performative contradiction inherent in an ideology critique that outstrips itself" (PDM 127). Adorno in particular strikes Habermas as admirably consistent, for Adorno remains inside this performative contradiction and shows why it cannot be escaped (PDM 119–20). Nevertheless Habermas rejects the "purist intent" behind the Frankfurters' hypercritique. It prevents their developing "a social-scientific revision of theory," lands them in "an uninhibited scepticism regarding reason," and forecloses on the possibility that an always already impure reason can nevertheless "break the spell of mythic thinking" without losing touch with "the semantic potentials also preserved in myth" (PDM 129–30).

Remembrance of Nature

Given such a wide array of serious charges from Adorno's own successor, one wonders why *Dialectic of Enlightenment* remains an important text for Habermas. But one also wonders which text he has read. Other readers might barely recognize his portrait of it as a critique of instrumental reason that, cut loose from its normative foundations and making wild aesthetic gestures, drifts into the maelstrom of performative self-contradiction. My own alternative reading singles out two issues on which Habermas and Adorno disagree. I provide my own interpretation of *Dialectic of Enlightenment* with respect to those issues, and propose a critical retrieval that does not replicate central problems in Habermas' theory of communicative action. The first issue concerns the scope and imbrication of domination. The second pertains to connections between economic exploitation and societal differentiation. In response, I introduce the idea of "differential transformation" as a post-Habermasian renewal of Adorno's social vision for an age of globalization. My approach emerges from a selective commentary on "The Concept of Enlightenment,"[23] Horkheimer and Adorno's first chapter, on which Habermas is strangely silent.[24]

Unyielding Theory

The difference between Habermas' critical interpretation and my own shows up around the sentence from which he quotes concerning the "mindfulness of nature." Jephcott translates it as follows:

> Through this remembrance of nature [*Eingedenken der Natur*] within the subject, a remembrance which contains the unrecognized truth of all culture, enlightenment is opposed in principle to power [*Herrschaft*], and even in the time of Vanini the call to hold back enlightenment was uttered less from fear of exact sci-

ence than from hatred of licentious thought, which had escaped the spell of nature by confessing itself to be nature's own dread of itself. (DE 32/64)

Habermas and his followers interpret this "mindfulness" or "remembrance" of nature as a "magically invoked" aesthetic relation to nature, a relation that can only be juxtaposed to a totally instrumental rationality. I find little textual basis for their interpretation. The "remembrance" in question is not an aesthetic gesture. It is a process of critical self-reflection no less conceptual and "rational" than any critical social theory that Habermas would endorse. Further, what enlightenment remembers or recollects is not nature in its amorphous nonidentity but rather nature as that which takes distance from itself in fear of its own power, and thereby blindly embraces power.

My interpretation is borne out by the surrounding sentences. Horkheimer and Adorno claim that each "advance of civilization" renews both domination and "the prospect of its alleviation." This prospect depends, they say, "on the concept"—not on aesthetic conduct. Why does it depend on the concept? Because, as good Hegelians, Horkheimer and Adorno think that the concept is inherently critical and self-reflective.[25] As "the self-reflection of thought," the concept can measure the distance that economically driven sciences foster between human beings and nature, a distance that "perpetuates injustice" (DE 32/63–64). Accordingly, to "remember nature" in this context is nothing other than conceptually "to recognize power [*Herrschaft*] even within thought as unreconciled nature" (DE 32/64). Such conceptual recognition is precisely what Horkheimer and Adorno attempt in their book. Nor do they think conceptual recognition stands outside the scientific enterprise. Rather it is a hidden and suppressed dimension of science itself, without which science loses its emancipatory potential. Although in a "social context which induces blindness" science becomes an instrument whereby people embrace the status quo, science could just as readily let enlightenment fulfill itself by daring "to abolish [*aufzuheben*] the false absolute, the principle of blind power [*Herrschaft*]. The spirit of such unyielding theory would be able to turn back from its goal even the spirit of pitiless progress" (DE 33/65).

To understand the confidence that Horkheimer and Adorno place in "the concept" and in "unyielding theory," one needs to recall three earlier passages where embers of redemption flicker.

Each section in "The Concept of Enlightenment" has such a passage. Together they set a stage for the concluding pages from which
I have just quoted. In the first section (DE 1–12/25–39), which traces
the origins of enlightenment in myth, the diremptions that make
enlightenment possible are considered inherently dialectical (DE
10–11/37–38). They are inherently dialectical because, in its pre-
animist origins, language already "expresses the contradiction"
that something "is at the same time itself and something other
than itself, identical and not identical": a tree addressed as a location of *mana* is both a tree and not a tree. Bound up with language,
the concept too originates as "a product of dialectical thinking, in
which each thing is what it is only by becoming what it is not" (DE
11/37–38). Hence enlightenment goes wrong not by originating in
myth but by suppressing its own dialectical character, in fear of
nature's power. So long as enlightenment continues along the path
of "mythical fear radicalized," it duplicates rather than recognizes
the power of nature: "But this dialectic remains powerless as long
as it emerges from the cry of terror, which is the doubling, the mere
tautology of terror itself" (DE 11/38). From the circle of power and
fear arises the fundamentally unjust principle of equivalence (*Prin-
zip der Gleichheit*, DE 12/39) that eventually governs monopoly capitalism as the principle of exchange (*Tauschprinzip*). Already here,
then, Horkheimer and Adorno point to a countervailing tendency
within enlightenment—dialectical thinking—and a normative basis
for their critique of Western society—justice that would "originate
in freedom" (DE 12/39) rather than in fear.

The second section (DE 12–22/39–52) maps an enlightenment
path from symbolic myths through cultural separations to mythicized scientific symbols (such as mathematical formulas and
fetishized facts). In this context the authors introduce "determinate
negation" as an enlightening alternative to myths and symbols (DE
17–18/46–47). Whereas mythic symbols fuse not only sign and image
but also reference and referent (DE 12/39–40), the mythicized symbols of positivist science and capitalist culture both isolate the sign
and eliminate reference. In this way they render "the powerless"
mute and "the existing order" unassailable: "Such neutrality is more
metaphysical than metaphysics" (DE 17/45). The alternative suggested by Horkheimer and Adorno is neither to deny nor to hypos-
tatize the enlightening separation between sign and image (and the

concomitant separation between science and art, DE 12–13/40), and neither to deny nor to endorse the admixture of oppression and sociality "precipitated in intellectual forms" (DE 16/44). They point instead to the dialectical path of "determinate negation." According to their allegorical interpretation, this path opens in the *Bilderverbot* of the Jewish religion (DE 17/46). While rendering concepts expressive, determinate negation "discloses each image as script," so that language "becomes more than a mere system of signs" (DE 18/46–47). This implies a continual effort to elicit the unfinished meaning of the referent, to grasp "existing things as such . . . as mediated conceptual moments which are only fulfilled by [unfolding] their social, historical, and human meaning" (DE 20/49). Without the authors explicitly saying this, such mediation of image and concept, and such eliciting of unfinished meaning, are precisely what *Dialectic of Enlightenment* attempts. Far from being the self-contradictory performance of gloomy aesthetes, it is a risk-taking foray into dialectical social criticism, without the Hegelian safety net of "totality . . . as the absolute" (DE 18/47).

The third section (DE 22–34/52–66) diagnoses the societal shape of enlightenment-turned-mythical, especially the impact of monopoly capitalism on labor and human consciousness. There Horkheimer and Adorno make an extraordinary claim: domination is inherently self-limiting, they say, due to the tools it requires (DE 29–32/60–63). This claim presents a variation on the Hegelian dialectic of master and slave that organizes the entire section and gets refigured in the commentary on Homer's *Odyssey*, book 12 (DE 25–29/55–60).[26] Whereas in Hegel's struggle for recognition the slave achieves freedom through working upon nature under the master's power, Horkheimer and Adorno suggest that, despite the experiential impoverishment of both "master" and "slave" in a capitalist society, the instruments through which power operates resist being controlled by the ruling class: "The instruments of power [*Herrschaft*]—language, weapons, and finally machines— which are intended to hold everyone in their grasp, must in their turn be grasped by everyone" (DE 29/60). The thought here seems to be twofold. First, the purposive character of instruments gives rise to questions about ends that go beyond the restricted "goals" toward which profiteering points them.[27] Second, as machines, instruments open up a horizon in which neither forced labor nor class division would be necessary.[28] Far from mounting an all-out assault on instrumental reason, then, passages like this suggest that instrumentalization is itself a potential source of liberation.

Placed side by side, these three passages explain why Horkheimer and Adorno put their confidence in "unyielding theory." For if the concept is dialectical in its origins, if determinate negation provides a conceptual alternative to neutralized rationality, and if the instruments of domination themselves resist domination, then the "disaster" (*Unheil*) radiating across the "enlightened earth" is not inevitable. If it is not inevitable, then a dialectical critique of enlightenment makes sense. In fact, the real antipodes to such a critique are not positivism and the culture industry, but political and economic rulers who desperately attempt, at this late stage, to pose "as engineers of world history" (DE 30/61). It would not be far-fetched to regard the rulers' desperation as a hopeful sign: not even those who benefit most from class-based domination believe in its necessity.

This makes it easier to grasp why necessity does not have the last word in thought either. Given its dialectical character, thought, as an "idea-tool," can rightly insist on separations, say, between subject and object, yet, when applied to itself, can also recognize separations as an "index" both of thought's own untruth and of truth. Proscribing the fusions of superstition, enlightenment has always both promoted and opposed domination. And from this the "remembrance of nature" flows. Let me quote at some length:

> Enlightenment is more than enlightenment, it is nature made audible in its estrangement. In mind's self-recognition as nature divided from itself, nature, as in prehistory, is calling to itself, . . . no longer directly by its supposed name, . . . but as something blind and mutilated. In the mastery of nature, without which mind does not exist, enslavement to nature persists. By modestly confessing itself to be power [*Herrschaft*] and thus being taken back into nature, mind rids itself of the very claim to mastery [*der herrschaftliche Anspruch*] which had enslaved it to nature. (DE 31/63)

For this, only unyielding theory will suffice, theory that neither mistakes existing institutions and practices "for guarantors of the coming freedom" (DE 31/63) nor succumbs to nature's thrall by accepting the necessity of blind domination.

Domination and Exploitation

Elsewhere I have expressed reservations about Adorno's objectification of transformative hope. I have suggested that Adorno bases his hope for societal transformation upon nonidentical objects because he fails to distinguish sufficiently between societal evil and the violation of societal principles such as justice and solidarity.[29] Habermas has the same tendencies in view when he takes issue with what he sees as a theoretical totalizing of reification in *Dialectic of Enlightenment* and in Adorno's subsequent writings. Yet I do not think that Adorno actually totalizes reification in the way Habermas describes, nor does Adorno put the emphasis on reification that Habermas alleges. Indeed, Adorno's *Negative Dialectics* very clearly calls reification "an epiphenomenon," compared with "the possibility of total catastrophe."[30] The theoretical moves that lead to Adorno's objectification of transformative hope cannot be explained along Habermasian lines. They have to do, rather, with the two issues I wish to examine: the scope and imbrication of domination, and connections between economic exploitation and societal differentiation. To set the stage, permit me two remarks of a systematic nature. The first has to do with the much-disputed relation between subject and object. The other has to do with the status of normative judgments about economic systems.

Adorno's insistence in *Negative Dialectics* on "the priority of the object," and Habermas' relative neglect of this Adornian theme, are equally noteworthy. The point to Adorno's insistence is both to recall normative limits to the subject's ability to "constitute" the object and to remind us that the subject is itself an object at its core. Missing in Adorno's account, however, and even more strikingly absent in Habermas' theory of communicative action, is any indication that the object can also be a subject. Both Adorno and Habermas omit this because they have epistemological notions of "subject" and "object." That is to say, they define the object primarily as what human beings can know and, by extension, what they can (try to) make, control, or influence.[31] But this leaves out of account an entire range of relations within which human beings and their "objects" are mutual subjects. Animals, for example, perceive us just as much as we perceive them, and they have needs and emotions that no mere "object" could have. So too, humans share biospheres with plants and animals. Although dramatically shaped by human activity, for better and for worse, biospheres are co-constituted by nonhuman life. In that sense plants and animals have an "agency," or at least a subjectivity, that exceeds mere "objecthood," and on which human "subjects" depend. The relevance of this remark for the question of domination will become apparent shortly.

Closely connected to the disputed relation between subject and object is the question of normative judgments about economic systems. Is it appropriate to evaluate and criticize an economic system in terms of societal principles such as solidarity and justice and in terms of an economy's contribution to human flourishing? Ambivalence about this question in critical theory goes back to Hegel and Marx. It surfaces, for example, in ongoing debates about whether there are "moral" underpinnings to Marx' critique of capitalism. Adorno's resistance to the "exchange society" implies a critique of economic exploitation and of the needless suffering it creates. To that extent *Dialectic of Enlightenment* and *Negative Dialectics* suggest, but do not elaborate, normative judgments about capitalism as an economic system, from the perspective of "damaged life." Habermas seems less concerned about damage that is internal to the capitalist economy. Under the theme "colonization of the lifeworld," he shifts the focus of normative critique outward, to the economic system's impact on noneconomic practices and institutions.[32] It seems to me, by contrast, that neither implicit nor external normative judgments suffice. For if the nerve center of societal evil in its modern form lies in a capitalist economy, then a theoretical diagnosis needs to be explicit in its normative critique of the economy as such. What this entails will emerge a little later.

Both the subject/object relation and the question of normative critique are at work in "The Concept of Enlightenment." This can be seen from the prominence given to a pattern of blind domination when Adorno and Horkheimer explain the "disaster triumphant" that has befallen "the wholly enlightened earth." In their account, blind domination occurs in three tightly interlinked modes: as human domination over nature, as domination over nature within human existence, and, within both of these modes, as the domination of some human beings by others. To provide terminological markers for these three modes of domination, I use the terms "control," "repression," and "exploitation," respectively. Critics of Adorno either downplay one of these modes or argue that they are not tightly interlinked in the manner he suggests. My own response is that all three modes do actually characterize modern Western societies, and that understanding their interlinkage is crucial for a transformative social theory. But I want to propose that each mode of domination deserves its own form of normative critique. *Dialectic of Enlightenment* hovers near the trap of a totalizing critique of reification precisely because it does not differentiate sufficiently in its critique of domination. Although Habermas has called attention to insufficient differentiation, he does so at the cost of ignoring continuities among control, repression, and exploitation.

According to *Dialectic of Enlightenment*, violence is systemic in modern Western societies. This systemic violence has emerged in a specific configuration, namely, in the imbrication of control (*Naturbeherrschung*) with repression and exploitation. Further, Western exploitation involves a class-based division of labor that traces back to wars of territorial conquest and the establishment of a social order based on fixed property (DE 9/36). The differentiation of cultural spheres, and particular advances within science, art, and morality, are neither separate from nor reducible to such societal tendencies. In order for all of these developments to deliver what they promise— for so-called progress not to be cursed with "irresistible regression" (DE 28/59)—systemic violence needs to be recognized and resisted. That, in my own language, is the truth to Adorno's "remembrance of nature," and a blind spot in Habermas' critique.

Yet systemic violence becomes difficult to recognize and resist if control, repression, and exploitation become fused in the critical concept of "domination." Let me begin with the notion of control. Adorno does not consider all control of "nature" to be illegitimate. In fact he regards some control to be necessary if human freedom is to be possible. One wonders, then, how the distinction should be drawn between legitimate and liberating control, on the one hand, and illegitimate and destructive control, on the other. In other words, what is askew in the enlightenment vision of "liberating human beings from fear and installing them as masters"? Adorno suggests that enlightened mastery gets distorted in being driven by a fear of nature's power. But what would be the alternative to fear? Presumably it would be a form of recognition, as Adorno's "*Eingedenken der Natur*" suggests. Yet it cannot be a straightforward recognition of "nature" as "other" than human, nor can it be merely a recognition of nature's power as the object of fear. The first would not support discriminations between legitimate and illegitimate control, and the second would provide little basis for distinguishing liberation from destruction.

The recognition required pertains to the mutual intersubjectivity of human beings with other creatures in the dimensions of life they share. It pertains, for example, to the mutual interdependency of all organisms in the biospheres they inhabit. Human control of other organisms becomes illegitimate when it no longer promotes their interconnected flourishing. It becomes destructive when it promotes human flourishing at the expense of all other organisms. Although it is not necessarily illegitimate and destructive for human beings to treat other organisms as objects in dimensions they do not share, to treat them as no more than objects, and to ignore the dimensions of subjectivity we share with them, are forms of violence. Unfortunately, as Horkheimer and Adorno suggest, such violence has permeated Western civilization from its earliest stages. To base the pursuit of human freedom on misrecognition of other creatures is to violate the very meaning of freedom. Freedom is not a freedom to dominate but a freedom to flourish.

As a second mode of domination, repression is closely linked to the first. But the two differ in significant respects. Adorno's excursus on the *Odyssey* describes repression as the introversion of sacrifice. The emergent self attains its masterful identity by sacrificing its own happiness:

> The identical, enduring self which springs from the conquest of sacrifice is itself the product of a hard, petrified sacrificial ritual in which the human being, by opposing its consciousness to its natural context, celebrates itself. . . . In class society [*Klassengeschichte*], the self's hostility to sacrifice included a sacrifice of the self, since it was paid for by a denial of nature in the human being for the sake of mastery [*Herrschaft*] over extrahuman nature and over other human beings. . . . The human being's mastery [*Herrschaft*] of itself . . . practically always involves the annihilation of the subject in whose service that mastery is maintained. . . . The history of civilization is the history of the introversion of sacrifice—in other words, the history of renunciation. (DE 42–43/77–79)

Yet Adorno does not think that all self-mastery is illegitimate, or that all delayed gratification is destructive. Sensuous nirvana is not the same as human freedom. In what does the difference consist?

For Adorno the crucial difference seems to lie between repression and sublimation. In repression, our urges and desires are ignored or denied. In sublimation, they are accepted and redirected. But the accepting and redirecting of urges and desires raises a normative question that Adorno avoids: what makes our urges and desires acceptable and worthy of redirection? To answer requires an account of basic needs, not merely my needs or yours, but needs whose satisfaction, with suitable cultural inflections, would characterize any human flourishing. Among these would be needs for adequate food and drink, for shelter and clothing, for affection and companionship, and the like. On my account, those urges and desires are acceptable and worthy of redirection which lead to the satisfaction of such basic needs. Moreover, because their satisfaction rarely occurs outside the context of other human beings, a culture that represses our urges and desires is just as problematic as a societal formation that grants satisfaction on the part of some human beings by denying it to others.[33]

Such a society would be exploitative. According to *Dialectic of Enlightenment*, the various societal formations that have characterized Western civilization, from Homeric times to the twentieth century, have been exploitative. Further, the advances brought about by the process of enlightenment have occurred not *despite* exploitation but *by way of* exploitation.[34] By "exploitation" I mean a one-sided social distribution of power in which the apparent flourishing of one group persistently occurs at the expense of another. Although such a distribution need not require a class-based division of labor, I accept Adorno's Marxist claim that it has been class based in Western societies. I also share Adorno's intuition that exploitation is always illegitimate and destructive—directly destructive for the exploited and indirectly destructive for the exploiters. I would assert more explicitly than Adorno does, however, that the reason why exploitation is illegitimate is that it violates fundamental principles of solidarity and justice without which societal freedom cannot be attained.

Accordingly, I distinguish three forms of violence in Western societies and posit a distinct normative basis for criticizing each. The control of nature becomes violent when it does not promote the interconnected flourishing of all creatures but promotes human flourishing at the expense of all other creatures. The formation of the self becomes violent when it represses urges and desires that would lead to the satisfaction of basic needs. And the social distribution of power becomes exploitative, and therefore illegitimate and destructive, when it persistently promotes the apparent flourishing of one group at the expense of another.

Evaluating Globalization

How should we understand the interlinkage among these three modes of domination? If Adorno does not totalize the domination of nature (contra Honneth) and does not project reification back into the dawn of humanity (contra Habermas), and if such a collapsing of distinctions cannot in any case support a transformative social theory, how should we thematize the connections among control, repression, and exploitation? My response is this. Although exploitation, as it has taken shape in modern Western societies, requires a high degree of repression and destructive control, repression and destructive control are not peculiar to Western societal formations. Nor would they automatically disappear if Western-style exploitation ended. Yet, because capitalism as an economic system depends so heavily on patterns of repression and destructive control, it would be very difficult to disrupt these patterns today if economically anchored exploitation were not dismantled.

Normative Critique

To envision a dismantling of exploitation, a transformative social theory needs to include a normative critique of capitalism as an economic system. This critique would have two themes. First, it would need to come to grips with the totalizing character of the "logic" of capitalism. Despite the pitfalls introduced by Adorno's critique of "identity thinking" and the "exchange society," he has recovered Marx' insight into the inexorably expansive character of a capitalist economy. Such an economy is not simply one system within a larger and differentiated societal whole, as Habermas often seems to suggest. It inherently tends to dominate the whole, an expansionary drive that Adorno succinctly captures in his famous parody of Hegel: "The whole is the false."[35] To stop growing would eventually spell the end of capitalism. The commodification of culture, the militarization of space, and the perpetual destruction of biospheres are simply different manifestations of this systemic imperative at work. It is a real question whether capitalism as such leaves room in the long term for "sustainable development."

The imperative to expand presupposes a second troubling feature of capitalism, namely, its channeling intrinsically collective and public goods into private and privileged pockets. Despite problematic aspects to Marx' labor theory of value, his account of "surplus value" identifies this feature with remarkable clarity and insight. In nontechnical language, the secret of capitalism, which mainstream economic theories occlude, is that it must continually generate excess returns for those who occupy positions of economic power, whether they be individual investors, transnational corporations, or the most prosperous countries in the world economy. Attempts to rectify resulting imbalances in the distribution of wealth—charity, progressive taxation, debt relief, foreign aid, and the like—do not challenge the continuation of this inherently exploitative system.

It is one thing to identify the totalizing and exploitative character of capitalism, however, and quite another to say how the economic system should be transformed. Recognizing this difference, Adorno has little to say about the sorts of changes needed. Yet he insists on the historical possibility of such a transformation, and he consistently indicates that a postcapitalist economy will need to be neither totalizing nor exploitative. It will also need to be an economy that does not heavily depend upon repression and destructive control. In my own terms, what is needed is a differential transformation of Western society.[36]

Differential Transformation

By "differential transformation" I mean a process of significant change in contemporary society as a whole that occurs at differing levels, across various structural interfaces, and with respect to distinct societal principles. The primary levels in question are social institutions, cultural practices, and interpersonal relations. The primary structural interfaces lie among economy, polity, and civil society. The most relevant societal principles in this context are those of resourcefulness, justice, and solidarity. Given the tight links among exploitation, repression, and destructive control, no single societal site can suffice as an arena in which to promote creaturely flourishing. Yet changes in many diverse sites also will not suffice if they do not move in mutually reinforcing directions. As I shall elaborate, the transformation of society as a whole needs to be an internally differentiated and complementary process. The differentiation of

levels and principles in Western society provides a historical basis
for such a process.

Seen from this perspective, the debate between advocates and
opponents of "globalization" misses some of the central issues at
stake. Few would deny that the world is caught up in an "expanding scale, growing magnitude, speeding up and deepening impact
of transcontinental flows and patterns of social interaction," such
that "distant communities" are more directly linked and "the
reach of power relations [expands] across the world's regions and
continents."[37] But this does not tell us which direction these changes
should take and on what historical basis they are possible. The idea
of differential transformation provides a historically informed
basis for attempting a normative critique of globalization, in three
respects.

First, globalization needs to be evaluated with regard to different
levels of social interaction. Two considerations come into play. One
is that the tasks of differentiated institutions—schools, businesses,
governments, families, worship communities, and the like—and
of differentiated practices—practices of art, communication, education, and so forth—need to be strengthened rather than undermined. Moreover, the intrinsic worth of interpersonal relations
cannot be forgotten. Accordingly, patterns of globalization that turn
cultures into economic war zones need to be identified and resisted
by organizations and agencies within them, in the name of upholding societal differentiation and interpersonal connections. The "no
logo" slogan of antiglobalization activists points in this direction,
although their anarchist formulations often suggest a communalist
and dedifferentiating agenda. The second consideration is that, to
maintain and strengthen societal differentiation, economic alternatives to the capitalist juggernaut must be fostered. In the absence
of nonprofit, cooperative, and community-based modes for securing
resources and providing goods and services, noncommercial organizations and agencies will not thrive. So another basis for evaluating
patterns of globalization is the extent to which these permit and
promote economic alternatives.

Globalization also needs to be evaluated in terms of the structural interfaces among economy, polity, and civil society. Arguably
an achievement of modernization has been to create societal subsystems that follow their own imperatives. The result is a society in
which, for example, law and politics are not supposed to serve merely

private economic interests, and the organizations and agencies of civil society are not supposed to serve merely the interests of state. Admittedly, the integrity of these subsystems is constantly threatened. The economically and politically powerful regularly subvert it in their pursuit of greater wealth and power. Yet the subsystems remain mostly intact, and their boundaries are relatively clear. This provides a basis for evaluating patterns of globalization. As Habermas' thesis about the "colonization of the lifeworld" suggests, patterns that subsume one subsystem under another are inherently destructive and unstable. The two obvious examples are economic imperialism and political authoritarianism, which recently have joined forces in a volatile and violent American empire. Clearly, if globalization simply means the spread of this empire, all bets are off. Yet even a critique of globalization as a "new imperialism" needs to go beyond a sort of reverse nationalism.[38] It needs to insist on the integrity of distinct subsystems, and it needs to detect those spots where structural interfaces have been weakened or overridden. For a subsystem cannot maintain its integrity if it does not open properly toward the imperatives of the other subsystems.

Finally, globalization needs to be evaluated with respect to societal principles that are pervasive, distinct, and mutually complementary. I have mentioned three such principles: resourcefulness, justice, and solidarity. Being pervasive, these principles pertain to all of the levels and subsystems of a differentiated society. Yet each of them holds in a special way for a distinct range of levels and subsystems. Resourcefulness, for example, has decisive relevance for economic institutions and the economy as a whole; justice, for political institutions and the state; and solidarity, for cultural practices and civil society. The theoretical challenge, and a practical one as well, is to envision normative integration across these differentiated zones without either allowing one to dominate the others or exempting any zone from the requirements of all three principles. Specifically, given the expansionary drive of capitalism, economic institutions and patterns need to demonstrate resourcefulness without promoting injustice and alienation.

Two insights are crucial in this regard. The first is that, for the most part, resourcefulness is not the operative imperative of contemporary capitalist economies. Capitalism distorts the principle of carefully stewarding human and nonhuman potentials for the sake of interconnected flourishing. Capitalism twists this principle in the direction of efficiency, productivity, and maximal consumption for their own sakes. Consequently considerations of justice and solidarity become economic afterthoughts. They turn into belated attempts to alleviate the damage necessarily done by a system that does not prize resourcefulness in the first place.

The second insight, closely connected to the first, is that a society must follow all three principles at the same time in order to follow any one of them. Dutch economist and social philosopher Bob Goudzwaard calls this "the simultaneous realization of norms."[39] According to Goudzwaard, the industrial revolution and the development of capitalism problematically gave "well-nigh *absolute* priority" to "technical and economic progress" of a certain sort, while turning societal principles such as justice and solidarity into mere means to achieve such "progress." Let me quote a central passage from his critique:

> *Capitalism is subject to critique insofar as, for the sake of progress, it is founded on independent and autonomous forces of economic growth and technology, that is, forces which are considered isolated, sufficient, and good in themselves. These economic and technological forces are indeed related to norms of ethics and social justice, but in such a manner that these norms cannot impede the realization of those forces and the promotion of "progress." These norms are consciously viewed as dependent upon and secondary to the forces of progress: they are placed in the service of the expansion of technology and the growth of the economy.*[40]

According to Goudzwaard, the instrumentalizing of societal principles and the failure to pursue a "simultaneous realization of norms" have two effects. First, they distort the meaning of economic resourcefulness. Second, they turn all institutions and interpersonal relations into means to "economic" ends. Given the dominance of capitalism, Western society has become a "tunnel society" in which "everything—people, institutions, norms, behavior—contributes to the smooth advance toward the light at the end of the tunnel. But the end of the tunnel never appears to be within reach; the light shines forever *in the future*. Nevertheless, it keeps everything and everyone in the tunnel on the move. . . . *Functional streamlining* [is] imposed on the social order in each of its aspects. Nothing is of essential value in any social relationship unless it is a means to advance in the tunnel."[41]

In my own terms, Goudzwaard points up a central requirement for the differential transformation of society. Differential
transformation will not occur unless distinct and pervasive societal principles such as resourcefulness, justice, and solidarity are in
effect across the board and are not relegated to separate zones. The
intrinsic meaning of each depends on the simultaneous holding of
the others. Here "holding" means both that the principles hold for
the members of a society and that the members, amid their social
struggles and conflicting interpretations, hold these principles in
common.[42] In other words, the principles are mutually complementary, and existing societal patterns need to be evaluated in that
regard. Although, like Goudzwaard, I find Western societies woe-
fully lacking in this respect, I also judge that modern differentiation creates conditions that would allow greater complementarity
in the future. But this is not the occasion to make a detailed case in
support of this judgment.

We can summarize the argument of this essay as follows. Whereas
Habermas rightly criticizes Adorno for missing the potential of modern differentiation to promote human flourishing, Habermas has an
inadequate analysis of the systemic violence that accompanies this
differentiation. Conversely, whereas Adorno rightly calls attention
to systemic violence in its several and interconnected modes, he
tends to totalize it in a way that seems to preclude genuine change
in a societal formation. On my own account, the change required
will be a differential transformation. It will occur across different
social institutions, cultural practices, and interpersonal relations.
It will rearticulate the structural interfaces among economy, polity,
and civil society. And it will ensure that distinct societal principles
such as resourcefulness, justice, and solidarity are neither played
off against one another nor instrumentalized into means to a single discrete end. Instead, these societal principles will be mutually
complementary, not only in the economy, where they are often violated or ignored, but also in the state, in civil society, and, indeed, in
society as a whole.

What Adorno articulates more eloquently than his successors
is that "the whole is the false." In the long run, we cannot resist
the repression of desire and the destruction of nature unless we
dismantle economic exploitation. What he needed to say more vig-
orously, however, and with greater nuance, is that the whole is not

wholly false. This is the valid point to Habermas' otherwise over-
wrought critique. Like the book over which the ways of critical
theory seem ever to part, the dialectic of enlightenment is an alienated masterpiece. To disalienate both, to turn their mastery toward
differential transformation, would be signs of hope in the face of
"disaster triumphant."

Part III

BOUNDARIES AND BORDERS IN A GLOBALIZED WORLD

Chapter 6

Space, Place, and the Gospel
Theological Exploration in the Anthropocene Era

Iain Wallace

Prologue

I want to start by drawing on two biblical stories: the Tower of
Babel (Genesis 11) and the Good Samaritan (Luke 10). In the Tower
of Babel narrative, the people say, "Let us build ourselves a city, and
a tower with its top in the heavens, and let us make a name for ourselves" (Gen 11:4). They believe nothing is impossible: they have the
resources, they have the technology. They don't need God. In fact,
they don't even want him around. They are masters of Nature and
are intent on constructing an edifice that embodies their expansive
sense of their own importance. They are, you might say, thoroughly
modernist!

Of course, you know how the story ends. God scatters them.
Their bravado in defying their creaturely limits, and the deep insecurity underlying it, leads to precisely the conclusion the narrator
tells us they feared. They are cut down to size.

The second story is about relationships. A traveler on a deserted
stretch of highway has been set upon by thugs. He is badly beaten up
and left half-dead in a ditch. Eventually other travelers come across
him. The first two are stalwart members of the religious community,
and I'm sure you've come across imaginative reconstructions of their
rationalizations for not getting involved. The third traveler is not
part of the religious community. Instead, he is a despised member of
a heretical sect. Yet it is this man, a Samaritan, who shows practical

love, a response Jesus holds up as fulfilling the second great commandment: to love your neighbor as yourself.

So what has all this to do with space, place, or the Anthropocene? I approach the theme of secularity and globalization from the perspective of a geographer, a social scientist given to integrating the often separated worlds of humanity and Nature and encouraged in that quest by trust in the One in whom all things hold together.[1] I want to argue for reading the narrative of the Tower of Babel as an example of secular reason and its technological prowess being applied to avoid acknowledging the creator God and living with appropriate humility in the world in which humankind has been set. The recently introduced concept of the Anthropocene (which I define below) helps us think more clearly about some of the novel challenges that being creatures in the universe pose in our time. They are challenges that stem from a crisis many secular observers are all too aware of and which I suggest a biblical worldview is well equipped to diagnose.

My reading of the parable of the Good Samaritan, on the other hand, contains the important lesson that members of the faith community can behave in ways that discredit their calling. In doing so, they call into question the character of the God they proclaim. The hero of this story was not, strictly speaking, secular, but he certainly represented a belief system rejected by the religiously orthodox. Yet it was this despised "other" who embodied an ethic of human relationships that Jesus commended to those who would follow him. I want to propose, then, that Christians reflecting on the issues addressed in this volume need to be alive to the possibility that convictions condemned in some quarters of the faith community as heretical capitulation to secular values may come closer to God's intent for the world than those believers who are censorious of them may currently be able to acknowledge. Our contemporary crisis is not only environmental—how the people of the world are to live in harmony with the biosphere—but also social—how we are to live in harmony with each other, as those made in the image of God.

I develop this argument by first elaborating geographical perspectives on globalization. This serves to identify the insights that can be obtained by working with the distinctive concepts (space, place, and the Anthropocene) contained in my title. After exploring some contemporary efforts to frame the dynamics of relations between humanity and the biosphere and noting their limited impact on the course of global development, I step back to consider underlying challenges to the welfare of the planet presented by the worldview of secular modernity, and equally by the postmodern culture that has selectively replaced it. One of the consequences of the loss of innocence about the modernist scientific worldview has been the emergence of localized (in a social or geographical sense) alternative narratives that challenge it. These movements have equally forced Christians to reflect on the modernist characteristics of their own theologies, prompting novel questions about the implications of space and place within the church. The chapter concludes by noting similarities between current controversies about environmental sustainability and homosexuality that illustrate some of the tensions Christians face in discerning the mind of Christ in the world today.

Geographical Bearings

For the sake of those unfamiliar with contemporary geographical literature, I begin by defining the specific meanings that geographers attach to the commonplace terms, "space" and "place." They distinguish two complementary ways of looking at the globe, seen primarily as the home of humanity. The world as "space" is a field of interaction: an arena of flows—of people, commodities, and ideas—between locations, points on the surface of the earth where constellations of social power and human activity set these flows in motion and spread their economic and cultural influence. Manuel Castells[2] captures the essence of this perspective in his concept of the "network society," in which what matters most of all are the many forms of linkages binding societies and economies together over distances that modern technologies have shrunk. This process of convergence, termed "space-time compression" by David Harvey,[3] is recognized by most observers as an essential element of the broader dynamics of contemporary globalization.

"Place," in contrast, enshrines the perspective that the world is still fundamentally made up of distinctively different local settings—where people, their cultures, and their livelihoods have developed specific characteristics over time, born of the interplay between societies and the geographical environments in which they are set and the cumulative results of local past decisions and events. For this reason, the distinctiveness of places is not easily dissolved, even when it is inundated by waves of powerful external cultural or economic influences.[4] Geographers therefore resist the suggestion that processes of globalization are inevitably processes of homogenization. Rather, they are equally processes of differentiation, as the local settings (places) from which forces of change originate play a role in determining the form of what may eventually become global effects (operating over space); and conversely global influences are refracted differently when they encounter the embedded particulars of individual places.

It is easy to grasp these interdependencies between the global and the local when considering a phenomenon such as the fast-food industry. A localized American solution to consuming a meat-based meal in a highly mobile culture has been transformed into a global eating option, however unrelated it may be to local food resources and traditional dietary preferences in the places where it has been introduced. But at the same time, the McDonald's menu is not universally the same: it acquires locally distinctive profiles (such as lobster burgers in Atlantic Canada) wherever regional tastes and dietary staples can be incorporated into the globalized corporate production system.[5]

More challenging is the question of how far the dynamic interactions of space and place inform our understanding of the gospel. We may acknowledge that God's dealings with humanity recorded in the Old Testament took shape within a specific historical and regional context that is reflected in the literary style and content of the narratives (the genealogies, the legal structure of the covenant; the desert, sheep, monarchy, etc.); or that the growth of the early church benefited from the judicial and transportation infrastructure of the Roman Empire. But have we reflected deeply enough on what difference the features of the local environments in which our faith took shape have made to our understanding of it? Or how the complex variety of geographically localized characteristics evident in the contemporary places that we now inhabit shapes what is heard there and how the gospel message is interpreted?

Suppose Christ had indeed set foot, in the words of the hymn, in nineteenth-century England's "green and pleasant land"[6]; or if God's chosen people had been Latin Americans, led into a promised land situated in Paraguay rather than in Palestine? What difference might a narrative originating in such alternative geographical contexts have made to our understanding of God's purposes? Or how would the hermeneutics that have shaped Christian belief as developed in the Greek and Roman cultures of the West been different

if the church of the first millennium had been centered in India?[7] I
return to these questions of the gospel's geographical enculturation
below; they pose inescapable challenges to the church in a world
shrunk by technologies of "space-time compression" and pluralized
by currents of cultural postmodernity, yet constituted by people
and peoples varyingly attached to place and to traditions that have
been elaborated therein.[8]

First, though, the "Anthropocene" needs defining. Coined a
few years ago by Nobel Prize–winning atmospheric chemist Paul
Crutzen,[9] it takes up the vocabulary of the major geological eras
that trace the evolution of our planet. The geologically brief period
since the end of the most recent Ice Age, some twelve thousand
years ago, is commonly referred to as the Holocene. But according
to Crutzen, a decisive milestone has now been reached that justifies
the recognition of a new era, the Anthropocene, characterized by
the emergence of human capabilities to transform the Earth on such
a scale that they equal the power of geological processes. One simple
measure of expressing this shift is that humans now displace more
Earth material each year than all the world's rivers put together.
More precisely, the burning of fossil fuels leads to twice the volume
of sulfur dioxide being released into the atmosphere than the sum of
all natural emissions, and more nitrogen is now captured syntheti-
cally and applied as agricultural fertilizer than is fixed naturally in
all terrestrial ecosystems.[10] In other words, human impacts on the
global environment have reached a level that matches or exceeds
the workings of "Nature," a realm traditionally viewed as ontologically distinct from humanity and whose threatening forces have
long been associated with "acts of God."

The Babel Imperative

On a narrowly literalistic reading of Genesis 1:28, to "fill the earth
and subdue it," the Anthropocene stands as the culmination, in our
current generation, of the divine mandate to our forebears. The
consequences have scarcely begun to be grasped. Of course, the cultural values of the industrialized societies that have brought the
Earth to its present state are far removed from those of the authors
of the early chapters of Genesis, and from the richly nuanced treatment of society/environment relations that the Old Testament as a
whole conveys.[11] Yet the levels of material consumption now threatening to disrupt the global biosphere have until recently been most

assiduously pursued in "Christian Europe" and in a United States that has self-consciously framed itself as deserving of God's blessing. And while mainstream Christian witness has invariably warned of the spiritual dangers of accumulating worldly wealth, the church in the global North has largely become complicit by domesticating secular economic priorities.[12]

To explore what an Anthropocene perspective can contribute to our understanding of the world today, I expand here on its image of humanity matching Nature as an environmental agent by drawing on related models that bring into clearer focus the implications for societies in the twenty-first century. We need to start by noting that human dependence on the natural environment is a truth the social sciences (outside of anthropology and geography) have for the most part chosen to ignore.[13] This is most obvious and critical in the field of economics, where land (as a proxy for the natural environment as a whole) ceased to be of central theoretical interest by the early twentieth century, even though it had been one of the three basic factors of production identified by the late-eighteenth-century classical economists (Adam Smith, David Ricardo, et al.). With the global spread of the steamship and the steam locomotive, lack of access to agricultural land and natural resources was no longer a constraint on the economic development of the politically dominant industrialized economies. Viewed from New York or London, there was no limit to what the lands or resources of the Earth could offer to the production process. There was always (and there still is) somewhere new to open up, and there would always be (well, there always has been so far) resources available for an acceptable price.

That there might be absolute limits imposed on human activity by the very structure of the universe is a concept that became not only foreign to mainstream economic theory in the second half of the twentieth century, but one that, when articulated in the early 1990s by then–World Bank economist Herman Daly, was condemned as heretical and dangerous by his senior associates.[14] Such attitudes have led British author Jeremy Seabrook to claim, "The secularism claimed by the [W]est is no such thing. It is built on an arbitrary act of faith. The cosmic wager made by this belief is that human ingenuity will always be equal to the consequences of its own actions."[15] This secular religion, highly resonant of the mind-set that sought a tower in Babel, is at the root of the current global environmental crisis.

Modern comprehension of the extent and consequences of human-induced environmental change developed initially in the wake of publication of *Limits to Growth*.[16] This study of the Earth as a complex system by a modernist think tank, the Club of Rome, ushered in the era of computer modeling of the biosphere. Like all such exercises, the outcome was significantly shaped by its assumptions, which were oversimplified and essentially Malthusian (that population growth, resource consumption, and the resultant pollution would lead to a "crash" that would severely reduce the world's population and standard of living). It was not difficult for critics, including most economists, to undermine confidence in its conclusions. But infinitely more sophisticated computer modeling of the Earth as a biophysical system underlies the scenarios of prospective global climate change that have given birth to the Kyoto Protocol and the faltering international steps to limit greenhouse gas emissions.[17] The capability of modeling economy-environment interactions at a geographically disaggregated scale, one that takes place and space seriously, is something toward which much effort is now being expended. All these demanding enterprises remain essentially modernist in their conception of the world, treating the Earth and the human activity within it as mechanistic systems; a lively debate has developed around the representations of Nature these models entail, the values embedded in their construction, and the politics of their interpretation.[18]

The convergence of empirical and ethical paths to understanding the intensifying crisis facing the inhabitants of the Earth is assisted by a second set of images. Herman Daly proposes a simple distinction between the "Empty Earth" and the "Full Earth" as a way of articulating the critical relationship between economic activity and the biosphere.[19] In its preindustrial ("Empty") state, human transformation of the Earth was limited in scope, as ultimately all societies were dependent on natural environmental processes for their food and energy. But an industrialized global economy, drawing on nonrenewable resources and novel transformative technologies, has reached scales of production and consumption that fully exploit humanity's ecological niche. Evidence is accumulating that in the "Full Earth" of the Anthropocene Era, the global material economy is stressing and degrading environmental systems and pressing against the biosphere's ultimate limits. This is seen at a

macro scale in terms of the rising concentration of atmospheric car-
bon dioxide at the root of global warming, and at regional scales
in the destruction of fish stocks, depletion of groundwater aqui-
fers, and threats to life in all its forms from toxic levels of exposure
to industrial chemicals. The distribution of material benefits and
the costs of "Full Earth" conditions are marked by vast disparities
between world regions and social classes. By developing a methodol-
ogy, the "ecological footprint," to calculate the demands being made
on components of the global biosphere by societies defined at various geographical scales, Rees and Wackernagel have imaginatively
portrayed the disproportionate claims made by affluent nations on
the shared ecological endowment of humankind.[20]

Further insights into the apparent intractability of the global
environmental crisis come from the work of geographers such as Noel
Castree and Bruce Braun.[21] "Social Nature" is a postmodernist conceptual framework that captures the hybridity of the natural world
which contemporary societies inhabit. There is no pristine Nature,
untouched by human hand: for not only does the whole Earth bear
some material imprint of human presence, the very discourse that
posits and bounds "Nature" is a malleable and ideologically powerful
social construct. For example, even in the remote high Arctic, air-
borne industrial pollutants and pesticides gather in the food chain,
such that the boundary between humanity and the natural world
is rendered ambiguous. Equally, what counts as wilderness in many
parts of the world is almost entirely a biological hybrid reflecting
previous human environmental modification, such as by fire. But
the fundamental idea of Nature is increasingly recognized as having
been framed within, and to advance, the social values of dominant
social groups. This has been clearly evident in North America, in the
imbuing of Nature with positive moral qualities in ways that erase
(and thereby devalue) the indigenous occupants of spaces deemed
"empty," while simultaneously facilitating evasion of the demands
of social justice to ameliorate the social and built environments of
cities, the categorically distanced unnatural other.[22]

A final model for relating humanity to Nature derives from
acknowledging that the evolution of the biosphere has involved
interdependence between the living and the nonliving elements
within it. James Lovelock's "Gaia" concept explores the mutuality of
these components in what he identifies as a self-regulating system
that has brought about and maintained chemically improbable plan-

etary conditions to sustain life.[23] The name Gaia, drawn from the ancient Greek goddess of the Earth and adopted by Lovelock apparently unwittingly, has frightened away both scientists and theologians who feel their cosmologies threatened by the association.[24] Yet one could argue that each of the conceptual frameworks briefly introduced above focuses on an aspect of human activity cocreating its environmental setting. In place of the image of a God who makes the Earth and then places humankind upon it, there is a very real sense in which Nature is seen in part as a human product, and one that co-evolves with human society. This has led many Christians to interpret the Gaia model in particular as a postmodern pantheistic concept that undermines the sovereignty of a creator God. Yet the clear inference of Deuteronomy 28 is that the faithfulness or otherwise of Israel codetermines the fertility of the promised land: so concepts of cocreation and hybridity are hardly theologically heretical.

However, the biblical images of human stewardship of the environment do not seem immediately to anticipate the scale of human powers of intervention that are captured by the concept of the Anthropocene. And as Daly stresses, the most frightening aspect of the current situation is the refusal by those with the power to consume the Earth's resources to take seriously the limits of the biosphere.[25] Bob Goudzwaard has suggested that this inability or refusal of the world's richest inhabitants to come to terms with their material appetites typifies nothing more closely than teenage immaturity.[26] The refusal by leading economists, in the era of a "Full Earth," to engage Herman Daly's question, "What is the optimum size of the global economy?" points to a similar conclusion. With little serious consideration having been given to the ability of the Earth to support human populations at specified levels of resource consumption, or what geographical distribution of resource demand might approach equity, it is not surprising that attempts by theological and secular thinkers alike to flesh out concepts of environmental and social "sustainability" at a global scale have been inconclusive.[27]

For indeed, the crisis of globalization is a crisis of material consumption. Over the past two hundred years, a fossil-fueled economy has devoured natural resources and degraded environmental systems. The values driving this activity have been essentially secular, defining human security in terms of the amassing of goods and, latterly, experiences. And as Christian and Marxian critics alike have shown, the capitalist fixation on economic growth has entailed a moral evasion: the promise of wealth eventually trickling down to all has been used to silence more immediate claims by the poor against the unjust practices of the rich.[28] Within the Christian tradition, voices challenging this state of affairs have often been marginalized, as the Church has been too complicit in supporting the growth dynamic.[29] Many writers in the Judeo-Christian tradition have pursued the biblical theme of stewardship to explore paths to provide for human needs in a less destructive manner.[30] But the fact is, even where this sort of thinking has made some political headway, the global economy continues to run full-tilt into the constraints of the biosphere. Even secular multinational corporations, such as those in the insurance industry, are taking note of the losses associated with symptoms of global warming, such as intensified tropical storms and flooding.[31] In light of the theological lessons of the Babel narrative, the church cannot afford to give up on serious engagement with the deteriorating state of the global environment.

The Culture of Modernity and Postmodernity

The revolutions of the late eighteenth century, notably in the United States and France, crystallized the dominant values of the increasingly secular societies that were emerging in the West. We can identify three secular religions characteristic of modernity: political nationalism, economic freedom, and human rights (initially, the "rights of man"). Fred Hirsch has traced how the supposed benefits of the revolutionary period were delivered unevenly, both socially and temporally.[32] In general, the development of market economies, freed from medieval institutional constraints, proceeded more rapidly than the expansion of the franchise to those men without property (and ultimately to women). But it was the increasingly powerful state that defined the society within which populations strove to realize the promise of modernity. With the expanding franchise, democratic nations became increasingly governed by regimes that reflected the priorities of the majority and hence moderated the socioeconomic polarization that unregulated market economies generate. The widespread economic privation of the 1920s that gave legitimacy to strong government, combined with the theoretical justification for public-sector intervention in the economy outlined by John Maynard Keynes, promoted a social-democratic cast to postwar governments on both sides of the North Atlantic. Certainly the political engagement of Christian social conscience was active in creating a climate that encouraged these developments.[33]

However, the fascist nationalism of Germany and Japan that precipitated the Second World War was a prime motivation for the establishment of postwar institutions to tame nationalism and promote the global diffusion of economic prosperity. The creation of the United Nations and subsequently of the European Union were two of the major outcomes of this period. But national and international organizations devoted to the protection and expansion of human rights, the third secular religion of modernity, also took decisive shape in the postwar years. Since the 1970s, the balance between state and market has shifted, as political philosophies of possessive individualism have gained ascendancy from the disappointing experience of bureaucratic socialism. For many commentators, the freeing of economic activity from national regulation is the essence of contemporary globalization.

The increasingly evident shortcomings of modernity as a societal project have given rise to diverse reactions that collectively constitute the cultural expressions of postmodernity. Deconstruction of the modernist universals that had ideologically erased the complexity of the world (as "space") has brought back into prominence the great variety of natural environments and human experience (embedded in "place"). The modernist discourse of development elaborated after 1945 imagined the remaking of all parts of the world in the image of the industrialized nations.[34] But this faith was grounded in an economic model that discounted both real environmental differences (leading, for instance, to ill-conceived transfers of European agricultural practice into tropical Africa) and the dynamics of wealth creation and distribution (that established interests would generally claim the bulk of new wealth). Similarly, development gave first place to the role of the state in providing the societal context in which growth could take place. Yet in the majority of the nations of the South, the state as a group of citizens was significantly fractured along ethnic or tribal lines, and the state as an institution was usually treated as the fiefdom of the dominant elite. Postmodernity in its political dimension has thus questioned the legitimacy of the state in the name of more fundamental identities than nationalism. These identities, often associated with religious difference and often regionalized, have frequently produced armed conflict as groups have fought over territory and resources. The concept of civil liberties in the Western tradition has rarely been championed by elites, being cynically identified as one of those luxuries that only affluent nations can afford. But their denial has greatly strengthened the profile and moral authority of nongovernmental organizations promoting human rights, such as Amnesty International.

Significantly, postmodernity is also associated with the radical questioning of the benefits of a scientific worldview. The experience of technologies that have proven to be toxic to people or the environment, whether at the macro level of nuclear weapons testing or the micro level of pesticide applications, has increasingly discredited science in the popular imagination. This has been facilitated by ever-closer links between scientific research and national defense or corporate commercial interests. The distinction between science as epistemological practice and the political economy of institutionalized science has not registered with the majority of people. The politicization of science, evident in debates about climate change, genetically modified organisms, and stem cell research, makes it difficult for the layperson to know where "the truth" lies. A positive outcome of the dethroning of social confidence in the modernist applications of science typical of the 1960s is that traditional ecological knowledge, born of long experience of people living harmoniously with their natural environment, has become more widely valued.[35] And this noninstrumentalist knowledge has made it easier to gain acceptance for concepts such as stewardship to enter into resource management decisions. But the undermining of popular confidence in the epistemology of science has come at a cost, as shown below.

The cultural dimensions of globalization include the increased interpenetration of different value systems as corporations and migrants place themselves in unfamiliar societal contexts. One consequence of this forced mixing of the global and the local has been the emergence of resistance to the "Coca-colonization" of developing countries, as institutions spreading a foreign material culture and proselytizing the values it embodies have given rise to oppositional movements.[36] Some are straightforward nationalist efforts to maintain a place for domestic entrepreneurship, but others are defined by religious or ethnic allegiances that regard the arrival of Western culture as a threat to their identity and values. Most of today's less-developed countries, especially those in Africa, have recent memories of colonial elites who suppressed indigenous allegiances. The ongoing interracial struggles in states such as Zimbabwe are illustrative of these tensions. But they are not confined to situations of conflict between descendants of Europeans and indigenous populations. Interethnic tensions in states such as Nigeria, invariably inflamed by disparities in prosperity or political power sharpened by religious difference, have been just as destructive. Does this imply that the increased mixing of peoples which globalization facilitates is unavoidably a recipe for increased ethnic tension?

Questions for the Church

The global church is not immune from these challenges. Under colonial regimes, the European or North American framing of Christianity was exported, in nearly every instance, with far too little attempt to comprehend and respect local cultures. Indeed in many contexts, local culture was actively dismissed as pagan, and seen to have nothing valuable to teach the Christianity that was being implanted. The emergence of liberation theology out of biblical reflection on the polarized social context of the Catholic Church in Latin America was a landmark in terms of bringing Southern perspectives to bear on the thinking of the Western church, one that was subsequently muzzled by the Vatican. More recent theological work of a postcolonial (as in the case of Palestinian Christians)[37] or indigenous peoples' origin (as in North America)[38] has required mainstream expositors to rethink some of their fundamental assumptions. These challenges to received frameworks of interpretation have been entirely healthy, forcing the global church to reflect much more carefully on how it frames its theology. At the same time, they open up the complexity of questions of place: of how differences that arise from lives being lived in particular locations with particular pasts and particular contemporary challenges inform our understanding of the gospel, in an era of globalization and of the postmodern valuing of all expressions of personal and societal difference.

This is illustrated particularly acutely in the current internal conflict within the worldwide Anglican Communion concerning that church's understanding of homosexuality. As Philip Jenkins[39] points out, the center of gravity of global Christianity—and this is certainly true of Anglicanism—is now unmistakably in the South, where the church faces different challenges from those it faces in

North America and Europe. The argument being voiced by leading Anglican spokespersons from Africa and Asia is that those parts of the Northern church which interpret the gospel as calling for inclusiveness toward all people (including traditionally ostracized homosexuals) should refrain from acting in opposition to the majority in the South, whose theology and cultural values deny, almost uniformly (except notably in South Africa), a legitimate place for homosexuals in the church, or even in the wider national society. The rigid defense of what is understood to be traditional biblical teaching on this topic is claimed to reflect the local context of churches facing a missionary Islam among populations that hold to traditional interpretations of sexuality.[40] The local context of the Northern churches, on the other hand, is that they are in contact with populations for whom the language of human rights is a secular religion, and where the local evangelistic challenge is to frame the gospel as an inclusive theology in the face of religiously sanctioned hostility to homosexuals.[41] What is presented by most Anglican churches in the South as the North's apostate accommodation of secular thinking and a pernicious departure from the gospel is defended by its proponents as a fulfillment of the inclusive promises implicit in passages such as Galatians 3:20, that in Christ all exclusionary forms of othering are abolished. The continuing subordination of women and homosexuals in the majority of developing societies is thus framed in the North as a perversion of the gospel that needs to be acknowledged as such, rather than having criticism inappropriately stifled by church leaders in the South in the name of resisting the imposition of liberal Northern theology or secular Western values.

In the background is the fact that the lack of human rights and indeed of personal safety for homosexuals has a clear colonial pedigree in many countries, especially former British territories. The rampant homophobia in Jamaica[42] that is celebrated in popular reggae music is implicitly sanctioned by the Offences Against the Person Act, which criminalizes consensual same-sex relations between males. This legislation is embodied in the postcolonial constitution of independent Jamaica of 1962; yet the relevant wording of the Act comes straight from the colonial Act of 1864, itself derived from the English Act of 1861. Jeremy Seabrook observes that the leaders of the independent Caribbean nation thus "honoured their former rulers by preserving colonial values . . . [that] had their roots in Victorian morality."[43] A similar legal genealogy can be found elsewhere in the former British Empire: the Indian Penal Code and its Malaysian equivalent each contain a Section 377 forbidding "sexual acts against the order of nature," and in most of former British Africa (except South Africa) the wording of the legislation is virtually identical. In other words, what is represented as a set of indigenous values (which correspond with traditional theological orthodoxy) toward different others has its roots in a transplanted elite culture steeped in the worldview of nineteenth-century British Protestantism at least as much as in precolonial social structures. (We leave for now the postmodern deconstruction of an "order of nature.")

The language of twentieth-century human rights may be presented in this context as a secular intrusion, but it is here that I see echoes of the ethic of the Good Samaritan. Regrettably, among Christian and Islamic fundamentalists alike, radical opposition to social change invariably targets selective aspects of sexual morality to the exclusion of almost all other values and notably of issues of human dignity and social justice. The continued acceptance of treating women as second-class citizens and the religiously sanctioned marginalization of gays and lesbians display a set of values that reverses the priorities of the Minor Prophets. The World Bank acknowledges that human development is achieved most successfully in societies that are inclusive rather than exclusive of women and minorities:[44] it is a scandal that churches are more often found opposing rather than endorsing this liberating perspective.

Let me draw the threads of this reflection together with an observation that links the contested discourses in the disparate worlds of climate change and inclusiveness toward homosexuals. In both areas, there is an emerging scientific consensus about the nature of the phenomena under review. The Intergovernmental Panel on Climate Change (IPCC) has provided a carefully structured mechanism for sifting the scientific publications of thousands of specialists and for reaching conclusions about what future global environmental conditions they point to.[45] There can be no absolute certainty about how complex, chaotic earth systems will behave, and data and interpretations challenge the consensus picture with respect to particular elements. However, almost uniformly, those few spokespersons (some scientists, many not) who deny or denigrate the scientific consensus position do so with clear ideological intent in an environment that is highly politicized. Very many of them are financially assisted by the multinational oil industry (most notoriously

ExxonMobil Corporation) or conservative groups opposed to the increased government regulation entailed in responding to the threat of climate change.[46]

I see a very strong parallel in the responses of many Christian groups to homosexuality. Human sexuality is as complex a phenomenon as climate change, and debates around it are even more politicized. But there is accumulating scientific evidence that homosexual orientation is at least in part genetic: it is a form of being human, not an optional pattern of social interaction.[47] As a result, legislation based on prescientific understandings and on religious scapegoating that has ghettoized homosexuals is gradually being repealed in Western societies.[48] The church has a long history, however, of being on the wrong side of human rights movements and has been lamentably slow to see the fulfillment of the gospel in efforts to release the captives of social power structures based on race, sex, and so on. Those who denigrate the scientific understanding of human sexuality (and the testimony of countless individuals who have struggled with the truth of their sexual orientation in a climate of social and religious ostracism) invariably do so for other than scientific reasons and with a noticeable lack of grace toward their fellow human beings. It is consistent with the argument of this paper that the societal expression of the issues at stake present themselves differently in different places, but the gospel challenge comes to every Christian wherever we are. This is not a new situation: an insightful reading of Acts 10 by Gary Hauch, of how the early church in Jerusalem came to discern the work of the Holy Spirit in the scandalous inclusion of the Gentiles that had taken place in Caesarea, suggests one possible route for the global church to find a way forward.[49]

The challenge of the current period of history is to identify ways of coming to terms with the finiteness of the world we live in and doing so in ways that are seen to be just. So long as the dominant religious system is a secular one of economic growth, there is little hope of a solution that is widely acceptable. The churches of the world have not articulated a convincing vision of how this challenge might be accomplished in terms of a biblical worldview. The obvious alternative to capitalist globalization, a socialist alternative compatible with the vision of liberation theology, contains prophetic warnings about the idolatry of the status quo but has not provided a convincing political solution in a world of fallen human beings. The dominant consuming nation, the United States, has a particular religious history that has ideologically framed national progress as advancing the kingdom of God. In both its economic and geopolitical dimensions, this has been widely critiqued but not effectively undermined. And to some extent, all affluent Christians are complicit in maintaining the status quo.

The challenge of the Anthropocene is to face us with the reality that we are cocreators of the natural world and therefore have a heightened responsibility to direct our energies justly. Of the three dominant secular religions—market economics, nationalism, and human rights—only the latter speaks the language of justice.[50] Yet many Christian communities are uncomfortable with what they see as its secular premises, despite its historical foundation in a view of human beings as bearers of the image of God. And the global institutions most supportive of expanding human rights have proved to be, so far at least, weaker than the institutions supportive of expanding the market economy or maintaining national security.

But globalization has provided the means for both markets and justice-seeking nongovernmental organizations to increase their power by linking the local to the global. For example, increased opposition by leading Southern nations to the power wielded by rich nations in the World Trade Organization is evidence of how local initiative, brought together, can effect change at the global level. There are examples of similar local-global coalitions in the human rights arena, as was evident, for instance, in the global campaign to eliminate apartheid in South Africa. The Jubilee 2000 campaign to reduce poor country indebtedness is a further example of how Christian churches have capitalized on their ability to link local efforts with international agendas.[51]

Conclusion

My first attempt to introduce a theological dimension into the secular disciplinary literature of geography made this claim: that because a biblical worldview acknowledges humanity's pervasive unwillingness to internalize a stewardly ethic toward the natural environment and to follow an ethic of love and justice, Christians are saved from promoting a utopian idealism about the possibilities for change in this world. Yet they are still able to maintain their eschatological hope.[52] I admitted that, as a result, the Christian social scientist is more likely to be cast in the role of a prophet than a policy maker, invariably dismissed (or worse!) by those in power who do not wish to hear a divine challenge. I feel some of that impotence now, a generation later, when confronting the global embeddedness of societies dedicated to material consumption. God knows, of course, that as creatures of the biosphere we need food and clothing and shelter, and too many people in the world lack these basic necessities. But when even affluent "Christian" nations put maintaining their economic way of life above the well-being of the planet that supports them and of its less affluent members, one wonders just what a new round of theological analysis may achieve. Elijah voiced a similar sense of futility and was chastised for his lack of confidence in God's power to act through faithful people, so I don't want to leave my readers without any hope!

David Smith[53] suggests we see the current state of the Western church as one of liminality, an anthropological concept that denotes a time of transition or rite of passage. This is a confusing and often frightening state, which may well be met by a deep desire to return to what is seen as a safe past. But for growth to take place, the passage to greater maturity must first be navigated. Smith warns that a church finding itself increasingly marginalized within its home culture (in place) instead tends to relapse into a reactionary conservatism, when transformation is what the situation demands. It doesn't look for new and more strategic models of being a missionary church (and place, in the form of hallowed buildings, can be a powerful trap!). Moreover, it doesn't reflect on its own biblical blind spots, for, as he argues, "a knowledge of church history confirms all too clearly the limited and partial nature of our human perceptions of the truth of Christ and the Gospel."[54] He claims that Christians from the global South can be a "key resource" in helping the church in the global North discover its shortcomings.

I affirm that conclusion wholeheartedly. But globalization is a concept that encourages us to conceive of the world networked by flows in multiple directions and linking across geographical scales. An appropriate postcolonial humility on the part of Christians in the North does not mean that they have nothing to offer the church in the South. Respect for the dignity of all persons and elaborating the theology underpinning it is perhaps one of those gifts the North has to share, even as it learns from the South to temper the excessive individualism that contributes to its complacency about material consumption.

The concept of the Anthropocene reminds us that we are living in a critical period for the Earth and for its inhabitants. I have outlined the modern world's three dominant secular religions. These embody idolatries that Christians need to resist, but among them are ethical signposts the church would do well to heed. Faithfulness to the gospel demands that we each from our own place respond to the challenges of globalization and environmental change in ways that are consistent with the well-being of the Earth and of all its people—as long as we recognize that each person, near and far, gay and straight, is our neighbor.

Chapter 7

The Duty of Care to Refugees, Christian Cosmopolitanism, and the Hallowing of Bare Life

Luke Bretherton

Introduction

Some speculate that one outcome of contemporary globalization is the decline of the nation-state and the emergence of global, post-national forms of citizenship underwritten by human rights and international law. However, attention to the treatment of refugees suggests that, despite the globalization of economies and cultures, nation-states will remain the primary location of political belonging and organization for the foreseeable future. Yet attention to refugees also unveils a deep crisis in the nation-state, especially liberal democratic nation-states, one not brought about by globalization, but arising from the basis of modern sovereignty itself. In contrast to unwarranted accounts of global citizenship, which mask the plight of refugees, and overly protectionist accounts of national politics, which exclude refugees, this article draws on the Christian cosmopolitan tradition, the theology of personhood, and the practice of prayer in order to present a series of responses to the situation of refugees in the contemporary context.

The first section critically reviews the debate on how liberal democracies should respond to refugees. The second section, following Georgio Agamben's characterization of refugees as "bare life," argues that refugees unveil a deep contradiction in contemporary patterns of political sovereignty. It is this contradiction that makes the current debate on the duty of care to refugees so intractable and yet so pressing. The article closes by arguing that while a theological account of political authority points to some roads beyond the crisis, the first task of the church is to properly order its own duty of care to refugees. It concludes with an exegesis of the second clause of the Lord's Prayer as a way of giving an account of what such care might involve.

Theological Politics and the Liberal Democratic Response to Refugees

In debates about appropriate ethical and political responses to refugees in liberal democratic polities, three key issues emerge. The first is the very definition of a refugee. The second is whether refugees should receive a priority of attention and resources as compared with the claims of economic migrants. The third is whether governments owe a greater duty of care to existing members than to those who exist beyond its formal boundaries. Directly related to this last issue is the question of whether borders and a defined territory are themselves moral.[1]

Definitions and the Priority of Refugees

There is some debate about how to define who and what is a refugee and how this contrasts with related terms, notably the term "economic migrant." The most accepted definition is given in the 1951 UN Convention on Refugees, which states that a refugee is

> a person who is outside his/her country of nationality or habitual residence; has a well-founded fear of persecution because of his/her race, religion, nationality, membership in a particular social group or political opinion; and is unable or unwilling to avail himself/herself of the protection of that country, or to return there, for fear of persecution.[2]

There are several things to notice about this definition. In the contemporary context the close interrelation between violent political conflict and severe economic and social disruption makes it difficult to distinguish between refugees and economic migrants. Technically, refugees move to save their lives and economic migrants move to improve their economic and social prospects. However, most migration—of which refugees are a subcategory—involves mixed motives stimulated by a variety of economic, social, and political pull and push factors.[3] Yet the UN Convention is specific. As Gil Loescher points out,

> The key criterion determining refugee status is *persecution*, which usually means a deliberate act of the government against individuals, and thus excludes victims of general insecurity and oppression or systematic economic deprivation, and people who have not crossed national frontiers to seek refuge.[4]

Thus a refugee must be outside his or her country of origin and without the protection of one's government. This excludes internally displaced persons and those moving because of forced migration (either because of social, economic or political disruption or low-intensity conflicts which exacerbate such disruption). The convention is also individualistic in its assumption, requiring that the individual personally must face persecution. For example, someone who moves because of civil war or famine is not covered by the convention and so cannot, according to the UN Convention, be granted refugee status. For these reasons a number of other, broader definitions are currently operative. Notable among these are those of the Organization of African Unity and of Sweden, both of which widen the focus to include victims of generalized states of violence and events that severely disrupt public order, such as natural disasters.[5] Some, for example, Andrew Shacknove, seek to broaden the definition even further so as to include all those whose basic needs are not protected by their state.[6] However, as Gibney comments, we should "resist the temptation to define all threatened peoples as 'refugees.' There are other ways of drawing attention to the plight of people in need of protection and assistance than lumping them into a single amorphous category."[7] At a certain point, if the definition of who qualifies for refugee status is too broad, then it becomes meaningless. While there is much to be said for broadening the definition to take account of contemporary geopolitical realities, the crucial point to keep sight of is that, in order to be of any critical or practical use, the definition needs to be able to distinguish the moral status and claims of refugees from other categories of those in need in order that the appropriate forms of care can be given and the specific need met.

The qualitative difference between refugees and, for example, destitute economic migrants or those caught up in environmental catastrophes, arises from the primarily political cause of their placelessness.[8] By implication, this affirms the trajectory of the UN Convention but widens it to include those rendered placeless due to both civil war and political policies deliberately designed to cause deterritorialization, such as forced collectivization. For example, those dislocated because of the tsunami in 2004 or the 2005 famine in Niger are not refugees but destitute and in need of various forms of direct assistance. While there is a political dimension to these events, political authority is not the causal factor. Those rendered placeless by ongoing warlordism in Liberia or Afghanistan are refugees even though their life may be economically sustainable. The political basis of their placelessness, I want to argue, is the defining feature of a refugee, which means that the primary need of the refugee is, as Gibney puts it, "the security of a new state within which to reside,"[9] as distinct from social welfare, economic investment, access to education, or some other good.

It is vital to properly locate the status and need of refugees and asylum seekers in order to make sense of subsequent debate about the duty of care to refugees as well as to identify how best to help them.[10]

The Duty of Care to Near and Distant Neighbors

If the primary need of refugees is for a new polity, this immediately raises the questions of whether the political authority of any given state has a greater duty of care to its existent members than to non-members who make a claim to participate in its jurisdiction and protection. Thus, to state the obvious, the need of refugees may be for a new polity, but it does not necessarily follow that all polities have a duty of care to refugees.[11] The fulfillment of the refugees' need is dependent upon a duty of care being recognized by another polity. Two issues related to this are whether border controls are moral and whether proximity has moral implications. In this section the agency of refugees themselves is deliberately bracketed in order to examine the moral and political responsibilities of the "host."

Liberal utilitarians and deontologists argue that liberal democracies, in principle, owe an equal duty of care to all humanity and by implication, that borders should, in principle, be open. Representative of these two approaches are the utilitarians Peter and Renata Singer, and the deontologists Michael Dummett and Joseph Carens. The Singers argue that immigration policy in general and refugee policy in particular should give equal consideration to the interests of all those affected, and where the interests of different parties conflict, priority should be given to those with the most pressing claim.[12] Michael Dummett argues that the requirements of justice are such that "all states ought to recognize the normal principle to be that of open borders, allowing all freely to enter and, if they will, to settle in, any country they wish."[13] Joseph Carens extends the logic of John Rawls' original position to include humankind as a whole.[14] On this basis he argues that free movement is essential for the realization of an individual's other liberties and thus should be considered as a basic human right with open borders a direct implication of this right.[15]

Gibney provides a telling critique of the inconsistencies at work in each of these arguments, but he overstates the extent to which these writers argue for open borders per se.[16] None of these writers argue for completely open borders, and all recognize limits to freedom of movement and how this freedom can conflict with other rights that may necessitate its legitimate restriction. The continuance of borders and the need to balance duty of care to existing members with the duty of care to all humans qua humans is emphasized by the fact that none of them argue for world government. Rather they should be characterized as liberal internationalists who, while universalistic or cosmopolitan in outlook, hold that intermediary political entities—notably, the nation-state—are the means through which the good of humanity is best served. However, proximity has little or no moral bearing upon their conclusions. It is also difficult, on the basis of their arguments, to say whether the claims of refugees should receive priority over those of destitute economic migrants. A contrast can be drawn with the work of Walzer and Gibney.

Michael Walzer notes how entrance policy goes to the heart of political sovereignty and the ability of a community to sustain a common life.[17] He argues that the primary duty of care that members of a political community owe to each other is the communal provision of security and welfare.[18] Central to this provision is the need for community itself, which inherently involves culture, religion, and politics.[19] Maintenance of security and welfare, which inherently involves maintenance of the community itself, justifies entrance policies. In relation to refugees, the provision of security and welfare gives rise to a conflict. What refugees need is a new state; however, the very thing they need cannot be exported, but takes historical and determinate form in particular places.[20] Thus, should the numbers of refugees ever threaten the provision of security and welfare, there is a strong case for refusing entry of the refugees.[21]

Like Walzer, Gibney sees entrance policies as a site of conflicting moral claims.[22] For Gibney, the needs of refugees should be privileged over and against the claims of other foreigners in need of help.[23] However, the claims of refugees must be balanced against the need for states to protect the institutions and values of the liberal democratic state.[24] Gibney goes on to argue, "Liberal egalitarian principles can only be realized in communities where relations amongst citizens are characterized by solidarity and trust, relations which develop over time and can be jeopardized by large, short-term changes in membership."[25] Gibney proposes a "humanitarian principle" for adjudicating between the rival claims of citizens and refugees. This principle holds that "states have an obligation to assist refugees when the costs of doing so are low."[26] In concert with liberal utilitarians and deontologists, this principle recognizes the duties that arise from membership of a single human community, but specifies that priority be given to those in greatest need—that is, refugees. It recognizes also that, at times, other values and interests may need priority which may in turn lead to the exclusion of refugees, including asylum seekers already present within the borders of a given state.[27]

In contrast to liberal utilitarians and deontologists, Gibney and Walzer do attempt to give some account of how to order the duty of care to refugees in relation to the duty of care to existing members. They do this by a minimal account of the common good of liberal democracies.[28] However, neither Gibney nor Walzer gives an account of how the common good of liberal democracies finds its fulfillment beyond itself in some higher good or in the good of humanity. Thus, if the likes of Singer, Dummett, and Carens underemphasize the value of the common life of a nation, Gibney and Walzer maroon that common life, making of it a self-subsisting good and thereby overinvesting it with significance.

Within the multifarious strands of the Christian tradition there is a common teleology that orders the good of a particular community as being fulfilled in the good of humanity which is itself fulfilled in communion with God.[29] This common teleology can be represented by two deliberately diverse and disparate figures: Dante Alighieri and Wolfhart Pannenberg. In Dante's *Divine Comedy* we find an example of how, from Augustine onward, the local and universal horizons of Christian mission and ecclesiology were integrated. The cosmic history of the body of Christ may only be appropriated and entered into through the particularity of one's local language (Dante writes in the vernacular) and one's local political community (the history and destiny of Florence are a central preoccupation of the work), but that history is set within a wider imperial Roman history, and finds its fulfillment in cosmic salvation history. Thus, the local is not absolutized or made an end in itself; instead, it is the necessary beginning point for the pilgrim's journey that culminates in communion with God and redeemed humanity.[30]

The Christian cosmopolitanism of Dante's *Divine Comedy* and its subsequent development from the early modern period onward must be distinguished from its rationalist rival. Both are deeply influenced by Aristotle and notions of the *ius gentium* and natural rights. However, in the development of the former (witnessed in the likes of Vitoria, Saurez, and Grotius), rather than a world government or empire, there is a commonwealth of nations, Christian or otherwise, that can seek a common good of nations and which ultimately finds its *telos* beyond itself in the communion of all humans together with God.[31] In the latter (witnessed in the likes of Montaigne, Jean Bodin, Locke, Leibniz, and eventually coming to fulfillment in Bentham and Kant), *pietas* is not teleologically ordered to the love of humanity, but is subsumed within it: that is, love for humanity precedes and has priority over love of one's immediate neighbor.[32] This latter view is best summarized by Leibniz' statement, "I am indifferent to that which constitutes a German or a Frenchman because I will only the good of all mankind."[33] In short, *pietas* for humanity is understood as overriding the respect that is owed to one's particular community or to God. It is the rationalist cosmopolitan tradition that informs the work of Singer, Dummett, and Carens and those who call for open borders.[34]

A Christian cosmopolitanism also contrasts with Walzer and Gibney, who see the common life of a nation or particular group as an end in itself. Wolfhart Pannenberg argues that the cultivation of a distinctive national life must be subordinated to the concern for an international order of justice and freedom.[35] However, this order can only begin in particular communities that then form unions with other nations, of which Pannenberg cites the European Union as a good example. However, like nations themselves, such unions

should be orientated beyond their own bounds towards the idea
of an order of justice and peace that should one day include all
humanity, that is, not only the world of our friends but also our
present enemies. Thus this sequence of specific unions, which
must have their beginnings in the internal political life of each
people that is involved . . . points toward the universal goal of a
peaceful world that encompasses all mankind.[36]

It is the comprehensive goals of regional and then world peace that
"determines the boundary between the justifiable cultivation of
distinctive national features and nationalistic exaggerations."[37] It
should be noted that Pannenberg conceives world peace as a wholly
provisional, political, and penultimate form of peaceableness that
is in no way equivalent to the peace of God but is rather an echo
of the kingdom Christ inaugurates and which finds its *telos* in that
kingdom.[38] Thus, in contrast to Walzer and Gibney, there is no inherent or necessary conflict between the duty of care to refugees and
the duty of care to existing members. Rather, the duty of care to
refugees must be ordered in relation to pursuit of the common good,
which itself must be ordered in relation to the universal and cosmic
good of humanity. The true end of humans lies in neither the family,
nor a particular culture, nor a nation, nor in some kind of worldwide
polity or universal society, but in the City of God.

Within a Christian cosmopolitan framework, the *telos* of humanity is neither a return to an original state of blessing nor a movement
beyond the materiality of creation. Rather, it is a movement, via differentiation and development through history, to an eschatological
fulfillment of creation. Unlike the rationalist cosmopolitans whose
Platonic, protological teleology posits a return to a undifferentiated
"humanity," a properly theological cosmopolitanism must incorporate the fulfillment of humanity via differentiation into particular
sodalities of persons that involve differences of language, kinship,
and territoriality and a myriad of other aspects of creation. Without
discrete identities that take up and play with creation in particular
ways through history there can be no communion of persons, no
interplay of persons in relation. However, this is not to say that all
patterns of differentiation are good. There can be false and destructive patterns of binding and loosing creation; that is, humans can be
set apart and bound together in ways that are orientated to chaos
and nothingness rather than eschatological fulfillment. Nationalism constitutes one such false form of binding and loosing. Diversity

in unity of relationship to God is the way in which creation is to be properly ordered; all other attempts at unity, whether national or global, constitute a "totalitarian project to centralize, homogenize and control."[39]

The loss of the above, or, for that matter, any teleological framework, renders debate about the ethics of refugee policy incoherent because there is no way to integrate or reconcile the moral claims of citizens and refugees. The absence of such a teleological framework means rational deliberation about what is just is haphazard, and the interests of the strong—the existing members of a polity—tend to prevail over the interests of the weak.

The plight of refugees brings to the fore many of the salutary features of liberal democracy in comparison to other political regimes. Yet, while one does not have to accept a full-scale critique of liberal democracy such as MacIntyre's, it is clear that the current refugee policies adopted by most liberal democracies are morally problematic, favoring the strong over the weak. The crucial point at issue in relation to the formulation of a just and generous refugee policy goes back to Augustine's account of what constitutes a true *res publica*. For Augustine, it is the ends or loves of the polity which form the basis of its common life. Thus the difference between the earthly city and the City of God rests in their different ends or objects of love.[40] An earthly city cannot be a true *res publica* because the nature of its loves means that it can never be a truly harmonious society; rather, it always involves individual and group competition and hostility. For Augustine, the politics of any instance of the earthly city is about negotiating what is necessary for a tolerable earthly peace to exist within which the gospel can be preached and which the heavenly city makes use of for a time. The earthly city is not an end in itself, but serves an end—communion with God—beyond itself. The role of political authority is to establish the conditions for human flourishing through the promulgation and enforcement of law.[41] Liberal democracies are good insofar as they provide a limited peace. However, as the treatment of asylum seekers makes clear, they have made an end in and of themselves and their common lives are based on objects of love—notably, individual and collective self-fulfillment and autonomy—that inherently tend toward hostility to needy strangers. They tend toward hostility to needy strangers because the pursuit of such goods directs us away from the just and generous consideration of the needs of others. Yet, on a conception of the polity within the Christian tradition, there should be no incompatibility between welcoming refugees and pursuit of the common life of the polity.

As previously argued, the primary or defining need of the refugee is political; it is the need for a stable arena of law and order. This need coincides with how, for the most part, the Christian tradition, following Augustine, conceives the defining purpose of a polity, whether it be a city-state, a nation-state, or a confederation of states. Within the Christian political tradition, it is neither territory, nor ethnic/linguistic homogeneity, nor economic power that defines the political identity of a society, even though each of these contributes toward it.[42] Rather, as Joan Lockwood O'Donovan puts it, after the advent of Christ's kingdom, "We can discern the defining aspect of the earthly nation to be the concrete rendering over time of legal justice, that is, the ongoing practice of judgment conducted through the medium of law."[43] Thus the need of the refugee coincides with the raison d'être of the polity. The just political judgment to be made in relation to refugees is at what point the inclusion of more refugees threatens to destabilize any given arena of law and order and not, as so many other responses to refugees suppose, the point at which either territorial integrity, ethnic or cultural homogeneity, or economic power is threatened. Nevertheless, attention to territory, culture, and economics will properly and necessarily be factors in the deliberation process. It is just that they should not be primary or determinative.

It may be objected that to make the criteria of exclusion the point at which law and order becomes untenable is simply to make law and order an end in itself, something which, in the shadow of totalitarian and authoritarian politics, sounds like a license to justify anything. This is not the intention of this argument. Neither is it the intention of this argument to justify the securitization of refugee policy. Current approaches to security as part of the "war on terror" seem to militate against concern for legal process and the rule of law. To make law and order the criteria for exclusion is simply to draw out the logic that it can hardly be moral to will the destruction of that which is the very basis of the remedy sought. It is also to recognize that no single polity is responsible for all refugees. As is actually the case, the provision of asylum necessarily involves all nations. At the same time, there is an urgent need for further attention to how the burden of care is currently distributed, both between North and South and between Western liberal democracies.

The above discussion of the purpose of an earthly polity points toward an inherent contradiction in the modern liberal democratic nation-state, a contradiction that greatly magnifies the suffering of refugees. It is a contradiction on which Hannah Arendt and Georgio Agamben are the most perceptive commentators. Inherent in the justification and legitimation of modern, liberal, democratic nation-states is the upholding of individual or human rights. Yet, whether it is based on *jus solis* or *jus sanguinas*, rights are only extended to members of the nation-states and not, despite the rhetoric, to humans qua humans.

Refugees as Bare Life

There are numerous studies that point to how, within the current context, refugees are labeled, stigmatized, and made scapegoats so they can be dehumanized, abstracted, and empathy toward them diminished.[44] Crossing borders and transgressing the maintenance of boundaries refugees bring into view the contested and contingent nature of national limits and identities. Asylum seekers are literally matter out of place. They do not conform to the established order, and cannot be domesticated; thus, they emerge as dirt or pollution in need of purification from the social body.[45] Such dehumanizing processes allow for a grotesque inversion in perception whereby the vulnerability and powerlessness of asylum seekers is masked and instead, they are seen as a force of nature capable of swamping a country like some human tsunami.

These social processes are mirrored in politics and law. Around the world, refugees and asylum seekers are increasingly stripped of what little political and legal rights they had. Some examples from North America and the European Union will suffice to illustrate this. In the 1994 case, *Sale v. Haitian Centers Council*, the U.S. Supreme Court ruled that it was neither a violation of U.S. domestic nor international law to interdict Haitian boats before they reached U.S. territorial waters and return them to Haiti without assessment of their asylum claims.[46] Effectively, this puts an end to the principle of *non-refoulement*. On the back of the public furor following the revelation that one of those involved in the 1993 bombing of the World Trade Center in New York was in the process of applying for refugee status, the 1996 Illegal Immigration Reform and Immigrant Responsibility Act was signed by Bill Clinton. This reasserted political control over asylum and introduced a system of "expedited removal" that gave immigration officers the authority to remove "improperly documented aliens" arriving in the United States "without further hearing or review."[47] In 1999, in a ruling that set an ominous precedent, the Eleventh Circuit Court of Appeals determined that aliens held at Guantanamo Bay "had no legal rights under the domestic law of the U.S. or under international law" because those rights were only available to persons on U.S. territory.[48]

In the European Union, the 1990 Schengen Accord established a common set of restrictive policies with regard to those coming into the signatory states. The most significant of these was that refusal of asylum in one country meant refusal of asylum in all of them. Geddes notes that Schengen created a buffer zone and displaced the burden of dealing with immigrants and the dilemma of control outside the jurisdiction of the states of Western Europe. It allows EU states to uphold the commitment to the 1951 UN Convention and maintain civil rights for members while achieving illiberal asylum policies via diverting the problem to countries less concerned with human rights. As Geddes put it: "Externalization allows members states to pursue domestic migration policy objectives by other means."[49] The flouting of the UN Convention on Refugees is not restricted to Europe and America. Gaim Kibreab notes that in most of Africa the principle of *non-refoulement* is a dead letter.[50] In terms of the application of the 1951 UN Convention, Caroline Moorehead points out, "The Refugee Convention is in the odd position of being the only major·human-rights treaty that is not externally supervised—all other key UN human-rights accords have some mechanism to ensure the states are held accountable for what they have signed up to."[51]

Denuding asylum seekers of their legal rights is not a new phenomenon. It directly mirrors the process of denaturalization and denationalization undertaken by European states after World War I. Beginning with France in 1915, which denaturalized citizens of "enemy origin," it culminated in the 1935 Nuremberg Laws which divided Germans into those citizens with full rights and those without political rights.[52] This legislation resulted in a situation of mass statelessness and formed the background to the Final Solution.[53] Making this link is not to imply that Western liberal democracies are about to ship refugees off to extermination camps.

However, it does draw out how, like the Jews under the Nazi regime, we encounter refugees as those whose human face is locked away in the iron mask of stereotype and stigma and who are without political rights. They are, to use Georgio Agamben's phrase, reduced to "bare life."

Agamben develops the ancient Roman legal category of *homo sacer* and relates it to the Jews under the Nazis and to contemporary refugees. The *homo sacer* was someone who, though human, could be killed with impunity or without the charge of homicide but could not be sacrificed to the gods nor submitted to sanctioned forms of execution.[54] The *homo sacer* was naked or bare life, neither simply *zoe* or natural life nor *bios*, a participant in a particular form of life.[55] Rather, the *homo sacer* exists in a zone of indistinction, life exposed to death, life that is excluded or banned from participation in both the divine and human community. It is as bare life that refugees raise their most pressing moral claim and unmask the deep contradictions at work in modern political regimes.[56]

Hannah Arendt was the first to see clearly how refugees unveil a contradiction at the heart of modern politics. Arendt argues that in the new, secular, emancipated societies of modernity humans were no longer sure of their social and human rights which "until then had been outside the political order and guaranteed not by government and constitution, but by social, spiritual and religious forces."[57] A consensus emerged that human rights needed to be invoked whenever individuals needed protection "against the new sovereignty of the state and the new arbitrariness of society."[58] Yet the question of human rights became inextricably blended with the question of national emancipation so that the individual could only be protected as a citizen. Agamben points out that the ambiguity between human rights and citizenship is implicit in the 1789 French Declaration of the Rights of Man and Citizen. He states, "It is not clear whether the two terms *homme* and *citoyen* name two autonomous beings or instead form a unitary system in which the first is always already included in the second."[59] In theory humans were supposed to bear rights simply by membership of humanity. However, as Arendt states:

> The conception of human rights, based upon the assumed existence of a human being as such, broke down at the very moment when those who professed to believe in it were for the first time confronted with people who had indeed lost all other qualities

and specific relationships—except that they were still human.
The world found nothing sacred in the abstract nakedness of
being human.[60]

Refugees should have been precisely those to benefit from inborn
and inalienable rights. Their treatment by nation-states, both after
World War II and today, demonstrates that the opposite is the case.
For all the talk about global human rights regimes and deterritorialized forms of citizenship, the individual still depends upon a
sovereign state for the upholding of their legal status.[61] Arendt concludes, "It seems that a man who is nothing but a man has lost the
very qualities that make it possible for other people to treat him as
a fellow-man."[62] Thus, the very thing that justifies and legitimates
a liberal democratic nation-state—the upholding and protection of
human rights—it proves incapable of upholding and protecting at
the greatest point of need. Refugees both unveil the inherent link
between nativity, nationality, and human rights and represent its
crises because, as a mass phenomenon, they cannot be assimilated
to this order. Agamben states, "The refugee must be considered for
what he is: nothing less than a limit concept that radically calls into
question the fundamental categories of the nation-state, from the
birth-nation to the man-citizen link."[63]

Part of the response to this crisis is to separate humanitarian concern from politics and thus maintain refugees as bare life,
excluded from the political community and exposed to death at
every turn. According to its statute, the actions of United Nations
Human Rights Commission are not to be political. Its mission is solely
humanitarian and social.[64] For Agamben, the separation of humanitarian concern from political action means that, despite themselves,
humanitarian organizations "maintain a secret solidarity with the
very powers they ought to fight."[65] The most pointed outworking
of this is the neutrality of the International Committee of the Red
Cross and its refusal to comment on the actions of political regimes.
In the United Kingdom, this distinction simultaneously makes plausible and obscures the perverse inversion of sympathy whereby
the general populace demonstrate great compassion to those suffering abroad, giving millions of pounds to fund humanitarian aid,
while showing great hostility to those same suffering faces when
they are more proximate strangers. There is, however, a discernable
shift wherein humanitarian aid is seen as intrinsically political. The
contrasting strategies of Band Aid and its subsequent incarnation

as Live 8 linked to the Make Poverty History campaign is a case in point. Likewise, newer agencies such as *Médecins Sans Frontières* deliberately eschew an apolitical stance.[66] The inverse of this shift is the political justification of war as humanitarian intervention, for example, in Kosovo, East Timor, and more controversially in the second Gulf War; the deliberate targeting of aid agencies in militarized conflict—for example, the bombing of the UN headquarters in Iraq in 2003; and the militarization of the delivery of aid itself. Yet, even given such shifts, it is crucial that the primarily political nature of the needs of refugees be kept to the fore and neither occluded by their representation as humanitarian need nor marginalized by economic, territorial, cultural, or more recently, security concerns. Any such move makes the refugee an exception, albeit a permanent exception, who can be dealt with outside of the rule of law.[67]

Hallowed Be Thy Name

It is the identification of how refugees are rendered as bare life that points to how the church can makes sense of its own duty of care to refugees and move beyond humanitarian concern. I argue here that the involvement of churches with refugees should be characterized as the hallowing of bare life. The hallowing of bare life is intrinsic to the command to hallow the name of God (Exod 20:1-7). As Karl Barth argued, the second clause of the Lord's Prayer—"Hallowed be thy name"—carries within it the declaration that God establishes God's name. Yet, in the call to hallow the name of God there is also the permission and command for the church to stand against the "twilight and ambivalence that characterizes our present" by bearing witness to the glory of God and making known "the promise of morning without evening."[68] To hallow the name of God involves us in standing against that which desecrates God's holy name.[69] The rendering of creatures as bare life constitutes just such a desecration.

The verb "to hallow" has two definitions. The first is to call or summon with shouting. The second is to make holy and sanctify or to bless a thing so that it is under the protection of a deity. The response of the church to refugees encompasses both of these definitions: it summons forth bare life from exclusion by abiding with refugees as persons able to express themselves within and act upon a common world, and it names refugees as creatures called by God to participate as persons in divine communion. The hallowing of God's name sets the pattern for how the church is to hallow bare life and involves recognizing bare life as gift, as judgment, and as promise.

Bare Life as Gift

Arendt suggest that one of the reasons nation-states find it so difficult to assimilate refugees into the political order is that as a form of human civilization nation-states cannot cope with the sheer givenness of human existence. What cannot be organized and domesticated reminds us of the limitations of human activity. The other, in their sheer givenness, emerges as a threat that arouses "dumb hatred, mistrust, and discrimination because they indicate all too clearly those spheres where men cannot act and change at will, that is, the limitations of the human artifice."[70]

By contrast, to hallow something means recognizing the irreducible worth of what is before one. To hallow a name is to recognize a person and value that person's "external self-outworking and self-expression in relation to all other beings."[71] To hallow one with a name is to identify someone who is free to act in and of herself, who is not simply a passive recipient, but someone who brings herself to expression in the world (either potentially, actually, or latently). A person with a name is one who is differentiated, distinct, and deserving of honor that is their due. Barth identifies hallowing the name of God with glorification and transfiguration. Barth takes these to mean the overcoming of "all misunderstanding and obscurity concerning someone and to set forth and display his true being openly and clearly" so that he may be known "distinctly and unmistakably as the one he really is."[72] To hallow one made in the image of God, imaging being understood in relational terms, involves this same dynamic of overcoming misunderstanding and obscurity. Thus, within discussions of refugees and asylum seekers we are to avoid characterizing them as passive subjects. Rather, they are persons with a name possessing their own complex agency and motivations. The church's duty of care must thence involve creating places for the recognition and expression of that agency.

In hallowing the name of God we recognize both the otherness of God and that God is intimately related to us. The One we hallow is named to us as Father. Thus, the two dimensions of divine personal being—otherness and relation—are encompassed in the prayer. Likewise, if hallowing bare life involves recognizing another person with a name who is distinct and other, it also involves recognizing relationship as constitutive of creaturely personhood.[73]

Personhood in the image of God is constituted by relations of gift and reception.[74] Such relations, however, necessarily involve particularity, limit, and points of exchange. The particularity of creatures is, to a large extent, constituted by their place—that is, their social, economic, political, and historical location in creation. As John Inge argues, scripture, and preeminently the Incarnation, emphasize that places are "the seat of relations or the place of meeting and activity in the interaction between God and the world" and are thus fundamental to human being.[75] The interrelationship between personhood and the dense fabric of place—that refugeehood represents the rupture of and asylum represents the gift of—suggests the necessity of borders to relations of gift and reception. A sense of place and the existence of borders resist the homogenizing collectivism and abstraction of a cosmopolitan egalitarianism (whether capitalist or communist) that would make everyone the same and thereby eradicate the possibility of gift-exchange. The parable of the Good Samaritan, a frequent reference point in philosophical discussions of the duty of care of refugees, is instructive here.[76]

The parable of the Good Samaritan is often read as justifying a universalistic ethic of unconditional love. However, while the parable suggests that aid knows no boundaries—all may be counted as neighbors—the extension of solidarity is particular: care is given by one person to another. Proximity and location are directly relevant: the Good Samaritan responds to one he finds nearby, not some generalized "Other" who exists nowhere and everywhere. The one in distress is presented as a fleshly body to be hosted through costly personal involvement. To abstract or objectify this particular body and so pass on by without encountering them is a sin. Moreover, that the Samaritan comes from a particular place that has a particular relationship to the hearers of the story and the other characters in the parable is central to its dramatic force. Oliver O'Donovan notes, "It is essential to our humanity that there should be always foreigners, human beings from another community who have an alternative way of organizing the task and privilege of being human, so that our imaginations are refreshed and our sense of cultural possibilities renewed."[77] The parable explicates, among all its hearers, both ancient and modern, precisely how someone from another place can renew our false constructions of what constitutes neighbor love. As the parable suggests, while the church must uphold the worth of places as intrinsic to personal relations, it must also recognize that all our human constructions of place are under judgment.

Bare Life as Judgment

Just as the hallowing of God's name reorientates the community of prayer to God, so the hallowing of bare life reorientates the church's existence, calling into question patterns of sedentary exclusivity. Refugees, like the fetus and the suffering dying, call us to recognize bare life as human life worthy of respect and to be afforded dignity as a potential or existent participant in a particular human community. Refugees call us to extend human solidarity and question our limits as to whom we recognize as persons—that is, whom we include in the relations of gift-exchange in a particular place. The primary moral claim of the refugee is the claim to personhood through the restoration of their ability to express themselves within and act upon a common world. Yet, our response to refugees unveils our propensity to retreat and withdraw in order to protect "our" property or "our" way of life, thereby turning place from gift to possession and render refugees as bare life. Our response to refugees unveils the deeply embedded economy of scarcity and equivalence that informs Western society. It is an economy that refuses the possibility of a generative, overabundant future and conforms to the logic of fate rather than faith. The emphasis in current refugee policy on deterrence rather than prevention is indicative of such fatalism.[78] John Milbank suggests that Jesus can be characterized as a *homo sacer*.[79] As *homo sacer* Jesus unmasks the exclusionary violence and self-justification at work in human society. Analogous to how the church is to receive Jesus and so repent and turn away from its participation in systems and structures of sin and "idolatrous security," refugees, as *homo sacer*, decenter and disrupt our sedentary lives and our refusal to live as pilgrims within the earthly city.[80]

Bare Life as Promise

The hallowing of bare life involves trusting that we will see God's kingdom come and his will be done on earth as it is in heaven. "Hallowed be thy name" is an expression of eschatological hope for that time when God will be all in all.[81] The Lord's Prayer as a whole can be read as a summons to live according to the reign of God. The gift of kinship with God that is established in Christ is the beginning of a new community whose pattern of life is set out in the Lord's Prayer. This new community generates new forms of solidarity. Bernd Wannenwetsch notes how the formation of the *ekklesia* overcame the antinomies of *polis* and *oikos* to form a hybrid, the *oikos-polis*.[82] The new political space that was the church refigured all existing social relations. Women, slaves, and children, who were previously excluded from the public political realm, are now addressed as citizens.[83] Men, the only ones who had political agency, and who in their homes were the *paterfamilias*, are now asked to identify themselves as brothers to slaves, women, and children. As Galatians 3 suggests, ethnic, sexual, political, and economic differences do not count when it comes to being included as a citizen in the City of God; and as the Gospel of Matthew puts it, it is "whoever does the will of my Father in heaven [who] is my brother and sister and mother" (Matt 12:50). The hallowing of bare life involves just such a refiguring of social relations in the contemporary context.[84] A good example of this is the sanctuary movement in North America.[85] Indeed, churches throughout the world have, for most part, been at the forefront of arguing for the political rights of refugees, providing sanctuary, visiting them in detention centers, and trying to overcome their dehumanization in contemporary debates.

The new forms of solidarity that emerge through the hallowing of bare life necessarily involve a two-way reconfiguration. Openness to the other involves changing the status quo in order to accommodate the otherness of the other. Likewise, the "guest" must adapt and change as they, with their host, together seek communion with God. This is to spell out the dynamics of gift-exchange. However, such mutual transformation necessarily involves loss as the familiar, and what counts as "home" is renegotiated. In order for new forms of solidarity to emerge, a process of grieving is necessary as both guest and host emigrate from the familiar. Such grieving is the prelude to the formation of shared memories and an interdependent identity narrative. Without any account of loss and grief, racist politics and an exclusionary nostalgia gain legitimacy and so the promise of bare life is never fulfilled.

It must be remembered, however, that eschatology is neither utopian nor idealistic. Thus, the hallowing of bare life is not a call to be overwhelmed by what cannot be done. We are not to fret that we are not gods. We can only take little steps operating within the framework of opportunities and possibilities open to us. The church cannot solve the refugee problem, and it cannot present itself as the bearer of a solution to the complex interplay of factors that result in huge numbers of refugees. Yet, as Karl Barth notes, "Measured by whether it is analogous or not to the hallowing of God's name for which we pray, a supposedly great step might be a fairly small one. Measured by the same criterion, a supposedly little step might really be a very big one."[86] Stories of five thousand fed from a few loaves and fishes, of mustard seeds turning into great trees, of new life gestated in crucifixion and death should open our eyes to the reality that, within an economy of grace, small steps can bear manifold fruit.

Conclusion

This article constitutes an assessment of the contemporary debate on the duty of care to refugees and presented a number of theological responses to this debate. The needs of the refugee are distinct from those of the economically destitute or those displaced due to natural disaster. They are political. The needs of refugees being for a new polity means that in relation to migration, refugees are the most vulnerable because their needs cannot be met in any other way except by inclusion in a new polity. Thus, in relation to policies of admittance, they should receive priority even over destitute economic migrants (although distinguishing between the two is often difficult in the contemporary context). Others, with other needs, should be aided by a variety of different means. Indeed, churches should call on governments to emphasize the needs of refugees over and against current policies which favor certain types of skilled economic migrants yet are increasingly restrictive toward asylum seekers. Policies that favor those who make an economic contribution over those whose need is for a new polity are, on this account, immoral and raise larger questions about what ends any given polity seeks: that is, is it a community that seeks justice or simply a way of organizing economic competition?

Refugees, by definition, need a relatively stable and just regime of law and order. As relatively stable and just regimes of law and order, liberal democracies are called upon to provide asylum. However, a question thus arises about how to reconcile a duty of care to refugees with the ongoing duty of care to existing members of liberal democracies. Debates about how to respond to this question appear irresolvable because contending parties lack any teleology by which to make a just judgment between different claims. On a Christian account of political authority there is no necessary conflict between welcoming refugees and the pursuit of the common life of a polity. There is, however, a need for just and generous political judgment. Such a judgment is only possible when the pursuit of the goods of a particular polity are ordered to the good of humanity as a whole and the common good of humanity is itself ordered in relation to communion with God. The tragedy of the contemporary context is that, despite their best intentions, liberal democratic polities render refugees as bare life, life exposed to death at every turn. Conversely, refugees unveil how humans only possess rights when they are counted as participants in a nation-state—whether as citizens or as putative citizens. The response of the church must be to move beyond the antinomies of humanitarian concern and political exclusion and refuse to link inclusion of the most vulnerable in a common life with participation in a nation-state.[87] Refusing to see refugees as an exception, churches must overcome the exclusion of refugees by abiding with them as persons able to express themselves within and act upon a common world. Such action can be characterized as the hallowing of bare life. Hallowing bare life involves being open, first, to the sheer givenness of those seeking asylum; second, to how refugees disrupt patterns of idolatrous security; and third, to how they call the church to witness to the in-breaking reign of God. To conclude, what is presented here is not a comprehensive theological account of how churches should respond to refugees. It is, however, a necessary prolegomena to such an account, for it sets out the central terrain of the moral debate about the duty of care to refugees and situates a theological response within that territory.

Chapter 8

"Faith" as Mediator in Legitimizing Global Market Integration?

A Preliminary Probe

J. David Richardson

Prolegomenon

In this very preliminary paper, prologue for a longer monograph along similar lines, I set for myself two tightly bounded tasks:

- To begin to explore Christianity's historic role in forging and sustaining sociopolitical acceptance of economic market integration across borders,

and in that light,

- To speculate on Christianity's potential future role in helping to "legitimize" modern global market integration, which has deepened in contentiousness almost as sharply as it has deepened in reality.[1]

The first task is largely descriptive and historical, with a focus on the late nineteenth-century United States and the late twentieth-century European Union. The second task, though also descriptive, involves the normative judgment that legitimate global market integration is on balance a good thing. "Legitimacy" will be defined below as social acceptance and embeddedness, but not necessarily social justice (as normally conceived).[2]

I would also call these tasks modest except for my conviction that they are vitally important, inadequately explored, unappreciated domains of social science. They can also be addressed for other major religious and ethical traditions, but I do so here only very casually and speculatively.[3]

So what is the distinctive content of this paper? I try to make a case for global religion's unique role in envisioning, modeling, debating, and building global institutions and processes to legitimize and socially embed the global market. I begin descriptively and retrospectively, and conclude with some prospective prescription. Compared to existing literatures, this paper purports to be more historically rooted and social-scientific, and more prescriptively constructive.

What gap is the paper hoping to begin to fill? The gap into which this material fits is the surprising absence of global counterparts to a well-developed literature on national markets, social embeddedness, and justice. For just one of many examples, Blank and McGurn give a recent and prominent treatment of these themes, yet it is almost entirely national in its perspective, with four pages of attention to global markets.[4] And even the pope's recurrent and thoughtful encyclicals about the market system, *Centesimus Annus*, for example, premise their discussions implicitly on the appropriateness and effectiveness of countries' juridical and social systems, with no explicit discussion of intercountry counterparts.[5]

What I claim in the previous paragraph may surprise some readers, sated over the past thirty years especially with the recurrence of ringing, stinging indictments of globalization in the name of justice. Yet such literature is nearly entirely, prophetically diagnostic.[6] Almost none of it proposes or prescribes viable institutional sequences of solutions or structures, or tactical mechanisms to attain them. Very little of it uses national histories of gradually "legitimized" internal integration as a template for what might be done at a global level. Nor does this literature ask what elements of national religious histories hold cautionary conclusions or are unsuitable as a template for socially embedding globalism. Almost none of this vast, angry literature is social-scientific.[7]

Meanwhile, global markets continue to grow without legitimizing support. They grow because of incentives. They grow because the costs of travel, communication, coordination, and information continue to decline precipitously. They grow at what economists call the extensive margin: more and more activities become open to cross-border supply and demand that used to be localized, such as trade in standardized surgery and secondary-school tutoring. And they grow at the intensive margin, too: larger and larger market shares for globally owned and managed firms and for cross-border transactions in activities that are already open, such as accounting, banking, retailing, and tourism.

But growth without legitimacy is inherently self-limiting. Justice-oriented critics find that limitation a good thing. I think they are demanding too much perfection. Socially acceptable globalization is my orientation, because I read the recent literature on "genuinely human" development (economic, political, social) to conclude that global openness is a key contributor to such integral development.[8] In this light, to sustain deeper and deeper global market integration is better than to limit it, as long as some sort of social embedding is in place, presumably evolving at a roughly comparable rate to openness.

I argue below that norm-driven religion, Christianity in particular, has played and could play a fruitfully constructive role in discourse and scaffolding that legitimizes markets that otherwise begin to grow dangerously faster than polities or societies.

Christianity's important role in legitimizing historic American and modern European market integration is in fact the most surprising (to me) discovery in what follows. I will trace it in two capsule histories, then speculate on how it and other religions might play a similarly constructive role in global market integration. Or should they play such a role? The weight of the rest of history, beyond the favorable-but-important American and European cases, invites caution. Before these core sections of the paper, the next section defines important terms and roots my perspective in recent research.

Antecedents and Foundational Concepts for this Paper

With political scientist Craig Parsons, I have argued that the striking economic success of the single-market quest of both the European Union and the United States at the turns of the last two centuries is not actually the most noteworthy feature of their sweeping experiments in national and regional integration.[9] The most noteworthy feature is the legitimacy and public support for the single-market experiment that is firmly grounded in the United States and evolving fitfully in Europe.[10]

"Legitimacy" is the key to sustained market integration. Parsons and I argued that there is a necessary nexus between social stability, political participation, and legitimacy on the one hand

and the growth of a single market on the other.[11] We characterized legitimacy in a nuanced way by the degree to which members of a society are free to criticize but choose not to challenge institutions or processes. This characterization is broader than democratic legitimacy but narrower than moral legitimacy—and also more observable empirically than the latter. Thus we were able to discuss mechanisms for eliciting popular acquiescence that were quasi-democratic at best. In this paper, I focus more on the role that religion has played in observable social scaffolding, and less on religion's role in helping to build social ethics.

Parsons and I also argued that the content of the markets-legitimacy nexus includes certain necessary and ubiquitous elements (like courts that implement and enforce commercial law), whereas the historical mechanisms—the sociopolitical processes—by which legitimacy is attained are far more varied (and often even autocratic). We distinguished three such processes, which we labeled pluralism, commercialism, and developmentalism. All three are normatively instrumental, that is, "good," because they enhance an objective. Only the first is unambiguously democratic. The second, commercialism, involves a business-government coalition initiating as much integration as the rest of society can stand,[12] and the third, developmentalism, involves top-down initiatives in which market integration is the principal means by which a government builds a viable state, a common East Asian model.

What was missing from our instrumental account of the three mechanisms is the possibility that civil society, and Christian (or other) religion in particular, may have had a particularly important role both in modulating the public debate over the goods and "bads" of market integration, and in designing and maintaining the institutions, respect for laws, due process, and symbols that serve as mediators of the nexus between market integration and legitimacy. This paper reminds readers of the historical evidence for such a role, with Christian influence particularly in view, and then speculates on the potential for a similar future role at the global level.[13]

In still earlier work,[14] I have observed that at its foundation, the market system is socially populated, socially rooted, socially conditioned, and socially constructed[15]—far, far away from the chaotically competitive "law of the jungle" with which it is rhetorically confused. I then argued, more controversially, that an economically and politically sustainable global market system will have to be socially constructed and conditioned, too, by global discourse and policy design, including labor-relations and competition law, as well as policies to promote dissemination of innovation.

This progressive view that specific types of social regulation can support markets (or augment or embed them, to use terms associated with modern scholars such as Mancur Olson and John Ruggie) has deep roots in economic history and philosophy, in the institutional school,[16] in liberal political theory, and in the American social gospel and its European counterparts, as described below.[17] The view is most naturally applied to nation-states or subnational societies. But the progressive view has acquired very little recent traction in discussions of global market integration, despite high-level attempts to give it visibility and indefatigable, coherent campaigning by prominent public intellectuals.[18]

More important for this paper, the Christian provenance of the progressive view—and what the activist Christian religion may have added to the embedded legitimacy and effectiveness of the historic market system—seems to have been denied[19] or forgotten by all but a few lonely commentators, Fogel being the most prominent among Americans, and Pope John Paul II among Europeans.[20]

I argue next that to remember the constructive role of religion in this regard is instructive, encapsulizing histories of the late-nineteenth-century United States and the late-twentieth-century European Union. Later I outline the promising constructive role of serious religion in facilitating the legitimacy and sustainability of a global market system.[21]

Two Capsule Histories, Suggestive Insights, Doubts[22]

The American Capsule History

For much of the first half of the nineteenth century the United States' own national economy was poorly integrated. Rather than displaying broad and diffuse patterns of domestic exchange, economic activity was mostly either localized in fairly distinct regions or flowed through parallel networks to ports for export. Mountains, settlement gaps (empty geographical spaces bounded by "the frontier"), and a lack of navigable rivers kept markets quite separate from each other.

Variation in state-level regulation further encouraged economic fragmentation. As a reaction to the pervasive trade disputes under the Articles of Confederation, the U.S. Constitution had given the federal government broad power to regulate commerce. But it also authorized states to maintain distinct regulation for health, safety, or welfare reasons. Combined with a decentralized monetary system—the federal government had the sole legal authority to coin and regulate currency, but no mandate to oversee a banking system with its money-equivalent deposits—the early American regulatory framework provided openings for an agenda of national market integration, but did not immediately challenge the fragmented status quo.

As the mid-century approached, slow change in economic and regulatory patterns began to accelerate. First the canals and then, even more strongly, the telecommunications and railroad booms, followed by internal migration, merged markets that had been local and regional. With improved technology and infrastructure came the growth of cross-frontier trade and "national"[23] corporations now able to contemplate profitable sales and division of labor across a wider geographical scope. Firms began consolidating and competing in one another's backyards with similar ("best-practice") production techniques and product arrays, whose prices gradually converged from region to region. Vertical integration, facilitated by refinements in best-practice corporate governance, made regions increasingly interdependent, as did the rationalization of national finance and insurance.

The basic facts about the regulatory and institutional content of responses to these American integration trends are familiar.[24] Less familiar and more contentious are the mechanisms by which legitimizing content evolved. Least familiar is the prominent role of Christian writing and civic and political activism in both content and mechanisms.

Content

As to content, the chartering of national banks and banknotes after 1863 began to reduce monetary chaos—replacing the eight thousand or so state-chartered banks that had been issuing different notes as of 1860. Business actors mobilized to seek favorable regulation (or no regulation) at the national level. In parallel, a growing social reform movement emerged to seek national fixes for robber-baron capitalism and corrupt machine politics. They were amply catalyzed by muckraking journalists, pamphleteers ("mugwumps"), and novelists of the era. Some of them, in turn, were moonlighting from day jobs as pastors (Washington Gladden) and administrators (Jane Addams). Regulatory experiments at the state and local levels were quickly superseded by federal government counterparts, including the Interstate Commerce Act, the Sherman and Clayton antitrust acts, the Interstate Commerce Commission, and the Federal Trade Commission. Though initially symbolic because the Supreme Court limited their application and because American political institutions lacked any tradition of rational public administration, the eventual result was a broad framework of regulatory laws and institutions.

Waiting in the wings were ensuing innovations in redistributive justice—in public education, industrial and labor relations, and fiscal and social policies, all provoked by growing inequality of wealth, rural-urban dislocation, workplace violence, and immigration. The broader political agenda attached to these regulatory and distributional regulations included pressure for direct primaries and election of senators, women's suffrage, civil-service reform, and procedures for initiative, referendum, and recall.

Mechanisms and Christian Influence

While there was American market growth and reform in this period, there is considerable disagreement over the mechanisms that generated the story and their respective emphases and causal links. Little recollection remains of the prominent roles of Christians and their faith-inspired words and actions.

One account of legitimizing mechanisms emphasizes pluralism. American market integration generated broad resistance from elements of society that benefited only marginally or who actually seemed to lose—for example, farmers, squeezed between the late-1800s decline in agricultural prices and the rise in the price of credit and manufactured inputs. Open, flexible democracy enabled bargaining and policy responses that redistributed these gains adequately enough to enlist the legitimate consent of most of the populace.

Fogel (2000) and McGerr (2003), in two definitive accounts, emphasize such pluralistic mechanisms.[25] These include the reformist election campaigns of William Jennings Bryan, appealing strongly to serious Protestants, and the catalytic role of a radically crusading, progressive Christian middle and professional class, who found their voice and political agenda initially in the social gospel of Richard T. Ely, Washington Gladden, and Walter Rauschenbusch[26] and in the examples of civic activism pioneered by the Salvation Army and Jane Addams.

Fogel describes the subsequent commandeering of the moral force of the social gospel movement by secularly minded humanists, and attributes their takeover partly to factionalism within American Protestantism and conflict between it and nascent American Catholicism.[27] We speculate below that sharp Christian disunity always undermines Christianity's potential to modulate and contribute constructively to the social scaffolding that undergirds market integration and the market system.[28] But none of this should obscure the important place of serious Protestantism in the early American progressive movement, nor of serious Catholicism in the later progressivism of labor relations and social transfers.

However, a second account of the mechanisms by which Americans legitimized national economic integration gives less credit to pluralism than to business and political elites. Cohen, for example, focuses on elites, in her case elite liberal intellectuals who mediated the reconciliation of "economic consolidation" and an "active liberal state"—in our language, "who articulated the legitimization of national economic integration."[29] Serious Christians were prominent among these dominating elites, from business (John D. Rockefeller), politics (William Jennings Bryan), and civil-society media and scholarship (Washington Gladden and the academic social reformers).

Bensel emphasizes the primal importance of the post–Civil War "national" project—the reconstruction of an economically prosperous yet legitimately democratic nation-state.[30] American Christians, with strong commitment to healing and reconciliation, were supportive and ready to be led. In Bensel's view, which combines commercialist and developmentalist mechanisms, national market integration was first and foremost a political construction. The U.S. Supreme Court and the business-backed Republican Party (that maintained the Court) were the political agents (the presidency and the whole executive branch were still weak). Pro-business, pro-development internal transportation systems were enabled by land grants, sympathetic regulatory policies, and the hard-fought battle for a single, gold-based hard currency. The Supreme Court was packed with justices who vigilantly defended the rights of commercial firms to be treated the same as persons with respect to property rights and who struck down state regulatory challenges to unfettered markets on the constitutional grounds that the federal government controls interstate commerce.

Yet legitimacy could not be neglected in American democracy; parties (especially the Republicans) "purchased" popular acquiescence (however fitfully) by raising tariffs against foreign manufactures, then irregularly redistributing the tariff revenues as needed to win grudging acceptance. The tariffs helped maintain Northern support, and their redistribution placated the South and West. In Bensel's account, the legitimacy of the national project to develop prosperous internal market integration was essentially bought from above, not born from below. But it could never have happened without Christian priority for reconciliation.

The EU Capsule History

Postwar reconstruction, reintegration, and reconciliation, envisioned and pursued by activist Christians, also played a central role in twentieth-century European integration, with the American model in mind. But the historical roots go back to the nineteenth century. At the same time that religiously rooted American progressivism was fitfully growing and subdividing, European Christian democracy was born as a political movement. It grew globally into the Christian Democratic parties that still compete in Europe (and Latin America). In its early decades, its legitimizing influences were intranational, and similarly again to the United States, its religious foundations (in Pope Leo's XIII's pathbreaking *Rerum Novarum*) were commandeered by nationalist, pragmatic, and secular fellow travelers.[31]

Christianity's direct impact on integrated Europe-wide markets, institutions and mechanisms was slight until after the great Euro-global wars of the twentieth century. In the face of those crushing assaults on human solidarity and goodwill, Christian Democratic parties rose again as strong supporters of nascent European economic integration in the 1950s and beyond—integration that was broad, deep, growing, and socially embedded—to tie warring Europe together so tightly that continental war was ultimately unthinkable.[32] Christian Democrats—Konrad Adenauer and Robert Schuman—were prominently represented. Weigel calls them, along with Alcide de Gasperi and Jean Monnet, "serious Catholics who saw European integration as a project of Christian civilization."[33] Wallace implicitly outlines European integration as a project of *re*-civilization, inspired by pre-Reformation visions of a culturally united, Western Christian Europe, the successor to Charlemagne's empire.[34]

Content

European economic integration began on a small sectoral scale; its purpose was, after all, sociopolitical. The European Coal and Steel Community (ECSC), set up in 1952, amounted to a experiment in institutionally centralized and substantively deeper market integration. The goal of full sectoral liberalization was supported by a social fund for compensating those who bore the economic burdens and by a variety of other conditional safeguards. Embedded into it was an autonomous market regulator (the High Authority), a court for dispute resolution, a political assembly, and an intergovernmental organ (the Council of Ministers). Broad sectoral antitrust, including oversight of state subsidies and other "beggar-your-neighbor" support, was the High Authority's key policy tool to integrate and rationalize these sectors within an arguably fair rule of (competition) law.

As is familiar, the ECSC birthed an institutionally centralized, *multi*-sectoral experiment, also with well-developed mechanisms for adjudication and side payments to those burdened. The largest continental economies extended the ECSC institutional framework into a general Common Market in the European Economic Community (EEC) in 1958. A court, assembly, and intergovernmental body again flanked an autonomous market regulator (now the European Commission), for which broad antitrust remained a key integrative tool with a rule-of-law underpinning to gain social acceptance across otherwise competitive nation-states..

As in the American case, justice-motivated redistribution followed the regulatory scaffolding that supported early legitimacy. To the social fund was added a promise, realized in the 1960s, for a much larger set of compensatory payoffs to farmers (the Common Agricultural Policy [CAP]).[35] The other major development of the 1960s (though little recognized at the time) was judicial: the EEC's European Court of Justice declared itself supreme to national law, resolving (by unchallenged fiat) ambiguities in the EEC treaty. Within this framework the EEC achieved full customs union in the early 1970s. British accession encouraged still more cross-country redistribution; since it received few CAP subsidies, EEC "Structural Funds" would go largely to British deindustrialized areas. These funds were then greatly expanded with the accession of Greece, Spain, and Portugal in the 1980s, all of which insisted on adjustment money before opening themselves to single-market EEC competition.

In the mid-1980s the EEC added an ambitious new "Single Market 1992" agenda of elimination of nontariff barriers, harmonization of standards, and capital liberalization—again to be socially modulated by an aggressive European Union competition policy. More majority voting in the Council of Ministers decreased the political obstacles to this push. A few short years later the member-states agreed on a schedule for monetary union (though with an opt-out clause for the less enthusiastic members). With these massive integrative commitments the poorer members successfully demanded hugely increased payoffs in the Structural Funds, which doubled in 1988 and again in 1992. Richer actors insisted that monetary union be accompanied by significantly greater powers for the EEC assembly—now known as the European Parliament—a new social protocol on working conditions, and stronger environmental standards.

This basic content changed little in the later 1990s. Negotiations over the accession of twelve mostly postcommunist states seemed to threaten the EU payoff systems—the cost of extending the CAP and Structural Funds to the east looked prohibitive—but clever formulae were found to preserve the benefits to current members while offering more modest subsidies to new members.[36] Mechanisms of majority voting among member-states and Parliamentary influence were slightly strengthened in the treaty modifications of 1997 and 2000 that readied the institutions for larger membership.

Further-reaching reforms were envisioned in the constitution proposal of 2003–2005, but they foundered in what have been widely interpreted as protest votes by French and Dutch citizens. The many commentators who have argued that they were as much disillusioned with their own national leaders and problems as with any aspect of the EU pay a high compliment to the effectiveness of the EU's traditional institutions of embedded legitimization. They have worked well enough; if they were not seriously broken, there was no compelling benefit in buttressing them constitutionally.

That today's deeply integrated European Union developed this content in this basic sequence of events is a matter of widely accepted historical record. Why and how and with what mechanisms this framework appeared, however, is much more contested.

Mechanisms and Christian Influence

The dominant view—what we call the pluralistic mechanism, and what its proponents call a liberal account—is that this legitimizing scaffolding emerged from a set of pluralistic deals between those who stood to profit from market integration and those who stood to lose.[37] A second, more commercialist view sees the European institutional framework itself as a calculated mechanism to foment "ever deeper" regional market integration, a mechanism propelled by Euro-societal interest groups, especially business.[38]

A third view of EU history is central to this paper for the role played by Catholic thinkers and Christian Democratic activists, as outlined at the beginning of this subsection. In this view, the construction of the EU was led by a minority of national political elites who were ideologically committed to the development of supranational European institution-building.[39] Market integration was an ancillary by-product of a top-down political agenda for strong European institutions that would make the conflicts of the early twentieth century extremely unlikely. Only a top-down ideological crusade for the development of European institutions carried Europe to such profound integration.

This marriage of convenience was forced on European business throughout the postwar period. Many business actors preferred freer trade and deregulation, but they generally opposed the creation of supranational institutions to manage that economic agenda. Yet to get the market prizes they really wanted, they were willing to learn to live with the unwelcome institutional costs that the supranational enthusiasts pressed on them.

This account connects poorly to conventional norms of popular democratic legitimacy and to the pluralist legitimizing interpretations that others use to explain the legitimization of American and European market integration. Yet in an unusual way, this account features the influence of a visionary civil society, unelected indeed, but importantly norm-driven and heavily populated by Christians, using persuasion as well as opportunity and power when they presented themselves, to pursue peaceful prosperity that broad American and European publics have come to embrace—however little they claim to understand it and however little they feel they created it or that it is adequately just. They own it today, however accidentally and reluctantly.

Suggestive Insights and Doubts

But how exactly did all this evolve? Important omissions in the capsule histories above are the roles of civil society, including its discourse and communications outlets, and a consideration of how much Christian perspectives influenced them.

With regard to civil-society discourse, its importance seems clear. American newspapers, books, and novels were vital in awakening middle-class American consciousness; many of them were written by high-profile Protestants, though not in any way elites.[40] European discourse, though more dominated by elites, was also vital, but so also was political service by Catholic activists like Adenauer and de Gasperi (Jean Monnet, by contrast, never held elective office). No elected American political leader matched them in the seriousness of their Christian commitments.[41]

But church-commissioned discourse, as opposed to that written for broad-audience outlets by serious Christians, seems to have had little impact on the institutions and mechanisms of market integration's social modulation. Even the papal encyclicals had indirect rather than direct influence on European integration.

Nor did fitful market integration elsewhere—for example, Latin America—ever reach sustaining momentum, much less socially embedded legitimization. Two things seem possibly to stand in the way, pending deeper research. One is the intensity of political corruption, which *de*-legitimizes the social scaffolding that a market system needs, and which was strongly disciplined by civil-service reform in both the American[42] and European cases. The other is visceral contention within or across the dominant religions of a region, as discussed briefly below.

Duly noting these unanswered questions, we speculate next on whether this account of less pluralistic, more development-oriented American and European economic integration has some surprising potential promise for future legitimizing institutions and mechanisms that will socially embed global market integration and spread its benefits more broadly.

How Global Religion Ought Naturally Help Legitimize Global Market Integration

Religion, like business itself, is all too reflexively excluded from civil society—and not just excluded, but often shunned. A widespread prejudice has it that religion is irrational and *un*civil and doesn't belong, just as commercial (read: crass, uncivil) business itself doesn't belong.

Whatever one thinks of this marginalizing posture as a normative preference, it is ahistorical.[43] And it ought to seem more than
a little foolish as a tactic of *realpolitik*, disparaging coalitions rather
than developing them. After shunning both transcendent sources
of values and no-nonsense efficiency reasons for conserving scarce
resources, the remaining reed of sociopolitical negotiation for managing values seems to be dangerously thin, unstable, weak, and
vapid. It may also be mindlessly (or innocently) exclusive, marginalizing also the political voices of children, the unborn, and others
who are spatially outside current political constituencies.[44]

Better it seems, for several reasons, to draw religion explicitly
into the legitimizing debate, mechanisms, and institution building.
Elliott, for example, emphasizes how community identity contributes directly to trust, and then how trust, in turn, contributes to
legitimacy and helps support the transparency that is necessary for
formal, market-embedding institutions and processes to be themselves socially accepted and supported.[45]

Any global community, therefore, including global religion, has
a natural advantage in contributing to the building of global institutions and practices that socially embed deeper and deeper global
economic integration.

But how might this be done? The question does not seem to me
to be unduly academic, because historical case studies already provide some guidance, and because some religious activism to legitimize is still alive in contemporary Europe.

In Europe, a confluence of recent events seems to be thrusting
religion forward for a prominent constructive role, a role anticipated presciently by John Paul II, in an exhortation entitled *Ecclesia in Europa*.[46] One marker event is that constitutional momentum
in the European Union has stalled, in part according to some commentators because of widespread popular mistrust of policy elites
and their values. A second marker is that the strictly secular French
model ("laïcité") of national integration seems to be reaching its
limits in meeting its objective to integrally embed all social inter-
course within French borders under the umbrella of French secular
citizen-culture. Third, two largely Orthodox countries, Bulgaria and
Romania, have joined the EU in 2007, and Muslim Turkey has been
accepted into the beginning of its accession negotiations. Finally,
two large cross-border ecumenical groups, one Roman Catholic and
one Protestant/Orthodox, scheduled a twenty-month "pilgrimage"

series of meetings across Europe and at the grass roots during 2006–2007 that founded an ongoing discussion of renewal and unity in Europe and the Christian churches' potential role in it.[47]

Furthermore, historic Christian Democracy seems to be enjoying some renaissance and renewal at a Europe-wide level. A federated "group" (not willing yet to call itself a party) of national Christian Democratic parties[48] now occupies more seats in the European Parliament than any similar group. A movement of more evangelical, observant Christian individuals, many from newer EU members, has formed for discussion, reflection, and activism across ethnic and national lines under the name European Christian Political Movement.[49] And some see in growing Roman Catholic youth and social movements not merely a reconverted Europe, but a Europe now naturally and integrally (i.e., with integrity) able to socially embed and integrate change of all kinds—in technology, in markets, and even in the ethnic makeup of the European population.[50]

But it is not clear that any of this is beginning again yet in the United States. American Christianity seems mired in myopic disarray in regard to any constructive agenda by which to engage further global economic market integration, much less to attempt its legitimization. Prophetic voices exist, but it is not clear that they are being widely heard, much less translated into an activist sociopolitical agenda.[51] Americans seem to be turning away from global integration (e.g., in agriculture, immigration, inward foreign investment, and white-collar services trade) rather than trying to deepen and embed it further. The outlook is not positive, however pregnant the history is.

Conclusions and Extensions

History cautions us about any single answer to this paper's principal question: is religion a help or hindrance in legitimizing cross-border economic forces? History's most positive examples beckon us toward continuing to ask the question hopefully, with both the future and a global domain in mind. But the "rest of history" seems to hold few such examples, making it an open question whether the positive examples are exceptions or models.

Adding to the hopeful side of this inquiry is the simple fact of religion as norm-oriented global civil society. Why should it not help legitimize globalization?[52] History has at least two important examples in which organized Christian religion has facilitated the legitimization of sustained economic integration across borders. American Protestantism and European Catholicism were both constructive and catalytic contributors to the nineteenth- and twentieth-century social embedding of ambitious and continuing experiments in continental single markets. Methods and mechanisms of influence differed in these two examples, but the institutions they constructed and the holistic overall result were remarkably similar, and continue to exist, many decades after their initiation.

Nascent contemporary Islamic parallels also seem to exist but are beyond the scope of this paper.[53] Indonesia, Malaysia, Tunisia, and possibly Egypt and Turkey may be paving the way for widely accepted (if not Western democratic) regional integration in the East and South Mediterranean and in East and Southeast Asia. More speculative still is the place of parallel Christian and Jewish influence in the same regions—even perhaps in collaborative effort with Muslims.[54] Israel's, Jordan's, Lebanon's, and South Korea's monotheistic populations seem poised for constructive, if not necessarily cooperative, contributions, to say nothing of China's underground counterpart.

Nevertheless, other history and other speculation point in less hopeful directions. The ebb and flow of eclectic Catholic and Protestant influence in Latin America, as well as the historical conflict between their partisans, has contributed little to legitimate economic integration there.[55] Nor is it easy to see any constructive contributions by the fragmented Orthodox, Catholic, and Protestant brands of Eastern European Christianity in Russia, Ukraine, and neighboring states to legitimizing the transition to political-economic integration there. For all the aforementioned constructive African and Asian examples of monotheistic contributions, there are the apparent countercases of the Congo, Iran, Iraq, Pakistan, the Philippines, and Sudan.[56]

Looking ahead, it is not clear whether Christianity's constructive face or its chaotically critical face will dominate world momentum for more regional integration. Much may depend on which face American Christianity adopts in the coming decades, given the central leadership of the United States in global economic integration. If American Christians learn from the nascent ecumenical European activism and perhaps form transatlantic joint ventures, the constructive legitimizing cooperation could easily spread across the Pacific to eager and energetic churches in China, Indonesia, and Korea. On the other hand, if American Christians turn increasingly fractious and the country turns increasingly insular, then global economic integration may not only decelerate, but shrink in both depth and legitimacy.

In sum, to look ahead expansively, it is not yet clear whether monotheism or religion of any or all types has a hope of contributing to the great challenge of globally embedding modern globalization in a scaffolding of reinforcing and stabilizing sociopolitical supports. On the other hand, I see little hope that modern secular ethics is any more likely to succeed! So looking ahead as a Christian disciple, I'm still hopeful . . . and hopefully prayerful.

Chapter 9

Globalization and the Problem of the Nature/Culture Boundary

Janel Curry

Inherent to any discussion of human-environment relations are the interrelated issues of the globalization of the market, the nature of reality (ontology), and our understanding of how we gain knowledge of nature (epistemology). Both regulation and the marketing of aspects of nature, fueled by the forces of the global market, involve assumptions about the ontological state of nature, and thus our ability to divide and bound aspects of it. Second, our beliefs about our ability to know and understand the workings of nature have given us the hubris to enhance the marketing and use of these aspects for the purpose of participating in the forces of global market. Views on the nature of reality, particularly views on the relationship between nature and humans, or what is often called the nature-culture boundary, have concrete expression in policies that shape both this regulation and commodification of nature. Furthermore, these policies are undergirded by a particular view of knowledge. The result is a further transformation of human-environment boundaries, and the boundaries among humans, portrayed as neutral in terms of its approach and result through the lack of transparency of underlying views of reality and knowledge creation.[1]

Joan Tronto, in her book *Moral Boundaries*, shows how central the issue of boundaries is to morality and challenges the neutrality of much that underlies boundaries related to the nature-culture boundary and natural resource policy. She identifies two moral boundaries that are particularly pertinent to the issue of nature-culture relations and natural resource policy. The first is the boundary between morality and politics. In an Enlightenment, modernist worldview, morality refers to what one thinks is important to do and how to conduct one's relations with other people. Politics, on the other hand, within the Western tradition, is the realm in which resources are allocated, public order is maintained, and disputes about how these activities should occur are resolved.[2] Politics becomes a means to achieve moral ends, or morality becomes a means to achieve political ends. In this tradition, the notion that politics and morality have similar ends and means is incomprehensible.[3] Thus the allocation of resources through natural resource policy is seen as a neutral political question that does not involve questions of morality.

The second moral boundary concerns the moral point of view. This contemporary modernist Enlightenment boundary requires that moral judgments be made from a point of view that is distant and disinterested, and these requirements are identified as the requirements of reason.[4] Several consequences of this latter boundary are, first, that morality becomes a realm beyond the world of emotions and feelings; second, that it is not allowed to be shaped by local custom, and third, that local customs and variations are defined, necessarily, as inferior or defective modes of moral understanding.[5]

Tronto unmasks these assumptions and argues that politics and morality cannot be separated, just as knowledge arising out of the local or attachment does not reflect a lower level of moral or intellectual understanding. Radical orthodoxy proponent John Milbank likewise calls into question the dominant paradigm that, while claiming to merely describe society and human relationships, in reality has embedded within it an a priori account of human relationality which is atomistic.[6]

The relevance of Tronto's discussion to our understanding of such geographical concepts as the bounding of property rights can be seen when we turn to the work of William Cronon. He writes, "To define property is thus to represent boundaries between people; equally, it is to articulate at least one set of conscious ecological boundaries between people and things."[7] Cronon sees the bounding of property as ultimately representing a society's view on the boundaries between people and between people and nature. Both of these points are significant. First, the act of bounding property and resources cannot be separated from the building of boundaries between and among people. For example, a legal system that emphasizes individual property rights results in a society that also emphasizes the boundary between individuals over against a more communal sense of property and personhood. Second, boundary construction reflects our views about the relationship between nature and humans, the nature-culture boundary. Natural resource management policy has to involve drawing exactly these sorts of boundaries between different groups of people and between the social and the natural. Cronon's principles allow us to see that these boundaries are choices, not timeless, predetermined absolutes. Once we recognize that they are choices, Tronto reminds us that they are not neutral, but choices weighted with heavy moral baggage. Relationship to nature is intertwined with human society. Policy creates boundaries and rules related to permeability of human-nature boundaries and boundaries among people.

The issue of the nature-culture boundary is intertwined with that of globalization. Globalization refers to the present-day neoliberal capitalist perspective that claims that the global market economy and the bundle of freedoms that are attached to it (political, economic, and personal) is the best vehicle for achieving universal human aspirations—what all people on earth are presumed to desire.[8] Through the force of the global market, the economy becomes deterritorialized, while the importance and control of the nation-state is reduced.[9] And through this process, the scale and complexity of social organizations change, disempowering local communities in favor of a globally integrated economic system."[10] Through this process, neoliberal government policies encourage and extend economic reason into more and more aspects of society and life.[11]

In this paper, I explore the relationship between society and nature through the use of the concept of boundaries in an analysis of New Zealand's marine resource management policies and their impact on a local community. This analysis critiques the assumptions of the policy framework that arises out of the modernist, Enlightenment ontology of autonomous individualism as well as the Enlightenment, modernist view of rationality that rejects the local and attachment in terms of its ability to form the basis for moral judgment. The purpose that orients the modern state and the forces of globalization is its mission at serving as mediator or peacemaker among competing autonomous individuals.[12] This purpose is fundamentally based on an ontology of social atomism.[13] A reductionistic epistemology follows this social atomism. Radical orthodoxy critiques this epistemology of secular modernity, claiming that its ontological framework gives "autonomy to things such that it is supposed that the world can be properly understood in itself without reference to its transcendent origin, the Creator."[14] Their alternative, closer to the alternative offered here, is one of a participatory ontology. A relational social anthropology, underlain by recent writings in Trinitarian theology, demands a broader understanding of methods of gaining knowledge, not entirely based on rational, universal, and reductionistic viewpoints, but rather ones that incorporate relational aspects of reality and knowing in all its complexity. Starting with different assumptions aids in understanding the promises and failures of our natural resource policies, policies that are concrete expressions of our views on the nature-culture boundary.

Case Study

The local community used in this case study is Great Barrier Island. Great Barrier Island is approximately sixty miles off the coast from Auckland, New Zealand. The island is approximately twenty-five miles by fifteen miles (forty kilometers by twenty-two kilometers) in size and has a population of less than one thousand people.[15] Highly dependent on marine resources for its economy, life on the island has been transformed through the development of a market- and property-rights-based marine resource policy regime driven by globalization (Figure 1).[16] Modernist policy, such as that which shapes New Zealand's marine policy, emphasizes the division and bounding of nature and human society. In the case of New Zealand, this policy regime was driven by the real problem of the "tragedy of the commons" in the fisheries. Prior to the implementation of the policies, the fisheries of the country were under tremendous stress from overfishing.

My focus is not so much on the right or wrong of globalization, but the assumptions underlying the policy structures that have shaped it in New Zealand. So while I am uncomfortable with Jagdish Bhagwati's unbridled support for the global market on the one hand, I believe he is correct in suggesting that environmental and social problems often attributed to the global market more often reflect a weakness in institutional structure within a country.[17]

Thus my argument follows at one level that of J. David Richardson in the previous chapter, where he states that the market system is "socially populated, socially rooted, socially conditioned, and socially constructed" and that "an economically and politically sustainable global market system will have to be socially constructed and conditioned, too, by global discourse and policy design." The question I address involves how such policy has been constructed, on what views of reality and knowledge in the case of New Zealand's ocean policy, and can such policies ever be morally neutral as modernism believes?

Policy regimes both reflect and transform relationships among people and between nature and culture. Beginning in the 1980s, fisheries policy across the world moved toward closed access to fisheries through the development of new forms of property rights, an approach called rights-based management. These changes have been made in the context of a global emphasis on market-based approaches to resource management in yet the larger context of neoliberalism. Neoliberalism is a "political economic approach that posits markets as the ultimate tool for achieving optimal use and allocation of scarce resources."[18]

New Zealand's rights-based system of management is its Quota Management System (QMS). It has two key structural pillars: Total Allowable Catch (TAC) and Individual Transferable Quota (ITQ). Individual Transferable Quota (ITQ) are transferable property rights allocated to fishers in the form of a "right of harvest" up to a particular tonnage of a species from a defined region. In addition, a permit is necessary to commercially harvest fish controlled by the QMS. To be eligible for a permit, commercial fishers must hold minimum quota amounts such as three tons for rock lobster and shellfish per quota management area, or region (QMA).[19]

The QMS system, as it has been implemented in New Zealand, illustrates how the bounding of property has an impact on relations among people and the natural world. The QMS system divides nature into pieces that are legally bounded. Ownership of pieces is individualized. For the purpose of establishing these property rights, nature is divided into single species catch, by ton. Noncommercial species are set outside these boundaries. Minimum species quota for a license also has constructed human interests by individual species and amount.

The Individualized Quota tonnage is also regionalized under the QMS. This regionalized ownership has further reordered who fishers are in relationship with, putting together regions as joint exploiters. These regions may bear no relationship to prior social relations. Great Barrier Island's quota management area covers the entire northeast portion of the North Island. In the past the small boats out of Great Barrier Island were limited by their size to a relatively small area, yet the quota system has opened up Great Barrier Island fishing grounds to those from off the island. Furthermore, after a decade or more under the quota system, the option of returning to a locally controlled system is no longer viable because of the individualistic decision making that resulted from the QMS. A local resident talked about how giving power to the local fisherman to manage the island fisheries at this point wouldn't work because locals didn't have the informal management system—the relationships—in place that was there fifty years ago.

Finally, and significantly, the QMS system has changed the relationship between local catch and commercial sales of catch. The QMS system requires that the catch around Great Barrier Island be recorded in Auckland, which means, among other things, that local restaurants cannot buy from local fishers. This rule has increased the social distance among locals on Great Barrier Island as well as increased the distance between nature and humans. No longer could locally caught fish be sold directly into the local economy, but rather the relationships had to be funneled through Auckland.

The impact of New Zealand's QMS on social boundaries is particularly significant on those at the margins of society who often live along coastal margins. For example, the QMS undermined the survival strategy of life on Great Barrier Island, which involved part-time, multiple jobs. Individuals in places like Great Barrier Island have had a strategy for survival that involves crossing the land-ocean boundary as well as crossing standard employment boundaries through part-time employment and multiple jobs. This strategy sustained communities and has been particularly true of the indigenous people of New Zealand, the Maori.[20]

Great Barrier Island is a microcosm of these larger changes brought by the QMS. In the early 1990s Great Barrier Island had twenty-five locally owned fishing boats and another fifteen from the mainland that unloaded catch on the island. By 2002, only two full-time resident fishermen remained. Commercial fishers were either forced out of fishing because they could not establish their right to quota, or they were given amounts of quota that were under the limit to obtain a permit to fish.[21]

The Quota Management System policy offers a clear example of Cronon's and Tronto's points. It offers us a policy that views nature and society as divisible and boundable. Nature is not seen as tied to the local human community any more than to the nation. In fact the interests of the local community are seen as biased. Thus, in order for policy to be rational and disinterested, decision making must be protected from the interests of the local community. The market, enhanced by the QMS distribution of property rights to individuals, is thought to serve as the morally neutral arbitrator of the distribution of goods.

Fisheries, Boundaries, and Marine Reserves

The idea of freedom is at the very heart of neoliberalism, and the modernist roots of neoliberalism define freedom in part as the separation (disembedding) of the economic from the rest of society. Mansfield, citing Polanyi, argues that for each move toward economic liberalism, there is a countermovement toward social protection.[22] This idea can also be applied to nature-culture relations. In the case of the commodification of nature as seen in the QMS in New Zealand, this countermove is toward environmental preservation. An emphasis on freedom through the QMS system has led to a countermove of restrictions on freedom through the establishment of marine reserves as no-take zones. The development of protected areas is part of a worldwide movement.[23] The development of marine reserves on the surface appears to be the opposite of the division and portioning of nature via the QMS system. However, both assume very rigid nature-culture boundaries. Humans are not seen to be integrated with nature, but rather separate. Great Barrier Island has also been subject to this policy.

New Zealand passed a Marine Reserves law whose purpose was to establish a series of marine reserves in response to worries about overfishing and decreasing marine biodiversity. The New Zealand government is committed to putting 10 percent of New Zealand's marine environment in reserves as a way to preserve biodiversity.

To date, only 0.1 percent of the coastline is protected within fifteen marine reserves.[24]

The most isolated part of Great Barrier Island is the northeastern tip, with more populated ports and sheltered areas on the western shore. The isolation of this area, combined with the Department of Conservation's ownership of much of the land in this area, has led to a proposal to make a portion of the area a marine reserve (Figure 1). The creation of this reserve has been controversial, and the debate surrounding its possible establishment illustrates, again, how boundary construction reflects views on the nature-culture boundary. The Department of Conservation and the marine reserve legislation emphasize no-take marine protected areas, separating the human community from nature. This separation is based on a view of nature-culture which concluded that humans must be removed from nature to ensure the protection of biodiversity, imply-

FIGURE 1

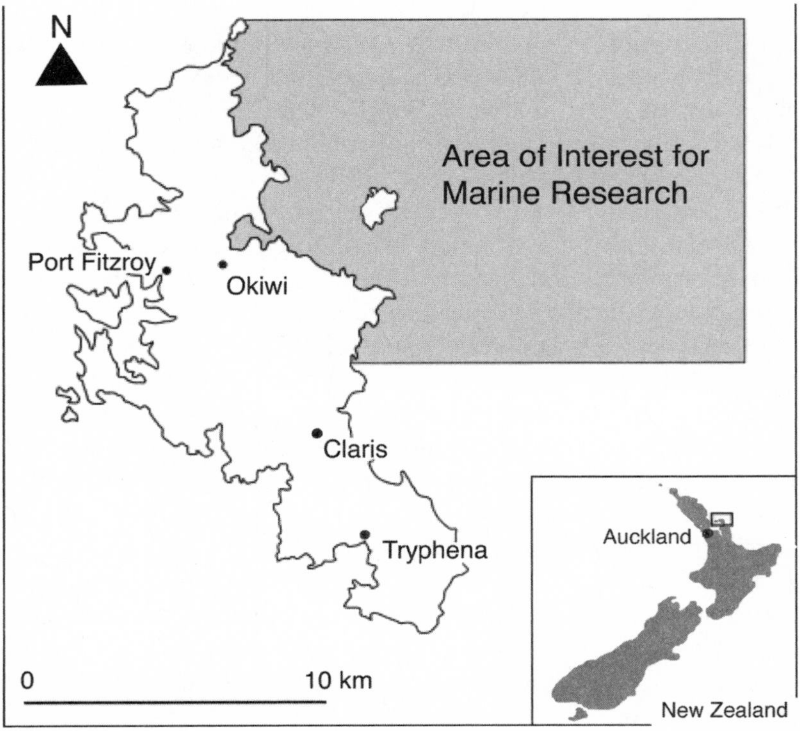

Great Barrier Island, New Zealand

ing that humans exploit nature through their action, leaving it in a degraded state. Thus, in order to save nature, we must set a "boundary between pristine wilderness and modified, humanized stretches of land."[25] This preservation is based on scientific justifications.[26]

In interviews with locals on Great Barrier Island, it was clear that they did not perceive such a strict separation between nature and the human community, but view reality as the integration of nature and the human community with community health and the well-being of the surrounding environment intertwined. They would often speak of how the management of the environment around them was directly related to the health of the community and economy. In this view of reality, science does not stand apart from the political, but includes deeply held values based on assumptions that all parties need to discuss.[27] Their exclusion from meaningful participation in decisions related to the management of the environment thus was a constant area of frustration.

Debates over the establishment of a marine reserve on Great Barrier Island illustrate the same largely modernist, nature-culture dichotomy seen in fisheries management. The proposal assumes a spatial dichotomy between the protection of the inside from the threat by those outside and a clear distinction between nature and culture.[28]

Mussel Farms

The picture of nature inherent in, and established by, the QMS has changed social relations on Great Barrier Island. The QMS splits nature into pieces of a bundle of property rights. These property rights have been distributed in such a way as to transform social relations between people and the nonhuman world and relations among people. The countermove has been to create more protected areas. Science has been a part of this process of division, tending to fragment both biological and human systems into parts in the application of management policies. This leaves science and policy grasping for means for reconnecting the pieces of nature into a whole, and reconnecting this whole with human society.[29]

What, then, integrates these pieces back into some kind of whole? What force is the mediator for the boundaries constructed? Neoliberalism, the dominant ideology of government in New Zealand since the 1980s, sees the free market as the integrator.[30] The market is expected to behave as the mediator of boundaries, and the individual thus contributes to the community via market competitiveness. Yet rationalistic and market-oriented policy structures allow for no local consideration to be taken into account in terms of who gets the benefits of policy. Such considerations are thought to be biased.

The proposed expansion of aquaculture for mussel farms around Great Barrier Island shows these tensions within this structuring of policy. Mussel farming is one of the major commercial fishing industries on Great Barrier Island, with tremendous pressures for expansion due to high prices and the high quality that can be produced on the island. Green-lipped mussels are grown on lines suspended from floats on the surface of the water, and such mussel farms on Great Barrier Island produce fifteen hundred tons annually.[31] The Auckland Regional Council (ARC), the local planning entity, grants permits for the establishment of such aquacultural farms. However, ARC is not allowed to take into account in its decision making the residency of the applicant. If a local person gets such a license, they are allowed to turn around and sell it to a nonlocal person at a huge profit. Rationalistic and market-oriented policy structure allowed for no local consideration to be taken into account in terms of who could get permits. A person who owned a Great Barrier Island mussel farm but was from Auckland was equal to a mussel farmer who lived on Great Barrier Island itself. Embedded in this policy is the neoliberal ideology of progress.[32]

This policy has created great internal conflict among locals. Some locals would have been willing to support an increase in mussel farm permits, if these could be maintained by locals. But policy, based on the liberalism, does not allow for such local accountability or recognition of interest. The same applies to tourism-related concession contracts with the Department of Conservation. No guaranteed benefits to the local community are ensured. The use of the market as integrator of society with the emphasis on bounding the individual has led to the necessity of placing the boundary of "community" around the nation as a whole. This is stated regularly; for the good of the country, one would not want to incorporate prejudicial local consideration.

Breaking Conceptual Boundaries

If social-local-economic-ecological considerations are intertwined and exhibit multiple connections rather than being clearly separable, what is left out by acting as if they were boundable? The unknown and uncertainty are left out of policy. If something is not known or bounded via policy, its existence is not recognized. Bounding individualized commercial interests leaves out ecosystems as a whole, including noncommercial aspects of nature. A radical orthodoxy critique of this view of the world might be that it assumes that we can "know" and the other is "knowable" without reference to the Creator. Thus, the social entity of community—the relationships in between individuals—are also excluded in this approach to resource management. Because of the way nature and society have been divided in policy in New Zealand, the only answer to the problem of the nature-culture relationship problem is strict bounding through preservation. This is the only way to keep nature as a whole. Yet by doing so, humans and "the local" are once again left out of nature.

In order to overcome the conceptual and policy boundaries built by modernism and the neoliberal economics of globalization, the boundary between objective science and local knowledge must be permeable. Knowledge creation must include the processes of objective science but be placed in dialogue with local knowledge. Our objective science demands the universality of distance and objectivity, but we also need local knowledge—contextualization—to form effective policy. The growing literature and research in natural and social sciences supports the idea that there are many valid ways of knowing.[33]

To remove science from its context—concrete problems in actual places—decontextualizes science and allows it to become an ideology rather than a practice, an ideology that is allowed to ignore the consequences of its work.[34] The conservation community is largely made up of professionals trained in such a way as to give priority to scientific explanations and strategies for protecting biodiversity. However, science arises out of a particular intellectual and philosophical tradition, and often discredits other ways of knowing, creating a barrier to dialogue with local communities and the possibility for finding a common language. In addition, protectionist, scientific perspectives often claim national or even global interests, trumping local interests. Wilshusen claims that this argument "assumes that both types of interests (local and nonlocal) are of the same order and carry the same weight. . . . Many people living in and near protected areas perceive their interests as tangible and immediate and the 'common' interest as unclear and intangible."[35] For example, on

Great Barrier Island, local people continually said of the DOC and their scientific studies, "They never ask us! I've sat here every day for forty years observing the estuary and the brown teal ducks, and ecologists come in and do a one-month study, demand I change some type of activity, without ever asking me what I've observed, and then leave."

So why is this local knowledge needed alongside the more distant objective knowledge? It is the bridge between objective science and ideological policy, contextualizing science and policy. Knowledge creation must include the processes of objective science but dialogue with local knowledge, because knowledge and context are ever-changing. Care theorist Nel Noddings calls for the movement between the abstract and the concrete. She says that one of the greatest dangers may be premature switching to a rational-objective mode. If rational-objective thinking is to be put in the service of caring for nature and the human community, we must at the right moments turn it away from the abstract toward which it tends and back to the concrete. The rational-objective mode must continually be reestablished and redirected from a fresh base of the concrete. Otherwise, we become deeply enmeshed in procedures that somehow serve only themselves; our thoughts are separated, completely detached, from the original context.[36] Noddings' call to turn back to the concrete parallels the concept of "hybrid geographies," where thinking involves the concrete rather than recognizing only the abstract. Practice becomes a craft over against abstract reasoning alone.[37]

Great Barrier Island is an example of a case where local knowledge may provide information to contribute to objective, scientific studies, limited in time and space. Scientists cannot be there all the time. As with the proposed marine reserve, consensus at the local level is the only means of policing the reserve. No other way exists of protecting an area extending out eighteen kilometers (twelve miles) from the coastline from poaching at night. A constant criticism of the Great Barrier Island marine reserve proposal is the problem of policing the reserve. The Department of Conservation wants to establish the reserve only on its scientific merits, as delineated in the original legislation, without presenting as part of the package the contextual plan on policing and ensuring benefits to the local community. This lack of contextualization remains the largest barrier to locals. Protection of biodiversity can only take place through the vehicle of human institutions such as laws, organizations, or cultural practices.[38] Our objective science demands the universality of distance and objectivity. In reality, we can benefit from seeing nature, human nature, and our understanding of knowledge intertwined.[39]

The character of globalization and its unevenly distributed benefits has given rise to the "cultural turn" in the social sciences toward greater sensitivity to the role of cultural context and identity.[40] Nurnberger's work has also incorporated a more ecologically grounded viewpoint where the outcomes of the global market system are assessed by their impacts on specific geographical settings.[41]

Relational Ontology and Theology

If knowing involves a relational and contextualized aspect, then a universalized, "distant" morality that consists of a set of principles that are universalized and impartial also reflects a particular view of reality, one in which the state is seen as the mediator among autonomous individuals. This view of morality assumes conditions of life that prevail in a geographically large, diverse, market-oriented world, and build policies that, in fact, make life to be so.[42] In fact, radical orthodoxy calls into question not only the naïve assumption regarding the state's neutrality, but also the difference between the kinds of people the state wants to create and the kind of persons that we wish to form through the Spirit's work through the church.[43] The alternative is a relational, rather than an individualistic understanding of ethical agency, and call for a grounding of ethical systems in an embodied form, over against the abstracting tendencies of universality.[44] Such a view sees nature as intertwined with human society, in contrast to the universalizing nature of science, which abstracts nature, humans, and their interrelationships from our more thickly nuanced, intricately interactive reality.

In this relational ontology, humans are viewed "not as an individually held static quality of mind, but as a relational achievement which is constituted between others-in-relation."[45] Several theoretical movements are simultaneously arguing for this very thing. Care theorists, arising out of feminist ethics, work out of a relational framework.[46] Likewise, Action/Actant-Network Theory (ANT), a field of sciences studies, begins with a relational ontology. ANT incorporates both humans and nonhumans, technological and artificial, as it develops a view that all these entities acquire their attributes as a result of their relations with "others."[47] Latour and others question the ability of humans to be persons "without the multiplicity of nonhumans with whom we share our collective existence."[48] Likewise, Sarah Whatmore's use of the concept of hybridity describes this reality as a "mode of worldly inhabitation that precedes the urge to separate out the social from the natural" but rather is a "gesture towards their reconciliation."[49] What it is to be human cannot be conceived apart from these relationships, and the same can be said of nature.

Radical orthodoxy claims that modernism is undergirded by an anthropology of individual self-determination which is theologically promoted in that it appropriates the Christian *imago Dei* with a conception of radically autonomous individuals while taking the concept of covenantal relationships and turning it into contractual ones.[50] Their proposed ontology of participation recognizes dependence of the creation on the Creator, affirms immanence as such, and recognizes the essential embodiment of human beings, accounting for sociality and intersubjective relationships that are oriented around charity, not power.[51]

Radical orthodoxy's ontology of participation has its parallels in the theological thought of Douglas Hall, who argues that while traditional theological reflection has centered on traits possessed by humans which image God, a minority tradition has identified the image of God not as a quality of being but as a quality of relationship. Hall proposes a biblical ontology of communion, community, and ecology, similar to Joseph Sittler.[52] Hall states, "We are created for relationship. Relatedness—and specifically the modality of relatedness designated by the biblical word 'love'—is the essence of our humanity as the Creator-Redeemer of this tradition intends it."[53] And in this relatedness, nature is not a neutral backdrop, but rather God, humanity, and nature are inextricably bound up with one another.[54] To start from the assumption that humans are interdependent means that the terms for our moral discussions must shift. Local community health and wholeness is one measure of the fulfillment of that relational aspect of human nature as well as in the relationship between humans and land.[55]

Hall is part of a group of so-called social Trinitarians, namely, those who argue that God is who God is only by virtue of the relationships among the persons of the godhead—God is a community of Love, a family of interpenetrating perichoretic Love. Thus, a relational ontology arising out of secular streams of thought is backed by a relational theology. Colin Gunton goes so far as to say that whereas Descartes and his successors destroyed the understanding of the symbiosis of social and universal order, "We shall not understand our place in the world unless we face up to the way in which we are internally related to the rest of the world."[56] Not only is it wrong to abstract humans from their social context, Gunton argues that abstracting the environment from its inhabitants leads to a world that is emptied of its personal meaning.[57]

Can there be a rebuilding on the new theological foundation suggested by the Trinitarians?[58] The key to Gunton is an appreciation for the role of the spirit in which the spirit is to do the crossing of boundaries while maintaining and even strengthening particularity. "It is not a spirit of merging or assimilation—of homogenization—but of relation in otherness, relation which does not subvert but establishes the other in its true reality."[59] In contrast, the modern notion of particularity loses that particular when it is deprived of its concrete subsistence and meaning.[60]

Growing Trinitarian dialogue promises to reshape the way we see our relations to God, to the earth, and to each other. But it also reveals a deep human desire to be connected to each other and to the Earth.[61] All entities are what they are only by virtue of their relationships to other entities. In Christian terms, all being is being-with; all existence is coexistence, because the God who makes and sustains all things is a triune community of mutually engendering and indwelling love.[62] The challenge is to build natural resource policies that invite this communion, extending it to the rest of creation.[63]

So what does theology have to teach about fisheries management? A relational ontology and theology make it possible to develop a view of boundaries as places for relationship building and avoid the problems of both modernists who see boundaries as demarcating differences, and postmodernists who view boundaries as settings of aggressive incursions. A relational ontology suggests that rather than looking at boundaries as something that divide, they should be seen as opportunities for dialogue and relationship building that deepen understanding of ourselves, our place in the world, and our relationship to nature. With this view, boundary crossing is to be encouraged through the development of processes, monitoring, and trust building.[64] And it follows that "knowing" also is only possible through understanding relationships, whether it is the relationship among entities, or between creations and the Creator.

New Zealand's marine management strategies favor a universalized policy regime with equitable treatment of each individual, individuals who are assumed to have no basis for continuing relationships with each other. This fits the model of disconnected if not globalized concerns.[65] The alternative, relational model must be built on more flexibility, and assume ongoing relationships within the human community as well as between the human community and environment. The reality of ecological systems is that their long-term stability requires models that integrate nonlinearity, complexity, flexibility, quick feedback, and change.[66] In the former, the public becomes an abstract concept, one more element to add to a technical question, allowing the expert to remain above the fray.[67] The relational model requires natural resource agencies to make clearer distinctions, acknowledging its on-the-ground reality.[68]

Community management strategies of a variety of types have been initiated in the management of fisheries.[69] Environment Canada has replaced its basic management model with a more flexible approach in its development of its Atlantic Coastal Action Program (ACAP). The program stresses community involvement in dealing with coastal problems.[70] Community involvement goes beyond participation to what are referred to as community-based initiatives.[71] The role of Environment Canada has changed to allow for local ownership of decision making and actions. In the case of the ACAP, environmental monitoring activities are often done by unpaid volunteers because government funding is not sufficient.[72] Yet government agencies still need to empower the local community, support their initiatives, and provide some funding.[73] The relationships across scales are important.

Common characteristics underlie the success of these initiatives. Local stakeholders and the government must mutually recognize the existence of the resource problems, and this mutual recognition serves to initiate a joint management arrangement. Local interests and knowledge must be recognized. Local institutional capacity must exist or be built. User rights must be clearly defined, and enforcement must be effective through the provision of legal and policy support. The objects of the management scheme must be clear and agreed upon by local and government interests with tangible, mutually agreed-upon results. In the end, the combination of these characteristics leads to positive attitudes toward rules and toward collective action rather than their being undermined.[74]

A relational ontology, undergirded by a relational theology lead to a fundamental need for building of trust as a fundamental building block for any management scheme. Trust is achieved through verification, and verification is achieved through monitoring, not just of biodiversity, but of ecological, biological, social, and economic conditions. Such monitoring is embedded in local community initiatives because it is essential for building trust, for discussion, and for knowing if actions have led to desired objectives.[75] Trust building is a process, not an outcome, just as monitoring is a continuous process.[76]

The move toward further commodification of nature leads us in the opposite direction. It is a policy regime that views nature as divisible and boundable and fails to conceive of its being tied to the local human community. Human society is likewise divided into individual interests with national interests seen as the sum of abstract individuals. The local community is not seen as relevant to rational decision making.

The picture of nature inherent in, and established by, the QMS has changed social relations on Great Barrier Island. The Individual Quota System has split nature into pieces of a bundle of property rights. These property rights have been distributed in such a way as to transform social relations between people and the nonhuman world and relations among people. The countermove has been to create more protected areas. Science has been a part of this process of division, tending to fragment biological and human systems into parts in the application of management policies and then left science, policy, and the market as the means for reconnecting the pieces of nature into a whole and reconnecting this whole with human society.[77]

We are in need of a Trinitarian imagination and a relational ontology in constructing our future on this Earth. Nature and culture are not separate, objective entities. But neither are they social constructions. "They are socio-material fabrication in which the histories and geographies" are made flesh.[78] And boundaries are the key to understanding the relational nature of this "fleshiness."

Conclusion

Inherent to any discussion of human-environment relations are the interrelated issues of the globalization of the market, the nature of reality (ontology), and our understanding of how we gain knowledge of nature (epistemology). Regulation and the marketing of aspects of nature, fueled by the forces of the global market, first involve the bounding of aspects of "nature," and second, the transformation of global and national governmental structures to enhance the marketing and use of these aspects. Views on the nature of reality, particularly views on "human nature," the relationship between nature and humans, or what is often called the nature-culture boundary, have concrete expression in policies that shape this regulation and commodification of nature. Furthermore, these policies are undergirded by a particular view of knowledge. The result is a further transformation of human-environment boundaries and the boundaries among humans, portrayed as neutral in terms of its approach and result through the lack of transparency of underlying views of reality and knowledge creation.

A Christian ontology is not built on a dualistic and oppositional structure of culture and nature. Rather culture and nature are viewed as inherently relational and representing a whole which in turn has its origins in, and is sustained by, God. The challenge is to build policies that recognize this reality.

Part IV

PRACTICES OF RE-ENCHANTMENT

Chapter 10

Religion after Democracy

Graham Ward

Globalization, like secularization, is proving to be an ideology—that is, a myth masquerading as natural law, even divine providence.[1] But it is only as it discloses itself as such that we begin to observe and are able to analyze the various elements that constitute its potency, and analyze the imaginative strengths that create credencies, enjoin belief, and capture hopes, dreams, and desires. Foremost, in global-ism, is its appeal to a universalism that not only sublates space (in its internationalism) but also sublates time (in its transhistoricism). This is an appeal wrapped in the mythemes of religion, most partic-ularly those associated with Christian eschatology. My contention in this essay is that unless we appreciate and examine this connec-tion between globalism and transcendence we will not understand how the phenomenon of globalization is profoundly associated in our time with two other prominent aspects of Western culture: the demise of liberal democracy and the new visibility of religion in the public sphere.

But allow me first to clarify a central relationship before con-tinuing to examine what I mean by the demise of liberal democracy and the new visibility of religion. This is the relationship between globalization and secularization. If by secularization is understood a process of rationalization that defined the nature of being human without recourse to theological notions such as being made "in the image of God" and defining the world as a self-regulating organism without recourse to being created and sustained by God, then the

expansion of global trade and what Chadwick termed the secularization of the European mind develop simultaneously. Whatever the
avowed intentions of Columbus (and Isabella of Spain) to missionize
the Indies and create a wealth that would enable the pope to embark
again on a campaign of Crusades, the voyages of discovery in the
fifteenth and sixteenth centuries opened world trade and brought
quantities of gold, silver, and spices into Europe that radically transformed national economies. At this point, we have to recognize two
aspects of this trading transformation: (1) It was allied to the universalist injunction of the Christian faith ("Go therefore and make
disciples of all nations"—Matt 28:19) and a Christian eschatology in
which the return of Christ was predicated on the "good news of the
kingdom [being] proclaimed throughout the whole world, as a testimony to all the nations"—Matt 24:14). This universalism was being
given powerful expression prior to, throughout, and following the
opening up of a world market by Christian theologians as diverse as
Raymond Lull, Marsilio de Ficino, and Hugo Grotius, who were developing the idea of Christianity as the one true and perfect expression
of the religious. In other words, this globalization was not itself, yet,
a secular phenomenon. (2) The trading transformation was inseparable from advances in technology (and instrumental reasoning);
shipbuilding and navigation developed to make such long journeys
into *terra et mare incognita* possible. But as the trading and colonizing
fostered new international relations throughout the seventeenth
and eighteenth centuries, the ideology that legitimized its ambitions slowly also changed. Not to say that missionizing stopped; it
still continues today.

But the nature of the change that was slowly emerging can be
witnessed in Hume and Kant, both of whom saw globalization as the
international extension of "benevolent tendencies" (Hume) and the
mediation of a cosmopolitan peace (Kant). The secular eschatology
of early Enlightenment liberal humanism now informed the visions
for a world market. What I mean by a secular eschatology here is
that the transcendent role of divine Providence yields to the purely
immanent teleology of history and economics, but the absolutism
and the utopianism remain the same: the theological myth of all
being made one in Christ gives way to the secular myth of Kenichi
Ohmae's "borderless economy"[2] in which warring nation-states are
transcended and a new international democracy announces itself.
Bryan and Farrell write, "Increasingly, millions of global investors,

operating out of their own economic self-interest, are determining interest rates, exchange rates, and the allocation of capital, irrespective of the wishes or political objectives of national political leaders."[3]

I would contend that this myth of free global market capitalism and the new world culture it inaugurates is religious on several counts, each of which is associated with modern developments in Christian eschatology. The modern understanding of Christian eschatology emphasized the *modo*, the now, the present as the time of fulfillment. It emphasized a realized eschatology that was radically detraditionalized; in fact, with theologians like Harvey Cox and Johann Baptist Metz, it embraced secularism as a development brought about and fostered by Christianity. This detraditionalized religion, and the Gnosticism it invokes, finds itself expressed in globalism as a cultural, not simply economic, phenomenon in six particular ways. First, it invokes a new vision of infinite freedom—understood economically as being able to pursue one's own desires, control one's own destiny liberated from dependencies and political, social, and local needs. Second, it fosters belief in an eternal sustainability promising unlimited consumption. It is not just that this kingdom (and its everlasting banquet) can be established and bring history to an end; the kingdom will be governed by a perpetual progressive motion. Third, this motion is determining and inevitable. It is a transcending force beyond human control that human beings have to embrace: not so much a Providence as a pagan understanding of fate to be loved. Fourth, this force is dematerializing. As Marx already saw, money is not a natural substance; it is a virtual reality that Marx could only describe in metaphors drawn from religious fetishism and mysticism. Coins and notes are the nominal tokens of a sovereign power that is ultimately ungraspable. There is a metaphysics of money, an appeal to a transcending ontology. The less we see of the actual coins and notes that gave us the illusion of money as a natural substance, the more transactions concern electronic figures transcribed in cyberspace, the more the material is transcended. The eclipse of time and space in this new internationalism and the access to such an eclipse via the Internet assist in this dematerialization. Fifth, it offers an all-encompassing worldview in which credit and *credo* are again inseparable. That is, globalism is not just a historical process; it is a universalist vision of the truth about human beings and the civilizations they nurture and are nurtured by—the truth about a cosmological community that recognizes what Live 8 set out to proclaim: our radical intradependence. It is a vision of a community stable and beyond conflict. Sixth, finally, a Protestant moral vision informs its reforming mission; the *amor fati*, though an intense discipline (as Nietzsche understood) will bring about the rejuvenation of an economy and its people. This is the message still being given the third-world countries by the G8, who have the power to cancel the vast burden of their debts. It is this "religious" eschatological undertow to globalization that is turning Weber's disenchantment of the world through rationalization into a new reenchantment. And in doing this, it is helping to reverse the processes of secularization founded upon an adherence to the material and the rational. John Rawston Saul has recently written, "What we are dealing with here is a type of religious fundamentalism."[4] This understanding is important for the way globalism is situated within the second of my phenomena: the new visibility of religion in the public sphere.

For the moment, let me conclude this section by emphasizing that this globalism is a myth formed out of the universalisms of Christianity, and this is why it is significant for theologians. In fact, from John Gray's analysis in *False Dawn* to Joseph Stiglitz' confessions in *Globalization and Its Discontents*, and, most recently, Saul's analyses in *The Collapse of Globalism*—globalization is "an end-state towards which all economies are converging. A universal state of equal integration in worldwide economic activity"[5] has been recognized as an illusion. But that is not the point here. As a myth it governs and generates cultural imaginings; it fashions hopes, beliefs, dreams and desires. As such, despite the counterfactual evidence of globalism's "achievements"—the accumulating evidence that it does not result in "a universal free market but an anarchy of sovereign states, rival capitalisms and stateless zones"[6] or what Saul describes as "a vacuum . . . between two unreasonable uncertainties"[7]—the myth can remain powerful. It can remain socially and culturally determinative. Furthermore, the effects of the myth already remain with us (most notably in terms of advanced social disaffection, depoliticization, and insecurity), even while the market fundamentalists in their designer offices and book-lined studies are changing their minds and spinning other prognostications.

Now let me return to those two other dominant contemporary Western phenomena, the demise of liberal democracy and the new visibility of religion in the public sphere, and relate them to the operational myth of globalization. My working hypothesis is that they are profoundly interrelated, and the question I am asking in and through this examination, then, is what are the nature and consequences of this interrelation? I'm going to suggest that what we are witnessing and experiencing is one more cycle in the permanent identity crisis that we call democracy, but this crisis may be permanent for what is being challenged is the liberal philosophy that has nurtured all modern notions of democracy. It is an identity crisis insofar as we are, once more, unsure what a democracy is or upon what it is founded. And in this crisis, as in others, there is, yet again, a yearning heard (and amplified for political use) for the return of the king. There is an appeal for strong, dictatorial leadership that, in the words of one political scientist, provokes "a tendency to theologize political conflicts."[8]

Let me begin by just expanding a little on these two other phenomena. First: the new public face of religion. I suggest there are, broadly speaking, three forms of this visibility. The first form has been the most widely discussed and examined: religious fundamentalism. There have been a number of studies in English of Christian fundamentalism as it grew out of American evangelical movements in the early part of the twentieth century and the present-day impact, say, of charismatic Christianity in Latin America, biblicalism in South Korea, the work of *Opus Dei*, and Alpha-courses in Britain. Like laissez faire capitalism, it mainly arises, though not exclusively, from the Protestant and nonconformist traditions. But though the word "fundamentalism" is most particularly forged within this Christian heritage, after the Salman Rushdie affair it was applied as a term to describe certain forms of militant Muslim regimes and even forms of militant Judaism. More recently, this use of "fundamentalism" has been employed to describe certain forms of Hindu aggressiveness, such as surfaced with the massacre of almost fifteen hundred Muslims in Gujarat. Now at this point I don't wish to enter into whether there are structural similarities between these forms of fundamentalism or structural similarities between these forms of militarism and other forms of believing that constitute communal, even tribal, identity: the various nationalist parties, for example. At this point, all I am doing is sketching out some major differences in the new visibility of religion. Much has already been written about the resurgence of religious fundamentalism as a response to the radical insecurity, inequalities, and detraditionalization enforced by economic modernizations that have profoundly affected traditional communities, their value, and their identities. We can point to the work of Manuel Castells as just one example of a sociologist examining religious fundamentalism in terms of resistant communities. I would only wish to point to the religious nature of globalism itself and problematize what is a cause and what is an effect here.

The second form of visibility can be defined in terms of the return of religion to the public sphere. The story of the rise of secularism has been told in terms of the development of a public sphere that aimed to be religiously and ideologically neutral in order to operate most effectively, that is, inclusively. Institutions forged as means of administrating, safeguarding, and producing this public sphere—the judiciary, schools and universities, hospitals, the media and forms of government local and national—all explicitly espoused this notion of neutrality. Religious beliefs were a matter of private devotion. Now, as political scientists like Graham Maddox and Charles Taylor have pointed out (among others), this is a very reductive account of the relationship between religion and civil society. In fact, we may reverse the notion that the state banished religion into the private sphere, as Maddox does when discussing the rise of the state in the United States; it was more a matter of religion wishing to withdraw from any interference by the state.[9] Nevertheless, most historians of the eighteenth and nineteenth century will testify to the profound public interaction of church and state, which is important, because the great disassociation of religion from public life is possibly as recent as post–Second World War. This then becomes represented, and defined as the prevailing condition of modernity, by certain liberal thinkers working at that time. Foremost among them would be John Rawls. So when we begin to examine the way in which a new confessionalism is, once again, entering into the public arena we have to recall that its absence from the public arena is not that old, and the idea that this absence goes back to the late seventeenth century is nonsense.

A further question arises: when, then, the religious once again enters the public domain and questions "secular neutrality," who is making it visible, why, and what are the effects? Let me give a concrete example: In France, *la cité*—what Jacques Chirac termed "the principle of secularism"—was not coined until 1903 in a law concerned with the abolition of religious education in state schools.

The law forbade the placing of religious symbols in public places, including graveyards, and ended any financial or political support from the government to any religious groups (which, in effect, meant Catholics). This followed the closure of most Catholic schools in France by Prime Minister Emile Combes. But this law lay dormant until post-9/11 when, in 2003, the French government commissioned the Stasi Report concerning the application of *la cité* in France. This report made the recommendations that have caused so much international trouble since. The revisions to the law turned the spotlight on the Muslim population of France, making the public visibility of wearing the veil even more public. The Muslim population in France, as in Germany, arose from economic policies inviting guest workers to become the new working classes of European society. France has the largest such population, and the state, far from being neutral, now made moves to legislate for civil society. Two observations need to be made here. First, this is an antidemocratic and antiliberal move, for the liberal democratic state is supposedly there to safeguard civil society, and not impinge upon its liberties, notably the liberties of its religious conscience. Second, the appeal to the law of *la cité* in fact made visible the sectarianism and, therefore, ideology of "the principle of secularism" itself. It made manifest that such liberalism is hegemonic. The cry went up that such secular neutrality was actually a form of racism. The point of this examination is to show that there is a question of both the economics and the politics of this new confessionalism (and those who challenge it).

Of course, the reverse of the French situation is evident in any number of speeches by George Bush or even Tony Blair, where private convictions are seen as involved in internationally public actions—like declaring war. The three televised debates between Bush and John Kerry prior to the presidential election of 2004 focused on key issues all of which—whether abortion, the use of stem cells, or the war with Iraq—were inseparable from religious issues. The explicit questions regarding their personal faith were then apposite. What is significant, given the outcome, is that Bush drew attention to the strong correlation between his religious practices and sovereign action, his prayer life and his decisions. Kerry, while informing the public of his Catholicism, said exactly the opposite—repeating a formula first used by John F. Kennedy when he said he would not be a Catholic president but a president who happened to be Catholic. He rehearsed, that is, a liberal line such that Bush, rather than Kerry, drew the support of important and influential Catholic bishops. Again, there is a politics of making religion visible in which neoconservative religion is allied to neoliberal economics.

I have called the third form of the visibility the "commodification of religion," drawing upon specific analyses by Marx of the processes of reification and fetishism associated with the cultural dominance of capitalism. I view this as the greatest single source of the desecularization of Western culture. It is a phenomenon that cannot be divorced from the globalization that makes such commodification possible. If you like, it is the manifestation of the market in a spirituality that a culture based upon the universalist dreams of unfettered consumer freedoms, bound to the unpredictable but inevitable destinies of vast and virtual flows of currency speculation, will necessarily produce. The religiosity of the market reflects upon itself in the commercialization of religion—the manufacture of religion as a special effect. Although in 1985 the French political scientist Marcel Gauchet could write about "the disappearance of enchanters and powerful supernatural beings,"[10] the cultural scene since has been overpopulated with enchanters from Gandalf to Harry Potter, and whole armies of angels and demons, vampires, ghosts, and superheroes. Zygmunt Bauman is not the first to write about the reenchantment of the postmodern world. Others have written about the reawakening of the Gothic imagination, a neo-Romanticism, even a postsecularity. From Hollywood films representing the afterlife—like *Gladiator* and *American Beauty*, to the phenomenal success of *The Da Vinci Code* and the names of bars and shops locally like the Font, Gaia, the Eighth Day, the Parting of the Waves—religion does not live in and of itself anymore. It lives in commercial business, gothic and sci-fi fantasy; in health clubs, theme bars, and architectural design; among happy-hour drinkers, tattooists, ecologists, and cyberpunks. Religion has become a special effect, inseparably bound to an entertainment value. It plays two mutually implicated roles in contemporary Western and North American culture. On the one hand, as symbolic capital with a certain charismatic past, it can give places, goods, even people, a mystic charge. Those allured by this charge are not buying religion, they are not consuming the religious or being consumed by it; they are consuming the illusions or simulations of religion. On the other hand, these simulations of religion, religion as symbolic capital, are used as an aesthetic diversion from the profound uncertainties, insecurities, and indeterminacies of postmodern living. The religious is used rhetorically in the creation of the illusions of transcendence, to help simulate euphoria in transporting events. It is in sync with the religious eschatology of globalism itself.

There are other forms of this new visibility I haven't accounted for; for example, new age movements, kabbalah bracelets, the frank espousal by some of what was once called paganism, and its links to eco or green parties. The schema simply develops heuristically the findings of the 1999 European Values Study, which claims, "In all countries, young people who declare themselves Christian, appear more religious in 1999 than in 1990 and 1981 . . . regardless of whether the indicators are personal religiosity (being a religious person, getting comfort and strength from religion, beliefs, especially in a personal God and life after death) or of institutional religiosity (attachment to ceremonies, appreciation of the spiritual and moral contributions of churches)."[11]

The new commodification of religion is not simply an economic matter, for in a capitalist democracy (and I'll come back to that term in a moment) economic matters cannot be disassociated from political and social ones. There are two ways in which this commodification, and the subsequent remythologization of the Western imagination is political. First, as we have learned from the work of the Frankfurt School, these cultural artifacts are not simply products (mirror reflections), they are producers (transforming the cultural or social imagination). They are technologies implicated in social processes that change the nature of our perception, our senses of space and time, our appreciation of the visible and the invisible, our understandings of what the world is and what it is to be human in such a world. In this way they must be treated as political apparatuses that govern not just our bodies (certain physical shapes are desired and others not) but also our minds. These technologies, along with the technologies that have nurtured economic globalism, structure our dreaming and desiring. Second, as tied to consumerism and as related to the dramatic rise in eclectic customized spiritualities, they foster what Antonio Negri defines as "zero degree dialectic."[12] Where there is no dialectic, where there is the continual suspension of judgment, and where the citizen as customer or client is merely requested to be satisfied with the services provided, there is rampant depoliticization that endangers democracy; there is self-determined disenfranchisement in favor of leisure, personal lifestyle, and entertainment. Dialectic means discussion, and as Carl Schmitt noted, politically "where there is no discussion there is dictatorship."[13]

These three forms of the visibility of religion leads me to the third of the phenomena that we are examining here: the changing nature of democracy. Democracy has been used as an indicator of globalism's success and failure. On the one hand, globalism has been viewed as countering the pretensions of the nation-state and promoting a universalism that transcends the borders of any one country. For Fukuyama the opening of the world market will bring about international franchise, a world democracy that negates the warring of individual states. On the other, the failure of globalism is signified in the rise of new nationalisms and the increase in warfare between such nations. But whether nations are being eclipsed by globalism or asserting their strengths in a way that announces the end of globalism, what I wish to focus on is what cultural scientists like Colin Crouch are elaborating as our evolving postdemocratic condition. The key characteristics of this postdemocratic condition are as follows:

- The will of the people is not obtained but created by various means of persuasion—politics are mediatized, particularly by the new telecommunications that gave economic globalism its life-force.[14]

- The political sphere is dominated by economic questions—such that the rise of global capitalism has produced a self-referential political class more concerned with forging links with wealthy business interests than with pursuing political programs.[15]

- Depoliticization and atomism have occurred to such an extent there is the decline among and between those social classes which had made possible an active and critical mass politics so that the concept of society is now radically questionable.[16]

- There is a crisis of representation such that powerful minority interests get far more attention, and politicians are increasingly speaking not for their constituency but for their own concerns or at the behest of a party line.[17]

- There is an increased outsourcing to private companies of what once were held to be primary state tasks (the welfare, education, protection, and health of the people), which has

rendered government increasingly opaque rather than trans-
parent and responsible to its electorate.[18]

I certainly recognize these contemporary characteristics, but
if there is a problem with the postdemocratic thesis it lies, to my
mind, in the stability of the modern concept of democracy that it
employs: that democracy in the past is so self-evident we can now
talk about its demise. Ironically, Bush and Blair suffer from the same
problem: democracy is itself unproblematic; it is an unreflected category. But from the early reflections upon this form of government,
by Tocqueville, the instability of democracy and its latent dangers
have been all too evident. For Tocqueville observing America, as
for Carl Schmitt observing interwar Weimar, the fundamental difficulty with democracy lay in the tension between liberalism's commitment to fostering individualism and the homogeneity needed to
express a common will. Let me make this point through Tocqueville,
rather than Schmitt. Tocqueville writes:

> When authority in the matter of religion no longer exists, nor
> in the matter of politics, men are soon frightened at the aspect
> of [this] limitless independence. This perpetual agitation of all
> things makes them restive and fatigues them. As everything is
> moving in the world of the intellect, they want at least that all
> be firm and stable in the material order; and as they are no lon-
> ger able to recapture their former beliefs, they give themselves a
> master.[19]

Democracy needs religious authority, Tocqueville concludes.[20] Without it there will be servility. If man is to be "free, he must believe,"
he writes.[21] This believing is not intrinsic to freedom—as it was to
older Catholic notions of being free to serve. This believing is necessary because freedom now is being defined as being subject to no
one. Believing then (and Tocqueville is an ardent supporter of why
democracy needs Christianity) is a safeguard against libertarian-
ism. The libertarian possibilities within democratic cultures require
that masters be found—require, that is, authoritarianism. Totalitarianism or absolute sovereignty, against which democratic polity
defines and legitimates itself, is actually latent within democracy's
very possibility and practice. While then proclaiming and enforc-
ing the universal values of equality and emancipation, democratic
culture dreams, secretly, of the return of the king. This dreaming
is the result of a certain suppressed relation between absolutism

and liberalism that can be examined historically (the transposition in nationhood from absolute monarchy to the absolute state)[22] and philosophically (the atomized sovereignty of the self-grounding subject).[23] French political scientist Claude Lefort takes this tension further, clarifying what is at issue. In the move from the sovereignty of the monarch to the sovereignty of the people, the body of the king (the focus and raison d'être for the first form of sovereignty) is replaced by "the image of an empty space impossible to occupy, such that those who exercise public authority can never claim to appropriate it."[24] The king's body (as the body of Christ before it) provides the symbolic grounding for the construal of oneness: difference contained within homogeneity. The social body, on the other hand, is nebulous and ungraspable such that the "people will be said to be sovereign, of course, but whose identity will constantly be open to question." In this sense I spoke earlier of democracy being in the throes of a permanent identity crisis. Lefort opines that totalitarianism is a response to the questions raised by the paradoxes within democracy itself.[25] The egocrat or dictator offers his or her body as a materialization of democracy's own need; he or she embodies the fantasy of democracy's own coherence. In Tocqueville's word, the atomized and therefore ungraspable "people" give themselves a master. We can call this the first paradox destabilizing liberal democratic identity.

But what is it that facilitates the reassertion of a sovereignty needed to safeguard democracy? I think with this question we return to Crouch's analysis (and in fact also Schmitt's). Democracy has to recognize its own crisis, its own need for strong leadership. And this occurs when the democratic principle of egalitarianism is most clearly threatened. Equality, according to Aristotle, is always tenuous[26] for it is always and only the equality of those who are counted as equal. But the myth of universal equality can be placed under threat by an external force, and can use this threatening enemy of democracy. Totalitarianism fulfilled this function until 1989, rendering democracy as polemical concept.[27] But egalitarianism can also be threatened internally by a more powerful set of inequalities. Schmitt and Crouch point to the sphere in which today's inequalities are registered: economics. And economic globalism, as all political economists agree, has accentuated the inequalities between the haves and the have-nots, aggrandizing the inequalities of class, race, and gender. Furthermore, this internal undermining of egalitarianism is worsened when state democratic policy itself is being dictated by economics. This is because of a second paradox at the heart of liberal democracy identified in the 1930s by the British political scientist Harold Laski:[28] on the one hand, democracy requires the universal extension of franchise (to all the people), while, on the other, recognizing that liberal democracy is also capitalist democracy and therefore must and will protect some interests (the capitalists') to the detriment of other interests. This paradox has been at the heart of the socialist and Marxist critique of liberal democracy—that it is fundamentally a bourgeois ideology in which a minority rule over the majority. But the paradox is even more intriguing. For if democracy as the will of people could ever be realized, and all the people are franchised such that this could be made manifest, then the state and the people become one. The tension then between civil society and the governing state disappears, for there is zero-degree dialectic—which is Lefort's definition of totalitarianism and Antonio Negri's analysis of where we are today.

Allow me to sum up so far. We have three cultural phenomena that are profoundly interconnected:

1. Globalism, which continues a secularized eschatology that runs throughout modernity.

2. A new public visibility of religion, given prominence by the advanced technologies fast-tracking globalism; arising in part as a resistance against the detraditionalizations of globalism; partly giving expression to the spiritual ethos of globalism itself; and partly assimilated to the forces of commodification such that religion is used as a special effect for the global promotion of certain goods, events, and practices.

3. The crisis of democracy, which may or may not signal the crisis of globalism itself, but certainly is fueled by the privatization of what were once state-held monopolies, the mediatizing of politics, and the power of the world market and competition for deciding policy. It is a crisis aggravated also by religion insofar as liberal secularism is shown not at all to be neutral, but ideological; by the appeal made by certain religionists to an authority higher than that of the state and sometimes an ethnicity with allegiances transcending nation boundaries. The clash of civilizations, pace Huntingdon, is taking place *within* liberal democracies—witness the Paris riots as I speak.

The interpenetration of these three phenomena means that they cannot be reduced one to the other in a logic of a is the cause of b. For example, the commodification of Christian notions of sin and conceptions of angels in recent advertising campaigns by Jamaica Rum and Diesel point to an economic drive though that does explain why such a drive can itself be successful, why the sale of such mythemes can, in fact, be profitable. Similarly, the question, "Are we becoming less secular?" is too reductive, because I think part of what is happening is the realization we never had a particularly good grasp on what it was that we called "secularization" to begin with. It was a myth created by sociologists. There never was a pure form of secularity, and the more it is made a regulative ideal to strive toward (an idea that seems to lie behind statements like Chirac's about a fundamental principle) the more it announces itself as a Western, racist ideology. But what then is the logic that relates these three phenomena, and what does that logic portend? Allow me to make a suggestion.

Liberal democracy was born out of the struggle with absolute princes, but ironically its self-proclaimed triumph in the late 1990s revealed an imperialism hidden within its logics: an imperialism endemic to globalization. Democracy then announces its triumph at the zenith of its crisis, as Agamben observes.[29] For the prince wasn't overcome, he was sublated in the Hegelian sense of being negated by being taken up into liberal democracy. While this sublated absolutism could be, even can be, projected on to external forces—various historical and concrete fascisms, totalitarianisms, theocracies— then it could, even can, maintain its fragile, paradoxical identity. But because of its own fragility, and because it must always make visible the freedom and fraternity it is fighting to maintain, these external threats must be defeated. And so democracy has ceased to be one possible form of polity (as it is with Aristotle); it has a mission—an educational mission executed through what Schmitt termed "educational dictators."[30] Again it shares so much with the moralism, fundamentalism, and eschatology of economic globalization. The logic of its mission entails that the global triumph of democracy would announce a new empire, just as Negri and Hardt have shown us how globalization seeks total subjection to omnipotence of the world market. When the external projections of an inner crisis are no longer available, democracy will have conquered and subjected all things to its rule. Similarly, when globalism has forced open all national borders and erased all trading restrictions, it too will have realized its world of endlessly marketable commodities. And then the absolute prince within (who has always sat beneath a mystic baldachin, draped in myths of divinity, proclaiming visions of a future kingdom and the bearer of a spiritual charism) returns, and the kingdom is established. The political is theological—again—and economic. But it is no longer liberal nor humanist, and possibly not even democratic.

What relates these three phenomena perhaps more fundamentally than antiliberalism and antihumanism is the investment all of them make in mythologizing. I'm using myth and the imaginative power of myth here along the lines of Georges Sorel in his 1908 book *Reflexions sur la violence*[31]—images and narratives of heroes, ideals to die for, revolutions, missions for utopian kingdoms of eternal peace, homogeneities (national or ethnic), Gnostic battles between good and evil, apocalyptic struggles between civilizations, and perhaps most terrifying and fascinating of all: war, conquest, expansion, or its obverse, holocaust and infinite, inconceivable suffering. I may be wrong here, but what these three phenomena are, even in their interrelationship, are symptoms of what I want to call a remythologization in which the social dissolves into the cultural and aesthetic. I am tempted then, finally, to suggest the West is situated imaginatively, politically, even religiously, somewhere between the first trilogy of Lucas' *Star Wars* and the last part of Jackson's *Lord of the Rings, The Return of the King*—two of the most commercially and internationally successful films in cinema history. One other way to begin this analysis I have been undertaking between globalism, the new public visibility of religion, and the crisis of liberal democracy would be to submit these box-office mega-earners to a serious theological, political, and economic examination. I have to leave that for another time. What stills needs thinking through is: if this is where we are, what does that mean we do? Perhaps we can open the questions there.

Chapter 11

Celebrating the Church Year as a Constructive Response to Globalization

Scott Waalkes

A few years ago, I pulled a Granny Smith apple out of our family's refrigerator and began to peel a thumbnail-sized sticker off its waxy green skin—a sticker that said, "New Zealand, ENZA, Granny Smith, #4017." For once, at least, I stopped to think about what I was doing. New Zealand is nearly ten thousand miles from my family's home in Ohio, and yet we paid ninety-nine cents a pound for these apples. Without even thinking about it, I was eating in a global food economy.

My New Zealand apple helps tell the story of an already existing globalization—a quasi-liturgy, if you will—that has shaped all of us from childhood to the present through our buying, selling, producing, consuming, eating, voting, and viewing. Globalization is part of our everyday practices, and we are already responding to globalization in our daily lives, even if we are doing nothing consciously. Depositing our paycheck in the bank makes us part of global finance. Buying a T-shirt made in China connects us to the globalization of work. Eating food from the local grocery chain connects us to a global food supply chain. Shopping at a superstore turns us into a global consumer. Fueling up our cars ties us to a global political system. Buying foreign goods joins us to global trade patterns. Voting or joining a nongovernmental organization links us to global political communities. Viewing a Hollywood or a Bollywood film links us to cultural meanings accessed across the globe. We cannot escape being enmeshed in practices of globalization.

Although globalization does not dictate the way we live, it is something we engage daily.[1]

But what is globalization? More than a buzzword, it is a term describing our shrinking world. Drawing on the literature, we can define globalization as a process of increasing economic, ecological, political, and cultural contacts between peoples on the planet.[2] While such "transplanetary" contacts between peoples in different world regions are nothing new—humans have been migrating since the dawn of recorded history—the density, velocity, and numbers of supraterritorial social relations are increasing in unprecedented ways.[3] Supraterritorial contacts are "social connections that substantially transcend territorial geography" and create situations of "*transworld simultaneity* (that is, they extend anywhere across the planet at the same time) and *transworld instantaneity* (that is, they move anywhere on the planet in no time)."[4] Airplanes, television, and the Internet, among other technologies, have helped compress space and time in ways that Europeans and North Americans recognize in their daily lives. We call our computer tech support line and end up talking with a person in India. We log into our accounts and shift money in seconds. We download African music in minutes, and we can fly to Africa in hours. European converts to Islam join a "transnational and supranational" community, and radical members of that globalized community crash airplanes into skyscrapers.[5] Thomas Friedman may overstate the case when he writes, "The world is being flattened. I didn't start it and you can't stop it, except at a great cost to human development and your own future."[6] But there is no question that Western Christians live in a world that pushes them into the rhythms of the simultaneous and instantaneous more than into the rhythms of liturgical time. Friedman presents us with the reality of the world and restricts the imagination to the given. I argue here that Christian liturgy can liberate our imaginations and incorporate us into the drama of living in God's story, thereby countering the rival quasi-liturgies of globalization.

Many Everyday Globalizations as Rival Liturgies

Nonsocial scientists sometimes lump together under the umbrella of globalization a wide variety of phenomena that should be distinguished clearly in our shrinking world. Sloppy usage of the term can lead to any number of gross generalizations that allow us to avoid our personal connections to the many manifestations of globalization in our daily lives. Clearly distinguishing these manifestations will help us understand these globalizations better—the better to engage them constructively by seeing them as rival liturgies.

The first type of globalization is *economic*, and within this are the globalizations of finance, labor, consumption, and trade.[7] Each of these intermeshes with our everyday lives in different but related ways. We deposit money in financial institutions with global connections. We buy clothing made by workers laboring elsewhere in conditions unknown. We consume goods produced through outsourcing within business firms. We pay higher or lower prices depending on tariffs or quotas on trade.

The second type of globalization is *ecological*. By definition these types of connections between peoples—think of ozone depletion or global warming—are global.[8] They present potential or actual problems that affect the whole earth, but the nation-state system often fails to address them, because no one state has a compelling interest in resolving the problems. For instance, a majority in the U.S. Senate has no interest in ratifying the Kyoto Protocol, which requires reductions in greenhouse gas emissions, because they fear it would limit the American economy while not limiting India's or China's. Thus we drive our cars without facing the potential costs of our personal contribution to greenhouse gas emissions. We buy food grown overseas without considering the impact on fuel consumption or soil erosion.

The third type of globalization is *political*, tied directly to the nation-state as an institution. Globalization can refer to relations *above*, *between*, or *below* state structures across the globe. Interaction that occurs above or outside states implies truly supranational forms of authority; interaction at the level of states implies cooperation between states to carry out global actions; and interaction of peoples below and outside state structures implies cooperation between nongovernmental organizations in different countries or the migration of peoples from one state to another. Globalization above the state is nascent at best. In a world of nearly two hundred sovereign states, there is little true supranational political authority. We do not live in a single global political system; the United Nations or other international organizations have little, if any, authority to compel sovereign states to take actions that harm their interests. Governments are not legally accountable to any higher (earthly) political authority, although the trend seems to be toward a decentralized global system that structures or pressures the states to follow market-friendly or corporate-friendly policies.[9] Thus states and the global market seem to exist in a reciprocal relationship of tension, each dependent on the other.[10] One state in particular plays a dominant role in the global economy of the early twenty-first century at the second, interstate level: the United States acts as a hegemonic or imperial power in running a global system that favors its interests (or the interests of powers within the United States).[11] Hence when Americans vote for leaders who expand U.S. military engagements overseas, they vote for empire. When they support a global military, they support empire. By contrast, when North Americans join global nongovernmental organizations and increase their travel overseas, they join movements that may be encouraging new forms of political solidarity below the state.

The final type of globalization, then, is *cultural*. The explosion of information and media technology allows people to view television programs and films or read books produced from around the world. These shared contacts raise the question whether the world is facing U.S. cultural imperialism, a violent backlash against such imperialism, or some kind of increased common identity and shared cultural understanding.

Each of the four types of globalization, then, can be expressed in terms of observable categories, each of which involves everyday activities directly or indirectly.[12] Economic globalization can be detected in levels of foreign investment, outsourcing, consumer purchases of foreign goods, and international trade levels. Ecological globalization takes us over to the realm of the climate sciences, but widely debated measures of ozone depletion and global climate change suggest increasing global consequences to human actions.[13] When pollution from China shows up in the atmosphere above North America, we can measure ecological aspects of globalization.[14] Political globalization can be captured by numbers of sovereign states, abandoned currencies, tourist visits, nongovernmental organizations, or military bases overseas—as well as membership in international organizations, personnel and financial contributions to UN peacekeeping missions, international treaties ratified, and foreign aid transfers.[15] Cultural globalization shows up in exports and imports of books, periodicals, newspapers, films, and television programs.[16] My point here is not to say that globalization can be reduced to these measures, but to draw the reader's attention to the specific types of globalization in which we all participate when we save, buy, drive, vote, view, or read.

To put it another way, the everyday practices of globalization inculcate a kind of formation that mimics the formation that occurs in liturgies. The *Oxford English Dictionary* notes that the term "liturgy" in ancient Greece originally referred to public service. It can also refer to "public worship conducted in accordance with a prescribed form." Liturgists note that the Greek roots of the word "liturgy" mean the "work of people." It is this public dimension that allows us to speak of liturgies of globalization.[17] The major patterns of economic, ecological, political, and cultural integration that shape us today are publicly "prescribed forms." They are practices that shape us into certain ways of being: into *transplanetary* ways of being economically, ecologically, culturally, or politically connected. And departure from these ways of being is often considered to be departure from a sensible, taken-for-granted norm. From the dominant cultural view, only a curmudgeon avoids the Internet or only eats locally grown food. Few people want to eat root vegetables all winter, and few can return to old habits of preserving, canning, and storing up food until spring. If liturgy is partly a public work that shapes our habits, then globalization has been a liturgy shaping North American habits.

So how does one respond constructively when one has been shaped by these liturgies? We are already deeply immersed in globalization practices, and total escape is not possible. Hence Tom Friedman argues that opposing globalization is a bit like opposing the rising of the sun: "Even if I didn't much care for the dawn there isn't much I could do about it. I didn't start globalization, I can't stop it—except at a huge cost to human development—and I'm not going to waste time trying."[18] And he writes, "If you want to resist these changes [of globalization], that is your business. . . . But if you think that you can resist these changes without paying an increasingly steep price . . . then you are deluding yourself."[19] Yet liturgy can help us see how the many globalizations are not natural givens or orders of creation that we must accept as they are now.[20]

To borrow a metaphor from Samuel Wells, globalization seems to put the church in a position similar to a person who has received a gift they do not like. That person can reject the gift, and the church can say no to globalization, but this threatens "to deny the goodness of God's creation and to declare war on society." That person can accept the gift and ask what the gift is *for* and what one is *"supposed to do with it."* But this puts the church in the position of treating globalization as part of a natural order, which assumes that "when [the gift/globalization] is employed about its correct purpose all is well." By contrast, Wells argues for a third option:

> It is not a question of what the gift is *supposed* to be: it is a question of what the gift *can* be. One does not say, "What is this gift *for*?"—and even less, "Is this a good gift?"; one says, "How can this gift be understood or used in a faithful way? What does the way we accept this gift say about the kind of people we are and want to be? What can (or has) this gift become in the Kingdom of God?" The ethical issues are less about the gift itself than about where it is perceived to fit into the story of the way God deals with his people and how that fitting-in takes place.[21]

My purpose, similarly, will be to focus on how the gift of globalization fits into the church's story, a story beginning with creation and only ending in the eschaton. To use Wells' term, the church can "overaccept" gifts such as globalization. "Overaccepting," Wells writes, "is an active way of receiving that enables one to retain both identity and relevance. It is a way of accepting without losing the initiative."[22] It is neither blocking globalization nor finding a built-in purpose to it. It is incorporating it into God's purposes within the church.

The Church Year as Drama Helps Christians Reimagine Globalizations in God's Story

To reiterate, it is not a question of being for or against globalization; we cannot escape it. But it is a question of finding ourselves in the Christian story while facing the globalizations in our everyday lives. In *After Virtue* moral philosopher Alasdair MacIntyre writes, "I can only answer the question 'What am I to do?' if I can answer the prior question 'Of what story or stories do I find myself a part?'"[23] The enacted narratives of the liturgical seasons offer not just a resource for thinking about globalization, but also a way for the church to find itself in the Christian story and figure out what to do.

Living through the church year can help the church to reimagine the many globalizations and frame them within the always-being-enacted drama of God's work with God's people. The liturgical progression from Advent through Pentecost helps Christians find themselves in the story of "God's self-revelation in Jesus"—a story of God's "continual presence in the life of the church."[24] Christians are embedded in this story and their lives are shaped by virtues that breed fidelity to its author. Stephen Long frames the task well when he writes that "the first task of any Christian reflection on the economy is not to speculate whether Christianity sides with capitalism or socialism but to seek to interpret our 'economic activity,' that is, our producing, buying, selling, and consuming, within the larger narrative of God's economy."[25] But how do we place ourselves in that larger narrative?

One powerful way is through celebrating the Christian story—from Advent to Christmas, from Epiphany to Lent, from Lent to Easter, and from Pentecost to Ordinary Time. This calendar emerged from the Jewish liturgical calendar, notably in the feasts of Easter and Pentecost, which are tied directly to Passover and Shavuot (the Feast of Weeks), which are commanded in the Torah (Exod 34:18-25; Lev 23:4-8, 15-22).[26] Alexander Schmemann argues that the church maintained these Jewish festivals "not because they reminded it of Christ's resurrection and the coming of the Spirit . . . but because they were, even before Christ, the announcement, the anticipation of that experience of time and of life in time, of which the Church was the manifestation and the fulfillment."[27] The rest of the Christian year invites the church to participate in the dramatic reenactment of the Christian story each time. And this dramatic reenactment, with the Word and sacraments at its center, is not just a way of restating certain truths about the world but is a way of bringing the community into living contact with the author of its story.[28] This series of performances shapes Christians into a certain kind of people with a unique way of being-in-the-world. They are formed to emulate God as the author of their story; their imaginations are formed as they are brought into the drama of Christian worship.

Rodney Clapp writes, "What we [the church] need is not a new path but better language and sharpened imaginations to discern the path we are already following."[29] It is not a question, then, of coming up with new perspectives on globalization but of living out the gospel we already have. It is not a question of theoretical invention but of sharing what we already experience as true. It is a question of discovering what the church is: to quote Bill Cavanaugh, the church is "a series of dramatic performances, and not a state of being."[30] Or to use the language of Michel de Certeau, the church is not a place, but it is a space. A space, in Certeau's terms, "*is a practiced place.* Thus the street geometrically defined by urban planning [a fixed place] is transformed into a space by walkers."[31] Likewise, the performance of Christian worship transforms the fixed places of daily life into the altars or signposts of a journey. Without such performances, the places in which we live are filled with other meanings, other spaces. But through performance of the Christian story in the liturgical year, we reimagine our quotidian routines in ways that reconnect them to the larger narrative of God's action in the world. For *stories* convert "places into spaces or spaces into places."[32] The liturgical year reminds us that the church is a story, on a journey of movement from one place to another. Advent recapitulates the end in which we find our beginning,[33] and we travel through Pentecost, which sends us into the world until the end of the ages. These and all the movements of the drama in between help us reframe globalization as part of God's story.

Christian liturgy, after all, regularly reenacts the Christian story as an open-ended drama that involves the Spirit and the church wrestling with how to be faithful. The drama metaphor aptly bridges the liturgical year and globalization, for a number of reasons.[34] First, *God is the author of the drama,* and the Christian church responds to the promptings of the Holy Spirit in its worship, which may sometimes need God's correction. It is not as if the church always gets things right and has been a perfect example; we do not want to romantically idealize the church as the solution to globalization or any other political issue.[35] The church's practices alone are "not a Pelagian mechanism for making humanity holy without recourse to the grace of God: they are, on the contrary, a pattern of making that dependence regular and faithful over time."[36] The liturgical year alone will not give us all answers to globalization, but it will help us turn to the Author of the story. Second, a dramatic view, in Nicholas Healy's words, "acknowledges that Christian existence is never stable or resolvable in terms of purely theoretical constructions, but is ever-moving, always struggling along within the theodrama."[37] *The church's struggle to be faithful with regard to globalization is an open-ended one,* until the end of time when all struggles shall end. Third, then, *the church must know its place in the drama.* As the player in the drama between the birth of the church and the eschaton, the church must learn not to make the mistake of thinking that it is "in a one-act play rather than a five-act play."[38] Urgency to figure out globalization in a hurry may well reflect the idea that "everything must be squeezed into the unforgiving span of a single life" (55). Likewise, the church must place itself in the correct act. We are not the Creator, and we live after the time of Jesus, who takes the leading role in redeeming. "The most important things have already happened. The Messiah has come, has been put to death, has been raised; and the Spirit has come. This is a great liberation for the church. It leaves Christians free, in faith, to make mistakes" (57). We are liberated to do our best in the knowledge that the world's redemption is not up to us.[39] Finally, the notion of drama implies an *active participation on the part of the church as a community whose role is to improvise responses to ethical challenges of globalization in light of its worship of God.* Answers to globalization will require the church to engage with its heart, mind, soul, and strength with creative practices of communal discernment, attuned to the particular circumstances in which local churches find themselves, with an eye to the end of the story.

How does the drama of the church year—from Advent through Pentecost—help the church incorporate the many globalizations into its story? The church learns to anticipate the end of time in Advent, to embody the created gift of human incarnation at Christmas, to start its ecological work at Epiphany, to work for all after Epiphany, to rest and confess its sins in Lent, to resist temptation in Holy Week, to proclaim the gospel on Easter, to commune as a social body after Easter, and to go out to the ends of the earth as a "called out" community of witnesses after Pentecost. In the course of a liturgical year, one travels through the contours of the life of Christ and—one hopes—learns to traverse one's own life. This is true both personally and communally. One learns to live and find oneself in a story. More than that, one learns to live in an always-being-enacted drama that is part of the journey. Likewise the church body lives out of this drama that incorporates into its story. Table 1 summarizes the rest of the paper.

Table 1

THE CHRISTIAN YEAR VIS-À-VIS GLOBALIZATION

Liturgical season	Biblical theme	Dimension of globalization
Advent	Last things	Globalization in general
Christmas	Creation & Incarnation	Globalization of finance
Epiphany	Gift and stewardship	Globalization of food economics & ecology
Sundays after Epiphany	Jubilee work of Jesus	Globalization of work: overwork & oppressive labor practices
Lent	Sabbath and healing	Globalization of production & consumption
Holy Week	Overcoming temptation of power	Globalization of military power & U.S. hegemony
Easter Sunday	Gospel mystery of faith	Globalization of trade: gospel of free trade
Sundays after Easter	"Discerning the body"	Globalization of political institutions & migration
Pentecost & after	The church as *ecclesia*	Globalization of culture

A Sketch of How the Drama of the Liturgical Year Can Incorporate Many Globalizations[40]

Advent and the End of the Story: Globalization in General

Globalization evokes the end of the ages and is often proclaimed as an eschatological reality, the end of history.[41] Celebrating Advent challenges us to see the true end. Interestingly, most of the daily office readings in the *Book of Common Prayer*—as well as the first three weeks in the Sunday lectionary—relate to the end times. So the new church year begins by proclaiming the end of the story— the second Advent of Christ, and his return to the earth to judge the living and the dead. As Fleming Rutledge has said, "In a very deep sense the entire Christian life in this world is lived in Advent, between the first and second comings of the Lord, in the midst of the tension between things the way they are and things the way they ought to be."[42]

By reimagining pictures of the end of the story, the church remains watchful and hopeful, praying and waiting for the end. If we listen to the daily office and lectionary, we know that no one can know the day or the hour, so we can confidently declare that globalization itself is not the end of the story. And we can wait for the true hope that should give us patient endurance, as well as a heightened sense of the need to practice shalom here and now.[43] Active vigilance is a major point of Jesus' parables of the kingdom: We can be like the five foolish virgins who failed to bring extra oil, or the five wise ones, who did bring extra oil (Matt 25:1-13). We can be like the two who received the talents and multiplied them, or we can be like the fearful one who received one talent and buried it (Matt 25:14-30). We can be like the ones who failed to extend help to the hungry, the thirsty, the stranger, the naked, the sick, and the imprisoned—or those that did (Matt 25:31-46). We face a choice. Are our actions in this global world making us ready more each day to face the end?

Christmas: Globalized Finance and Its Earthly Limits

Globalized finance is a crucial part of economic globalization. It is the kind of world where your money "works" for you around the clock, around the globe, every day of the year. It is the kind of world where there is "a new power source in the world . . . made up of all the faceless stock, bond and currency traders sitting behind computer screens all over the globe, moving their money around from mutual funds to pension funds to emerging market funds, or trading on the Internet from their basements."[44] In the years since 1971, most major countries of the world have shifted to floating exchange rates and have dropped capital controls.[45] "The more capital controls have fallen between countries, the more everyone is offering everything for sale as stocks, bonds or derivatives." The world is moving toward "securitizing everything" and truly "offering everything for sale."[46] Even a mortgage on a house in the United States can be resold globally in markets. When mortgages secure bonds (borrowing upon borrowing), capital is detached from the "real" economy and can flow freely around the world.

Finance has been globalized and detached from tangible realities, but the lived-out stories of creation and Incarnation ground the church in real time and present place. When the church celebrates the mystery of the Incarnation at Christmas, it is reenacting the Word of God becoming flesh—an echo of God's creating humans out of dust in Genesis, affirming the earthiness of Adam and Eve's (and our) creation. Christmas reenacts these truths with the story of how God was born as a human (yet fully divine) child, embracing the same earthly limits all humans face. But anytime the church gathers in worship it affirms its limits. We cannot worship as disembodied spirits. We need to worship as physical beings together.

In 1996 a *Doonesbury* cartoon spoofed the Rev. Scott Sloane's Little Church of Walden. Showing an old friend around the church building, he says, "The old house is used for our spiritual wellness seminars and various 12-step recovery programs. In the new wings, we have a food court, a fitness center, and our interpretive dance studios."

His friend asks, "Um . . . where do people worship?"

"On our website. Keeps the heating bills down."[47]

Of course, the comic strip was a joke. A real church can't worship in any meaningful way over the Web. We must serve each other in the flesh—the very flesh that the Word entered.

Therefore, if our financial practice is to be consistent, it must likewise embody embodiedness. From a similar starting point, Long sums up the principle behind the ban on usury this way: "The principle is quite simple: money does no work, people do. So when we assume that our money is working for us to make more money, we are not describing accurately God's economy."[48] And yet much of what drives the globalization process is just the opposite principle: by putting capital to work globally, by following the "electronic herd" to find the highest returns on our money,[49] and by detaching money from any earthly limits, we are putting our money to work for us—without bothering to figure out who our money is affecting or how it is affecting them. Thus, writes Long, "We lose the ability to describe how our lives are embedded in the narratives of others. The food that we eat, the clothes we wear, the transportation available to us, clean restrooms, floors, and so on—all these things are provided for us without any awareness on our part of other people's practices which make such external goods possible. We cannot name our debts. Thus we cannot pray well."[50] A church ought to be a place where we know the relationships rooted in tangible realities of time and place that bring us the food, the clothes, the transportation, the clean restrooms, and all the rest. A church that reenacts the story of Christmas ought to form people who put earthly limits on their money.

Epiphany: Sharing Gifts and Glory in Stewardship of Global Ecology

The global food economy and the global environment may well be in a crisis of sustainability as our consumption threatens both to outstrip the "resources" on earth and to change the earth's climate. Yet the church responds by forming its members with virtues of stewardship. Genesis 1 links the creation of men and women "in God's image" to their calling to "have dominion" over the earth (Gen 1:27-28). Reformed theology has long emphasized the exercise of this cultural mandate as a high calling for human beings to live out as part of a calling to be good stewards. Viewing stewardship through the themes and practices of Epiphany adds another dimension to the Reformed view. To take on the language of the season, humans share in bearing God's image, and they reflect his glory when they work in the culture as a whole taking on the work of stewardship. They are icons reflecting God's glory, called to stewardship—to the cultural mandate to rule the earth, which after all comes immediately after the image of God language in Genesis 1:27. Epiphany is a day to ponder the gifts offered by the wise men in response to the gift of Jesus to the Gentiles. These wise men of the east "knelt down and paid . . . homage" to the baby Jesus, and so does the church (Matt 2:11).

In reminding itself of God's good gifts at Epiphany, the church is beginning to live out a stewardship wisdom that sees Creation as a gift, just as Christ was a gift. "Stewardship holds that the possessor of a natural resource should behave as a custodian, using the resource wisely but enjoined from destruction or disposal. . . . Stewardship identifies possessors as managers, servants, and beneficiaries rather than as masters."[51] Because Creation is not ours but a gift, the church must care for it with a light touch, learning to see it as a gift rather than as "natural resources" or "my property." Instead of buying apples from New Zealand, we might begin to eat locally or seasonally—even grow a home garden—in an effort to lessen the strains of unsustainable resource consumption.[52] A church living out the Epiphany story of shared gifts and shared glory fosters stewardship practices of simplicity and conservation in its members.[53]

Sundays after Epiphany: The Globalization of Work

We see evidence of the globalization of work in the outsourcing of production to low-cost factories all around the world, some of them relying on abusive labor practices. In the Sundays after the

Epiphany, the church first reenacts the story of the baptism of Jesus, the beginning of his work. The church also recalls the story of Jesus' first miracle: changing water into wine at the wedding in Cana, which "revealed his glory" to his disciples (John 2:11)—this theme of revealed glory being a key theme enacted in the season.[54] While his glory was being revealed in his work of healing, Jesus was unveiling a foretaste of things to come, and a present reality. So he proclaimed to the synagogue at Nazareth that he was the fulfillment of Isaiah's prophecy to "bring good news to the poor . . . proclaim release for the captives and recovery of sight to the blind, to let the oppressed go free," and to proclaim the Jubilee year (Luke 4:18-20). The work of the church is to do the same, especially in a world of globalized work. Our reenactments of Jesus' work in worship should help train us to work for Jubilee for others.

To take one instance, Christian "consumers" reenacting the post-Epiphany Jubilee vision could use their buying power to reshape the market; indeed, Ron Sider estimates that Christians worldwide annually spend $10 trillion on consumption.[55] If Christians sought to promote only products that reflect just work practices, they could have a significant impact. Christians, merely as part of living out their story, could move markets to penalize producers who harm their workers and reward those who treat theirs. Christ's jubilee work after Epiphany goes on. The question is whether our work will participate in this drama.

Lent and the Sabbath:
The Globalization of Consumption and Production

Consumption and production have both been globalized, as people worldwide can increasingly purchase products made worldwide. It is not unusual for families on a budget to buy inexpensive consumer goods sold at Wal-Mart, Costco, Kmart, or Target. Just by shopping at these stores, they are going global, because production of these items has been globalized. Workers in China do the work instead of workers closer to home, and an estimated 80 percent of the factories that supply to Wal-Mart are in China.[56] Yet economists find a direct link between our ability to consume ever-cheaper stuff and the outsourcing of production from high-wage countries.[57] By moving their production facilities to lower-wage areas, corporations are able to cut labor costs. As consumers, we benefit, because things stay cheap. But as producers we, and our neighbors, may well suffer. Even Friedman recognizes that Wal-Mart divides the human person into different selves:

> The Wal-Mart shopper in all of us wants the lowest price possible, with all the middlemen, fat, and friction removed. And the Wal-Mart shareholder in us wants Wal-Mart to be relentless about removing the fat and friction in its supply chain and in its employee benefits packages, in order to fatten the company's profits. But the Wal-Mart worker in us hates the benefits and pay packages that Wal-Mart offers its starting employees.[58]

Lower wages and cheaper stuff go hand in hand. While Wal-Mart helps drive the cycle of cutting "labor costs" for goods requiring low-skilled workers, it also helps us afford more with less. We are split into shoppers and producers. How can we restore wholeness to our lives in relation to globalization?

Lent, read as a Sabbath practice of restful confession, gives us the space to begin finding and living out answers. By fasting from temptations in the world for a season we develop the disciplines to live with openness to grace. The practice of confessing sin can also help us to see ourselves clearly, and one thing Americans might learn in examining their consumption habits is that they are global consumers.[59] Yet the Christian's identity should be in Christ and the living out of his story in one's life. But sin so often gets in our way that it must be confessed regularly. Repeatedly enacting the practices of resting, fasting, and confession—rooted in the many stories of wilderness journeys, from the Israelites' forty years to Jesus' forty days—can help lead some to true repentance, a real turnaround of thoughts and actions through habits of decreased consumption and greater reflection. Lenten fasting prepares the church for change rooted in receiving the Resurrection and the forgiveness of sins.

Holy Week and Baptism: Globalization of Military Power[60]

Military power has been globalized in the form of a global U.S. hegemony. To say that the current global economic order is based on U.S. military power is a truism among political scientists who advance the hegemonic stability theory, arguing that the United States created an "open" trading system after World War II to serve its own security and economic interests.[61] More recently, the description of the United States as an empire has gone public, with debate focusing on whether the United States is a *benevolent empire*.[62] But few question the fact that there is an empire, a global system backed by global U.S. military force, a system based on the threat or use of violence.

But the drama of Holy Week—especially Maundy Thursday and Good Friday—suggests that resisting the temptation to violence comes close to the heart of the Christian story. The context for Holy Week starts in comparing the temptation accounts of Genesis and Matthew 4. When Adam and Eve were tempted with the allure of being like God, they failed to resist, but Jesus managed to succeed where Adam and Eve failed. They saw that the fruit was "desirable for gaining wisdom" and succumbed, but Jesus resisted the temptation to take worldly power (Matt 4:8-10). One reading of the agony of Jesus in the garden of Gethsemane on Maundy Thursday is that Jesus' own will was to take the easy way out—the way of grasping power with the sword.[63] In the scene immediately following this, all four Synoptic Gospels quote Jesus rebuking Peter and denying that he was leading a rebellion (Matt 26:52-55; Mark 14:43-51; Luke 22:47-53; John 18:11). The baptized Jesus overcame the temptation to decline the roles of suffering servant and Passover lamb. And if baptized Christians are to emulate Jesus, they too are called to follow their savior, servant, and lamb. That is, they are to decline easy solutions in their journey toward unity with God. They are to die to the temptations to achieve their goals with power and to rise to the new life of practicing agape love and reconciliation. They are called to say also, "Father, forgive them, for they do not know what they are doing" (Luke 23:34). They may even need to dissent from U.S. military hegemony and be called out of the empire—perhaps even to the point of martyrdom.[64]

Easter: Globalization of Trade as Rival Gospel

When supporters of globalization preach good news to the poor, they preach the benefits of global free trade. A number of well-meaning advocates of free trade argue that it is good news for developing countries and poor people, because it allows countries to specialize in producing for export while benefiting from cheaper imports.[65] Incomes and the standard of living both rise—or so they argue. In a column interestingly entitled "Good News about Poverty," *New York Times* columnist David Brooks cites a World Bank report that described a "spectacular" decline in poverty in Asia. Brooks asks,

"What explains all this good news? The short answer is this thing we call globalization." Thus, he says, "The key task ahead is spreading the benefits of globalization. . . . Write this on your forehead: Free trade reduces world suffering."[66] Brooks is preaching here. But, while there is no disputing a simultaneous opening to international trade and an increase in economic growth in Asia, there is still a vigorous debate over whether globalization alone caused the so-called East Asian Miracle.[67] Sidestepping this debate, *Wall Street Journal* editorial writer William McGurn argues that theologians and religious leaders have missed the good news for the poor: free trade has lifted the incomes of millions of workers in Asian countries.[68] He blames educated elites, especially theologians, for this alleged failure.

But the preaching of the Easter gospel by the church challenges the gospel of free trade. From the church's founding, the good news has been that Jesus the Messiah died, rose again, and appeared to his disciples—just as he will someday appear again, and thus he instituted a new covenant. The mystery of faith—"Christ has died, Christ has risen, Christ will come again"—may well be a proto-gospel that predates the writing of the actual Gospels, and this story certainly structures the four Gospels. That Jesus' passion, death, and resurrection take up large parts each of the four Gospels makes sense (Matt 21:1–28:15; Mark 11:1–16:8; Luke 19:28–24:49; and John 12:12–20:31); as many have said, they are really "passion narratives with extended introductions." Easter is the center of the story. It is this core gospel message (the evangel) that the church proclaims and preaches. Following in the footsteps of the disciples, we are witnesses to the resurrection, and we want to share the good news that Christ is risen. "He is risen, indeed. Alleluia."

This gospel offers wholeness, security, and hope that liberalism cannot offer. While free trade might generate economic growth—and this can be good for the poor—it cannot match the full gospel, in two ways. First, Easter saves all who accept it. But free trade's benefits are at the macroeconomic level—the level of the national economy, and the expectation is that its benefits will be spread across the country to consumers. But does everyone really experience the benefits? At the microeconomic level of households and small businesses, there are no guarantees of benefits, only hypothetical ones, whereas the costs of "adjustment" to competition are all too clear. To use the technical terms of economists, an opening to trade can be defended as Pareto-optimal if the gains to the winners from trade are so great that they would allow the winners to compensate the losers (presumably for lost income) and still be better off. The problem is that in the real world this never happens fully. Trade displacement assistance is a luxury of industrialized countries, but workers displaced by trade in countries without social safety nets are on their own. Second, Easter presents a full gospel; the resurrection is sufficient to save us. But even liberals will admit free trade alone is not enough. As *The Economist* admitted, "Simply liberalizing poor economies, without giving them support during the transition, can be a recipe for economic instability."[69] Trade alone is not enough to save people. It must be a policy step that is part of a larger, holistic context, for understanding "economic development" requires a holistic approach that includes cultural, educational, technological, political, and—yes—communal-religious steps of discernment—including debates about what "development" means.[70]

Sundays after Easter and Communion: Globalization of Politics

In the age of globalization, then, questions about the location of political community naturally arise. Where is the political community that claims our highest allegiance? Is it a nation-state or a supranational entity or something else? If the state is under siege, or if it is maintaining its grip, where is our loyalty to be placed? Is community found in local identities or in global identities? Where does the church fit here?[71]

William Cavanaugh has made a compelling case for the "spatial story" of the Eucharist as the church's main response to globalization. In the Eucharist, he argues, the church is always enacting a story that is both local and global, and therefore it practices a politics of authentic integration (as opposed to the false universalism of globalization, which is actually based on the extension and entrenchment of state power). "It is Christ, not we, who tells the story. Each consumer of the Eucharist receives the whole body of Christ, though the body remains one throughout the whole world. This is only possible because the consumer is absorbed into the body. The consumer of the Eucharist begins to walk in the strange landscape of the body of Christ, while still inhabiting a particular earthly place."[72] For Cavanaugh, this remarkable ability to be both global and local while practicing a true universalism makes the church a uniquely hospitable place for the weak and vulnerable.

"Communion" nicely expresses this communal dimension of the celebration of the feast, while the term "Eucharist" (thanksgiving) properly places the celebration of the feast in the Response to the Word portion of a worship service. The mystery of unity with Christ is at the heart of the mystery of the church. J. M. R. Tillard puts it simply: "The nature of the church is to be communion."[73] In a world of shifting identities, this community, united in communion with its head, can be a compelling site of loyalty. Life after Easter requires discerning this body (of Christ and his church). The communal context of Paul's advice to the Corinthian church to "discern the body" is central here (1 Cor 11:29): it comes in the middle of a discourse on the need to overcome the shameful division between rich and poor Christians (vv. 17-22), and to focus on the body of believers (1 Cor 12 and 13).[74] In this context, the meaning of "discerning the body" is both vertical and horizontal: to touch Christ's broken body like the apostle Thomas and to comprehend the body of Christ within the communing congregation. After Easter, the church began to wrestle with both types of discernment, trying to understand what it meant to be united with Christ's body "in memory" and united with each other. This post-Easter community—the church—can be a truer community than any other. As Yoder says, emphasizing the literal sharing of bread, "the Eucharist is an economic act."[75] It forms a community of sharing that is more real than the communities of states or ethnic groups—a community that is deeply rooted in the local and yet global and universal at the same time.

Pentecost and After: Globalization of Culture

Therefore, the church offers a potent symbol of true and authentic globalization. Secular globalism promises increased choices, but what happens to community and identity in a globalizing world? Some fear that such globalization threatens to promise a false universalism of homogenization—the threat of a McWorld of strip malls, Disney, and movie theaters, while others fear a backlash—the threat of a "clash of civilizations" and a retreat to local communities.[76] What is the role of the church here?

As a community of identity with its own culture, the church is engaged already in cultural globalization, but in its own peculiar way. Yoder writes that "the original meaning of the word *ecclesia* [the New Testament Greek word for church] is political; it is literally a 'called meeting,' an assembly, such as a town meeting, convened to do business, to deliberate on behalf of the entire society."[77] In Cavanaugh's view, "*Ecclesia* is neither *polis* nor *oikos*, but an alternative which radically reconfigures the dichotomy between public and private used to domesticate the Gospel."[78] The church is sent out to "make disciples" and to "teach them to obey" until the "end of the age" (Matt 28:19-20). There is a world outside the communion with Christ, and the faithful are being sent to live and work in that world—still worshiping and serving, but in day-to-day contexts. Living after Pentecost means living out this work with the Spirit in ordinary time.

Lest we think that worship encompasses the Christian story, then, we must see that the church looks beyond its "ordinary time" to the end. Rodney Clapp makes the striking point that "the church is the only institution that regularly celebrates the hope of its demise, the hope that it will not endure forever." The church bears witness to a story that transcends the story of God's people on earth. It hopes for the day when, in Clapp's words, "There will no longer be any distinction between the church and the world."[79] When heaven is unveiled, the apostle John sees people of "every tribe and language and people and nation" worshiping the Lamb; this is the end of our story (Rev 5:9; 7:9). This end is already now becoming real. In fact, if we define globalization as integration across continents, we can see that the new church was global from the beginning at Pentecost.[80] When the Holy Spirit came, there were "devout Jews from every nation under heaven" in Jerusalem, and each of them heard the disciples speaking to them in their own language (Acts 2:5-6). Quite literally, the curse of Babel was overcome. So, too, heaven will be the final undoing of Babel's curse but with the multiplicity of tongues and nations preserved. Some of the first people to worship Jesus were Gentile wise men from the east. One of the first converts was from Africa (Acts 8:26-40). Paul traveled from Asia to Europe. Legend has it that the apostle Thomas traveled all the way to India preaching the gospel. From the start, this was a new transnational community with its own peculiar Jewish-Gentile-adaptive culture.

Hence, while alternative visions of local, self-sufficient communities offer compelling critiques of liberalism's false universal culture, it also falls short of the expansive nature of God's kingdom.[81] While these critics are correct to reject the false promise of cosmopolitanism in global liberalism, one must also admit that God loves the diversity of a global people. Admittedly, liberalism would create a global community in which "Each can be the architect of his own future—if he's allowed to be."[82] By contrast, the church in heaven will be a global community of love, in which people are ever free to live in God's presence. Liberalism would create a world of hybrids, in which everyone's identity is a mixed-up jumble of global and local. In heaven, the global and the local will be one. Already bearing witness to the worship of heaven, the worshiping church has been practicing "glocalization" since Pentecost.[83] In each place the church enters, it creates an embodied, local presence in its worship and work. In the real world, you can't break bread together over the Web. Therefore, Christian communities have always adapted to the local conditions in which they find themselves, and even the intellectual culture of Christianity has changed over time, as it shifted from Rome, to Ireland, to Europe, to North America, and now to Africa, Asia, and South America.[84] Rather than requiring people to convert to a culture in order to join the community, the church has always adapted its culture to local needs and concerns, while preserving its universal (catholic) core culture. Therefore, the church is a model of relatively healthy cultural adaptation, calling its people into a healthier blend of global and local that will only be fully achieved in the end. Which returns us to Advent. . . .

Conclusion

Observing its own seasons and rhythms through the church year, the church repeatedly reenacts its drama in relation to the many globalizations its members live within each day. The story begins with Advent, where the church waits for the true end (rather than the false end of globalization). It continues through Christmas where the church participates dramatically in God's affirmation of the finite dust of Creation (in contrast to dreams of disembodied finance). Observing Epiphany, the church lives out the reality that its members reflect the glory of God as his image bearers, a community called to stewardship of Creation (rather than its use as a resource to be owned and exploited). The Sundays after Epiphany reenact stories of Jesus' work, reminding us that his Jubilee work is not yet complete and not all are liberated. Entering Lent on Ash Wednesday, the church confesses its sins for forty weekdays, which could include its sins of complicity in a global consumption and production cycle—a cycle that continues to bring Western Christians abundance and technological change, but at the expense of rest and wholeness and peace for those left behind, made insecure, or split between worker and producer identity. Holy Week reminds us of baptismal promises to renounce sin and resist temptation to take the easy way out—notably the temptation to seize power by force. Like Jesus, the church is called to ride on a donkey rather than a white horse, in a spirit of forgiveness rather than a spirit of conquest. Most of all, the church is called to forgive its enemies in a way that the empires of the world find senseless and might only be possible for the baptized. The good news of Easter—the tomb is empty, he is risen—offers a true gospel that makes the gospel of free trade pale by comparison. While economic policies come and go, the hope of resurrection lives on for the church. The Sundays after Easter bring new meaning to the communion of the body and blood, as the church encounters the scarred lamb that is now risen and ascended. Discerning his body among the body of believers after Easter, communion re-knits true community (in a world of communities in flux). As Pentecost arrives, the church recalls that it is being extended to the ends of the earth (Acts 1:8) and that some day it will no longer need to exist. In the meantime, in ordinary time, its glimpses of Pentecost remind the church that it already unites global and local, universal and particular. When Advent approaches again, we are reminded of the true end of the story. Until the end arrives, the church reenacts a drama liturgically through the seasons—a drama that reimagines globalizations in the church's story and places the church's members within a larger narrative of God's economy, helping them understand what to do.

Chapter 12

Agrarianism after Modernity
An Opening for Grace

Norman Wirzba

We are what we are given
and what is taken away;
blessed be the name
of the giver and the taker.
For everything that comes
is a gift, the meaning always
carried out of sight
to renew our whereabouts,
always a starting place.
And every gift is perfect
in its beginning, for it
is "from above, and cometh down
from the Father of lights."
Gravity is grace.[1]

Modernity defies gravity.[2] In multiple ways the various trends of secularization, commodification, individualism, industrialism, urbanization, standardization, technological hype, and, most recently, global markets have torn asunder the gravitational threads that bind us to each other, to the earth, and to God. In the last several centuries we have all become witnesses to one of the greatest of cultural upheavals in which human and natural properties have been transformed and confounded into, among other things, monetary bits subject to manipulation and sale. In our practical and economic

lives, reduced as we now are to being spectators and consumers, we
are increasingly cut off and insulated from each other. Because of
"the demotion of public spaces"[3]—the meeting places where values
can be clarified, desires made attentive and patient, norms created,
and responsibilities learned and assumed—we find ourselves more
and more alone in worlds of our own making and fantasy. A sense
for the integrity of things, and for their interdependence, as well as
an appreciation for things having their beginning and end in God,
is mostly gone. We do not know who we are, do not welcome and
receive each other as gifts "from the Father of lights" (James 1:17),
nor do we know what the earth means—all because we have lost the
"art" of being creatures.[4]

Modernity also defies grace. In the summer of 1946, while lec-
turing amid the rubble of what was once the University of Bonn,
Karl Barth said, "The greatest hindrance to faith is again and again
just the pride and anxiety of our human hearts. We would rather
not live by grace. Something within us energetically rebels against
it. We do not wish to receive grace; at best we prefer to give ourselves
grace."[5] Barth was speaking about a culture that had come to ruin,
and speaking to survivors who would now need to learn to eschew
the arrogant, controlling, and violent character of modern life and
take up the difficult—because it is patient, humble, and responsible—path of faith. His observation about the human heart's refusal
of grace cuts to the core of what has long been and continues to be
our modern (but not only modern) crisis: namely, our preference for
life on our own terms. We have refused our status as creatures made
dependent upon each other and upon God, and instead have chosen
goals that satisfy self-chosen or media-manufactured desires. We
have done this most directly with technological, industrial means
that enable us to refashion the whole world according to our own
likeness. The world, rather than signifying as the graced realm of
God's creativity, is reduced to an idol that everywhere reflects a
human (narrowly pragmatic and economic) intention.

The combined refusal of gravity and grace qualifies modernity
as the time of perpetual crisis. Our failure to appreciate the wide
scope of social and environmental catastrophes, or to know the
signs of our common degradation—the erosion and toxification of
soils, the pollution of waterways, the chemical clouding of air, global
warming, the extinction of animal species, and the poisoning of
life habitats, but also the deterioration of communal structures of

nurture and upbuilding—is typical of people who are firmly within the chaotic mainstream. We have lost the vantage point that would offer a differing perspective or an alternative set of assumptions. We are simply unable to see the deep spiritual contradiction that exists between our professed belief in God as Creator and our consenting, whether intentionally or not, to creation's mutilation.

The scope and consequences of creation's mutilation have now, except to the willfully blind and obstinate, become extremely difficult to overlook or deny. Legions of scientific studies and cultural analysis are making it plain that the grand experiment to exercise complete control over the earth—to have life on our own terms—is ending in disaster: as glaciers, polar ice caps, and the Greenland ice sheet melt owing to global warming, people alternately face drought, dehydration, starvation, or drowning (as ocean levels rise to consume them);[6] as countries compete to gain entrance into global markets, local food economies and small-scale, sustainable agriculture are destroyed, with the result that millions are displaced from their homes and livelihoods and are compelled to find "work" in crowded, unprepared urban areas;[7] and as industrial methods of agriculture lace our soils and waterways with synthetic fertilizers and pesticides, all with the aim of maximizing production, the very ground and water that nourish us are rendered sterile and poisonous.[8] The natural, created sources that support and sustain all life, human and nonhuman, are being degraded or destroyed by us at an unprecedented rate. No wonder, then, that some people think it is only a matter of time before we are compelled to find another home in outer space!

What our destructiveness shows is profound blindness and outright refusal to trust in and abide by the grace of interdependent life, for what is our destructiveness if it is not an assault against God's goodness or the denial that God's grace is sufficient, even lovely? Our rejection of grace, of its possibilities and demands, and our substituting for it the cheap satisfactions of consumer and media culture, are the practical demonstration (often more honest than our verbal piety) of a prior hesitancy or refusal to live out the ways of faith. In other words, our destruction of creation, and the undermining of human health and conviviality that are its inevitable correlate—the clearest indicators of modernity's collective malfunction—raises the possibility that our religious faith may be little more than a deceptive play, however exalted or affirming, of words.

Two questions become paramount: (1) how are we to characterize this cultural and spiritual failure? and (2) what paths must
we follow if we are to practice a more authentic spiritual life, a life
of faith that honors creation and community and brings delight to
God? As I argue in this essay, we have been blinded to the precise
character of modernity's malfunction because we have not successfully refined an alternative perspective in terms of which to evaluate modernity's harvest. Too much of our analysis operates within
media-manufactured or abstract academic paradigms, and thus is
oblivious to another, better way.

If we are to gain a fresh perspective we need an approach from
the margins, an approach that does not share modernity's dominant
assumptions. Agrarianism represents one such approach.[9] Far from
being a Luddite-inspired throwback to some pastoral arcadia, or the
interest and prerogative of the few remaining farmers, agrarianism is
a comprehensive and compelling worldview that aims to understand
human life in terms of its practical and concrete interdependence
with all other life. It is a deliberate and intentional way of living and
thinking that takes seriously the failures and successes of the past as
they have been realized in our engagement with the earth and with
each other. Authentic agrarianism, which should not be confused
with farming per se (since severe economic pressure and the dash
for quick profits have often led farmers to compromise agrarian ideals), represents the sustained attempt to live faithfully and responsibly in a world of biological and social limits and possibilities. As
such it takes seriously what we know (and still need to learn) about
the earth (the scientific ecological principles that govern all the living) and what we know about each other (the social-scientific and
humanistic disciplines that enrich human self-understanding).

Agrarianism tests success and failure not by market share or
economic growth but by the health and vitality of a region's entire
human and nonhuman neighborhood. Agrarianism, we might say,
represents the most complex and far-reaching accounting system ever known, for according to it success must include a vibrant
watershed and soil base; species diversity; human and animal con-
tentment; communal creativity, responsibility, and joy; usable
waste; social solidarity and sympathy, attention and delight; and
the respectful maintenance of all the sources of life. In an agrarian
economy every cost, ranging from resource depletion or contamination to social conflict and personal ill-health, must fully register and

not be externalized (for someone else to pay). Given the complexity and magnitude of this task, it is clear that authentic agrarianism has only been attempted thus far. Its full realization still awaits us.

What makes agrarianism the ideal candidate for cultural and spiritual renewal is that it, unlike some environmental approaches that sequester wilderness and portray the human presence as invariably destructive or evil, grows out of the sustained, practical, intimate engagement between human and natural power and creativity. It holds together in a synoptic vision the health of land and culture, recognizing that neither can flourish at the expense of the other. In agrarian practices we see a deliberate way of life in which the integrity of peoples and neighborhoods, and the natural sources they depend upon, are maintained and celebrated. Agrarianism builds on the acknowledgment that we are biological and social beings that live *through* healthy habitats and communities. However much we might think of ourselves as postagricultural beings or disembodied minds, the fact of the matter is that we are inextricably tied to the land through our bodies—we have to eat, drink, and breathe—and so our culture must always be sympathetic to the responsibilities of agri-culture. If we despise the latter, we are surely only a step away from despising the former, too.

Moreover, agrarianism also represents one of the most honest and practical ways for us to become reacquainted with the grace of God. It does this by connecting us practically and intimately— through our mouths, nostrils, and stomachs, but also with our hands and feet—with God's sustaining action in the ways of creation. If we believe with the Psalmist that God makes "springs gush forth in the valleys," and causes "the grass to grow for the cattle, and plants for people to use, to bring forth food from the earth," and that if God's face were to be hidden from us all creation would return to dust (Ps 104:10-30), then we must look to creation and to each other in new ways so we can see there, however dimly and mysteriously, the ways of God in our midst.[10] Agrarian practices and responsibilities open up new lines of vision, lines that have increasingly been closed in the time of modernity.

Our vision has become most clouded with respect to the food we eat. Never before in history have so many people been so ignorant about food—where it comes from, how it is produced, what biological and social conditions are necessary for its long-term and safe production. This is astonishing, especially when we remember that food is absolutely fundamental. Everything that lives, eats. It is the particular merit of an agrarian approach that it compels us to keep our focus and energies on protecting, preserving, and enhancing the practical and biological conditions that contribute to a healthy food network. The modern, industrial food system, as has recently been shown by Michael Pollan, gives clear indication that we have reduced food to the status of a commodity. It is without grace, and thus made utterly cheap and wastable.[11] Given this profane context, it is hardly surprising that we are losing the ability to speak authentically the words of grace at mealtime.

To help us realize an agrarian-informed world, we first need to have an appreciation for what went wrong in key moments of modernity so as to distort our understanding of life and faith. To keep our investigation to a manageable size, this essay focuses in particular on what happens to the meaning of grace. Following this analysis I develop how an agrarian witness has the potential to correct and make concrete an authentic life of faith, one that brings healing and salvation to creation and delight to the Creator.

To speak about grace is to point to our being called into the intimacy of God's own life, an intimacy founded in God's intense desire to love the world into being, to be ever-present in it as its sustaining, vivifying life. Grace is not something we initiate. It follows from and expresses a divine summons to join with God in the celebration of creation wonderfully made. It is important that we not think of this summons as coming to us wholly from without since our very being is always already the visible testimony of God's creative, joyous speech. In the action of creating, God "makes room" for us within the divine life so that we can share in the blessedness that God is.[12] Grace is thus God's self-communication and self-dedication to us so that we might enjoy, here and now, relationships that are informed by God's life-building ways.

This brief description indicates that it is a mistake to reduce grace to the giving of a few divine gifts or benefits that we then have the option to accept or reject. Because we are members of God's creation, the material testimony of God's continuing care and concern, grace touches literally everything in its most profound depth. The intimacy of divine grace requires that we stop thinking about God as one who is unapproachably remote and distant. God is perpetually near to us as the one who sustains us in our being and desires for us lives characterized by peace, justice, and delight. Nicholas

Lash puts the point beautifully when he writes: "God's utterance lovingly gives life: gives all life, all unfading freshness; gives only life, and peace, and love, and beauty, harmony and joy. And the life God gives is nothing other, nothing less, than God's own self. Life is God, given."[13] Grace communicates the communion of all life with God as the one who brings everything into existence and then sustains it daily. When we properly acknowledge and respond to this grace, which is what we do when we live out our calling as creatures made in the image of God, we learn to highlight, promote, and make concrete God's loving, life-giving intentions for the whole world.

But God's intention does not end with mere sustenance. God's desire for creation is that its members together enjoy a "blessed conviviality" of relationships founded on peace and joy rather than violent struggle.[14] Indeed, without our capacity to share in God's own delight in creation we run the risk of severely misunderstanding who and where we are, and what we are to become. Consider here the words of David Bentley Hart: "It is delight that constitutes creation, and so only delight can comprehend it, see it aright, understand its grammar. Only in loving creation's beauty—only in seeing that creation truly is beautiful—does one apprehend what creation is."[15] Moreover, and by not adequately appreciating the beauty of creation, we risk misunderstanding who God is as the one who delights in creation and enjoins us to share in this divine celebration. Quite rightly, therefore, Hart advises us to supplement the traditional analogies of being (Aquinas) and faith (Barth) with an analogy of delight (*analogia delectationis*). The practice of delight forms the basis for an authentic approach to God and for responsible relations with our fellow creation.[16]

For Christians grace finds its climactic, definitive, and most practical expression in the life of Jesus Christ. Christ, from the beginning of all time, is the one through whom God's reconciling presence and intention are made known and manifest. In his ministries we concretely see (even if we do not fully understand) what the life of God among us amounts to: healing, feeding, exorcism, restoration of relationships through forgiveness, celebration, and the resurrection of the dead. His is not a ministry designed to take us out of creation or out of this life. It is, rather, a sustained invitation to be drawn into life in its innermost depth so that creation in all its fullness can be experienced and enjoyed. Because Christ is the one through whom all things are created (cf. John 1:3; Col 1:15-20), we should not be surprised to learn that in Christ "all things" will also be redeemed. Here we can see why Gnosticism, whether in ancient or modern forms, amounts to a denial of grace, and must resolutely be rejected as heretical.

The Christian path of redemption, however, is a path that goes through the cross. This means that all creation, owing to the sinful and destructive ways of humanity, now bears a cruciform character. But even as creation is subject to needless suffering and death, these are not the final word. Just as Christ is present in creation as the one through whom all things are made, so Christ is present in the midst of its suffering and death as the one who bears and transforms it into new, more abundant life. In order for creation to become whole or saved, to be liberated from the destructive effects of violence, envy, greed, and pride, sin itself must first be defeated and overcome through the redemptive work of the Holy Spirit. Once liberated, creation will again enjoy the freedom and glory of life with God (see Rom 8:19-23). Creation will once more be healthy and whole, a visible confirmation of the delight and celebration that marked the very first Sabbath.

The practical and ecological implications of this theological teaching are immense because as Christians who are led by the Holy Spirit our task is nothing less than to share in the divine work of healing, reconciliation, and celebration. Our most fundamental work is to bring a halt to those practices that disfigure creation or prevent it from achieving its full potential. Our ministry, like that of Jesus Christ, is to name, know, and love all the members of creation—ranging from the Gerasene demoniac to the lilies of the field—so that together, in spirit and in body, we can all be made whole.

For a variety of reasons, this characterization of grace as God's loving, redeeming presence within creation has fallen from cultural view. Grace has become abstract, something like a good feeling, a special gift or reward that is added as a bonus to those who try to get by in a profane world. Given that economic expansion and consumer satisfaction have become the dominant forces that shape identity, understanding, and desire, there are relatively few opportunities for us to experience God's self-involvement in the world. Everywhere we turn we see the marks of our own ingenuity and design, all imprints of a mostly utilitarian or pragmatic mind. The result is that we do not, for the most part, appreciate our life and our world as God's creation or as the site of divine hospitality and care. For many people God is either entirely absent or made to be manifest through vigorous, sometimes desperate, emotional effort. In this context faith becomes a work in which we project or invent a god who (we hope) can meet the worries or desires of an anxious or unsatisfied ego. It ceases to be a fitting response to grace appropriately appreciated and received.

The denial and dissimulation of grace, though always a human temptation, became especially pronounced and systematic in the modern world. While it is common to refer to this development as the "desanctification" or "disenchantment" of the world, the key element in this process is the emptying out of the world's divine referent. What begins to emerge is the idea of pure "nature," a conception that reduces material reality to a mathematical and mechanical core that operates according to "natural laws" and can be appropriated by us as a resource for our own ends. As natural, the world does not find its origin or end in God. It does not bear witness to a divine intention. If it has any purpose at all, it is of a wholly immanent sort that can be understood—and exploited—through scientific and technological effort. In the time of modernity, as Bruce Foltz describes it, nature comes to be understood as autonomous, self-subsistent, and self-contained. It is pure exteriority, only a surface, having no face or deep interiority (sanctity) that might challenge an idolatrous gaze or utilitarian grasp.[17]

Bronislaw Szerszynski has recently, and persuasively, argued that disenchantment of this sort does not amount to a complete break from religion. Instead what we see is the emergence of a "technological sublime" that exalts in the human power to dominate and manage nature. This power, rather than any divine intention, is seen as the way for humans to return to the Edenic condition of peace and harmony between people and nature. Technological mastery, in other words, depends upon the collapse of the sacred into the empirical world, a shift from seeing the world as created by God to suit a divine goal to an immanent, natural order that has as its only concern the continuation of life processes.[18] Indeed, technology becomes the new civil religion, the officially sanctioned path to salvation that promises to fulfill all the aspirations of the human heart.

What we need to appreciate is that this modern, technological orientation represents a denial of God's grace. This becomes especially evident when we consider the full significance of the incarnation of God in the person of Jesus Christ. As Philip Sherard has clearly indicated, when creation is reduced to brute nature what is lost is the sense of God's presence and involvement in the world. Because Christ is the concrete site in which the "intimate meeting and inextricable intertwining of the spiritual and material" becomes most pronounced and evident, we must believe that God forever enters into creation from within and is its dynamic, pulsating energy.[19] God's presence in the body of Jesus is also God's direct pledge to be present in every other body of creation too. This does not mean that God is to be identified with creation or that creatures somehow possess God. Rather, God is present to all creation as the gift of life. Were this gift or grace ever to be withheld, we would simply cease to be.

As we can now see, an understanding of the world *as creation*, as the concrete expression of God's abiding and sustaining grace, is significantly at odds with modern forms of civil religion that establish human ambition as the center of reference. Indeed, the religions of technology and economic expansion represent some of the most systemic distortions of the life of faith because they entail the eclipse of God and lead to the destruction of the earth. What began nobly as the Baconian dream to alleviate human misery and abolish superstition has resulted in unprecedented species and habitat loss and unparalleled ecosystems degradation. Given its wholly profane starting point, it is not surprising that salvation itself, once understood in terms of the divinization of creation, would come to be gnostically defined as the escape from a world now destined to be destroyed in a fiery oblivion.

If we are to avert this scenario of ecological and social doom, we will need to practice a more authentic faith, one that honors God and creation. We will need to avoid the displacement of God's grace from the world, a displacement that prompts us to reduce God's presence to the inner, private life of the anxious believer or religious consumer. Biblical faith claims the whole person and the whole world, for God is not simply interested in our detachable, immortal souls. Rather, God engages us on the wide level of our hearts, minds, and bodies as they interact in concert with other bodies. This is why we proclaim the resurrection of the body and the reconciliation of "all things" on earth and in heaven through the blood of Christ's cross (Col 1:20). True faith is not the occasion for an escape from the world, but is rather the invitation to draw nearer to the heart of reality and there discover the life of God at work. Dietrich Bonhoeffer said it best when he observed:

It is only by living completely in this world that one learns to have faith. . . . By this-worldliness I mean living unreservedly in life's duties, problems, successes and failures, experiences and perplexities. In so doing we throw ourselves completely into the arms of God, taking seriously, not our own sufferings, but those of God in the world—watching with Christ in Gethsemane. That, I think, is faith; that is *metanoia*; and that is how one becomes a person and a Christian.[20]

Bonhoeffer's call for a this-worldly faith is not a dismissal of God. It is rather the recognition that as we turn away from creation, perhaps in pursuit of a more abstract human ambition, we at the same time turn away from God's presence. In a 1932 sermon entitled "Thy Kingdom Come," Bonhoeffer made this explicit: "Whoever evades the earth does not find God. They only find another world; their own, better, more beautiful, more peaceful world [the world of death camps and dead zones?] . . . Whoever loves God, loves God as Lord of the earth as it is; and whoever loves the earth loves it as God's earth."[21]

False religion follows from the displacement of grace and leads to our common degradation. As grace is severed from God's involvement in the whole creation, and is relocated in the personal aspirations of the anxious believer—this being the "cheap" grace we give ourselves—what is lost is the sacramental sense that enables us to appreciate the earth as the created realm in which all life is given its meaning and purpose by God. What is lost is the hope of salvation in which we participate in the costly, precious, celebratory life of God as revealed in the ministry, suffering, and resurrection of Christ. Without God's grace we relegate ourselves to a dark, cold, wholly immanent universe in which we depend on ourselves for the creation of any heat or light. Given our histories, it is plain to see that fire and bombs have been our preferred means.

If we are to practice a better faith, one that honors creation and its Creator, we will need to become reacquainted with God's costly grace. This cannot happen in the abstract or through mere personal will or effort. What we need are daily practices that will draw us more honestly and deeply into creation, for it is here that we will find God at work. We cannot demonstrate an authentic faith if we are not in multiple ways in sympathetic alignment with the action of God, for faith—whether understood as the faith through which we believe (*fides qua creditur*) or the content of faith that is believed (*fides quae creditur*)—becomes false if it is not responsive and tuned to God's self-involvement in creation and community. Faith is a gift arising out of our meeting with God. What we most need, therefore, is to encounter God's grace in a fresh and concrete manner so as not to misunderstand who God is and what God expects of us.

If we return for a moment to Nicholas Lash's trenchant remark that "Life is God, given," the first thing that needs to be observed is that from an agrarian point of view, most of us are fairly cut off from life. In certain respects, we could say that the time of modernity is precisely the intensification of this experience of separation. Think here of Henry David Thoreau's observation: "Men nowhere, east or west, live yet a *natural* life, round which the vine clings, and which the elm willingly shadows. Man would desecrate it by his touch, and so the beauty of the world remains veiled to him. He needs not only to be spiritualized, but *naturalized*, on the soil of the earth."[22] This reference to a "natural life," while theologically problematic (a better formulation would be a "creaturely life"), is especially insightful today because it indicates the multiple ways we have devised—climate-controlled housing, automobiles, suburbia, fast food, virtual reality—to insulate ourselves from the very action of life processes. More than ever before, Thoreau's advice to us, as recorded in his *Journal* (March 12, 1853), still stands: "Dwell as near as possible to the channel in which your life flows." The point is not simply to experience "Nature," but to be open to and let oneself be inspired by God's economy of grace.

Today our living mostly occurs within a synthetic or stylized world of our own making, a world in which we are insulated from neighbors, farmers, and wetlands alike. The heavens, rather than declaring the glory of God, have become unavailable to us for all the shining of our city lights. The mountains and hills do not break forth into song, nor do the trees of the fields clap their hands in praise of God (Isa 55:12), because they have been reduced to stockpiles of resources to be used in praise of ourselves. Ours is an increasingly commodified and virtual world, a world driven by "the career of money" (Berry), with its relentless preying upon our natural and human neighborhoods. In this world of the "spectacle" (Guy Debord), our language of God readily becomes thin and forced, almost ornamental, because it has lost its home and inspiration in the action of God in our midst. If we (minimally) claim God to be the source and sustainer of life, and given our practical ignorance of life's richness, complexity, and mystery, how can we be sure that our ideas about

God are not simply the projections of a fanciful or fearful mind? Not surprisingly, we learn to depend more and more on emotional or stylistic props to keep theological language alive. Put rather bluntly, can we know or appreciate Jesus as the bread of life (John 6:35) when we are ignorant of the life of bread?

Another way to state this is to say that we live in an anonymous economy in which things ("goods") and relations ("transactions") are not properly named or clearly understood in terms of their reference to and dependence upon God's economy. The potential for abuse and desecration, given this anonymity, is huge. For most of us economic choices, ranging from the food we eat to the cars we drive and the products we buy, take place in an immense cloud of ignorance. We do not know where these "goods" come from, under what conditions they were produced, what their real or total costs were, or if the social and biological contexts of their production were compromised or not. Our connection with reality is mostly indirect and attenuated, reduced to the ease of pushing buttons, turning dials, or laying down a credit card. Besides being an economy of "the one-night stand" in which we have a good time but do not show any commitment to know or understand, our decision making reflects a profound failure of imagination. "Most of us cannot imagine the wheat beyond the bread, or the farmer beyond the wheat, or the farm beyond the farmer, or the [social and geo-biological] history beyond the farm. . . . Most people appear to assume that when they have paid their money for these things they have entirely met their obligations." Berry says we have in fact become superstitious in our thinking, for what could be more superstitious than to believe that "money brings forth food"?[23]

Our practical separation from the sources of life—photosynthesis, humus, earthworms, bees, chickens, communal memory and tradition, family nurture, neighborly support—is of immense theological significance because what is at issue is our separation from the ways of God at work there. As Berry understands it, religion is about binding us to the sources of life and to the energy that keeps life on the move. This may sound rather mundane until we recall that energy is "the only universal currency."[24] Literally everything, from the shining of stars to the movement of planets and microscopic bodies, depends upon it. No wonder, then that William Blake referred to energy as "Eternal Delight." It is the concrete manifestation of divine love that binds us to each other.

Think for a moment about Moses' encounter with God in the burning bush in Exodus 3. Burning is one of the most visible ways in which energy is released and made useful in the processes of life. Is it an accident that it is precisely at this moment, in a burning bush that gives heat and life but is not itself consumed or destroyed, that God's name as the one "who is" and "will be" is revealed? I like to think that this scene conveys in a most practical and intimate manner God's commitment to be with us in the fundamental processes of respiration and digestion, the perpetual cooking of food that is our body. God does not come to us from far off, but moves in the midst of the very unfolding of life itself, feeding us and sustaining us. And so when we burn energy indiscriminately or ignorantly, without regard for its origin in God, or when we presume to be in control of energy—as we clearly do in our nuclear and fossil fuel economies—we not only cheapen life by transforming energy's life-giving potential into a wasteful and destructive force. We also cheapen the grace of God.

If we are to recover a sense for the costly grace that is God's dedication to be with us, we must learn the daily, practical *metanoia* that is our turning toward the world and to each other. But what kind of "turning" is it that we are talking about? It must not be a forsaking of the world, for as Berry reminds us, "It is the mind / turned away from the world / that turns against it."[25] Think here of the well-intentioned religious sentiment that aspires to an otherworldly heaven. What makes this Gnostic sentiment dangerous is its potential to deny the divine logic of incarnation, and so bypasses or condemns the material world. "Though Heaven is certainly more important than the earth if all they say about it is true, it is still morally incidental to it and dependent on it, and I can only imagine it and desire it in terms of what I know of the earth. And so my questions do not aspire beyond the earth. They aspire *toward* it and *into* it. Perhaps they aspire *through* it."[26]

From an agrarian point of view our first priority must be to "turn toward" the world and to each other, and learn in this turning the ways of attention, care, compassion, mercy, forgiveness, and celebration. This positive turning cannot be reduced to a "back to the land" movement because what Berry is really after is a transformation of consciousness made possible by a change in daily habits, a repositioning of human life in terms of its larger biological, social, and divine contexts. This is why Berry has championed the domes-

tic arts—"the husbandry and wifery of the world"—and the cultivation of local economies. The goal to decrease the distance between
production and consumption, or to increase the familiarity between
workers, is not simply so that we can have more nutritious food, keep
more money in the community, or decrease our transportation costs
(as significant as these are). Rather, the goal is to build our affection
and faith, to give our love and our hope a more informed and honest
(less emotive or fanciful) context. It is to make our aspirations more
realistic by compelling us to live with, and thus potentially correct
and improve, the often destructive effects of what we do.

What this means and entails can be seen if we consider something as simple as the family meal. When we eat together we do
much more than simply consume fuel. We share the grace of nourishment and companionship. But to do this responsibly and faithfully we must first make sure that the food we eat has been grown,
produced, and prepared in ways that honor God as the giver of every
good and perfect gift. This will not be easy since most of us now eat
with unprecedented ignorance. We are not aware of how our modern
food industry is based on injustice, cruelty, destruction, and sacri-
lege. As we become more faithful participants in the food economy,
perhaps by growing some of our own food or by purchasing directly
from organic producers, we will see the costliness and loveliness
of God's many gifts, and thus perhaps be inclined to eat with more
gratitude and less waste. We will see how our own health depends
on the health of each other and the vitality of our ecological communities, and so take steps to protect and nurture the sources of our
collective life.

None of this is possible without a profound spiritual conversion.
On one level, we can understand this conversion in terms of a transformation of vision. In his Sabbath poems Berry describes our intel-
lects as ravenous in their desire to know. Our hunger, in so many
instances, stems from the desire to control the world, a desire amply
borne out in our highly monitored, managed, and manipulated
world. What this desire does, however, is lead to a kind of blindness
resulting from the imposition of the ego's designs upon the world.
The ego clouds or dims our apprehension of another because it
comes between self and other, can even turn into an imposition of
the self upon another. What is necessary, therefore, is a "knowing of
the dark":

> O bent by fear and sorrow, now bend down,
> Leave word and argument, be dark and still,
> And come into the joy of healing shade.
> Rest from your work. Be still and dark until
> You grow as unopposing, unafraid
> As the young trees, without thought or belief;
> Until the shadow Sabbath light has made,
> Shudders, breaks open, shines in every leaf. (*TC*, 31)

Becoming dark consists of a certain kind of halting, ceasing, or desisting from our controlling, comprehending ways so that a Sabbath light, what we should here call the grace of God, can show itself in the splendor of the leaf or in the smiling of a child. In becoming still, in practicing a Sabbath way of being—a practice entirely foreign to the modern ethos which knows no rest—we embark on a path that succeeds not by the force of our own might but by the grace of God. This is a path we travel by faith, love, and hope, by the humble work that resembles prayer because it is the grateful acceptance of creation understood as a divine gift. And so Berry continues:

> The mind that comes to rest is tended
> In ways that it cannot intend:
> Is borne, preserved, and comprehended
> By what it cannot comprehend.
>> Your Sabbath, Lord, thus keeps us by
>> Your will, not ours. And it is fit
>> Our only choice should be to die
>> Into that rest, or out of it. (*TC*, 7)

Of course, faith is not simply a form of halting. It is the dying of the ego so that the work of God can take root in us. True, abundant life, life that complements the grace of God at work all around us, begins when we realize that we are nothing alone, but become what God intends when we, like a grain of wheat, fall into the soil and die, thereby producing much fruit (John 12:24). This is the practice of resurrection.

It is important to emphasize that Berry is talking about the *practice* of resurrection. Resurrection, from an agrarian and Christian point of view, is not some abstract notion in which people are suddenly and mysteriously reborn or resuscitated. It is, rather, the effect of daily affection and care for the ecological and social communities in which we find ourselves. It follows from the responsibility we assume for each other and in the detailed, mundane generosity and gratitude we show and have for each other when we share a meal, comfort the sick, perform good work, and lend a helping hand. When we practice resurrection what we do is put our lives in sympathetic and practical alignment with the action of God as revealed in the flesh of Jesus Christ, with the result that our living, rather than bringing injury to creation's members, enlivens and builds up the neighborhoods of which we are a part. To practice resurrection is to redirect the ego so that instead of serving oneself one opens oneself to the needs and nurture of others, thus creating a network of relationships maintained by patient attention and long-term fidelity.

What this means practically speaking can be seen in Berry's advocacy for local economies. In a local economy producers and consumers know each other. They share a common life sustained by a region. Because face-to-face contact is regular and sustained, we make and purchase with greater care because we will have to live with the effects of our work. Nobody with any neighborly sense would sell a useless, defective, or destructive product to a friend, or compel them to live in a toxic dump! And so the members of a local community work with an eye to the improvement and protection of the entire neighborhood. In a local economy injustice is more readily averted because it is easily seen to be personally destructive. Sharing in a membership of parts we learn to appreciate how we are each "inextricably joined to each other, indebted to each other, receiving significance and worth from each other and from the whole."[27]

Communal upbuilding, what Paul called the work of the Holy Spirit, is our highest calling as creatures made in the image of God. What Berry's agrarian and Sabbath vision enables us to see is that the borders of community do not end with the human, but extend to the whole creation. When we move according to a Sabbath vision what we will discover is the inexhaustible love of God that renders the whole creation a delight. The seventeenth-century poet Thomas Traherne put it well when he wrote: "Lov is the true Means by which the World is Enjoyed. Our Lov to others, and Others Lov to us. We ought therfore above all Things to get acquainted with the Nature of Lov · for Lov is the Root and Foundation of Nature: Lov is the Soul of Life, and Crown of Rewards. If we cannot be satisfied in the Nature of Lov we can never be satisfied at all."[28] It is as we commit ourselves to practices of delight, as when we devote ourselves to the exacting care of particular plots of creation and the generous hospitality of neighbors and strangers alike, that we through faith receive and enter fully into the grace of God.

Berry's agrarian vision invites us to love the world deeply not because the world is all that there is. Rather, it is only through a patient, detailed, sympathetic engagement with others, what Bonhoeffer described as the throwing of ourselves completely into the arms of God, that we will ever come to see, appreciate, and give thanks for the love of God at work therein. This resolute, hopeful, humble, and faithful engagement leads us into what Berry calls "the country of marriage." Practical fidelity of this sort not only leads us "into the care of neighbors . . . into care for one another and for the good gifts of Heaven and Earth." [29] It also forms the indispensable, concrete context for faith that welcomes and lives by and through the grace of God.

Berry understands the life of faith is a dance:

> The way I go is
> marriage to this place,
> grace beyond chance,
> love's braided dance
> covering the world. (*CP*, 268)

And so he invites us:

> Come into the life of the body, the one body
> granted to you in all the history of time.
> Come into the body's economy, its daily work,
> and its replenishment at mealtimes and at night.
> Come into the body's thanksgiving, when it knows
> and acknowledges itself a living soul.
> Come into the dance of the community, joined
> in a circle, hand in hand, the dance of the eternal
> love of women and men for one another
> and of neighbors and friends for one another. [30]

Notes

CHAPTER 1

1   This is sometimes described as the "return of religion," but this seems like a return only for academics solidly ensconced within the purified confines of the (supposedly) secular university. In fact, religion never left. For a representative of this "return" model, see Jacques Derrida, "Faith and Knowledge: The Two Sources of 'Religion' at the Limits of Reason Alone," in *Religion*, eds. Jacques Derrida and Gianni Vattimo (Stanford: Stanford University Press, 1998), 1–77.

2   For select scholarly discussion, see Johan Meuleman, ed., *Islam in the Era of Globalization* (London: RoutledgeCurzon, 2002); Talal Asad, *Formations of the Secular: Christianity, Islam, Modernity* (Stanford: Stanford University Press, 2003); Khaled Abou El Fadl, *Islam and the Challenge of Democracy* (Princeton: Princeton University Press, 2004); and Scott M. Thomas, *The Global Resurgence of Religion and the Transformation of International Relations* (London: Palgrave Macmillan, 2005). For more charged and contested, though influential, accounts, see Samuel Huntington, *The Clash of Civilizations and the Remaking of the World Order* (New York: Simon & Schuster, 1996), and Bernard Lewis, *The Crisis of Islam: Holy War and Unholy Terror* (New York: Modern Library, 2003).

3   Philip Jenkins, *The Next Christendom* (Oxford: Oxford University Press, 2003). See also David Martin, *Pentecostalism: The World Their Parish* (Oxford: Blackwell, 2002); Lamin Sanneh, *Whose Religion is Christianity?* (Grand Rapids: Eerdmans, 2003); and Lamin Sanneh and Joel Carpenter, eds., *The Changing Face of Christianity: Africa, the West, and the World* (Oxford: Oxford University Press, 2005).

4   For a particularly scintillating account of the latter, see Bernard-Henri Lévy, *Who Killed Daniel Pearl?* (London: Melville House, 2003), which tracks Pearl's killer to his time in the halls of the London School of Economics.

5   See, for instance, the International Monetary Fund (IMF)'s definition of globalization as "the increasing integration of economies around the world, particularly through trade and financial flows. The term sometimes also refers to the movement of people (labor) and knowledge (technology) across international borders." As one would expect, the IMF sees this largely (almost entirely) as a positive cultural development for the flow of capital. See IMF Issues Brief, *Globalization: Threat or Opportunity?* (April 12, 2000), available at http://www.imf.org/external/np/exr/ib/2000/041200.htm. For a more recent and nuanced discussion in the IMF orbit, see M. Ayhan Kose et al., *Financial Globalization: A Reappraisal*, IMF Working Paper 06/189 (August 2006).

6   This tends to be the formulation most commonly found in antiglobalization literature, such as Naomi Klein, *No Logo*, 2nd ed. (New York: Picador, 2002), or Michael Hardt and Antonio Negri, *Empire* (Cambridge, Mass.: Harvard University Press, 2000).

7   One could also suggest a theological parallel: just as Stanley Hauerwas argues that "ethics" is always qualified (there is no "neutral" ethics), so too globalization is always qualified—it will always be a particular kind of globalization.

8   For a helpful overview of the literature on the secularization thesis, see Kevin M. Schultz, "Secularization: A Bibliographic Essay," *Hedgehog Review* 8 (2006): 170–77.

9   See Max Weber's seminal reflections in "Science as Vocation," in *From Max Weber: Essays in Sociology*, trans. and ed., H. H. Gerth and C. Wright Mills, 129–56 (New York: Oxford University Press, 1977). See also Marcel Gauchet, *The Disenchantment of the World: A Political History of Religion*, trans. Oscar Burge (Princeton: Princeton University Press, 1997).

10   Even former advocates are recanting. See especially Peter L. Berger, "The Desecularization of the World: A Global Overview," in *The Desecularization of the World: Resurgent Religion and World Politics*, ed. Peter L. Berger (Grand Rapids: Eerdmans, 1999). For other reassessments by former faithful of the secularization thesis, see David Martin, *On Secularization: Towards a Revised General Theory* (Aldershot: Ashgate, 2005)— already anticipated in Martin, "Towards Eliminating the Concept of Secularization," in *Penguin Survey of the Social Sciences*, ed. J. Gould (Hammondsworth: Penguin, 1965), 169–82—and Harvey Cox, *Fire from Heaven: The Rise of Pentecostal Spirituality and the Reshaping of Religion in the Twenty-first Century* (Reading, Mass.: Addison-Wesley, 1995). For a requiem with little eulogy, see Rodney Stark, "Secularization, R.I.P.," *Sociology of Religion* 60 (1999): 249–73. For something of a last-gasp but

nuanced defense of the secularization thesis (suggesting that the rumors of its death are perhaps a bit exaggerated), see Steve Bruce, *God Is Dead: Secularization in the West* (Oxford: Blackwell, 2002). For rather excited hopes for a new "secular" religion, see Luc Ferry, *Man Made God: The Meaning of Life*, trans. David Pellauer (Chicago: University of Chicago Press, 2002), and Gianni Vattimo, *After Christianity*, trans. Luca D'Isanto (New York: Columbia University Press, 2002).

11   For discussion of the case of Europe as an exceptional case of secularization, see George Weigel, *The Cube and the Cathedral: Europe, America, and Politics without God* (New York: Basic Books, 2005). Such European exceptionalism has been contested most rigorously by Grace Davie. See Davie, *Religion in Britain since 1945: Believing without Belonging* (Oxford: Blackwell, 1994), and more recently, Davie, "Is Europe an Exceptional Case?" *Hedgehog Review* 8 (2006): 23–33. Graham Ward also sees a certain desecularization in Europe; see Ward, *True Religion*, Blackwell Manifestoes (Oxford: Blackwell, 2003).

12   Another line of critique, or perhaps revision of the secularization thesis, emphasizes that neither "modernity" nor "secularization" are monolithic phenomena. Rather, we should speak of "multiple modernities" yielding multiple secularizations: thus secularization in France looks very different than it does in the United States; the same would be true in comparisons of India and Germany. For relevant discussion, see Martin, *On Secularization*, 123–40; Charles Taylor, *A Secular Age* (Cambridge, Mass.: Harvard University Press, 2007), 424–37; and Peter J. Katzenstein, "Multiple Modernities as Limits to Secular Europeanization?, in *Religion in an Expanding Europe*, ed. T. A. Byrnes and P. J. Katzenstein, 1–33 (Cambridge: Cambridge University Press, 2006).

13   For an analysis, see Derrida, "Faith and Knowledge."

14   Here the work of Michael Budde is particularly insightful. See Budde, *The (Magic) Kingdom of God: Christianity and Global Culture Industries* (Boulder, Colo.: Westview, 1998) and Michael Budde and Robert W. Brimlow, *Christianity Incorporated: How Big Business Is Buying the Church* (Grand Rapids: Brazos, 2002). There is also a growing school of thought that, in the face of the failure of the secularization thesis, accounts for the persistence of religion in economic terms. Thus Ekelund et al., in a way that confirms the persistence of modernist reductionism, claim that "the course of Christianity and its continuous evolution cannot be fully understood outside the context of Adam Smith's conception of economics and competition." Working from that methodological assumption, however, they nonetheless conclude that "[f]or all societies, due to the intimate connection between psychology and economics, markets for magic and religion of some form will continue to exist." See Robert B. Ekelund, Jr. et al., *The Marketplace of Christianity* (Cambridge, Mass.: MIT Press, 2006), 271.

15 Consider, for instance, the vestiges of religious language found in Bush administration's 2002 *National Security Strategy* which outlines a foreign policy driven by "freedom." For discussion, see James K. A. Smith, "The Gospel of Freedom, or Another Gospel? Theology, Empire, and American Foreign Policy," in *Political Theology* (forthcoming) and Wes Avram, ed., *Anxious about Empire: Theological Essays on the New Global Realities* (Grand Rapids: Brazos, 2004).

16 For a confessional appropriation and affirmation of the Nietzschean announcement of the death of "God," see Jean-Luc Marion, *Idol and Distance,* trans. Thomas A. Carlson (New York: Fordham University Press, 2001 [1977]), and Marion, *God without Being,* trans. Thomas A. Carlson (Chicago: University of Chicago Press, 1991 [1982]).

17 Here religious concerns about justice overlap with broader discussions concerning the ethics of globalization. Consider, for instance, John H. Dunning, ed., *Making Globalization Good: The Moral Challenges of Global Capitalism* (Oxford: Oxford University Press, 2004); David Held, *Global Covenant: The Social Democratic Alternative to the Washington Consensus* (Cambridge and Malden, Mass., Polity, 2004); Rebecca Todd Peters, *In Search of the Good Life: The Ethics of Globalization* (London: Continuum, 2004); and Peter Singer, *One World: The Ethics of Globalization,* 2nd ed. (New Haven: Yale University Press, 2004).

18 See Dwight N. Hopkins' provocative essay, "The Religion of Globalization," in *Religions/Globalizations: Theories and Cases,* ed. Dwight N. Hopkins et al., 7–32 (Durham, N.C.: Duke University Press, 2001). Hopkins argues that "globalization of monopoly finance capitalist culture is itself a religion," complete with its own god (the monopolistic concentration of wealth), its own theological anthropology (the consumer), and its own theology (neoliberalism). This "theological" account of globalization is persuasive, but his prescription for an antidote (liberation theology) is insufficient. For the reasons why, see Daniel M. Bell Jr., *Liberation Theology after the End of History: The Refusal to Cease Suffering* (London: Routledge, 2001).

19 See the exemplary analysis and discussion in William T. Cavanaugh, *Theopolitical Imagination* (Edinburgh: T&T Clark, 2003).

20 See Max Stackhouse, ed., *God and Globalization,* vol. 1, *Religion and the Powers of the Common Life* (Harrisburg, Pa.: Trinity, 2000); Stackhouse, ed., *God and Globalization,* vol. 2, *The Spirit and the Modern Authorities* (Harrisburg, Pa.: Trinity, 2001); and Stackhouse, ed., *God and Globalization,* vol. 3, *Christ and the Dominions of Civilization* (Harrisburg, Pa.: Trinity, 2003).

21 See Peter Heslam, ed., *Globalization and the Good* (Grand Rapids: Eerdmans, 2004), and Bob Goudzwaard, *Globalization and the Kingdom of God* (Grand Rapids: Baker, 2001).

22 Consider, for example, Cavanaugh, *Theopolitical Imagination*; Bell, *Liberation Theology after the End of History*; Avram, ed., *Anxious about Empire*;

Brian J. Walsh and Sylvia C. Keesmaat, *Colossians Remixed: Subverting the Empire* (Downers Grove, Ill.: InterVarsity, 2004). Because of its polemical tone—and because such discourses are so hastily dismissed—I have generally tried to avoid "empire" talk. However, the shape of concerns about religion and globalization cannot avoid the analyses articulated by Michael Hardt and Antonio Negri in *Empire* (Cambridge, Mass.: Harvard University Press, 2000) and *Multitude* (New York: Penguin, 2004). I engage their paradigm more directly in my essay, "The Gospel of Freedom, or Another Gospel?"

23 For a discussion, see John Milbank, *Theology and Social Theory: Beyond Secular Reason* (Oxford: Blackwell, 1990), 27–48. More recently, Milbank has diagnosed the antithesis between Catholic faith and "the central premises of liberalism which, as Pierre Manent says, are based in Manichean fashion upon the ontological primacy of evil and violence: at the beginning is a threatened individual, piece of property or racial terrain. This is *not* the same as an Augustinian acknowledgment of original sin, perversity and frailty—a hopeful doctrine, since it affirms that all-pervasive evil for which we really cannot account . . . is yet all the same a contingent intrusion upon reality, which can one day be fully overcome. . . . Liberalism instead begins with a disguised naturalization of original sin as original egotism." See John Milbank, "Liberality versus Liberalism," *Telos* 134 (2006): 2. Cf. chap. 2 below, "The Gift of Ruling."

24 This collection includes only select papers from the conference. For a complete list of research presentations, see the program at http://www.calvin.edu/scs/lfp. Some of the papers from the conference not included here have been published elsewhere. See, for example, Steven Bouma-Prediger and Brian J. Walsh, *Beyond Homelessness: Christian Faith in a Culture of Displacement* (Grand Rapids: Eerdmans, 2008), and Peter J. Jankowski, "Embrace: A Theologically Informed Peace Psychology," *Christian Scholar's Review* 36 (2007): 141–57.

25 Berger was the opening plenary speaker for the conference that engendered this book, and his intervention at the conference established a platform (or foil) for many of the conversations. For the basic shape of his talk, see Berger, "Desecularization of the World."

26 Peter Berger, *A Rumor of Angels: Modern Society and the Rediscovery of the Supernatural* (Harmondsworth: Penguin, 1969), 119.

27 Berger, *Rumor of Angels*, 30. Berger later conceded that, though his own work contributed to the literature which espoused the secularization thesis, it had become clear that the thesis was essentially mistaken. See Peter Berger, "Desecularization of the World," 2. Cf. also Peter Berger, *Questions of Faith: A Skeptical Affirmation of Christianity* (Oxford: Blackwell, 2004), 99.

28 Berger, *Rumor of Angels*, 39.

29 Berger, *Rumor of Angels*, 59.

30 Cf. Richard Ekins, "Secular Fundamentalism and Democracy," *Journal of Markets and Morality* 8 (2005): 81–93.

31 This does not preclude, however, something like Charles Taylor's project, which is a descriptive account of a shift that clearly happened in "the West," namely, "a move from a society where belief in God is unchallenged and indeed, unproblematic, to one in which it is understood to be one option among others, and frequently not the easiest to embrace" (*Secular Age*, 3). Thus, Taylor wants to tell the story of secularization not necessarily as a decline in religious belief or practice, or even necessarily as an institutional marginalization of religion, but in such a way that accounts for this shift in plausibility structures. For Taylor, we are secular to the extent that we accept that "belief in God is no longer axiomatic"—even if we do, in fact, believe in God. While Taylor has no truck with a prescriptive form of the secularization thesis, he takes it to be the case that we inhabit "a secular age" in this sense: "We live in a condition where we cannot help but be aware that there are a number of different construals, views which intelligent, reasonably undeluded people, of good will, can and do disagree on" (*Secular Age*, 11). What he gives us, then, is a nontriumphalist account of the shift in plausibility structures (in modernity, he'll emphasize) that ushered in this state of affairs, our secular age.

32 See Habermas, "Faith and Knowledge," a 2001 address upon his acceptance of the Peace Prize awarded by the German Book Trade; Habermas, "Religion in the Public Sphere," presented in April 2004 at the University of Lodz in Poland; and finally, Habermas' engagement with (then) Cardinal Ratzinger in *Dialektik der Säkularisierung: Über Vernunft und Religion* (Freiburg im Breslau: Herder Verlag, 2005).

33 See George Weigel, *The Cube and the Cathedral: Europe, America, and Politics without God* (New York: Basic Books, 2005), 110 and *passim*. What I suggest is similar between Habermas and Weigel (which might also explain, by a certain triangulation, how Ratzinger fits in this mix) is that both offer a somewhat genealogical reading of the secular that won't let the secular forget its religious roots.

34 An important piece of Ward and Milbank's project is a reinvigorated metaphysics of "participation" that, in a sense, "re-enchants" the world, issuing in what Ward calls a "sacramental worldview" (*True Religion*, viii, 12). This also involves a critique of the disenchanted metaphysics of modernity. In this respect, it is very interesting to note a passage from Berger's 1969 work, *A Rumor of Angels*: "It was only with the onset of secularization that the divine fullness began to recede, until the point was reached when the empirical sphere became both all-encompassing and perfectly closed in upon itself" (118). This echoes the later critique of univocal metaphysics articulated by Ward, Mil-

bank, and Catherine Pickstock. For discussion, see James K. A. Smith, *Introducing Radical Orthodoxy: Mapping a Post-Secular Theology* (Grand Rapids: Baker Academic, 2004), chap. 6.

35 Slavoj Žižek, *The Fragile Absolute—Or, Why Is the Christian Legacy Worth Fighting For?* (London: Verso, 2004); Žižek, "The Thrilling Romance of Orthodoxy," in *Theology and the Political: The New Debate*, ed. Creston Davis, John Milbank, and Slavoj Žižek, 52–71 (Durham, N.C.: Duke University Press, 2005).

36 Jeffrey Stout, *Democracy and Tradition* (Princeton: Princeton University Press, 2004). Also relevant here is Richard Rorty's recanting of a strict secularism in response to criticisms from Nicholas Wolterstorff. See Nicholas Wolterstorff, "An Engagement with Rorty," *Journal of Religious Ethics* 31 (2003): 129–39 and Richard Rorty, "Religion in the Public Sphere: A Reconsideration," *Journal of Religious Ethics* 31 (2003): 141–49.

37 William Connolly, *Why I Am Not a Secularist* (Minneapolis: University of Minnesota Press, 1999).

38 On the distinction, see Asad, *Formations of the Secular*, 21–66. For a critical discussion of Asad, see James K. A. Smith, "Secularity, Religion, and the Politics of Ambiguity," *Journal for Cultural and Religious Theory* 6 (2005): 116–22.

39 By a postmodern critique of knowledge, I do not mean only a deconstructive critique of modernity as articulated by Derrida—though this would be an important voice. By a postmodern critique of knowledge here, I just mean twentieth-century accounts of knowledge that articulated trenchant criticisms of the modern account of rationality as ahistorical and universal—what Gadamer famously described as "the Enlightenment prejudice against prejudice." With this understanding, a broadly postmodern critique of Enlightenment rationality was articulated by Heidegger, Gadamer, Kuhn, Lyotard, Geertz, and others.

40 Ward, *True Religion*, 1.

41 Connolly, *Why I Am Not a Secularist*, 6.

42 Ward, *True Religion*, 130–31.

43 Habermas' invocation of "the image of God" as a basis for thinking about human nature might be seen along the same lines (Jürgen Habermas, *The Future of Human Nature* [Cambridge: Cambridge University Press, 2003]). Consider also process thought as a movement basically internal to modernity that nevertheless challenges stories of disenchantment. See, for example, David Ray Griffin, ed., *The Reenchantment of Science: Postmodern Proposals* (Albany: SUNY Press, 1998) and Griffin, *Reenchantment without Supernaturalism: A Process Philosophy of Religion* (Ithaca: Cornell University Press, 2001). And one might also point to renewed discourses concerning "spirit" in the sciences. See Philip Clayton, *Mind and Emergence: From Quantum to Consciousness* (Oxford: Oxford University Press, 2004), and Amos Yong, "Discerning Spirit[s]

in the Natural World: Toward a Typology of 'Spirit' in the Religion and Science Conversation," *Theology and Science* 3 (2005): 315–29.

44 Connolly, *Why I Am Not a Secularist*, 15. He emphasizes pluralizing the sources of enchantment, such that he imagines a "nontheistic enchantment" as one possibility.

45 Berger, *Rumor of Angels*, 118.

46 Graham Ward, *Cultural Transformation and Religious Practice* (Cambridge: Cambridge University Press, 2005), 9.

47 Graham Ward, *Cities of God* (London: Routledge, 2001), chap. 3.

48 Slavoj Žižek, "I Plead Guilty—But Where Is the Judgment?" *Nepantla: Views from South* 3 (2002): 581. Žižek goes on to suggest that "paganism is the ultimate Christian dream."

49 J. R. R. Tolkien, "On Fairy-Stories," in *Tree and Leaf* (London: HarperCollins, 2001 [1964]), 7–17.

50 A notable exception is David Harvey, *The New Imperialism* (New York: Oxford, 2003).

51 Janel M. Curry, "Introduction to the Theme Issue" [on Geography in Christian Perspective], *Christian Scholar's Review* 31, no. 4 (2002): 353.

52 Curry, "Introduction to the Theme Issue," 355.

53 Iain Wallace, "A Christian Reading of the Global Economy," in *Geography and Worldview: A Christian Reconnaissance*, ed. H. Aay and S. Griffioen (Lanham, Md.: University Press of America, 1998), 37. Chapter 6 below is part of a research agenda on "Geography, Social Theory, and the Theological Turn," which has included earlier articles on such as Wallace, "Globalization: Discourse of Destiny or Denial?" in *Christian Scholar's Review* 31 (2002): 377–91, and more recently, Wallace, "Territory, Typology, Theology: Geopolitics and the Christian Scriptures," *Geopolitics* 11 (2006): 209–30.

CHAPTER 2

1 Pierre Manent, *An Intellectual History of Liberalism*, trans. Rebecca Balinski (Princeton: Princeton University Press, 1995), 3–10.

2 See Oliver O'Donovan and Joan Lockwood O'Donovan, *From Irenaeus to Grotius: A Sourcebook in Christian Political Thought, 100-1625* (Grand Rapids: Eerdmans, 1999), 231–40; 362–87; Henri de Lubac, "L'autorité de L'Eglise en matiére temporelle" and "Augustinisme Politique?" in *Théologies d'Occasion* (Paris: Desclée de Brouwer, 1984), 217–40.

3 Pierre Manent, *The City of Man*, trans. Marc A. LePain (Princeton: Princeton University Press, 1998), 25, 200–201.

4 Manent, *Intellectual History of Liberalism*, chap. 11, "Machiavelli and the Fecundity of Evil," 10–20.

5 O'Donovan and O'Donovan, *From Irenaeus to Grotius*, 1–228; Oliver O'Donovan, *The Desire of the Nations: Rediscovering the Roots of Political Theology* (Cambridge: Cambridge University Press, 1999), 193–285. For

the point about Paul and ruling by judgment alone, see 148. On *oikos* and *paideia*, see Milbank, *Theology and Social Theory*, 399.

6 For a synthesis of research on this question, see Catherine Pickstock, *After Writing: On the Liturgical Consummation of Philosophy* (Oxford: Blackwell, 1998), 140–58.

7 See O'Donovan and O'Donovan, *From Irenaeus to Grotius*, 169–231; Ernest H. Kantorowicz, *The King's Two Bodies: A Study in Medieval Political Theology* (Princeton: Princeton University Press, 1997), 42–273.

8 See Milbank, *Theology and Social Theory*, 9–27.

9 Manent, *Intellectual History of Liberalism*, 5–7; Augustine Thompson, *Cities of God: The Religion of the Italian Communes, 1125–1325* (University Park: Pennsylvania State University Press, 2005).

10 Dante, *Monarchy*, ed. Prue Shaw (Cambridge: Cambridge University Press, 1996), esp. 3.16, 91–94.

11 Manent, *City of Man*, 200–201; Thomas Aquinas, *Summa Theologiae*, II. II. Q. 129 a3 ad 4; Q 161 a1.

12 Milbank, *Theology and Social Theory*, 359–62; Aquinas, *Summa Theologiae*, II. II. Q8 a1; Q23 aa 1–7.

13 De Lubac, "L'autorité de L'Eglise en matiére temporelle" and "Augustinisme Politique?"; John Milbank, *Being Reconciled: Ontology and Pardon* (London: Routledge, 2003), 105.

14 See Pickstock, *After Writing*, 121–40.

15 See O'Donovan and O'Donovan, *From Irenaeus to Grotius*, 423–76; 517–30; Milbank, *Theology and Social Theory*, 9–27; John Neville Figgis, *From Gerson to Grotius, 1414–1625* (Cambridge: Cambridge University Press, 1907); Figgis, *The Divine Right of Kings* (Cambridge: Cambridge University Press, 1914). Also see Charles-Louis de Montesquieu, *Lettres Persanes*, ed. Jean Goldzink (Paris: PUF, 1989), where he displays a certain fascination for the absolutism of the *seraglio*. The *Encyclopédie* speaks of Islam as a more rational faith, though Voltaire eventually came to see it as intrinsically despotic. I am grateful for discussions with David Hart here.

16 See Isiduro G. Manzano O.F.M., "Individuo y Sociedad en Duns Escoto," in *Antonianium* 76 (2001): fasc. I, 43–79.

17 See Milbank, *Theology and Social Theory*.

18 See *Intellectual History of Liberalism*, chaps. 3–10, and conclusion, 20–119; *City of Man*, esp. part 2, 111–207; *Modern Liberty and Its Discontents*, ed. Daniel J. Maloney and Paul Seaton, 79–117, 197–231 (Lanham, Md.: Rowman and Littlefield, 1998).

19 Manent, *Intellectual History of Liberalism*, 65–119. Manent disallows that Rousseau is a liberal, since he seeks, albeit within modern, liberal terms, once again a mode of the positive liberty of the ancients, a coincidence of individual with civic virtue. However, the coincidence, whereby the

liberty of each would be immediately the liberty of all, is still put forward by Rousseau in terms of modern negative liberty of pure choice and survival, whether of the city or the individual. Certainly Manent admits that Rousseau and Marx after him were trying to resolve the *aporia* of liberalism—which comes first: represented civil society or the representing state?—and to this extent their ideological excesses were the consequences of liberal presuppositions. Yet because, at the limit, he himself accepts these presuppositions, Rousseau and Marx became for Manent nonliberals by virtue of their continued quest for antique *sittlichkeit* in modern guise. Yet if this quest leads logically to terror (and one can agree with Manent it does) and the problem is the perverted hybrid of liberalism with *sittlichkeit*, then the fault may lie with the impossibility of positive liberty in modern circumstances, or it may lie with liberalism itself, since an aporetic reality must periodically (or even ceaselessly) seek to resolve the dilemmas it generates. The latter view appears more logical, and on this understanding Rousseau and Marx represent part of the inevitable continuum of liberal philosophy. Manent's own Straussian perspective, which appears to combine a tragic recognition of the truth but impossibility of antique virtue, with a resignation to liberal aporias, appears every bit as postmodern as the views of the *soixante-huitardes* he would reject, since he is resigned to a kind of endless undecidability. But if this is indeed the end of history, it will always generate new perturbations beyond this end, and new post-liberal terrorisms. For Montesquieu, see *Intellectual History*, 53–65; for Tocqueville, *Intellectual History*, 103–14, and Alexis de Tocqueville, *Democracy in America*, trans. George Lawrence (New York: Doubleday, 1969), 235.

20   Thomas Aquinas, *Contra Impugnantes*, 1 cap. 4 para. 14. Here he cites Augustine in *De Doctrina Christiana*: "Everything that is not lessened by being imparted, is not, if it be possessed without being communicated, possessed as it ought to be possessed." Russell Hittenger notes that Aquinas always mirrors "every analogous use of the word *societas* by uses of the word *communicatio*: *communicatio oeconomica, communicatio spiritualis, communicatio civilis*, and so forth"; in his unpublished article, "The *Munus Regale* in John Paul II's Political Theology," 24.

21   See Natalie Zemon Davis, *The Gift in Sixteenth-Century France* (Madison: University of Wisconsin Press, 2000), 90–95.

22   One can contrast Montesquieu with James Harrington (the cavalier turned republican; never a roundhead) on this point. For Harrington, "the Senate" is not a sovereign legislative power sundered from the executive; it is rather an aristocratic assembly of the wise that offers disinterested advice to the sovereign democratic power. But the constitution of the United States was finally based more on Montesquieu

than on Harrington. See James Harrington "A System of Politics," 28–32 of chap. 5, esp. 28: "If a council capable of debate has also the result, it is oligarchy. If an assembly capable of the result has debate also, it is anarchy. Debate in a council not capable of result, and result in an assembly not capable of debate is democracy." Hence democracy, as opposed to anarchy, for Harrington/Toland contains an educatively "aristocratic" moment.

23 See Milbank, *Being Reconciled*, 192–93, and Ted V. McAllister, *Revolt against Modernity: Leo Strauss, Eric Voegelin and the Search for a Postliberal Order* (Kansas City: University Press of Kansas, 1995), 160–61. See also Seymour M. Hersh, "Annals of National Security" column in the *New Yorker* for May 12, 2003: "Selective Intelligence: How the Pentagon Out-witted the CIA," 44–52. Hersh points out that many of the neoconservative "cabal" who have set up their own intelligence network—Abram Schutz, Paul Wolfowitz, William Kristol, and Stephen Camtone—are Strauss' pupils and that Schutz together with Gary Schmitt had already developed in print a "Straussian" approach to intelligence gathering, which of course stressed that there are always more hidden secrets than one imagines. These are the very people who overrode the professional expertise of the CIA and the DIA (Defense Intelligence Agency) to insist that Iraq had massive concealed stores of weapons of mass destruction! Pointing out the predominance of German and German-Jewish names here is surely not racist, but rather a necessary indication of profoundly terrible and tragic historical ironies at work. Strauss was a German Jew who fled Hitler, yet his heirs along with many others have helped to insinuate an element of Germanic author-itarianism and paranoia at the heart of an Anglo-Saxon polity. Nor has Israel—perhaps from the outset—escaped this taint. Meanwhile a chastened Germany now has much politically to teach the Anglo-Saxon world.

24 See David Brooks' article on Whitman's essay "Democratic Vistas" in *Atlantic Monthly*, May 2003, 32–33. Brooks cites Whitman: "So will indi-viduality, and unimpeded branchings, flourish best under imperial republican forms." Brooks appears, however—like increasingly many left-of-center supporters of the U.S. Democratic Party—unperturbed by this sort of rhetoric.

25 *Intellectual History of Liberalism*, 80–114. See also Milbank, *Theology and Social Theory*, 66–71, 196–203, 408.

26 Pierre Manent, "Charles Péguy: Between Political Faith and Faith," in *Modern Liberty and Its Discontents*, 79–81. And see Romain Rolland, *Péguy*, vol. 1 (Paris: Albin Michel, 1944), 137–39, 309.

27 Milbank, *Theology and Social Theory*, 66–71, 196–203, 408; Alexander Dru, *The Church in the Nineteenth Century: Germany 1800-1918* (London:

Burns and Oates, 1963). One can also note here that Augustine's new definition of a *res publica* as foregathered around the object of its desire already tends to make the political a subcategory of the social: see *Theology and Social Theory*, 400–401.

28 John Wyclif, "Civil Lordship," book 1, chap. 715c, in O'Donovan and O'Donovan, *From Irenaeus to Grotius*, 488: "God gives only in the best way of which the recipient is capable; but every righteous man is capable of the best gift in general; so God bestows only in that way, for as long as one is righteous . . . and so God cannot give a creature any created good without first giving uncreated good"; chap. 716c: "God gives no gifts to man without giving himself as the principal gift."

29 Wyclif, "Divine Lordship," book 3, chap. 170, chap. 478a, in *From Irenaeus to Grotius*, 487–88.

30 See the O'Donovans' commentary on Wyclif in *From Irenaeus to Grotius*, 482–87, and Oliver O'Donovan, *Desire of the Nations*, again on Wyclif at 26, and on the ambivalence of Franciscan poverty at 207. See also on the same subject Milbank, *Theology and Social Theory*, 15–16.

31 See Hilaire Belloc, *An Essay on the Restoration of Property* (Norfolk, Va.: IHS Press, 2002). Belloc's distributist notions were clearly of more Dominican than Franciscan inspiration.

32 See *From Irenaeus to Grotius*, 530–41 and 743–57; on Wyclif and the late post-Ockham Oxford neorealism, see Alain de Libera, *La Querelle des Universaux: de Platon á la fin du Moyen Age* (Paris: Eds du Seuil, 1996), 402–10. One can sympathize strongly with O'Donovan's predilection for what one might call very early modern conciliar realists: Fortescue, Nicholas of Cusa, Hooker, etc. In their fusion of ancient natural law and modern constitution making, they seem to offer an alternative to either the medieval or the modern. But is it correct to speak as he does of "early modern liberalism" here, and to assimilate such currents to the undoubted liberalism (founded in subjective rights) of Grotius? In these earlier currents there is no subjective right proceeding primarily from the ground of will in the Hobbesian-Lockean sense, and no social contract in the Hobbesian-Lockean mode of an agreement between previously sovereign individuals and establishing a primarily formal legitimacy. Fortescue's "mystical 'compact'" is rather the issuing of the Aristotelian social impulse at the very "origin" of any conceivable humanity in the collective enterprise of shaping artificial and historically contingent institutions that nevertheless seek to express a substantive equity.

33 See Milbank, *Theology and Social Theory*, 197–200.

34 See Charles Péguy, *Basic Verities*, trans. Ann and Julian Green (London: Kegan Paul, 1943), 75–95, 101–19.

35 See Giovanni Arrighi, "Tracking Global Turbulence," *New Left Review* 20, 2nd ser. (2003): 5–73.

36 The ongoing researches of Paul Morris (of Victoria University, Wellington, New Zealand) are tending to show this. For further reflections on the relation between religion and the nation-state and the way the latter always has to re-recruit and define the former, see Talal Asad, *Formulations of the Secular: Christianity, Islam, Modernity* (Stanford: Stanford University Press, 2003).

37 Manent, *Intellectual History of Liberalism*, 104–5; Tocqueville, *Democracy in America*, 364.

38 Manent, *Modern Liberty and Its Discontents*, 105.

39 See James Barr, *Fundamentalism* (London: SCM Press, 1984).

40 See *Theology and Social Theory*, 20, and John Milbank, review of M. S. Burrows and Paul Rorem, eds., *Biblical Hermeneutics in Historical Perspective*, in *Journal of Theological Studies* 46, part 2 (1995): 660–70.

41 Asad, *Formations of the Secular*, 100–127.

42 Asad, *Formations of the Secular*, 127–59.

43 See Hittenger, "*Munus Regale.*" See also the papal encyclicals, *De Familiae Christianae Muneribus*, para. 63, and *Christifidelis Laici*, para. 14, as well as *Lumen Gentium*, para. 3b.

44 See Hittenger, "*Munus Regale*" for the correct comment that the principle of "subsidiarity" is *not* a liberal one that means "do everything that can possibly be done at a local level, only resorting to higher levels or the center in extreme necessity." Rather it means "do everything at the appropriate level." Hence, as Hittenger also says, liberals who think that subsidiarity should be applied to church government as a liberal principle are wrong, but conservatives who think that it should not be applied are also wrong, since it is not averse to hierarchy. Of course, Hittinger and I would probably disagree about "appropriate levels" in the case of church government.

CHAPTER 3

1 Cited by George Hunsinger, *Disruptive Grace: Studies in the Theology of Karl Barth* (Grand Rapids: Eerdmans, 2002), 42.

2 Frederic Jameson, "The Dialectics of Disaster," in *Dissent from the Homeland: Essays after September 11*, ed. Stanley Hauerwas and Frank Lentricchia (Durham, N.C.: Duke University Press, 2003), 59.

3 Allegorical interpretation arose especially in Alexandria, through Philo (who appropriated Middle Platonism for Judaism) and Origen, who did the same for Christianity. In Milbank's work, there is an apparent conflation of typological and allegorical. See Milbank, *Theology and Social Theory*, 20; "Sovereignty, Empire, Capital, and Terror," in *Dissent from the Homeland*, 70–71. The same conflation occurs in Ward's *Cities of God* (New York and London: Routledge, 2000), 230. Similarly, in "The Gift of Ruling: Secularization and Political Authority," *New Blackfriars* 996 (2004: 215. Milbank writes, "Catholic, orthodox

Christianity, by contrast [with Protestant fundamentalism] insists that the abiding truth of the Old Testament is allegorical: literal violence points figuratively to a future revelation of embodied peace in Christ" (235). Aside from what seems like an uncommon definition of allegorical interpretation, his historical claim is far too sweeping. As I point out in *Covenant and Eschatology* (Louisville: Westminster John Knox, 2002), 172–73, criticism of the Quadriga method (namely, historical, allegorical, moral, and anagogical interpretation of each passage) can be found throughout medieval scholasticism. Nicholas of Lara (1270–1340) championed the "sensus literalis" (ordinary sense) as the exclusive hermeneutic (*Literal Postill on the Bible*, cited by Beryl Smalley, *The Study of the Bible in the Middle Ages* [Oxford: Blackwell, 1952], 45–46). Thomas Aquinas lamented its marginalization in favor of allegorical readings, urging a restoration of the primacy of the ordinary sense: "For all the senses are founded on one—the literal—from which alone can any argument be drawn, and not from those intended allegorically, as Augustine says" (*Summa Theologica* 1:1a.1.10, trans. Fathers of the English Dominican Province [Westminster, Md.: Christian Classics, 1981]).

4   Milbank, "Gift of Ruling," 218.
5   Bill Clinton peppered speeches with references to America's "covenant with God," just as George W. Bush includes allusions to the nation's divine destiny to bring freedom to the world. On the day of this writing, President Bush, in his national radio address on the eve of Easter Sunday 2005, offered grieving families who have lost loved ones in the Iraq war the comfort that this holy day marks "the triumph of light over darkness."
6   William T. Cavanaugh, "The City: Beyond Secular Parodies," in *Radical Orthodoxy*, ed. John Milbank, Catherine Pickstock, and Graham Ward (London: Routledge, 1998), 182-200; 182.
7   Cavanaugh, "The City," 194.
8   Milbank, *Theology and Social Theory*, 9.
9   Milbank, *Theology and Social Theory*, 15.
10 Milbank, *Theology and Social Theory*, 19. While challenging the connection between Reformed theology and nominalism is beyond my scope here, it should be noted that Reformed and Lutheran scholasticism universally rejected nominalism's soteriology (justification by congruent merit), along with its ontology of univocity. Affirming analogical being and knowledge, they distinguished sharply between archetypal and ectypal knowledge. Calvin referred to nominalism's doctrine of absolute power as "a diabolical blasphemy," and most of the post-Reformation theologians were more sympathetic to Aquinas than to Scotus or Ockham.

11 At the same time, Milbank concedes, "As with ancient Rome, as Augustine in effect diagnosed, the empire may have corrupted the republic, but it was still the republic, with its agonistic and defensive understanding of virtue, that generated the empire" ("Gift of Ruling," 226).

12 Milbank, "Sovereignty, Empire, Capital, and Terror," 70-71.

13 Milbank, "Sovereignty, Empire, Capital, and Terror," 71.

14 Milbank, "Sovereignty, Empire, Capital, and Terror," 72.

15 Milbank, "Sovereignty, Empire, Capital, and Terror," 75.

16 Milbank, "Sovereignty, Empire, Capital, and Terror," 79–80 (emphasis added).

17 Milbank, "Sovereignty, Empire, Capital, and Terror," 82.

18 Ward, *Cities of God*, 257.

19 John Howard Yoder, *The Christian Witness to the State*, 3rd ed. (Newton, Kan.: Faith and Life Press, 1973), 13, cited by Hunsinger, *Disruptive Grace*, 125. Hunsinger adds, "From Barth's point of view, none of these statements would be possible. Where Yoder finds himself speaking of the church, Barth would insist on speaking of Jesus Christ. He would say that it is not the church which has 'absolute priority' over the state in the plan of God, but Jesus Christ."

20 Stanley Hauerwas, *Dispatches from the Front: Theological Engagements with the Secular* (Durham and London: Duke University Press, 1994), 105.

21 Milbank, *Being Reconciled*, 5.

22 Augustine, *City of God*, trans. Henry Bettenson (New York: Penguin, 1972), 19.27 (892).

23 James K. A. Smith, *Introducing Radical Orthodoxy: Mapping a Post-secular Theology* (Grand Rapids: Baker Academic, 2004), 133, cf. chap. 7.

24 Augustine, *City of God*, ed. David Knowles; trans. Henry Bettenson (New York: Penguin, 1972), 14.1, 547. Books 15–18 offer a summary of the "two seeds" and "two cities" issuing from Seth and Cain, leading all the way to Christ and the church. This redemptive-historical survey of the outworking of predestination sets the stage for the more familiar comparisons and contrasts between the two cities. This predestinarian grounding of Augustine's argument has been an embarrassment to Milbank, Ward, and Hauerwas. Their universalist ecclesiologies can only treat this as an incidental or intentionally mythological element.

25 Augustine, *City of God*, 19.25 (891–92).

26 Augustine, *City of God*, 19.26–27 (891–92).

27 Augustine, *City of God*, 11.2 (430).

28 Augustine, *City of God*, 15.4 (599).

29 Augustine, *City of God*, 15.4 (599).

30 Augustine, *City of God*, 19.12 (866–77).

31 Augustine, *City of God*, 19.21 (881).

32 Augustine, *City of God*, 19.24 (890).

33 Augustine, *City of God*, 19.24 (890).

34 Augustine, *City of God*, 19.15 (875).

35 Augustine, *City of God*, 19.26 (891–92).

36 Augustine, *City of God*, 19.27 (892).

37 Ward, *Cities of God*, 226.

38 Ward, *Cities of God*, 228.

39 Like Milbank, Ward (*Cities of God*, 226–28) associates liberal democracy with the Roman commonwealth and, with selective quotes, concludes that Augustine would have followed radical orthodoxy in disallowing their legitimacy. On both counts, I think this interpretation misses the nuances of Augustine's argument. Furthermore, if rights-talk originates in the decadent era of modern liberalism, why is it (a) present in Cicero's definition and (b) approved by Augustine as a legitimate concern?

40 Ward, *Cities of God*, 230.

41 Ward, *Cities of God*, 233.

42 John Calvin, *Institutes of the Christian Religion*, ed. J. T. McNeill; trans. F. L. Battles (Philadelphia: Westminster), 2.2.15.

43 Calvin, *Institutes of the Christian Religion*, 4.20.1–2.

44 Calvin, *Institutes of the Christian Religion*, 4.20.8, 14. The basic ligaments of Calvin's political theology can be found in 4.20.1–32.

45 Calvin, *Institutes of the Christian Religion*, 4.20.8, 14.

46 Calvin, *Institutes of the Christian Religion*, 4.20.8, 14.

47 Calvin, *Institutes of the Christian Religion*, 4.20.15.

48 Calvin, *Institutes of the Christian Religion*, 4.20.15.

49 William Klempa, "John Calvin on Natural Law," in *John Calvin and the Church: A Prism of Reform*, ed. Timothy George (Louisville: Westminster John Knox, 1990), 87, citing Calvin, *Institutes of the Christian Religion*, 2.8.55.

50 Oliver O'Donovan and Joan Lockwood O'Donovan, eds., *From Irenaeus to Grotius: A Sourcebook in Christian Political Thought, 100–1625* (Grand Rapids: Eerdmans, 1999), 662.

51 O'Donovan and O'Donovan, *From Irenaeus to Grotius*, 662.

52 In relation to Calvin especially, the historical link to nominalism has been decisively refuted by Catholic historian Alexandre Ganoczy, in his *The Young Calvin*, trans. David Foxgrover and Wade Provo (Philadelphia: Westminster, 1987), 173–78. See also David Steinmetz, "Calvin and the Absolute Power of God," *Journal of Medieval and Renaissance Studies* 18, no. 1 (1988): 65–79; Susan Schreiner, *Where Shall Wisdom Be Found? Calvin's Exegesis of Job from Medieval and Modern Perspectives* (Chicago: University of Chicago Press, 1994); Jelle Faber, "Nominalisme in Calvijns preken over Job," in *Een sprekend begin*, ed. R. ter Beek et al., 68–85 (Kampen: Uitgeverij Van den Berg, 1993). See also several summaries of the primary and secondary literature in Richard Muller, *The*

Unaccomodated Calvin: Studies in the Foundation of a Theological Tradition (New York and Oxford: Oxford University Press, 2000), 40–41, 48, 52–53; cf. Heiko Oberman, *The Harvest of Medieval Theology* (Durham, N.C.: Labyrinth, 1985), 30–57; Oberman, "Some Notes on the Theology of Nominalism," *Harvard Theological Review* 53 (1960): 47–76.

53 Calvin, *Institutes of the Christian Religion*, 1.17.2. Cf. the editor's note on the same page (n. 7), referring to Calvin's extended criticism of this nominalist position in *De aeterna Dei praedestinatione* (*Corpus Reformatorum* 8.361), as well as his *Sermons on Job* 88, on Job 23:1-7 (*Corpus Reformatorum* 34.339f.).

54 Calvin offers little assistance to those who seek to pigeonhole him into or force him to choose between either "intellectualist" or "voluntarist" sides of the medieval debate. For him, "with firm faith we embrace this mercy and rest in it with steadfast hope" (*Institutes of the Christian Religion*, 3.2.1). Faith is an embracing of Christ with all of his benefits, and therefore simultaneously and equally involves the whole person. "Now we shall possess a right definition of faith if we call it a firm and certain knowledge of God's benevolence toward us, founded upon the truth of the freely given promise in Christ, both revealed to our minds and sealed upon our hearts through the Holy Spirit" (3.2.7). This definition of faith as "a firm and certain knowledge" is found throughout his writings, so he is incapable of being interpreted as a voluntarist, much less a radical Scotist.

55 Milbank, "Gift of Ruling," 228.

56 Milbank, "Gift of Ruling," 231.

57 The names of Johannes Althusius, John Ponet, Philippe de Morney, and other sixteenth-century Reformed theologians figure prominently in the development of modern constitutionalism. See also the research in this area by David VanDrunen in "The Context of Natural Law: John Calvin's Doctrine of the Two Kingdoms," *Journal of Church and State* 46 (2004): 503–25.

58 Francis Turretin, *Institutes of Elenctic Theology*, trans. John Musgrave Giger; ed. James T. Dennison (Phillipsburg, N.J.: P&R, 1999), 2.1.7.

59 The Westminster Confession of Faith, in *The Book of Confessions* (Louisville: PCUSA, 1989), 19.4.

60 David Novak, *Covenantal Rights: A Study in Jewish Political Theory* (Princeton: Princeton University Press, 2000), 20. See also Novak, *Jewish-Christian Dialogue: A Jewish Justification* (New York: Oxford University Press, 1989), 27.

61 Novak, *Covenantal Rights*, 25.

62 Novak, *Covenantal Rights*, 25.

63 Osman bin Bakar, "Pluralism and the 'People of the Book,'" in *Religion and Security,* ed. Robert A. Seiple and Dennis R. Hoover (Lanham, Md.:

Rowman & Littlefield, 2004), 105, 108. Nevertheless, unlike Novak, bin Bakar exploits this universal dimension as a unifying religious factor among the "religions of the book." I would argue that law, whether natural or revealed, is a unifying factor for the human sense of justice, but that the gospel is the only unifying factor for redeemed humanity.

64	Augustine, *City of God*, 873.

65	Kevin J. Hason, "Neither Sacred Nor Secular," in *Religion and Security*, 152–53. A U.S. diplomat, Hason relates, "When delegates from the fifty-eight nations of the Human Rights Commission surveyed world leaders as diverse as Mahatma Gandhi, Pierre Teilhard de Chardin, and Aldous Huxley, they found surprising agreement on a basic enumeration of rights. Yet when the Commission began its debates, the wide range of members' philosophies and religious backgrounds precluded consensus on recognizing divine revelation or natural law as the source for human rights. However, human dignity was the one foundation all parties could agree on, even countries with poor human rights records."

66	Milbank, "Gift of Ruling," 217.

67	Jeffrey Stout, *Democracy and Tradition* (Princeton: Princeton University Press, 2004), 64.

68	Stout, *Democracy and Tradition*, 241.

69	Stout, *Democracy and Tradition*, 283.

70	Stout, *Democracy and Tradition*, 298.

71	Stout, *Democracy and Tradition*, 299.

72	Stout, *Democracy and Tradition*, 146.

73	Stout, *Democracy and Tradition*, 146.

74	Stout, *Democracy and Tradition*, 260.

75	Stout, *Democracy and Tradition*, 300.

76	Stout, *Democracy and Tradition*, 58.

CHAPTER 4

1	José Casanova, *Public Religions in the Modern World* (Chicago: University of Chicago Press, 1994), 30–31.

2	Max Weber, *From Max Weber: Essays in Sociology*, ed. and trans. H. H. Gerth and C. Wright Mills (New York: Oxford University Press, 1946), 155, 139. Whether he shares this attitude or is merely describing it, Weber here effectively illustrates the rather presumptuous modern understanding of premodern ritual and intellectual practice as so many versions of the same mistake, that is, as so many forms of failed empirical science. For a criticism of this understanding, see Ludwig Wittgenstein, *Remarks on Fraser's Golden Bough*, ed. Rush Rhees (Nottinghamshire: Brynmill, 1971).

3	Weber, *From Max Weber*, 328 (emphasis in original).

4 Casanova, *Public Religions in the Modern World*, 20. Weber connects the collapse of these religious walls to the pursuit of rationalization within religious culture itself. See Weber, *From Max Weber*, 351: "The more religion became book-religion and doctrine, the more literary it became and the more efficacious it was in provoking rational lay-thinking, freed of priestly control. From the thinking laymen, however, emerged the prophets, who were hostile to priests; as well as the mystics, who searched salvation independently of priests and sectarians; and finally the skeptics and philosophers, who were hostile to faith." For a similar argument, which traces the origins of modern atheism to Christian theological attempts to mount a rational defense for God's existence, see Michael J. Buckley, *At the Origins of Modern Atheism* (New Haven: Yale University Press, 1987).

5 Casanova, *Public Religions in the Modern World*, 21.

6 The WVS data are drawn from coordinated face-to-face interviews conducted in multiple societies, collectively representing more than 80 percent of the world's population and all six inhabited continents. See Ronald Inglehart, *Human Values and Social Change: Findings in the Values Surveys* (Leiden: Brill, 2003). Four rounds of the survey have been conducted thus far, covering a period from 1981 to 2000, thus making it possible to track changes in sociocultural, political, and religious values across time.

7 David Martin, *On Secularization: Toward a Revised General Theory* (London: Ashgate, 2005), 19. It is important to note here that both Martin and Casanova accept the sociological analysis of societal differentiation as the "viable core" of what they otherwise take to be an ideologically-overdetermined secularization thesis. See Martin, *On Secularization*, 17, and Casanova, *Public Religions in the Modern World*, 20–25.

8 Pippa Norris and Ronald Inglehart, *Sacred and Secular: Religion and Politics Worldwide* (Cambridge: Cambridge University Press, 2004), 4. Subsequent page references to this book will occur parenthetically within the text.

9 It is important to note here that, given Norris and Inglehart's qualification, it is easier to defend those claims of "American exceptionalism" that have been put forward to salvage the troubled secularization thesis. Obviously, the authors are aware of the problem that high levels of religious identification and participation in the United States present to their theory, and they attempt to account for these within the limits their theory imposes. See especially chap. 4, "The Puzzle of Secularization in the United States and Western Europe."

10 See Rodney Stark and Roger Finke, *Acts of Faith: Explaining the Human Side of Religion* (Berkeley: University of California Press, 2000), 36.

11 This broad understanding of religion, along with a concomitant critique of the possibility of religious neutrality, has been extensively

developed in the tradition known as the Amsterdam School of reformational Christian philosophy, which informs the work of such North American philosophers of religion as Nicholas Wolterstorff and Hendrik Hart. From the perspective of a different Christian tradition, one also finds a similar notion at work in Paul Tillich's definition of faith as "ultimate concern." See Paul Tillich, *Dynamics of Faith* (New York: Harper and Row, 1957). According to Hart, words like "spirit" and "spiritual" do not simply name occult entities, or describe beliefs in their existence and efficacy. More than this, these words describe those deep sources of historical and cultural orientation—whether "sacred" or "secular"—that demonstrate a power to shape, inspire, and organize people's lives (as captured in a phrase like "the spirit of the Enlightenment"). In this broader sense, says Hart, one can begin to understand words like "faith," "religion," and "spirituality" as connoting "a complex of values, attitudes, and hopes that guide and direct people in their evaluations, decisions, courses of action, and plans. Through such a spirit people imbue their lives with coherence as they relate to other people, institutions, and their culture." See Hendrik Hart, "Conceptual Understanding and Knowing Other-wise: Reflections on Rationality and Spirituality in Philosophy," in *Knowing Otherwise: Philosophy at the Threshold of Spirituality,* ed. James H. Olthuis (New York: Fordham, 1997), 20.

12 Reginald Bibby offers the following succinct summary of this version of the story: "With industrialization comes institutional specialization and changes in personal consciousness. Simply put, religion loses control over areas such as politics, economics, health care, and education. . . . Religion's role becomes increasingly specialized and is relegated to matters of meaning, morality, and mortality, as well as to performing rites of passage." See Reginald W. Bibby, *Restless Gods: The Renaissance of Religion in Canada* (Toronto: Stoddart, 2002), 9.

13 In a discussion of the problem posed by religious fundamentalism, Jürgen Habermas describes this cognitive pressure, which in religious fundamentalism he claims becomes a dissonance, as the loss of "the innocence of the epistemological situation of an all-encompassing perspective," a perspective that becomes increasingly less tenable under "conditions of scientific knowledge and of religious pluralism. . . ." These conditions, according to Habermas, make any "return to the exclusivity of premodern belief attitudes" problematic, if not impossible. See his interview in Giovanna Borradori, *Philosophy in a Time of Terror: Dialogues with Jürgen Habermas and Jacques Derrida* (Chicago: University of Chicago Press, 2003), 32.

14 See Neil Nevitte, *The Decline of Deference: Canadian Value Change in Cross-National Perspective* (Peterborough: Broadview Press, 1996); Ronald Inglehart, "Postmodernization Erodes Respect for Authority, but

Increases Support for Democracy," in *Critical Citizens: Global Support for Democratic Governance*, ed. P. Norris (Oxford: Oxford University Press, 1999); Russell J. Dalton, *Citizen Politics: Public Opinion and Political Parties in Advanced Industrial Democracies*, 4th ed. (Washington: Congressional Quarterly Press, 2006).

15 See Nicholas John Ansell, *The Annihilation of Hell: Universal Salvation and the Redemption of Time in the Eschatology of Jürgen Moltmann* (Carlisle, U.K.: Paternoster, 2005); Jürgen Moltmann, "The Restoration of All Things," in *The Coming God: Christian Eschatology*, trans. Margaret Kohl, 235–55 (London: SCM Press, 1996).

16 Weber, *From Max Weber*, 350–51 (emphasis in original).

17 This is a conclusion that Habermas, of course, most strongly resists, and it motivates his attempt to conceive of a more differentiated understanding of rationality and rationalization. It is also important to note that religious culture and institutions themselves can devolve under the influence of the sort of calculating rationalism that Weber had in mind, especially if they submit to, rather than challenge, currently dominant modes of social organization. Perhaps some such situation led Theodor Adorno to quip: "Religion is on sale, as it were. It is cheaply marketed in order to provide one more so-called irrational stimulus among many others by which the members of a calculating society are calculatingly made to forget the calculation under which they suffer." See Theodor Adorno, "Theses upon Art and Religion Today," *Kenyon Review* 7, no. 4 (1945): 677–82.

18 It is important to note that Norris and Inglehart believe that the security that explains declining levels of religious involvement is a measure of overall human development as opposed to being a measure of simple economic development: "The most crucial precondition for security, we believe, is *human* development even more than purely *economic* development: it involves how far all sectors of society have equal access to schooling and literacy, basic healthcare, adequate nutrition, a clean water supply, and a minimal safety net for the needy" (53).

19 See Jürgen Habermas, "Faith and Knowledge," in *The Frankfurt School of Religion: Key Writings by the Major Thinkers*, ed. Eduardo Mendieta (New York: Routledge, 2005), 328.

20 See Weber, *From Max Weber*, 331–35.

21 See Christopher L. Walton, "Is Disenchantment the End of Religion?" in *Philocrites: Commentary on Religion, Liberalism, and Culture* (2000), available at http://www.philocrites.com/essays/weber.html.

22 Habermas' appreciation of the "semantic potential" and "lifeworld resources" housed within religious tradition can be found throughout his work, from early to late. See Jürgen Habermas, "On the Difficulty of Saying No," in *Religion and Rationality: Essays on Reason, God, and Modernity*, ed. Eduardo Mendieta (Cambridge, Mass.: MIT Press, 2002); "Religious

Tolerance—The Pacemaker for Cultural Rights," in *Philosophy* 79 (2004): 5–18; "Israel and Athens, or to Whom Does Anamnestic Reason Belong?" in *Frankfurt School on Religion*, 293–301; "Faith and Knowledge"; see also Ronald A. Kuipers, "Reconciling a Shattered Modernity: Habermas on the Enduring Relevance of the Judeo-Christian Ethical Tradition," in *Faith and Enlightenment: Friendly Enemies?* ed. Hendrik Vroom (Amsterdam and New York: Editions Rodopi, 2006). Norris and Inglehart also seem to be aware of this side of religious culture, yet such awareness does little to alter their defense of the secularization thesis. See Norris and Inglehart, *Sacred and Secular*, 191, where they say that the WVS data "confirm social capital theory's claim that the social networks and personal communications derived from regular churchgoing play an important role, not just in promoting activism within religious-related organizations, but also in strengthening community associations more generally." We are left wondering why Norris and Inglehart do not conceive of this aspect of religion, its function as a community-energizing moral resource, as an additional driving factor for religiosity in those societies that face an even greater degree of survival-threatening risks than do those in affluent advanced industrial societies. We think this issue stands in need of further examination.

23 Ludwig Wittgenstein, *Culture and Value*, ed. G. H. Von Wright, trans. Peter Winch (Chicago: University of Chicago Press, 1980), 5 (emphasis in original).

CHAPTER 5

1 Max Horkheimer and Theodor W. Adorno, *Dialectic of Enlightenment: Philosophical Fragments*, ed. Gunzelin Schmid Noerr, trans. Edmund Jephcott (Stanford: Stanford University Press, 2002), 1; *Dialektik der Aufklärung*, in Max Horkheimer, *Gesammelte Schriften*, vol. 5, *"Dialektik der Aufklärung" und Schriften 1940–1950*, ed. Gunzelin Schmid Noerr (Frankfurt am Main: Fischer Taschenbuch, 1987), 25; translation modified. In-text citations use the abbreviation DE, followed by the pagination from first the Jephcott translation and then the Horkheimer *Gesammelte Schriften* edition.

2 Jürgen Habermas, *Autonomy and Solidarity: Interviews with Jürgen Habermas*, ed. Peter Dews, rev. ed. (London: Verso, 1992), 222.

3 Theodor W. Adorno, "Alienated Masterpiece: The *Missa Solemnis* (1959)," *Telos* 28 (1976): 113–24; quotation from 113, with the word "abuse" (in square brackets) substituted for "admiration."

4 Adorno, "Alienated Masterpiece," 113.

5 This essay, in a slightly different version, forms a chapter in my book *Social Philosophy after Adorno* (Cambridge: Cambridge University Press, 2007), and it appears here with the kind permission of Cambridge University Press. The book explains what is meant by "a democratic politics of global transformation."

6   I shall focus on Adorno, even though he and Horkheimer cowrote substantial portions of the book. For a succinct overview of Adorno's thought, see my online entry "Theodor Adorno," in *The Stanford Encyclopedia of Philosophy*, ed. Edward N. Zalta, Summer 2007 ed., available at http://plato.stanford.edu/archives/sum2007/entries/adorno/. A revised version of this entry appears as an appendix in my book *Social Philosophy after Adorno*.

7   Jürgen Habermas, "Theodor Adorno: The Primal History of Subjectivity—Self-Affirmation Gone Wild (1969)," in *Philosophical-Political Profiles*, trans. Frederick G. Lawrence, 101–11 (Cambridge, Mass.: MIT Press, 1983), quotation from p. 109. For similar passages in other publications from the 1960s, see *Knowledge and Human Interests* (1968), trans. Jeremy J. Shapiro (Boston: Beacon, 1971), 32–33, and *Toward a Rational Society: Student Protest, Science, and Politics* (1968, 1969), trans. Jeremy J. Shapiro (Boston: Beacon, 1970), 85–86. It is interesting that already in 1963, in a tribute to Adorno on his sixtieth birthday (not included in the English translation of *Philosophical-Political Profiles*), Habermas portrays Adorno's intellectual biography and *Dialectic of Enlightenment* as centrally ambivalent about the link between human emancipation and a resurrection of nature. See "Ein philosophierender Intellektueller," *Philosophisch-politische Profile* (Frankfurt am Main: Suhrkamp, 1971), 176–84.

8   Habermas, *Philosophical-Political Profiles*, 110.

9   Albrecht Wellmer, *Critical Theory of Society*, trans. John Cumming (New York: Herder and Herder, 1971) (translation of *Kritische Gesellschaftstheorie und Positivismus* [Frankfurt am Main: Suhrkamp, 1969]).

10   Albrecht Wellmer, "Communications and Emancipation: Reflections on the Linguistic Turn in Critical Theory," in *On Critical Theory*, ed. John O'Neill (New York: Seabury, 1976), 231–63; quotations from 244, 245.

11   Axel Honneth, "Communication and Reconciliation: Habermas' Critique of Adorno," *Telos* 39 (1979): 45–61; quotations from 46–47. The longer German version of this essay was written in 1976, and has been retranslated as "From Adorno to Habermas: On the Transformation of Critical Theory," in Axel Honneth, *The Fragmented World of the Social: Essays in Social and Political Philosophy*, ed. Charles W. Wright, 92–120 (Albany: State University of New York Press, 1995).

12   Friedemann Grenz, *Adornos Philosophie in Grundbegriffen. Auflösung einiger Deutungsprobleme* (Frankfurt am Main: Suhrkamp, 1974).

13   Thomas Baumeister and Jens Kulenkampff, "Geschichtsphilosophie und philosophische Ästhetik. Zu Adornos 'Ästhetischer Theorie,'" *Neue Hefte für Philosophie* 5 (1973): 74–104.

14   Honneth, "Communication and Reconciliation," 47.

15   Honneth, "Communication and Reconciliation," 50.

16   Axel Honneth, *The Critique of Power: Reflective Stages in a Critical Social Theory*, trans. Kenneth Baynes (Cambridge, Mass.: MIT Press, 1991), xii.

17 Honneth, *Critique of Power*, 35–37.
18 Honneth, *Critique of Power*, 58.
19 Seyla Benhabib, *Critique, Norm, and Utopia: A Study of the Foundations of Critical Theory* (New York: Columbia University Press, 1986), 220.
20 This is not to deny that these authors have significant criticisms of Habermas, but simply to indicate that all three see his theory of communicative action as a necessary and fruitful advance that extracts critical theory from the abyssal aporias in *Dialectic of Enlightenment*.
21 Jürgen Habermas, *The Theory of Communicative Action* (1981), trans. Thomas McCarthy, 2 vols. (Boston: Beacon, 1984, 1987). Cited as TCA 1 and TCA 2.
22 Jürgen Habermas, *The Philosophical Discourse of Modernity: Twelve Lectures* (1985), trans. Frederick Lawrence (Cambridge, Mass.: MIT Press, 1987). Cited as PDM.
23 In one of many noteworthy revisions from the hectographic edition of 1944 to the published edition of 1947, the title of this chapter changed from "Dialectic of Enlightenment" to "The Concept of Enlightenment." For a detailed discussion of such revisions and their significance, see the "Editor's Afterword," DE 217–47/423–52.
24 In fact, the section in TCA where Habermas takes *Dialectic of Enlightenment* as his "point of reference" for discussing Horkheimer and Adorno's "reception of Weber" (TCA 1:450n2) relies much more heavily on Horkheimer's *Eclipse of Reason* than on *Dialectic of Enlightenment*. Perhaps that helps explain why Habermas titles this section "The Critique of Instrumental Reason," even though the term "instrumental reason" does not occur in *Dialectic of Enlightenment* and does not capture the target of Adorno's negative dialectic. Significantly, this section in TCA cites only two passages from "The Concept of Enlightenment" [see TCA 1:379 (453n45) and 384 (454n57)]. The second, about "mindfulness of nature in the subject," is cited again in PDM 119–20. In addition, PDM cites three other passages from "The Concept of Enlightenment." Neither TCA nor PDM offers much analysis of what these passages say.
25 J. M. Bernstein, *Adorno: Disenchantment and Ethics* (Cambridge: Cambridge University Press, 2001), gives an instructive elaboration of Adorno's emphasis on "the concept," with a view to developing a modernist ethic. On the roots of this emphasis in Kant and Hegel, see Brian O'Connor, *Adorno's Negative Dialectic: Philosophy and the Possibility of Critical Rationality* (Cambridge, Mass.: MIT Press, 2004).
26 It would be worthwhile to read all of "The Concept of Enlightenment" as a refiguring of themes from Hegel's *Phenomenology of Spirit*. See in this connection the highly illuminating essay by J. M. Bernstein, "Negative Dialectic as Fate: Adorno and Hegel," in *The Cambridge Companion to Adorno*, ed. Tom Huhn, 19–50 (Cambridge: Cambridge University Press, 2004). Bernstein interprets *Dialectic of Enlightenment* as

"a generalization and radicalization" of the dialectic between pure insight and religious faith in the chapter on "The Enlightenment" in Hegel's *Phenomenology of Spirit*.

27 In the authors' words: "The thing-like quality of the means, which make the means universally available . . . , itself implies a criticism of the domination from which thought has arisen as its means" (DE 29/60).

28 As Horkheimer and Adorno put it: "In the form of machines, however, alienated reason is moving toward a society which reconciles thought, in its solidification as an apparatus both material and intellectual, with a liberated living element, and relates it to society itself as its true subject" (DE 29/60–61).

29 Lambert Zuidervaart, "Metaphysics after Auschwitz: Suffering and Hope in Adorno's *Negative Dialectics*," in *Adorno and the Need in Thinking: New Critical Essays*, ed. Donald Burke et al. (Toronto: University of Toronto Press, 2007), 133–62.

30 Theodor W. Adorno, *Negative Dialectics*, trans. E. B. Ashton (New York: Seabury, 1973), 190; *Negative Dialektik* (1966, 1967), in *Gesammelte Schriften* 6 (Frankfurt am Main: Suhrkamp, 1973), 191. For a thorough commentary on this remark that shows why Habermas' interpretation of Adorno is mistaken and his "linguistic turn" is problematic, see the master's thesis by Matthew Klaassen, "The Nature of Critical Theory and Its Fate: Adorno vs. Habermas, Ltd." (Toronto: Institute for Christian Studies, 2005). Steven Vogel also emphasizes Adorno's reservations about Lukács' theory of reification, but he claims that Adorno's alternative relies on a highly problematic appeal to immediacy. It seems to me that Vogel's claim echoes Habermas' failure to understand the Hegelian dimensions to Adorno's "priority of the object." See Steven Vogel, *Against Nature: The Concept of Nature in Critical Theory* (Albany: State University of New York Press, 1996), 69–90.

31 Prior to the publication of TCA, Joel Whitebook, "The Problem of Nature in Habermas," *Telos* 40 (1979): 41–69, had already identified tendencies that make it very difficult for Habermas to regard nonhuman creatures as anything other than epistemological and instrumental objects. Whitebook's essay points up the need to find a more viable way to address the "ecological crisis," but it does not provide a significant alternative to Habermas' approach.

32 For a comparison of Habermas and Adorno that is critical of Habermas on this score, see Deborah Cook, *Adorno, Habermas, and the Search for a Rational Society* (New York: Routledge, 2004), 39–70.

33 To relate my account of sublimation to Adorno's more cautious approach would require a lengthier discussion, especially of two manuscripts that Adorno wrote in 1942 when he and Horkheimer were working on *Dialectic of Enlightenment*. Titled "Reflexionen zur

Klassentheorie" ["Reflections on Class Theory"] and "Thesen über Bedürfnisse" ["Theses about Needs"], these were published posthumously after Adorno's *Soziologische Schriften I, Gesammelte Schriften 8* (Frankfurt am Main: Suhrkamp, 1972), 373–91 and 392–96, respectively. The first as a translation appears in *Can One Live after Auschwitz? A Philosophical Reader*, ed. Rolf Tiedemann, trans. Rodney Livingstone et al. (Stanford.: Stanford University Press, 2003), 93–110. For a different and more psychoanalytic account of sublimation, see Joel Whitebook, *Perversion and Utopia: A Study in Psychoanalysis and Critical Theory* (Cambridge, Mass.: MIT Press, 1995), esp. 217–62. I share Whitebook's dissatisfaction both with Adorno's failure to spell out a theory of sublimation and with Habermas' failure to take seriously the need for such a theory.

34 The term "exploitation," used frequently in the 1944 hectograph, is replaced by less loaded terms, such as "enslavement," in the 1947 published version. For the theoretical debates about "state capitalism" informing this change, see Willem van Reijen and Jan Bransen, "The Disappearance of Class History in 'Dialectic of Enlightenment': A Commentary on the Textual Variants (1947 and 1944)," in DE 248–52/453–57. I have revived the term "exploitation" because it more precisely indicates the societal mode of domination that Horkheimer and Adorno have in mind.

35 Theodor W. Adorno, *Minima Moralia: Reflections from Damaged Life*, trans. E. F. N. Jephcott (London: NLB, 1974), §29, p. 50. *Minima Moralia: Reflexionen aus dem beschädigten Leben, Gesammelte Schriften*, vol. 4, 2nd ed. (Frankfurt am Main: Suhrkamp, 1996), 55. Hegel's dictum was "The True is the whole." See G. W. F. Hegel, *Phenomenology of Spirit*, trans. A. V. Miller (Oxford: Oxford University Press, 1977), 11.

36 From the description of "differential transformation" that follows, it should be clear that, like Max Pensky, I recognize three challenges facing an attempt to "globalize critical theory" in order to theorize globalization: to develop a highly reflexive social theory, to pursue a new form of interdisciplinarity, and to explicate the socially embedded grounds of normative critique. See Pensky's "Globalizing Theory, Theorizing Globalization: Introduction," in *Globalizing Critical Theory*, ed. Max Pensky, 1–15 (Lanham, Md.: Rowman and Littlefield, 2005).

37 David Held and Anthony McGrew, *Globalization/Anti-Globalization* (Cambridge: Polity, 2002), 1.

38 See David Harvey, *The New Imperialism* (Oxford: Oxford University Press, 2003).

39 Bob Goudzwaard, *Capitalism and Progress: A Diagnosis of Western Society*, ed. and trans. Josina Van Nuis Zylstra (Grand Rapids: Eerdmans, 1979), 65–68, 204–23. Goudzwaard, in turn, derives the idea of a simultaneous realization of norms from the work of Dutch economist T. P. van

der Kooy (see 65n30) and the philosopher and legal theorist Herman Dooyeweerd.

40 Goudzwaard, *Capitalism and Progress*, 66 (emphasis in original).

41 Goudzwaard, *Capitalism and Progress*, 183–84 (emphasis added).

42 For a fuller description of societal principles as commonly holding and commonly held, see Lambert Zuidervaart, *Artistic Truth: Aesthetics, Discourse, and Imaginative Disclosure* (Cambridge: Cambridge University Press, 2004), 96–100.

CHAPTER 6

1 Colossians 1:17.

2 Manuel Castells, *The Rise of the Network Society* (Cambridge, Mass.: Blackwell, 1996).

3 David Harvey, *The Condition of Post-Modernity* (Oxford: Blackwell, 1989).

4 J. Nicholas Entrikin, *The Betweenness of Place: Towards a Geography of Modernity* (Baltimore: Johns Hopkins University Press, 1991).

5 Peter Atkins and Ian Bowler, *Food in Society: Economy, Culture, Geography* (London: Arnold, 2001), chap. 7.

6 "Jerusalem" (words by William Blake, 1804).

7 See Christopher J. H. Wright, "Interpreting the Bible among the World Religions," *Themelios* 25, no. 3 (2000): 35–54.

8 Philip Jenkins, *The Next Christendom: The Coming of Global Christianity* (New York: Oxford University Press, 2002).

9 Paul J. Crutzen and Eugene F. Stoermer, "The Anthropocene," *IGBP Newsletter* 41 (May 2000), available at http://www.mpch-mainz.mpg.de/~air/anthropocene/ (accessed November 2, 2005).

10 Crutzen and Stoermer, "Anthropocene."

11 H. Paul Santmire, *The Travail of Nature: The Ambiguous Ecological Promise of Christian Theology* (Philadelphia: Fortress, 1985).

12 David Smith, "Junction or Terminus? Christianity in the West at the Dawn of the Third Millennium," *Themelios* 25, no. 3 (2000): 55–68.

13 Egon Becker and Thomas Jahn, eds., *Sustainability and the Social Sciences: A Cross-Disciplinary Approach to Integrating Environmental Considerations into Theoretical Reorientation* (London: Zed, 1999).

14 Herman Daly, *Beyond Growth: The Economics of Sustainable Development* (Boston: Beacon, 1996).

15 Jeremy Seabrook, "We Dodged the Real Issue," *The Guardian* (UK), May 6, 2005, available at http://www.commondreams.org/views05/0506-28.htm (accessed November 2, 2005).

16 Donella Meadows et al., *Limits to Growth* (New York: Universe, 1972).

17 Stephen D. Norton and Frederick Suppe, "Why Atmospheric Modeling Is Good Science," in *Changing the Atmosphere: Expert Knowledge and Environmental Governance*, ed. Clark A. Miller and Paul N. Edwards, 67–105 (Cambridge, Mass.: MIT Press, 2001).

18   David Demeritt, "The Construction of Global Warming and the Politics of Science," *Annals of the Association of American Geographers*, 91 no. 2 (2001): 307–37.

19   Herman E. Daly, "Operationalizing Sustainable Development by Investing in Natural Capital," in *Investing in Natural Capital: The Ecological Economics Approach to Sustainability*, ed. A. Jansson et al., 22–30 (Washington D.C.: Island, 1994).

20   William E. Rees and Mathis Wackernagel, *Our Ecological Footprint: Reducing Human Impact on the Earth* (Gabriola Island, B.C.: New Society, 1996).

21   Noel Castree and Bruce Braun, eds., *Social Nature: Theory, Practice, and Politics* (Oxford: Blackwell, 2001).

22   Bruce Braun, *The Intemperate Rainforest: Nature, Culture, and Power on Canada's West Coast* (Minneapolis: University of Minnesota Press 2002); H. Paul Santmire, "Historical Dimensions of the American Crisis, in *Western Man and Environmental Ethics: Attitudes Toward Nature and Technology*, ed. Ian G. Barbour, 66–92 (Reading, Mass.: Addison-Wesley 1973).

23   James Lovelock, *Gaia: A New Look at Life on Earth*, 3rd ed. (Oxford: Oxford University Press, 2000).

24   James Lovelock, "Gaia Warning" (interview with Pete Moore), *Third Way*, June 2005, 18–22.

25   Daly, *Beyond Growth*.

26   Bob Goudzwaard, *Globalization and the Kingdom of God* (Grand Rapids: Baker, 2001).

27   Gro Harlem Bruntland, ed., *Our Common Future* (Oxford: Oxford University Press, 1987); Ian Drummond and Terry Marsden, *The Condition of Sustainability* (London: Routledge, 1999); Harold Coward, ed., *Population, Consumption, and the Environment: Religious and Secular Responses* (Albany: State University of New York Press, 1995).

28   Ulrich Duchrow, *Alternatives to Global Capitalism: Drawn from Biblical History, Designed for Political Action* (Utrecht: International, 1995); Peter L. Berger, *Pyramids of Sacrifice: Political Ethics and Social Change* (New York: Basic, 1974).

29   Charles Elliot, *Inflation and the Compromised Church* (Belfast: Christian Journals Ltd., 1975).

30   Max Oelschlaeger, *Caring for Creation: An Ecumenical Approach to the Environmental Crisis* (New Haven: Yale University Press, 1994).

31   Allan Chen, "Climate Change and the Insurance Industry," Lawrence Berkeley National Laboratory, Environmental Energy Technologies Division, *Newsletter* 6, no. 3 (2005), available at http://eetd.lbl.gov/newsletter/nl22/2clim.htm (accessed January 4, 2006).

32   Fred Hirsch, *Social Limits to Growth* (Cambridge, Mass.: Harvard University Press, 1976).

33   Ronald H. Preston, *Church and Society in the Late Twentieth Century: The Economic and Political Task* (London: SCM Press, 1983).

34 Walt W. Rostow, *The Stages of Economic Growth, a Non-Communist Manifesto* (Cambridge: Cambridge University Press, 1960).

35 Rachel Carson's *Silent Spring* (Boston: Houghton Mifflin 1962), revealing the negative human and environmental consequences of using industrial agrichemicals, was a landmark work in undermining naïve confidence in the benefits of commercialized science and in preparing the way for the modern environmentalist movement.

36 Steven Flusty, *De-Coca-colonization: Making the Globe from the Inside Out* (New York: Routledge, 2004).

37 N. S. Ateek, "A Palestinian Perspective," in *Voices from the Margin: Interpreting the Bible in the Third World*, ed. R. S. Sugirtharajah, 280–86 (Maryknoll, N.Y.: Orbis, 1991), 86.

38 R. A. Warrior, "A North American Perspective," in *Voices from the Margin*, 287–95.

39 Jenkins, *Next Christendom.*

40 Archbishop Peter Akinola, primate (head of) the Anglican Church in Nigeria, was formerly bishop of Abuja, which placed him on the front line of tensions between Christian and Muslim adherents in the northern half of the country. He has recently attracted condemnation from many quarters, both inside and outside the Christian community, for his role in advocating repressive legislation against Nigerian homosexuals. This violates commitments he and his fellow Anglican primates made to engage in a process of "mutual listening" with homosexual members of the church and abandons any responsibility for their pastoral care, as noted by Bishop John Chane of Washington D.C., http://www.episcopal-life.org/26731_73898_ENG_HTM.htm (accessed May 4, 2006).

41 Most notoriously represented by Pastor Fred Phelps, leader of an unaffiliated church in Topeka, Kansas, whose hateful pronouncements at the time of the homophobic murder of Matthew Shepard in 1998 were widely publicized and have been perpetuated on his web site, godhatesfags.com. But the unwelcoming message to gays and lesbians sent by congregations espousing much more orthodox theologies cannot be ignored, as is acknowledged in a carefully worded discussion of homophobia in the church by Andrew Goddard, of Wycliffe College, Oxford, who holds to a traditional evangelical view of homosexuality; see http://www.fulcrum-anglican.org.uk/news/2006/20060524goddard.cfm?doc=108&CFID=7984126&CFTOKEN=c7ba5d4ef85a47b1-D0AE215B-D908-84CF-8FA105D992B401F0#matter (accessed June 8, 2006). My own experience of the tenor of public encounters between those campaigning for, and against, the inclusive treatment of homosexuals in the church and in society at large reflects my location in Ottawa, Canada's, capital.

42 Amnesty International USA, "OUTfront! Lesbian, Gay, Bisexual & Transgender Human Rights," available at http://www.amnestyusa. org/outfront/jamaica_report.html (accessed November 2, 2005).

43 Jeremy Seabrook, "It's Not Natural: The Developing World's Homophobia Is a Legacy of Colonial Rule," *The Guardian* (UK), July 3, 2004, available at   http://www.guardian.co.uk/gayrights/story/0,12592,1253130,00. html (accessed November 2, 2005).

44 World Bank, *Integrating Gender into the World Bank's Work: A Strategy for Action* (Washington: World Bank, 2001), available at http://siteresources.worldbank.org/INTGENDER/Resources/strategypaper.pdf (accessed November 2, 2005).

45 Paul N. Edwards and Stephen H. Schneider, "Self-Governance and Peer Review in Science-for-Policy: The Case of the IPCC Second Assessment Report," in *Changing the Atmosphere*, 219–46.

46 ExxonMobil's funding of groups scornful of the scientific mainstream and its actions to denigrate individual scientists is documented by critics at http://www.exxonsecrets.org/ (accessed June 8, 2006) and http://www.dontbuyexxonmobil.org/background?text_id=sabotage (accessed June 8, 2006). Its corporate stance toward climate change science continues to stress the uncertainties and question the methodologies of mainstream science; see http://exxonmobil.com/Corporate/Citizenship/CCR5/climate_science.asp (accessed June 8, 2006).

47 Ryan D. Johnson, "Homosexuality: Nature or Nurture," *AllPsych Journal* April 30, 2003, available at http://allpsych.com/journal/homosexuality.html (accessed November 2, 2005). See also American Psychological Association, "Sexual Orientation and Homosexuality," http://www. apahelpcenter.org/articles/article.php?id=31 (accessed June 10, 2006); Timothy F. Murphy, "The Search for the Gay Gene," *British Medical Journal* 330 (2005): 1033, available at http://bmj.bmjjournals.com/cgi/content/full/330/7498/1033.

48 The BBC provides a list of countries and discussion: "Gay Marriage around the Globe," December 22, 2005, available at http://news.bbc. co.uk/2/hi/americas/4081999.stm (accessed June 11, 2006).

49 Gary Hauch, "Same Sex Unions and Biblical Fidelity: Discerning the Spirit in Text and Context," April 15, 2005, http://www.ottawa.anglican.ca/documents/Gary%20Hauch%20on%20Scripture1.htm (accessed May 20, 2005).

50 David Harvey, *Spaces of Hope* (Berkeley: University of California Press, 2000).

51 Jubilee Research, "About Us," http://www.jubilee2000uk.org/about/ about.htm (accessed November 2, 2005).

52 Iain Wallace, "Towards a Humanised Conception of Economic Geography," in *Humanistic Geography: Prospects and Problems*, ed. D. F. Ley and M. S. Samuels, 91–108 (Chicago: Maaroufa, 1978).

53 Smith, "Junction or Terminus?"
54 Smith, "Junction or Terminus?" 67.

CHAPTER 7

1 Related issues, not directly addressed in this article are: first, the morality of deterrence and prevention policies that aim to reduce the numbers of asylum seekers arriving in a country; second, the ethics of detention centers; third, the ethics of dispersal policies that isolate refugees from fellow countrymen and whether these contravene a fundamental aspect of what it means to be human (i.e., the ability to express oneself in relationship with others); and fourth, the question of what can be expected or required of refugees when they are participants, whether temporary or permanent, of a given "host" society (i.e., the duties of "guestship" and residence). This last point relates to the debate about citizenship in a plural society.

2 For a history of the origins and development of the international refugee regime, see Gil Loescher, *Beyond Charity: International Cooperation and the Global Refugee Crises* (Oxford: Oxford University Press, 1993), 11–128.

3 Loescher, *Beyond Charity*, 16–17, 141.

4 Loescher, *Beyond Charity*, 6 (emphasis in original).

5 For the OAU definition, see Myron Weiner, *The Global Migration Crises: Challenges to States and to Human Rights* (New York: HarperCollins College Publishers, 1995), 188. Since 1997 in addition to grounds for recognition given in UN convention, Sweden has recognized a well-founded fear of capital or corporal punishment; protection from nonstate persecution (civil war, external conflict, or environmental disaster); and a well-founded fear of persecution because of gender or sexual orientation (see Andrew Geddes, *The Politics of Migration and Immigration in Europe* [London: Sage, 2003], 110).

6 A. Shacknove, "Who Is a refugee?" *Ethics* 95, no. 2 (1985); 274–84.

7 Matthew Gibney, *The Ethics and Politics of Asylum: Liberal Democracy and the Response to Refugees* (Cambridge: Cambridge University Press, 2004), 8.

8 It should be noted, however, that the line between political policy and natural disaster is not hard and fast. The work of Amartya Sen calls into question quite how "natural" many natural disasters are. See, e.g., Amartya Sen, *Poverty and Famines* (Oxford: Clarendon, 1981).

9 Gibney, *Ethics and Politics of Asylum*, 9.

10 For the purposes of this article an "asylum seeker" is someone who is fleeing persecution in his or her homeland, has arrived in another country, made him- or herself known to the authorities, and exercised the legal right to apply for asylum under the UN Convention. It should be noted that it is not technically possible in the United Kingdom to seek asylum illegally. Passage from a country of origin into another

country may be illegal, but, once in the United Kingdom, anyone may legitimately claim asylum under current legislation. A "failed asylum seeker" is someone whose asylum application has been turned down and is awaiting return to their country of origin. In U.K. law, failed asylum seekers are entitled to appeal and remain until a final decision has been made. The Home Office recognizes other reasons why it may not be able to remove someone from the United Kingdom immediately, ranging from illness and imminent childbirth to refusal by the country of origin to accept the person back without documentation or if it is not safe for unsuccessful asylum seekers to return. For any of these reasons they may be granted leave to stay. An "illegal immigrant" is someone who has arrived in another country, intentionally not made him- or herself known to the authorities, and has no legal basis for being there.

11 Likewise, the right to emigration does not entail a right to immigration in another country. On this see Michael Walzer, *Spheres of Justice: A Defense of Pluralism and Equality* (New York: Basic Books, 1983), 39–40; and Gibney, *Ethics and Politics of Asylum*, 68.

12 Peter and Renata Singer, "The Ethics of Refugee Policy," in *Open Borders? Closed Societies? The Ethics and Political Issues,* ed. Mark Gibney (New York: Greenwood Press, 1988), 121–22.

13 Michael Dummett, *On Immigration and Refugees* (London: Routledge, 2001), 80, 26–27.

14 Rawls himself does not develop the "original position" in this way. For his critique of a global original position see John Rawls, *The Law of the Peoples* (Cambridge, Mass.: Harvard University Press, 1999), 82–83, 119–20. Rawls argues that boundaries are a necessary feature of political association (38–39). In his account of the "Law of the Peoples," he sees the right of self-determination and the preservation of a particular way of life as goods in and of themselves, advocating a "proper patriotism" (111–12). By implication the preservation of these goods necessitates admission policies and, within his account of distributive justice, priority should be given to existing members of a given country, with inequality between peoples dealt with on a society-to-society basis rather than an individual basis (115–19).

15 J. Carens, "Aliens and Citizens: The Case for Open Borders," *The Review of Politics* 49, no. 2 (1987): 251–73. However, more recently, Carens has shifted his position, arguing that the right to move freely across borders is not absolute and that there can be justifiable reasons for restricting it (Carens, "A Reply to Meilaender: Reconsidering Open Borders," *International Migration Review* 33, no. 4 [1999]; 1088–89).

16 Gibney, *Ethics and Politics of Asylum*, 65–76.

17 Walzer, *Spheres of Justice*, 62.

18 Walzer, *Spheres of Justice*, 64.

19 Walzer, *Spheres of Justice*, 65.
20 Walzer, *Spheres of Justice*, 49.
21 Walzer argues that while all humans owe each other mutual aid, political membership is a distributive good that is necessarily distributed unequally.
22 Gibney, *Ethics and Politics of Asylum*, 82.
23 Gibney, *Ethics and Politics of Asylum*, 84.
24 Gibney, *Ethics and Politics of Asylum*, 83.
25 Gibney, *Ethics and Politics of Asylum*, 83. This argument, however, can be applied to what any polity, whether liberal democratic or not, holds to be a good.
26 Gibney, *Ethics and Politics of Asylum*, 231.
27 Gibney, *Ethics and Politics of Asylum*, 231.
28 Such an account intrinsically recognizes the situated or embedded nature of a liberal account of the good life.
29 For account of the deep scriptural and doctrinal logic that this teleology draws on, see Oliver O'Donovan, *The Desire of the Nations: Rediscovering the Roots of Political Theory* (Cambridge: Cambridge University Press, 1996), 66–73; Jon D. Levenson, "The Universal Horizon of Biblical Particularism," in *Ethnicity and the Bible*, ed. Mark Brett, 143–69 (Leiden: E. J. Brill, 1996); Karl Barth, *Church Dogmatics: The Doctrine of Creation* vol.3, part 4, trans. A. T. Mackay et al. (Edinburgh: T&T Clark, 1961), 309–23; and Nigel Biggar, "The Value of Limited Loyalty: Christianity, the Nation, and Territorial Boundaries," in *Boundaries and Justice: Diverse Ethics Perspectives*, ed. David Millar and Sohail Hashimi, 38–54 (Princeton: Princeton University Press, 2001).
30 Theologically, Dante is a deliberately ambiguous or borderline figure given that in his more explicitly political writing, he divorces human fulfillment from its fulfillment in communion with God such that it becomes an autonomous end. On this see Oliver O'Donovan and Joan Lockwood O'Donovan, *From Irenaeus to Grotius: A Sourcebook in Christian Political Thought 100–1625* (Grand Rapids: Eerdmans, 1999), 413–14, 423–24.
31 There is a strand of Christian political thought that justifies empire—Eusebius, for example. Even here empire is framed as a fulfillment of the local where the local is part of a hierarchy of rule rather than simply being overridden. Within modern theology, arguments for world government were put forward by Jacques Maritain, whose work informs much contemporary Catholic social thought, most notably *Pacem in Terris*. However, for the most part, the tradition equates world government with oppressive empire or the beast of Revelation. For a critique of Maritain and *Pacem in Terris*, see Joan Lockwood O'Donovan, "Subsidiarity and Political Authority in Theological Perspective," in *Bonds of Imperfection: Christian Politics, Past and Present*, ed.

Oliver O'Donovan and Joan Lockwood O'Donovan, 225–45 (Grand Rapids: Eerdmans, 2004).

32 *Pietas* denotes the reverence and concern for that to which one owes the possibility of one's own development, be it God or one's family, city, or country.

33 Quoted from Schlereth, *The Cosmopolitan Ideal* (Notre Dame, Ind.: University of Notre Dame, 1977), xxiv–xxv.

34 See, for example, Teresa Hayton, *Open Borders: The Case against Immigration Control* (Sterling, Va.: Pluto, 2000).

35 Wolfhart Pannenberg, *Ethics*, trans. Keith Crim (Philadelphia: Westminster, 1981), 147.

36 Pannenberg, *Ethics*, 148.

37 Pannenberg, *Ethics*, 148.

38 Pannenberg, *Ethics*, 151–74.

39 Miroslav Volf, *Exclusion and Embrace: A Theological Exploration of Identity, Otherness, and Reconciliation* (Nashville: Abingdon, 1996), 226.

40 *City of God*, xiv, 28

41 Oliver O'Donovan, "Government as Judgment," in *Bonds of Imperfection*, 207–24.

42 Joan Lockwood O'Donovan, "Nation, State and Civil Society in the Western Biblical Tradition," in *Bonds of Imperfection*, 287.

43 O'Donovan, "Nation, State and Civil Society in the Western Biblical Tradition," 286–87.

44 See, for example, David Morley, *Home Territories: Media, Mobility and Identity* (London: Routledge, 2000); and Paul Statham, "Understanding Anti-Asylum Rhetoric: Restrictive Politics or Racist Publics?" in *The Politics of Migration: Managing Opportunity, Conflict and Change*, ed. Sarah Spencer, 163–77 (Oxford: Blackwell, 2003).

45 On this, see Mary Douglas, *Purity and Danger: An Analysis of the Concept of Pollution and Taboo* (London: Routledge, 1966).

46 Gibney, *Ethics and Politics of Asylum*, 163.

47 Gibney, *Ethics and Politics of Asylum*, 164.

48 Gibney, *Ethics and Politics of Asylum*, 163. There is of course a direct parallel between the denuding of refugees of legal rights and the treatment of suspected terrorists after the bombings of September 11, 2001.

49 Geddes, *Politics of Migration and Immigration in Europe*, 127.

50 Gaim Kibreab, "Revisiting the Debate on People, Place, Identity and Displacement," *Journal of Refugee Studies* 12.4 (1999): 402.

51 Caroline Moorehead, *Human Cargo: A Journey among Refugees* (New York: H. Hold, 2005), 35–36.

52 Georgio Agamben, *Means without End: Notes on Politics*, trans. Vincenzo Binetti and Cesare Casarino (Minneapolis: University of Minnesota Press, 2000), 16–17.

53 Georgio Agamben, *Homo Sacer: Sovereign Power and Bare Life*, trans. Daniel Heller-Roazen (Stanford: Stanford University Press, 1998), 132.

54 Agamben, *Homo Sacer*, 103.

55 Agamben, *Homo Sacer*, 90.

56 The contrast between the situation of refugees, whose physical bodies are exposed to death at every turn, and that of transnational corporations (TNCs), those most abstract and ethereal of bodies, is instructive. While refugees are systematically denied or stripped of their international rights, TNCs are afforded more and more international legal protection. On this see B. S. Chimni, "Globalization, Humanitarianism, and the Erosion of Refugee Protection," *Journal of Refugee Studies* 13, no. 3 (2000): 243–63.

57 Hannah Arendt, *The Origins of Totalitarianism* (San Diego: Harcourt Brace Jovanovich, 1951), 291.

58 Arendt, *Origins of Totalitarianism*, 291.

59 Agamben, *Homo Sacer*, 126–27.

60 Arendt, *Origins of Totalitarianism*, 299.

61 This is a point that the exhortations of *Pacem in Terris* regarding refugees failed to grasp. John XXIII, *Pacem in Terris* (1963), para. 103–6.

62 Arendt, *The Origins of Totalitarianism*, 300.

63 Agamben, *Homo Sacer*, 134.

64 Agamben, *Homo Sacer*, 133.

65 Agamben, *Homo Sacer*, 133. For a critique of Agamben's account of the split between humanitarian concern and political action see Volker Heins, "Giogio Agamben and the Current State of Affairs in Humanitarian Law and Human Rights Policy," *German Law Journal* 6, no. 5 (2005): 845–60.

66 Similarly, the Sanctuary Movement in America and Canada, like many churches around the world, link political action with direct care.

67 On the centrality of the "state of exception" to modern sovereignty and contemporary politics see Agamben, *Homo Sacer*, 15–29.

68 Karl Barth, *The Christian Life: Church Dogmatics* IV, 4, *Lecture Fragments*, trans. Geoffrey Bromiley (Grand Rapids: Eerdmans, 1981), 175, 182.

69 Ulrich Luz notes that "hallowed be thy name" denotes both the sanctification of God's name by God himself (Lev 10:13; Ezek 36:22; 38:23; 39:7) and the sanctification of God's name by humans which intrinsically involves following God's commands and the pursuit of holiness (Exod 20:7; Lev 22:32; Isa 29:23). Ulrich Luz, *Matthew 1–7: A Commentary*, trans. Wilhelm Lins (Edinburgh: T&T Clark, 1989), 379.

70 Arendt, *Origins of Totalitarianism*, 301.

71 Barth, *Christian Life*, 154.

72 Barth, *Christian Life*, 160.

73 Colin Gunton, "Trinity, Ontology and Anthropology: Towards a Renewal

of the Doctrine of the *Imago Dei*," in *Persons, Divine and Human*, ed. Colin Gunton and Christoph Schwöbel (Edinburgh: T&T Clark, 1991), 59.

74 The question of whether gift within the divine-human economy is unconditional, as Kathryn Tanner contends, or involves gift-exchange, as John Milbank argues, is an important feature of contemporary theological debates. However, as David Albertson suggests in his discussion of patristic readings of the Lord's Prayer, one does not necessarily preclude the other (David Albertson, "On 'The Gift' in Tanner's Theology: A Patristic Parable," *Modern Theology* 21, no. 1 [2005]: 107–18).

75 John Inge, *A Christian Theology of Place* (Aldershot: Ashgate, 2003), 52.

76 See, for example, Gibney, *Ethics and Politics of Asylum*, 231–32; Walzer, *Spheres of Justice*, 33; and Dummett, *On Immigration and Refugees*, 69.

77 O'Donovan, *Desire of the Nations*, 268.

78 By giving priority to deterrence over prevention, states refuse the possibility of creative engagement with the causes of asylum and settle for containment, a policy that is inherently fatalistic and refuses hope in a different future.

79 Milbank, *Being Reconciled*, 92–97.

80 Denis Müller, "A Homeland for Transients: Towards an Ethic of Migrations," in *Migrants and Refugees*, ed. Dietmar Mieth and Lisa Sowle Cahill (London: Concilium/SCM Press, 1993), 143. Conversely, we should be wary of over-valorizing exile and mobility. Refugees point to the importance of home, place, and territory and call into question the "postmodern beatification of the nomad" (Morley, *Home Territories*, 230). See also Kibreab, "Revisiting the Debate on People, Place, Identity, and Displacement," 384–410.

81 See Ernst Lohmeyer, *The Lord's Prayer*, trans. John Bowden (London: Collins, 1965), 79–87.

82 Bernd Wannenwetsch, "The Political Worship of the Church: A Critical and Empowering Practice," *Modern Theology* 12, no. 3 (1996): 269–99.

83 See, e.g., Ephesians 2:19-22.

84 For an example of this in relation to the hallowing of the suffering-dying, see the discussion of hospitality and euthanasia in Luke Bretherton, *Hospitality as Holiness: Christian Witness amid Moral Diversity* (Aldershot: Ashgate, 2006).

85 The U.S. sanctuary movement operated from 1982 to 1992 in response to restrictive U.S. policy regarding Central American refugees from countries with regimes supported by the U.S. government. A similar movement began in Canada in 1983.

86 Barth, *Christian Life*, 172.

87 Even when the rights of refugees are respected, history suggests this respect is highly contingent and owes more to the vagaries of foreign policy than it does to concern for humans qua humans. An example

of this is the link between U.S. foreign and refugee policies during the Cold War. See Gibney, *Ethics and Politics of Asylum*, 146–54; and Loescher on the early development of UNHCR (*Beyond Charity*, 55–74).

CHAPTER 8

1 Many colleagues have contributed to this paper, some over the years, even decades, some with less attenuation. Craig Parsons is my coauthor of two papers that form the immediate basis for this one, and the principal author of indicated portions of the text below. Richard Mshomba and James K. A. Smith provided acute queries on earlier drafts. Kim Elliott, Ellen Frost, Brent Nelsen, Robert Rubinstein, and Mike Schneider have been ready and regular sounding boards for some of the ideas. Michael Barkun, Jim Halteman, P. J. Hill, John Mason, and Kurt Schaefer all provided key insights for literature on which to build. Alfonso Tolmos and Jessica Rosa Carmelia Silva Yon have been active interlocutors and colaborers on this entire draft, and are the authors of an extended Andean Case Study along these lines, slated to appear in a much-expanded planned-for-the-future version of this chapter.

2 Elliott, Kar, and Richardson document and explain the global backlash against global market integration and cross-reference a large literature that has the same purpose (Kimberly Ann Elliott, Debayani Kar, and J. David Richardson, "Assessing Globalization's Critics: 'Talkers Are No Good Doers???'," in *Challenges for Globalization*, ed. Robert E. Baldwin and Alan Winters, 17–60 [Chicago: University of Chicago Press, 2004]). Bhagwati's further purpose along these lines is to constructively answer and engage global-integration critics (Jagdish Bhagwati, *In Defense of Globalization* [New York: Oxford University Press for the Council on Foreign Relations, 2004]). Richardson describes the benefits and burdens of recent American globalization (J. David Richardson,"Some Measurable Costs and Benefits of Economic Globalization for Americans," in *Globalization and Its Outcomes*, ed. John O'Loughlin, Lynn Staehli, and Edward Greenberg, 182–92 [New York: Guilford, 2004]; Richardson, *Global Forces, American Faces: U.S. Economic Globalization at the Grass Roots* [Washington, D.C.: Institute for International Economics, forthcoming]).

3 Critics whose normative ideal is an economically just globalization may well be unsatisfied with this approach. My own feeling is that the task of "embedding" a market system in "social scaffolding" is logically and historically prior to the task of making the scaffolding "just" (by some "legitimate" definition), though there is almost always temporal overlap in real cases. The various fraught words in quotation marks will, I hope, be clarified in the text.

4 I will not, therefore, be addressing the more general—and natural and

important—ways that one might address the interface between religion and economics, such as whether whether there is an "economics
of religious adherence" (see Rachel M. McCleary and Robert J. Barro,
"Religion and Economy," *Journal of Economic Perspectives* 20 [2006]:
49–72; Laurence R. Iannaccone, "Economics of Religion: Debating the
Costs and Benefits of a New Field," *Faith and Economics* 46 [2005]: 1–23;
and commentators, with historical references), or whether religious
observance enhances economic performance for individuals or societies (see, e.g., Robert J. Barro and Rachel M. McCleary, "Religion and
Economic Growth," National Bureau of Economic Research Working
Paper 9682, May 2003, Cambridge, Massachusetts; Jonathan H. Gruber,
"Religious Market Structure, Religious Participation, and Outcomes:
Is Religion Good for You?" *Advances in Economic Analysis and Policy* 5,
no. 1 [2005]: Article 5, 1–30; McCleary and Barro, "Religion and Economy"; Marcus Noland and Howard Pack, "Islam, Globalization, and
Economic Performance in the Middle East," Institute for International
Economics Policy Brief Number PB04-4, June 2004, Washington, D.C.),
or whether strong economic performance enhances morality (Benjamin M. Friedman, *The Moral Consequences of Economic Growth* [New York:
Knopf, 2005]), or whether cross-country religious similarity enhances
both the acceptance and rejection of economic-reform ideas (as documented, for example, in both directions, by Beth A. Simmons and
Zachary Elkins, "The Globalization of Liberalization: Policy Diffusion
in the International Political Economy," *American Political Science Review*
98 [2004]: 171–89, for financial reform).

5   Rebecca M. Blank and William McGurn, *Is the Market Moral? A Dialogue
on Religion, Economics, and Justice* (Washington, D.C.: Brookings and
Georgetown University, 2004).

6   See John Paul II, *Centesimus Annus* (1991), available at http://www.
osjspm.org/cst/ca.htm. E. Malinvaud ("Duty of Democracies to Care
More about Intergenerational and International Solidarities," paper
presented at the Vatican City conference on The Call to Justice: The
Legacy of Gaudium et Spes 40 Years Later, March 16–18, 2005, available
at www.stthomas.edu/cathstudies/cst/conferences/gaudium/ among
the Selected Papers) observes a similar neglect in the sweep of Roman
Catholic social teaching, and also observes its surprising neglect of
intergenerational justice. I. M. D. Little, *Ethics, Economics, and Politics:
Principles of Public Policy* (Oxford: Oxford University Press, 2002), offers
an areligious example of the national-markets-and-justice theme (I
use the word "secular" below as a synonym for "areligious"), though
by design, not by neglect: "what is surely *unobtainable* is a moral
theory [and by implication a *political* philosophy] that applies universally. More than two thousand years of failure supports this view [xvi,

emphasis added]." In other words, Little would probably find the volu-
minous natural-law tradition and most of the forward-looking agenda
of the current paper to be a fool's errand. Yet if he were correct, the
world is left in the deeply uncomfortable position of having no ethical basis for legitimizing global markets. Secular philosophers such as
Peter Singer clearly are not *that* skeptical (*One World: The Ethics of Globalization* [New Haven: Yale University Press, 2002; 2nd ed., 2004]). Nor are
political economists such as Ethan B. Kapstein (*Economic Justice in an
Unfair World: Toward a Level Playing Field* [Princeton: Princeton University Press, 2006]). Nor are theologians such as John Milbank ("Liberality versus Liberalism," paper presented at the Vatican City conference
on the Call to Justice: The Legacy of Gaudium et Spes 40 Years Later,
March 16–18, 2005, available at www.stthomas.edu/cathstudies/cst/
conferences/gaudium/, among the Selected Papers)—to say nothing of
Aquinas and his successors!

7   Influential contributions to this narrowly "prophetic" literature (in
whole or in parts), from Christian and secular viewpoints, include
the following: Bob Goudzwaard, *Capitalism and Progress: A Diagnosis
of Western Society* (Toronto: Wedge, for Association for the Advancement of Christian Scholarship; Grand Rapids: Eerdmans, 1979; originally published in Dutch in 1978 as *Kapitalisme en vooruitgang* [Assen:
Van Gorcum, 1978]); Naomi Klein, *No Logo* (New York: Picador, 2002);
David C. Korten, *When Corporations Rule the World* (San Francisco: Ber-
rett-Koehler; West Hartford, Conn.: Kumarian, 1995); D. Stephen Long,
Divine Economy: Theology and the Market (London: Routledge, 2000); Jerry
Mander and Edward Goldsmith, eds., *The Case against the Global Economy*
(San Francisco: Sierra, 1996); National Conference of Catholic Bishops
(U.S.), *Economic Justice for All: Pastoral Letter on Catholic Social Teach-
ing and the U.S. Economy* (Washington, D.C.: U.S. Catholic Conference,
1986); Ronald J. Sider, *Rich Christians in an Age of Hunger: A Biblical Study*
(Chicago: InterVarsity, 1977; revised and republished as Sider, *Rich
Christians in an Age of Hunger: Moving from Affluence to Generosity* [Dal-
las: Word, 1997]); Singer, *One World*; World Council of Catholic Bishops,
Justice in the World (1971), http://www.osjspm.org/majordoc_justi-
cia_in_mundo_offical_test.aspx. J. Phillip Wogamon, *Economics and
Ethics: A Christian Inquiry* (Philadelphia: Fortress, 1986).

8   I have in mind a model of social science described cogently and ireni-
cally by Thomas F. Pettigrew (*How to Think Like a Social Scientist* [New
York: Harper Collins, 1996]). He emphasizes (1) theories of individual
and social behavior within the broader context of paradigms, (2) causal
accounts of similarity and difference in patterns over time and other
dimensions, as well as their nuances and philosophical difficulties,
and (3) sampling, inference, comparison, aggregation, and interac-

tions of patterns at "micro and macro" levels. Elegance notwithstanding, Pettigrew devotes only a little space to comparing social-science discourse and deliberation to that in humanities, and therefore does not wrestle in much detail with larger questions of method that concern epistemology and interpretation (assigning meaning).

9 See Johnson et al. for a very recent treatment (Simon Johnson, Jonathan D. Ostry, and Arvind Subramanian, "The Prospects for Sustained Growth in Africa: Benchmarking the Constraints," International Monetary Fund Working Paper No. WP/07/52 [March 2007]). See World Bank, *Globalization, Growth, and Poverty: Building an Inclusive World Economy* (Washington, DC: World Bank; New York: Oxford University Press, 2002), and Dani Rodrik, ed., *In Search of Prosperity: Analytical Narratives on Economic Growth* (Princeton: Princeton University Press, 2003) for more comprehensive treatments—the first supportive, the second skeptical. For varieties of documentation, see the annual *Human Development Reports* of the United Nations Conference on Trade and Development (UNCTAD) and the A. T. Kearney/Foreign Policy Globalization Index published annually in the journal *Foreign Policy*.

10 See Craig Parsons and J. David Richardson, "Lessons for Asia? European Experiences—in American Perspective—in Legitimizing Market Integration," *Journal of Asian Economics* 14 (2004): 885–907; Parsons and Richardson, "Lessons for Asia? Legitimacy and Quasi-Democratic Mechanisms in European and American Market Integration," in *International Economic Integration and Asia*, Advanced Research in Asian Economic Studies 3, ed. Erik Jones and Michael R. Plummer (Hackensack, N.J.: World Scientific Publishers, 2006). National and regional market integration are merely smaller-scale versions of global market integration—economic globalization.

11 Fitfully both historically and currently, as opposition to political and constitutional integration calls into question even the extant economic integration. For example, European integration of services markets, including public services and worker services (worker mobility), is raising new opposition from national governments and from professional educational, legal, and medical communities.

12 See also Kimberly Ann Elliott, who argues that economic incentives and strategic benefits (e.g., to draw a former Eastern-bloc country into the "West") go only so far in encouraging cross-border economic integration, and that social trust in market-modulating institutions and in cross-border political process is the necessary complement to make economic integration sustainable (Elliott, "The Role of Incentives, Trust, and Institutions in Sustainable Single Markets," presented at a conference on Lessons for a Globalizing World? Historical Experiences of Europe and the United States in Market Integration, European

Union Center of the Maxwell School of Syracuse University, Washington, D.C., September 25–26, 2002).

13 Parsons and Richardson describe a Polanyi-like "double movement" (K. Polanyi, *The Great Transformation* [Boston: Beacon, 1944]) that we find important in the American history of legitimizing the integration of national markets (as does Richard F. Bensel, *The Political Economy of American Industrialization, 1877–1900* [New York: Cambridge University Press, 2000], and, implicitly, Michael McGerr, *A Fierce Discontent: The Rise and Fall of the Progressive Movement in America, 1870–1920* [New York: Free Press, 2003]).

14 The contributors to John H. Dunning, ed., *Making Globalization Good: The Moral Challenges of Global Capitalism* (New York: Oxford University Press, 2003), make a valuable start at charting a role for religion in general. The five chapters of part 2 explore the moral challenge of global capitalism in the light of ethics from four major religious traditions. Dunning himself as editor, however, seems willing to embrace transcendental religion only for its energy and example, as a constructive catalyst in "making [economic] globalization good" (see "The Moral Imperatives of Global Capitalism: An Overview" and "Conclusions: In Search of a Global Moral Architecture," chaps. 1 and 16, respectively, in *Making Globalization Good*. But in rejecting without defining fundamentalist versions of monotheistic religion, Dunning runs the risk of undermining his hope for it by implicitly disparaging its integrity. This chapter and others in this book take Christian fundamentals more seriously than Dunning in undergirding a postsecular global society.

15 J. David Richardson, "The WTO and Market-Supportive Regulation: A Way Forward on New Competition, Technological, and Labor Issues," Proceedings of the Twenty-Fourth Annual Economic Policy Conference of the Federal Reserve Bank of St. Louis, *Federal Reserve Bank of St. Louis Review* 82, no. 4 (2000): 115–29; Richardson, "Designing a Market-Enhancing WTO," in *The World Trade Organization in the New Global Economy: Trade and Investment Issues in the Millennium Round*, ed. Alan M. Rugman and Gavin Boyd, 257–74 (Cheltenham, U.K.: Edward Elgar New Horizons in International Business Series, 2001).

16 The market system is a complex, vertical, and social network of purchases and sales, contracts and conventions among firms that are simultaneously cooperative and competitive. Firms are themselves cooperative social units, with socially granted rights (for example, to own property). The market system is thus a social organism (see Charles E. Lindblom, *The Market System: What It Is, How It Works, and What to Make of It* [New Haven: Yale University Press, 2001], and Neil Fligstein, *The Architecture of Markets: An Economic Sociology of Twenty-First Century Capitalist Societies* [Princeton: Princeton University Press, 2001]).

Economic regulations condition this competitive-cooperative market system, internally within a firm and externally across them. For example, company law enhances the market for corporate control; it establishes categories of voting rights and procedures for shareholders, and determines when and how a rival firm's managers can compete for the shareholders' allegiance (cooperation). Or, for example, labor-relations law enhances the market for cooperative representation—agency; it establishes workplace voting procedures for workers to be represented collectively by a union (a union is a specific type of firm), and when and how another union could compete for certification to organize the workers cooperatively. Among other goals, such economic regulations aim to make the market system work better and for a broader constituency. Designed properly, they are market-supportive and simultaneously part of the broader social infrastructure. They regulate the intensity of competition, the scope of cooperation, and define the due processes and legal boundaries for both, including the important boundary between coercive and voluntary transactions.

17 There are really several important institutional schools, of several vintages. For a modern sampling, with some retrospection, see Dani Rodrik, "Why Do More Open Economies Have Bigger Governments?" *Journal of Political Economy* 106, no. 5 (1998): 997–1032; or Douglass C. North, *Understanding the Process of Economic Change* (Princeton: Princeton University Press, 2005).

18 It is unfortunate that the progressive view is often submerged by both shallow, breathless defenses of "free" markets and alarmist, populist accounts of the war between greed and governance. Stigler's classic critique of the progressive confidence that regulation would desirably embed and discipline markets has spawned a much more thoughtful skepticism about the progressive confidence that underlies much of my own view (George J. Stigler, "The Theory of Economic Regulation," *Bell Journal of Economics and Management Science* 2 [1971]: 3–21).

19 See, for example, International Labor Organization, World Commission on the Social Dimension of Globalization, *A Fair Globalization: Creating Opportunities for All* (Geneva: ILO, 2004); Kemal Dervis, in cooperation with Ceren Özer, *A Better Globalization: Legitimacy, Governance, and Reform* (Washington, D.C.: Center for Global Development, 2005); David Held, *Global Covenant: The Social Democratic Alternative to the Washington Consensus* (Cambridge; Malden, Mass.: Polity, 2004); or David Held et al., *Debating Globalization* (Cambridge: Polity Press, in cooperation with openDemocracy [www.opendemocracy.net], 2005).

20 Robert H. Wiebe, *The Search for Order: 1877-1920* (New York: Farrar, Strauss, and Giroux [Hill and Wang], 1967), 208–9.

21 Robert Fogel, *The Fourth Great Awakening and the Future of Egalitarianism*

(Chicago: University of Chicago Press, 2000). American evangelicals, in contrast to European Catholics, may feel that riddance rather than remembrance is the proper fate of the social gospel, forgetting (or not knowing) the integral place it had in nineteenth-century de facto evangelicalism (social-gospel consolidator Walter Rauschenbusch was a pietist, poet, and hymn writer), and how the social-gospel movement was later corrupted and captured by secularizing and modernizing forces. On the richer and more nuanced American history, see Christopher H. Evans, *The Kingdom Is Always but Coming: A Life of Walter Rauschenbusch* (Grand Rapids: Eerdmans, 2004); David O. Moberg, *The Great Reversal: Evangelism and Social Concern*, rev. ed. (Philadelphia and New York: Lippincott, 1977), chaps, 1, 2; and Richard V. Pierard, *The Unequal Yoke: Evangelical Christianity and Political Conservatism* (Philadelphia: Lippincott, 1970; rev. ed. Eugene, Ore: Wipf and Stock, 2006). Some modern theologians may be equally dismissive of the social gospel, identifying it with mere civil religion. That it was, on the contrary, fervent, serious (even threatening), and transcendently motivated, see McGerr, *Fierce Discontent*. See also the important role of transcendent judgment in Robert N. Bellah's seminal articulation of civic religion ("Civil Religion in America," *Daedalus* (Winter 1967); reprinted as chapter 9 of Bellah, *Beyond Belief: Essays on Religion in a Post-Traditionalist World* [Berkeley: University of California Press, 1970]); the social gospel "had teeth." On contrasting European history, see Noll's brief Foreword to Evans, *Kingdom Is Always but Coming*, which has capsules on Anglican, Lutheran, and Reformed parallels to the succession of papal encyclicals, some celebrating the anniversary of others, starting with *Rerum Novarum* in 1891.

22 Anne-Marie Slaughter and Thomas N. Hale ("A Covenant to Make Global Governance Work," in Held et al., *Debating Globalization*, 130–33) include a brief endorsement of the value of exploring this idea. Scott M. Thomas endorses a variation of it forcefully (see *The Global Resurgence of Religion and the Transformation of International Relations* [New York: Palgrave/Macmillan, 2005], and "Whose Development, Which Rationality: *Gaudium et Spes*, Catholic Social Thought, and International Development Policy after MacIntyre," paper presented at the Vatican City conference on The Call to Justice: The Legacy of Gaudium et Spes 40 Years Later, March 16–18, 2005, available at www.stthomas.edu/cathstudies/cst/conferences/gaudium/, among the Selected Papers.

23 See Parsons and Richardson ("Lessons for Asia? European Experiences," and "Lessons for Asia? Legitimacy and Quasi-Democratic Mechanisms"), on which the capsule histories in this paper draw heavily, for a more detailed treatment of the content and mechanisms from an instrumental perspective.

24 One could provocatively call them "transnational" with only a tiny

rhetorical spin. The corporate form of governance blossomed during this era, for example, displacing less formal family ownership and partnerships.

25 See Richard Hofstadter, *The Age of Reform: From Bryan to F.D.R.* (New York: Random House [Vintage], 1955), and Robert H. Wiebe, *The Search for Order: 1877–1920*. New York: Farrar, Strauss, and Giroux (Hill and Wang), 1967.

26 See Fogel, *Fourth Great Awakening and the Future of Egalitarianism*, and McGerr, *Fierce Discontent.*

27 See Evans, *Kingdom Is Always but Coming*, for a definitive recent treatment of Rauschenbusch. Washington Gladden, though a pastor, was invited by Richard T. Ely, an economist, to the founding meeting of the American Economics Association, and became a charter member (Bradley W. Bateman, "Race, Intellectual History, and American Economics," *History of Political Economy* 35, no. 4 [2003]: 713–30).

28 Fogel, *Fourth Great Awakening and the Future of Egalitarianism*, 22–25, 171–73; see also Evans, *Kingdom Is Always but Coming*, chaps. 3, 11, 12.

29 See also Peter H. Lindert's magisterial treatment of the history and cross-country determinants of government social spending (*Growing Public: Social Spending and Economic Growth since the Eighteenth Century*, vol. 1 [New York: Cambridge University Press, 2004]). He finds (as have others he cites on 187) a negative relationship across countries and time, *ceteris paribus*, between government social spending as a share of overall output and an index of ethnic divisions (including religion).

30 Nancy Cohen, *The Reconstruction of American Liberalism, 1865–1914* (Chapel Hill: University of North Carolina Press, 2002).

31 Bensel, *Political Economy of American Industrialization.*

32 Leo XIII, *Rerum Novarum* (1891). http://www.papalencyclicals.net/Leo13/l13rerum.htm.

33 Worth addressing is the impression (and sometimes the prejudice) that religion—especially serious (pejoratively) fundamental versions of it in contrast to bland civil religion—has a negative influence on peace and prosperity. Many think viscerally that religion is at the heart of violent conflict and war, both among and within nations, with enormous carnage and economic loss. Recent research surveys have called this prejudice into serious question. One of the easiest to access surveys is Collier et al., who summarize research across fifty-two cases of civil war and a larger case sample of countries without civil war from 1960 to 1999 (Paul Collier, V. L. Elliott, Håvard Hegre, Anke Hoeffler, Marta Reynal-Querol, and Nicholas Sambanis, *Breaking the Conflict Trap: Civil War and Development Policy* [New York and Washington, D.C.: Oxford and World Bank, 2003], 3–4, 56–70). The research finds civil war most closely associated with geographically concentrated natural resources

and with devolution in territorial poverty, inequality, and economic decline. Religion itself has little correlation with civil war. In fact, ethnic and religious diversity is negatively related to civil war—though both dominance and polarization (roughly balanced binary diversity only) correlate positively with civil war. (Once conflict is under way, ethnicity is, however, commonly exploited as a tactic to maintain cohesion within the warring groups [Collier et al., 69–70]).

34 George Weigel, *The Cube and the Cathedral: Europe, America, and Politics without God* (New York: Basic, 2005), 70. See also Gary Marks and Carole Wilson, "National Parties and the Contestation of Europe," in *Legitimacy and the European Union: the Contested Polity*, ed. Thomas Banchoff and Mitchell P. Smith (London: Routledge, 1999), among many other references. My coauthor Craig Parsons is the original author of most of the rest of this subsection.

35 William Wallace, *Regional Integration: The West European Experience* (Washington, D.C.: Brookings, 1994), 19–27.

36 Farmers were also the key societal group needing compensation in the nineteenth-century United States.

37 Structural Funds, for example, had previously been distributed according to a region's level of poverty relative to EU averages. This had resulted in Greece, Spain, Portugal, and Ireland receiving as much as 4 percent of their GDP annually from the EU. To cut down subsidies to the East while preserving the appearance of fairness, the commission proposed that Structural Fund benefits be capped at 4 percent of any member's GDP—which in the much poorer East meant much smaller payments than the original formula would have implied.

38 For a much fuller account, see Parsons and Richardson, "Lessons for Asia? European Experiences," and "Lessons for Asia? Legitimacy and Quasi-Democratic Mechanisms."

39 See Ernst Haas, *The Uniting of Europe: Political, Social, and Economic Forces, 1950–1957* (Stanford: Stanford University Press, 1958), and Wayne Sandholtz and Alec Stone-Sweet, eds., *European Integration and Supranational Governance* (New York: Oxford University Press, 1998).

40 See Craig Parsons, "Showing Ideas as Causes: The Origins of the European Union," *International Organization* 56, no. 1 (2002): 47–84; Parsons, *A Certain Idea of Europe* (Ithaca: Cornell University Press, 2003).

41 See McGerr, *Fierce Discontent*, for a sustained argument that Progressivism was a middle-class social crusade.

42 Woodrow Wilson might be thought to come close, but his tenure was arguably marked by Progressive "over-reach" (McGerr, *Fierce Discontent*), and so was notably ineffective in pioneering new institutions or legitimizing mechanisms, as opposed to consolidating those that had been evolving for several decades, such as woman's suffrage. William

Jennings Bryan's highest elective office was two terms as a member of the U.S. House of Representatives.

43 Edward L. Glaeser and Claudia Goldin, eds., *Corruption and Reform: Lessons from America's Economic History* (Chicago: University of Chicago Press, 2006).

44 Robert N. Bellah's second wave of work on civil religion documents this point strongly (see Bellah and Phillip E. Hammond, *Varieties of Civil Religion* [San Francisco: Harper and Row, 1980]). And many commentators seem to have forgotten that Bellah's closing section ("The Third Time of Trial") of his foundational essay was devoted to envisioning and characterizing a global (civil) religion that could judge and/or legitimize global polities and structures ("Civil Religion in America").

45 See Malinvaud, "Duty of Democracies to Care More about Intergenerational and International Solidarities."

46 Elliott, "Role of Incentives, Trust, and Institutions in Sustainable Single Markets."

47 John Paul II, *Ecclesia in Europa, L'Osservatore Romano,* July 2, 2003; available at http://www.vatican.va/holy_father/john_paul_ii/apost_ exhortations/documents/hf_jp-ii_exh_20030628_ecclesia-in-europa_ en.html.

48 See especially Rudiger Noll ("European Integration: An Issue on the Churches' Agenda," in the *Study Guide for the Third European Ecumenical Assembly,* available at http://www.eea3.org/), on which this paragraph is based. The pilgrimage/assembly is the third in a series coorganized by the Conference of European Churches (CEC) (www.cec-kek.org) and the Concilium Conferentiarum Episcoporum Europae (CCEE) (www. ccee.ch). The first two assemblies in the series took place in 1989 and 1997.

49 The Group of the European People's Party (Christian Democrats) and European Democrats (EPP-ED) (www.epp-ed.org).

50 EPCM (www.epcm.info) aims to incorporate an "explicit Christian Social point of view" into European politics, along the lines of orthodox Protestantism, with full government guarantees therefore for freedom of religion that would include mainstream Islam (and implicitly Turkish EU membership) that was willing to abjure Islamist theocracy and violence.

51 See Weigel (*Cube and the Cathedral,* 146–53), who details a new generation's reassertion of Christian values in Catholic social teaching, reinforced by the Vatican and its decade of World Youth Days, as well as by activist, integrationist Catholic renewal and lay movements such as Focolaré and Opus Dei. Weigel's hopeful, perhaps wishful, scenario for what the "John Paul II generation" can constructively accomplish as successors to the Christophobic secularist "generation of 1968" is entirely consistent with the theme of this volume—postmodern,

respiritualized, socially sustainable, global integration. Weigel's second-to-last chapter is in fact entitled "A Different Modernity."

52 See, e.g., Ronald J. Sider, *The Scandal of the Evangelical Conscience* (Grand Rapids: Baker, 2005); James W. Skillen, *With or Against the World? America's Role among the Nations* (Lanham, Md.: Rowman and Littlefield, in cooperation with the Center for Public Justice, 2005); and Jim Wallis, *God's Politics: Why the Right Gets It Wrong and the Left Doesn't Get It* (San Francisco: Harper, 2005).

53 It is intriguing that Lindert (*Growing Public*, vol. 1, chap. 4; *Growing Public*, vol. 2, *Social Spending and Economic Growth since the Eighteenth Century* [New York: Cambridge University Press, 2004], chap. 17 and Appendix E) finds that global integration and government social spending go hand in hand positively across countries and time, *ceteris paribus*— replicating findings of Rodrik and other economists, historians, and sociologists (e.g., Brady, Beckfield, and Seelieb-Kaiser; Huberman and Lewchuk) for East Asian, Central Asian, and Central European transition economies also. See David Brady, Jason Beckfield, and Martin Seeleib-Kaiser, "Economic Globalization and the Welfare State in Affluent Democracies, 1975–2001," *American Sociological Review* 70 (2005): 921–48; Michael Huberman and Wayne Lewchuk, "European Economic Integration and the Labour Compact, 1850–1913," Centre Interuniversitaire de Recherché en Analyse des Organisations (CIRANO), Scientific Series 2002-s34.

54 But see, e.g., Khurshid Ahmad, "The Challenge of Global Capitalism: An Islamic Perspective," in Dunning, ed., *Making Globalization Good*; Timur Kuran, *Islam and Mammon: The Economic Predicaments of Islamism* (Princeton: Princeton University Press, 2004); Seyyed Hossein Nasr, *The Heart of Islam: Enduring Values for Humanity* (San Francisco: Harper-Collins, 2002); and William H. Thornton, *New World Empire: Civil Islam, Terrorism, and the Making of Neoglobalism* (Lanham, Md.: Rowman and Littlefield, 2005). Also beyond this paper would be a similar study of Hindu influence in Indian national and global integration (see Ramgopal Agarwala, "A Harmonist Manifesto: Hindu Philosophy in Action," in *Friday Morning Reflections at the World Bank*, ed. David Beckmann, Ramgopal Agarwala, Sven Burmester, and Ismail Serageldin [Washington, D.C.: Seven Locks, 1991], who begins laying a Hindu philosophical foundation) or Buddhist influence more broadly in East Asian integration (David R. Loy, "The Challenge of Global Capitalism: The Perspective of Eastern Religions," in Dunning, ed., *Making Globalization Good*, offers a beginning). The twenty-year-old ANZCERTA agreement between Australia and New Zealand may also be worth studying, to see if Christianity played any detectable legitimizing role. Likewise worth studying is the somewhat younger Southern African integration, the Southern African Development Community (SADC), in which the fractious

religious and cultural history of the region might be thought at first blush to hold back sustained successful social embedding.

55 See Milbank, "Liberality versus Liberalism," 6 and passim, for similar confidence that a common core of social embedding of markets can be discovered in each of the three great monotheistic traditions and in neo-Platonism. Milbank, however, differs diametrically from the current paper in his preference for localized markets, sufficiently insulated from global market integration that they can maintain elements of gift-exchange, beyond mere contracting for wants and desires.

56 The planned extension of this paper will include a detailed Andean case study, authored by Alfonso Tolmos and Jessica Rosa Carmelia Silva Yon.

CHAPTER 9

1 D. Liverman, "Who Governs, at What Scale and at What Price? Geography, Environmental Governance, and the Commodification of Nature," *Annals of the Association of American Geographers* 94, no. 4 (2004): 734–38, 734.

2 J. C. Tronto, *Moral Boundaries: A Political Argument for an Ethic of Care* (New York: Routledge, 1994), 6.

3 Tronto, *Moral Boundaries*, 8.

4 Tronto, *Moral Boundaries*, 9.

5 Tronto, *Moral Boundaries*, 9.

6 James K. A. Smith, *Introducing Radical Orthodoxy* (Grand Rapids: Baker Academic, 2004), 234.

7 William Cronon, *Changes in the Land: Indians, Colonists, and the Ecology of New England* (New York: Hill and Wang, 1983), 58.

8 Iain Wallace, "Globalization: Discourse of Destiny or Denial," *Christian Scholar's Review* 31 (2002): 377–91, 379.

9 Wallace, "Globalization," 382.

10 Iain Wallace, *The Global Economic System* (New York: Routledge, 1990), 12.

11 Smith, *Introducing Radical Orthodoxy*, 249.

12 Smith, *Introducing Radical Orthodoxy*, 133–34. For an expanded analysis of social atomism and how it impacts natural resource policy, see Janel M. Curry and Steve McGuire, *Community on Land: Community, Ecology, and the Public Interest* (Boulder, Colo.: Rowman and Littlefield, 2002); Janel M. Curry-Roper and Steven McGuire, "The Individualistic Imagination and Natural Resource Policy," *Society and Natural Resources* 6 (1993): 259–72.

13 Smith, *Introducing Radical Orthodoxy*, 136.

14 Smith, *Introducing Radical Orthodoxy*, 185.

15 R. Clough, "Introduction," in *Great Barrier Island*, ed. D. Armitage, 10–20 (Christchurch, N.Z.: Canterbury University Press, 2001), 19.

16　Janel M. Curry, "Contested Ocean Spaces: Great Barrier Island, New Zealand," *Focus* 48 (2006): 25–30.

17　J. Bhagwati, *In Defense of Globalization* (New York: Oxford University Press for the Council on Foreign Relations, 2004).

18　B. Mansfield, "Rules of Privatization: Contradictions in Neoliberal Regulation of North Pacific Fisheries," *Annals of the Association of American Geographers* 94, no. 3 (2004): 565–84, 565.

19　B. M. H. Sharp, "From Regulated Access to Transferable Harvesting Rights: Policy Insights from New Zealand," *Marine Policy* 21, no. 6 (1997): 501–17; C. J. Batstone and B. M. H. Sharp, "New Zealand's Quota Management System: The First Ten Years," *Marine Policy* 23, no. 2 (1999): 177–90.

20　P. A. Memon and R. Cullen, "Fisheries Policies and Their Impact on the New Zealand Maori," *Marine Resource Economics* 7 (1992): 153–67, 158.

21　Auckland City, Great Barrier Island (GBI) Overview and Strategy, Report to Directors, February 24, 2003, 5; L. Howie and A. Robertson, "Great Barrier Island Community Profile" (unpublished manuscript, 2002), 12.

22　Mansfield, "Rules of Privatization," 570.

23　J. Fall, "Divide and Rule: Constructing Human Boundaries in 'Boundless Nature,'" *GeoJournal* 58 (2002): 243–51.

24　New Zealand Department of Conservation, *A Marine Reserve for Great Barrier Island? Your Chance to Have a Say,* January 2003, 4.

25　Fall, "Divide and Rule," 245.

26　Fall, "Divide and Rule," 246.

27　C. A. Capitini, B. N. Tissot, M. S. Carroll, W. J. Walsh, and S. Peck, "Competing Perspectives in Resource Protection: The Case of Marine Protected Areas in West Hawai'i," *Society and Natural Resources* 17 (2004): 763–78, 776.

28　Fall, "Divide and Rule," 248.

29　G. A. Bradshaw and M. Bekoff, "Integrating Humans and Nature," *Trends in Ecology and Evolution* 15, no. 8 (2000): 309–10, 309.

30　Mansfield, "Rules of Privatization," 566.

31　Clough, "Introduction," 19.

32　P. Simons, "Going beyond Technicism and Neo-liberal Economism: What Is Involved in a Sustainable Long-term Care of Land and Sea?" Paper presented at Hui on "Caring for Land and Sea," Tamihana Foundation, June 12, 2004, 1.

33　Bradshaw and Bekoff, "Integrating Humans," 309.

34　L. Nader, "Anthropological Inquiry into Boundaries' Power, and Knowledge," in *Naked Science: Anthropological Inquiry into Boundaries, Power, and Knowledge*, ed. L. Nader, 1–25 (New York: Routledge, 1996), 3.

35　P. R. Wilshusen, S. R. Brechin, C. L. Fortwangler, and P. C. West, "Reinventing a Square Wheel: Critique of a Resurgent 'Protection Paradigm' in International Biodiversity Conservation," *Society and Natural Resources* 15 (2002): 17–40, 25.

36 N. Noddings, *Caring: A Feminine Approach to Ethics and Moral Education* (Berkeley: University of California Press, 1984), 26.

37 S. Whatmore, *Hybrid Geographies: Natures, Cultures Spaces* (London: Sage, 2002), 3.

38 S. R. Brechin, P. R. Wilshusen, C. L. Fortwangler, and P. C. West, "Beyond the Square Wheel: Toward a More Comprehensive Understanding of Biodiversity Conservation as Social and Political Process," *Society and Natural Resources* 15 (2002): 41–64, 46.

39 J. M. Curry-Roper, "Embeddedness in Place: Its Role in the Sustainability of a Rural Farm Community in Iowa," *Space and Culture* 4, no. 5 (2000): 204–22.

40 Wallace, "Globalization," 381.

41 Wallace, "Globalization," 391.

42 Tronto, *Moral Boundaries*, 29.

43 Smith, *Introducing Radical Orthodoxy*, 240.

44 Whatmore, *Hybrid Geographies*, 146.

45 B. Stephenson, "Nature, Technology, and the *Imago Dei*: Mediating the Nonhuman through the Practice of Science," *Perspectives on Science and Christian Faith* 57 (2005): 6–12, 7.

46 R. E. Groenhout, *Theological Echoes in an Ethic of Care*. Erasmus Institute Occasional Papers 2003-2 (South Bend, Ind.: Erasmus Institute, University of Notre Dame, 2003).

47 Stephenson, "Nature," 9.

48 Stephenson, "Nature," 11.

49 Whatmore, *Hybrid Geographies*, 98.

50 Smith, *Introducing Radical Orthodoxy*, 129–30.

51 Smith, *Introducing Radical Orthodoxy*, 188.

52 D. J. Hall, *Imaging God: Dominion as Stewardship* (Grand Rapids: Eerdmans, 1986), 124; Joseph Sittler in *Evocations of Grace: Writings on Ecology, Theology, and Ethics*, ed. Steven Bouma-Prediger and Peter Bakken (Grand Rapids: Eerdmans, 2000).

53 Hall, *Imaging God*, 113.

54 Hall, *Imaging God*, 129.

55 D. J. Hall, "The Spirituality of the Covenant: Imaging God, Stewarding Earth," *Perspectives* (December 1988): 11–14.

56 Colin E. Gunton, *The One, the Three and the Many: God, Creation and the Culture of Modernity* (Cambridge: Cambridge University Press, 1993), 15.

57 Gunton, *The One*, 16.

58 Gunton, *The One*, 155.

59 Gunton, *The One*, 18–82.

60 Gunton, *The One*, 193.

61   Wood et al., "Christian Environmentalism," 5.

62   J. Wood, J. Curry, M. Bjelland, S. Bouma-Prediger, and S. Bratton, "Christian Environmentalism: Cosmos, Community, and Place," *Perspectives on Science and Christian Faith* 57, no. 1 (2005): 1–5, 2.

63   Wood et al., "Christian Environmentalism," 5.

64   J. M. Curry and S. McGuire, *Community on Land: Community, Ecology, and the Public Interest* (Boulder, Colo.: Rowman and Littlefield, 2002), 209–34.

65   J. F. Handler, *Law and the Search for Community* (Philadelpha: University of Pennsylvania Press, 1990), 40.

66   James W. Crossley, "Managing Ecosystems for Integrity: Theoretical Considerations for Resource and Environmental Managers," *Society and Natural Resources* 9 (1996): 465.

67   B. J. McCay and S. Jentoft, "From the Bottom Up: Participatory Issues in Fisheries Management," *Society and Natural Resources* 9 (1996): 237–50, 243.

68   Nancy J. Manring, "Alternative Dispute Resolution and Organizational Incentives in the U.S. Forest Service," *Society and Natural Resources* 11 (1998): 75.

69   Anthony Davis and Conner Bailey, "Common in Custom, Uncommon in Advantage: Common Property, Local Elites, and Alternative Approaches to Fisheries Management," *Society and Natural Resources* 9 (1996): 255.

70   G. M. Robinson, "Theory and Practice in Community-Based Environmental Management in Atlantic Canada," paper presented at the International Rural Geography Symposium, St. Mary's University, Halifax, Nova Scotia, 1999, 1.

71   Robinson, "Theory and Practice in Community-Based Environmental Management," 3.

72   Robinson, "Theory and Practice in Community-Based Environmental Management," 3.

73   Robinson, "Theory and Practice in Community-Based Environmental Management," 5.

74   B. Katon, R. S. Pomeroy, L. R. Garces, and A. M. Salamanca, "Fisheries Management of San Salvador Island, Philippines: A Shared Responsibility," *Society and Natural Resources* 12 (1999): 777–95, 792–93.

75   G. Gray and J. Kusel, "Changing the Rules," *American* Forests 103, no. 4 (1998): 27–30, 29–30.

76   Michael P. Dombeck, Christopher A. Wood, and Jack E. Williams, "Focus: Restoring Watersheds, Rebuilding Communities," *American Forests* 103, no. 4 (1998): 26.

77   Bradshaw and Bekoff, "Integrating Humans," 309.

78   Whatmore, *Hybrid Geographies*, 98.

CHAPTER 10

1 "A law [against free trade] . . . interferes with the Wisdom of Divine Providence, and substitutes the law of wicked men for the law of nature" (Richard Cobden, *Speeches by Richard Cobden.* T. Fisher Unwin. 1908. Ed. John Bright and James E. Thorold Roger. Library of Economics and Liberty. 15 April 2008. http://www.econlib.org/library/YPD-Books/Cobden/cbdSPP5.html).

2 Quoted in John Gray, *False Dawn: The Delusions of Global Capitalism* (London: Granta Books, 2002), 68.

3 Gray, *False Dawn*, 68.

4 John Rawston Saul, *The Collapse of Global Capitalism* (London: Atlantic, 2005), 48.

5 Gray, *False Dawn*, 55–56.

6 Gray, *False Dawn*, 194.

7 Saul, *Collapse of Global Capitalism*, 6.

8 Thomas McCarthy, Editor's Foreword to Carl Schmitt, *The Crisis of Parliamentary Democracy,* trans. Ellen Kennedy (Cambridge, Mass.: MIT Press, 1988), viii. He is speaking, well before 9/11, of the tendency "to transform domestic and international adversaries into enemies who represent the forces of evil."

9 Graham Maddox, *Religion and the Rise of Democracy* (London: Routledge, 1996), 166.

10 Marcel Gauchet, *The Disenchantment of the World: A Political History of Religion*, trans. Oscar Burge (Princeton: Princeton University Press, 1997), 3.

11 Yves Lambert, "A Turning Point in Religious Evolution in Europe," *Journal of Contemporary Religion* 19, no. 1 (2004): 29–45, here 37–38.

12 Antonio Negri, *Time for Revolution*, trans. Matteo Mandarini (New York: Continuum, 2003), 41.

13 Carl Schmitt, *Politische Theologie*, Bd.1 (Duncker & Humbolt, 1996), 78.

14 This is ironic given that freedom of the press was one of the central axioms in the democratic defense against the abuse of power and absolute rule. Colin Crouch, *Post-Democracy* (Cambridge: Polity, 2004), 20, 26.

15 Crouch, *Post-Democracy*, 13, 43–46, 78–89.

16 Crouch, *Post-Democracy*, 9.

17 Crouch, *Post-Democracy*, 19.

18 Crouch, *Post-Democracy*, 94–101

19 Alexis de Tocqueville, *Democracy in America*, ed. and tr. Harvey C. Mansfield and Delba Winthrop (Chicago: Chicago University Press, 2000), 418.

20 See Maddox for a contemporary assessment of this democratic condition: "For democracy . . . is a gift of the spiritual realm to the temporal, set free to exercise its autonomous reign in the secular world. But it

bears within it its spiritual origin" (*Religion and the Rise of Democracy*, 219). Although the term "spiritual" is both too nebulous and too new age, this is an important observation when examining any new visibility of religion: a Western spiritual legacy haunts the democratic ideals of freedom, equality, community, and justice. What we may be witnessing, therefore, is a new legitimation for democracy that returns to its religious roots.

21 Maddox, *Religion and the Rise of Democracy*, 419.
22 See William T. Cavanaugh, "The Myth of the State as Savior," in *Theopolitical Imagination*, 9–52 (Edinburgh: T&T Clark, 2003), esp. 40.
23 For the logical progression from Bodin and Hobbes to Locke, see Milbank, *Theology and Social Theory*.
24 Claude Lefort, *Political Forms of Modern Society: Bureaucracy, Democracy, Totalitarianism* (Cambridge, Mass.: MIT Press, 1986), 279.
25 Lefort, *Political Forms of Modern Society*, 305.
26 Aristotle, *Politics* (1280a): "In democracies . . . justice is considered to mean equality. . . . It does mean equality—but equality for those who are equal, for not all are equal."
27 See Schmitt, *Crisis of Parliamentary Democracy*, 24.
28 Harold Laski, *Democracy in Crisis* (London: Allen and Unwin, 1933). "A democracy, in a word, must be led, and in a capitalist democracy the main weapons of leadership are in the hands of capitalists" (76). This is part of Laski's critique of representative institutions.
29 Giorgio Agamben, *State of Exception* (Chicago: University of Chicago Press, 2005).
30 "In material political and sociological praxis, those who have a higher consciousness and who believe themselves to be representatives of this great force will shake off the constraints of a narrow outlook, and will enforce the 'objectively necessary.' Here too their will forces the unfree to be free. In practice that is an educational dictatorship" (Schmitt, *Crisis of Parliamentary Democracy*, 57).
31 George Sorel, *Reflections on Violence*, trans. Jeremy Jennings (Cambridge: Cambridge University Press, 1999), 20–21. He quotes Newman appreciatively: "What imagination does for us is to find a means of stimulating these motive powers; and it does so by providing a supply of objects strong enough to stimulate them" (28).

CHAPTER 11

1 Here I am thinking of Michel de Certeau's focus on the uses that people make of social practices—their tactics. See *The Practice of Everyday Life*, trans. Steven F. Rendall (Berkeley: University of California Press, 1984), xii–xxii, 29–42.
2 David Held et al., *Global Transformations: Politics, Economics, and Culture* (Stanford: Stanford University Press, 1999), 14–21. The Globalization

Index published by *Foreign Policy* magazine and A. T. Kearney Company captures economics (measuring per capita levels of foreign investment and foreign trade) and politics (counting memberships in international organizations, personnel and financial contributions to UN peacekeeping missions, international treaties ratified, and foreign aid transfers). Technology is included in per capita numbers of Internet users, Internet hosts, and secure servers, but as, the next paragraph suggests, these are causes of globalization rather than manifestations of it. Notably absent from this list are measures of global ecological involvement and of cultural connections. See Robert Kudrle, "Globalization by the Numbers: Quantitative Indicators and the Role of Policy," *International Studies Perspectives* 5 (2004): 341–55; and Randolph Kluver and Wayne Fu, "The Cultural Globalization Index," *Foreign Policy* Website, February 2004, http://www.foreignpolicy.com/story/cms.php?story_id=2494 (accessed August 3, 2006).

3   Robert O. Keohane and Joseph S. Nye, "Globalization: What's New? What's Not? And So What?" *Foreign Policy* (Spring 2000),: 104–19; Jan Aart Scholte, *Globalization: A Critical Introduction*, 2nd ed. (New York: Palgrave Macmillan, 2005), 60–62. Scholte offers a comprehensive summary of rival definitions of globalization as well as a comprehensive description of "manifestations of globality" (67–75). His chapter on defining globalization is a seminal contribution in the literature.

4   Scholte, *Globalization*, 61 (emphasis in original).

5   Sarah Lyall, "Hungry for Fresh Recruits, Cult-Like Islamic Groups Know Just When to Pounce," *New York Times* Website, August 17, 2006, http://www.nytimes.com/2006/08/17/world/europe/17converts.html (accessed August 17, 2006). Olivier Roy, *Globalized Islam: The Search for a New Ummah* (New York: Columbia University Press, 2004).

6   Thomas L. Friedman, *The World Is Flat: A Brief History of the Twenty-first Century* (New York: Farrar, Straus and Giroux, 2005), 469. Also see Friedman, *The Lexus and the Olive Tree* (New York: Anchor, 2000), xxii, 104, 105, 109.

7   For a similar definition of economic globalization, see Jagdish Bhagwati, *In Defense of Globalization* (New York: Oxford University Press, 2004), 3.

8   Kudrle, "Globalization by the Numbers," 349.

9   For a strongly stated view, see Michael Hardt and Antonio Negri, *Empire* (Cambridge, Mass.: Harvard University Press, 2000), 31–32. For a contrary view, see Daniel W. Drezner, "Bottom Feeders," *Foreign Policy* 121 (2000): 64–70; and Drezner, "Globalization and Policy Convergence," *International Studies Review* 3 (2001): 53–78.

10 Immanuel Wallerstein, *The Politics of the World-Economy* (New York: Cambridge University Press, 1984), 27–30, 80–82, defines the global

capitalist system to include states that serve the interests of the world economy (the priority of the market and capitalist interests). While there is much truth in this depiction, I think it tends to underestimate the role of human agency and the autonomy of politics from economics. On the opposite side, Robert M. Gilpin, *Global Political Economy* (Princeton: Princeton University Press, 2001), 362–76, argues that states still dominate the world economy. Yet the historical coincidence of global markets and states in the modern period suggest a kind of reciprocal relationship in which economic interests or political interests dominate at different times and in different ways.

11   David B. Abernethy, *The Dynamics of Global Dominance: European Overseas Empires, 1415–1980* (New Haven: Yale University Press, 2000), writes: "Much is made today of globalization as if it were a recent phenomenon. To say this is to ignore the history of most of the world. For most ex-colonial countries a high degree of openness and vulnerability to economic trends elsewhere—including flows of capital and advanced technology—has been a reality for centuries.... Trade patterns between an industrialized north and primary product-producing south are difficult to change in the postcolonial era, in large part because they have deep roots in the formative colonial stage of the globalization process" (385).

12   For slightly different attempts to do just this, see "Measuring Globalization," *Foreign Policy*, May/June 2005, 52; and the review of the *Foreign Policy* index by Kudrle, "Globalization by the Numbers."

13   Rob Jackson, *The Earth Remains Forever: Generations at a Crossroads* (Austin: University of Texas Press, 2002), 69ff..

14   Terence Chea, "China's Air Pollution Reaches U.S. Skies," Associated Press Web site, http://apnews.myway.com/article/20060728/D8J53RV01.html (accessed August 3, 2006).

15   These latter four are part of the Foreign Policy index in "Measuring Globalization."

16   Kluver and Fu, "Cultural Globalization Index." They cite a UNESCO study that estimates that exports of Hollywood films take around 85 percent of the market. See UNESCO, *Survey on National Cinematography: Summary*, http://www.unesco.org/culture/industries/cinema/html_eng/survey.shtml.

17   Bernd Wannenwetsch, *Political Worship: Ethics for Christian Citizens*, trans. Margaret Kohl (New York: Oxford University Press, 2004), stresses how worship creates a public (7).

18   Friedman, *Lexus and the Olive Tree*, xxii.

19   Friedman, *Lexus and the Olive Tree*, 109.

20   For two examples treating globalization as a given, see Max L. Stackhouse, "General Introduction," *God and Globalization*, vol. 1, *Religion and*

the Powers of the Common Life, ed. Stackhouse with Peter L. Paris (Harrisburg, Pa.: Trinity, 2000), 18; and Bob Goudzwaard, *Globalization and the Kingdom of God* (Grand Rapids: Baker, 2001). For critiques of theologies of the natural that start with "the orders of creation," see John Howard Yoder, *The Politics of Jesus: Vicit Agnus Noster* (Grand Rapids: Eerdmans, 1972), 20; and Yoder, *Body Politics: Five Practices of the Christian Community Before the Watching World* (Scottdale, Pa.: Herald, 1992), viii.

21   Samuel Wells, *Improvisation: The Drama of Christian Ethics* (Grand Rapids: Brazos, 2004), 130 (emphasis in original).

22   Wells, *Improvisation*, 131.

23   Alasdair MacIntyre, *After Virtue*, 2nd ed. (Notre Dame, Ind.: University of Notre Dame Press, 1984), 216.

24   D. Stephen Long, *Divine Economy: Theology and the Market* (New York: Routledge, 2000), 232. These are among the "sources for a Christian economy" for Long.

25   D. Stephen Long, "Christian Economy," in *Virtues and Practices in the Christian Tradition: Christian Ethics after MacIntyre*, ed. Nancey Murphy, Brad J. Kallenberg, and Mark Thiessen Nation (Harrisburg, Pa.: Trinity International, 1997), 358.

26   See Peter G. Cobb, "The History of the Christian Year," in *The Study of Liturgy*, ed. Cheslyn Jones, Geoffrey Wainwright, Edward Yarnold, and Paul Bradshaw, 456–72 (New York: Oxford University Press, 1992).

27   Alexander Schmemann, *For the Life of the World: Sacraments and Orthodoxy* (Crestwood, NY: St. Vladimir's Seminary Press, 1973), 56.

28   John-Marie-Roger Tillard, *Flesh of the Church, Flesh of Christ: At the Source of the Ecclesiology of Communion*, trans. Madeleine Beaumont (Collegeville, Minn.: Liturgical, 2001), esp. 10–11, eloquently describes communion together among believers and with Christ as the heart of the church.

29   Rodney Clapp, *A Peculiar People: The Church as Culture in a Post-Christian Society* (Downers Grove, Ill.: InterVarsity, 1996), 188.

30   William T. Cavanaugh, *Torture and Eucharist: Theology, Politics, and the Body of Christ* (Oxford: Blackwell, 1998), 269.

31   Certeau, *Practice of Everyday Life*, 117. Emphasis in original.

32   Certeau, *Practice of Everyday Life*, 118.

33   An allusion to T. S. Eliot, "East Coker," in *Four Quartets*, 23–32 (New York: Harcourt Brace, 1943). The poem starts off with "In my beginning is my end," and concludes with "In my end is my beginning."

34   Some recent theology draws on drama as a way forward beyond narrow literalism and the postliberal theologies of Lindbeck and Frei. See Kevin J. Vanhoozer, *The Drama of Doctrine: A Canonical-Linguistic Approach to Christian Theology* (Louisville: Westminster John Knox, 2005), 16–19. Vanhoozer and others are drawing on the monumental five-volume work of Hans Urs von Balthasar entitled *Theo-Drama:*

Theological Dramatic Theory, trans. Graham Harrison, (San Francisco: Ignatius Press, 1988–1998).

35 This is an important critique against church-centered ethics by Nicholas M. Healy, "Practices and the New Ecclesiology: Misplaced Concreteness?" *International Journal of Systematic Theology* 5 (2003): 287–308.

36 Samuel Wells, *God's Companions: Reimagining Christian Ethics* (Malden, Mass.: Blackwell, 2006), 50.

37 Nicholas M. Healy, *Church, World and the Christian Life: Practical-Prophetic Ecclesiology* (New York: Cambridge University Press, 2000), 185.

38 Wells, *Improvisation*, 55. Subsequent references to Wells are in parentheses in the text.

39 Oliver O'Donovan, *The Desire of the Nations* (New York: Oxford University Press, 1996), 120, points out that in Jesus the kingdom *did* come in his person. Talk of humans helping usher in the kingdom or co-redeem the world often misses the point that we are witnesses to a kingdom that has already come (albeit a not fully present one).

40 The church year is only one of three different stories enacted across different time horizons. The other two are the story of the church gathered in Sunday worship—the framework for Stanley Hauerwas and Samuel Wells, *The Blackwell Companion to Christian Ethics* (Malden, Mass.: Blackwell, 2004)—and the story of scripture, reenacted and interpreted in the church. All of these—and more, including the stories of the worshipers and their leaders—come together in liturgical performance to create a dramatic horizon for story-formed understanding and action.

41 Francis Fukyama, *The End of History and the Last Man* (New York: Free Press, 1992) Friedman's argument that there is no alternative to free-market capitalism also proclaims an end to history.

42 Fleming Rutledge, *The Bible and the New York Times* (Grand Rapids: Eerdmans, 1998), 29.

43 A contextual reading of Revelation suggests that this is the main point of the unveiling (apocalypse): to give the early church hope. Likewise, our challenge is to read it as pastoral comfort. My understanding of these issues was greatly clarified by James William McClendon Jr., *Systematic Theology*: vol. 2, *Doctrine* (Nashville: Abingdon, 1994), 69–102. Interestingly, eschatology is the first doctrine McClendon explicates, but he does not link it to the focus on the last things at the beginning of Advent.

44 Friedman, *Lexus and the Olive Tree*, 109.

45 Interestingly, as of mid-2006, China had taken neither of these steps.

46 Friedman, *Lexus and the Olive Tree*, 120.

47 G. B. Trudeau, *Doonesbury*, November 26, 1996, available at http://www.amureprints.com/img1/doonesbury/1996/db961126.gif (accessed November 20, 2005).

48   Long, "Christian Economy," 357.

49   Friedman, *Lexus and the Olive Tree*, 53–60, 112–42.

50   Long, "Christian Economy," 357.

51   Christopher B. Barrett, "Markets, Social Norms, and Governments in the Service of Environmentally Sustainable Economic Development: The Pluralistic Stewardship Approach," *Christian Scholar's Review* 33 (2000): 440.

52   See Iain Wallace's analysis in chap. 6 of this volume. Also see Lauren Winner, *Mudhouse Sabbath* (Brewster, Mass.: Paraclete, 2003), 24–25, citing Barbara Kingsolver, "Lily's Chickens," in *Small Wonder: Essays*, 109–30 (New York: HarperCollins, 2002).. Kingsolver points out that global food transportation "guzzles some serious gas."

53   After the first draft of this essay was written, I discovered Orthodox theologians making just this argument. Vigen Guroian, *Ethics after Christendom: Toward an Ecclesial Christian Ethic* (Grand Rapids: Eerdmans, 1994), 155–74; and Kenneth Paul Wesche, "ΘΕΩΣΙΣ in Freedom and Love: The Patristic Vision," in *The Consuming Passion: Christianity and the Culture of Consumption*, ed. Rodney Clapp, 118–28 (Downers Grove, Ill.: InterVarsity, 1998).

54   The theme of Jesus' miracles as signs of his glory, recognized by some but not others, is of course an important theme in John's Gospel. See John 4:54; 6:14; 9:16; and 11:47. The Year 2 *Book of Common Prayer* Daily Office readings after Epiphany bring together Genesis and the Gospel of John.

55   Brian Fikkert, "Response," in Bob Goudzwaard, *Globalization and the Kingdom of God* (Grand Rapids: Baker Books, 2001), 72. Sider's estimate cited in Fikkert, "Response," 67.

56   Ted C. Fishman, *China, Inc.: How the Rise of the Next Superpower Challenges America and the World* (New York: Scribner, 2005), 154, citing Peter S. Goodman and Phillip P. Pan, "Chinese Workers Pay for Wal-Mart's Low Prices," *Washington Post*, February 8, 2004.

57   A recent study sponsored by Wal-Mart and conducted by eighteen economists found that Wal-Mart caused a decline in nominal wages (not inflation-adjusted) of 2.2 percent between 1985 and 2004, but this was offset by decreasing prices for consumer goods, which led to a 0.9 percent increase in real disposable income. Anne D'Innocenzio, "Wal-Mart Session Addresses Critics," *Repository* (Canton, Ohio), November 5, 2005, B-6.

58   Friedman, *World Is Flat*, 215.

59   Tom Beaudoin, *Consuming Faith: Integrating Who We Are with What We Buy* (Lanham, Md.: Sheed and Ward, 2003), offers a lively review of how identity is defined by brands we consume.

60 Keohane and Nye point out that World War II and the Cold War were high points of military globalization, defined as transcontinental contact between militaries.

61 Among others, see Stephen D. Krasner, "State Power and the Structure of International Trade," *World Politics* 20 (1976): 317–47; Robert Gilpin, *War and Change in World Politics* (New York: Cambridge University Press, 1981); and G. John Ikenberry, *After Victory: Institutions, Strategic Restraint, and the Rebuilding of Order after Major Wars* (Princeton: Princeton University Press, 2001), 163–214.

62 Friedman, *The Lexus and the Olive Tree*, 381–82, 463–68. Friedman writes, "America truly is the ultimate benign hegemon and reluctant enforcer" (467). Also see, among many others, Michael Mandelbaum, *The Case for Goliath: How America Acts as the World's Government in the Twenty-First Century* (New York: PublicAffairs, 2005); and Niall Ferguson, *Colossus: The Rise and Fall of the American Empire* (New York: Penguin, 2004). Ferguson is an unabashed supporter of an American empire in Iraq, Afghanistan, and elsewhere as a stabilizing force, following the precedent of the British Empire. Significantly, there seems to be a convergence here with the radical analysis of Hardt and Negri in *Empire*.

63 Yoder, *Politics of Jesus*, 45–48.

64 Brian L. Walsh and Sylvia C. Keesmaat, *Colossians Remixed: Subverting the Empire* (Downers Grove, Ill.: InterVarsity, 2004), esp. 159–68.

65 Martin Wolf, *Why Globalization Works* (New Haven, Conn.: Yale University Press, 2003), 173–219; Jay R. Mandle, *Globalization and the Poor* (New York: Cambridge University Press, 2003), 9–23; Tomas Larsson, *The Race to the Top: The Real Story of Globalization* (Washington, D.C.: Cato Institute, 2001), 53–60; and Jagdish Bhagwati, *In Defense of Globalization* (New York: Oxford University Press, 2004), 122–34 and 228–39.

66 David Brooks, "Good News about Poverty," *The New York Times* Web site (November 27, 2004), http://www.nytimes.com/2004/11/27/opinion/27brooks.html (accessed November 27, 2004).

67 E.g., see Joseph Stiglitz and Shahid Yusuf, eds. *Rethinking the East Asian Miracle* (New York: Oxford University Press, 2001); and Paul Kennedy, *Preparing for the Twenty-First Century* (New York: Random House, 1993), 193–202. Public investment in education and health care—as well as promotion of private savings and exports, rather than classic free trade—seems to have been key.

68 William McGurn, "Pulpit Economics," *First Things* 122 (2002): 21–25.

69 "Not by Their Bootstraps Alone," *Economist*, May 12, 2001, 52.

70 See Scott Thomas, *The Global Resurgence of Religion and the Transformation of International Relations* (New York: Palgrave Macmillan, 2005), 238–42.

71 See Paul S. Mills, "Globalization and the World Economy: For Richer for Poorer, for Better or Worse?" *Cambridge Papers* 14 (2005), http://www.

jubilee-centre.org/online_documents/Globalizationandtheworlde-conomy.htm (accessed June 8, 2006).

72   William T. Cavanaugh, "The Myth of Globalization as Catholicity," in *Theopolitical Imagination* (New York: T&T Clark, 2002), 119–20.

73   Tillard, *Flesh of the Church*, 79.

74   Cavanaugh, "Myth of Globalization as Catholicity," 121.

75   Yoder, *Body Politics*, 20–21.

76   Benjamin Barber, *Jihad vs. McWorld* (New York: Random House, 1992); Samuel P. Huntington, *The Clash of Civilizations and the Remaking of World Order* (New York: Touchstone, 1996).

77   Yoder, *Body Politics*, 2; Clapp, *Peculiar People*, 80–81.

78   Cavanaugh, *Torture and Eucharist*, 269.

79   Clapp, *Peculiar People*, 116.

80   Goudzwaard, *Globalization and the Kingdom of God*, 19–20.

81   See Jerry Mander and Edward Goldsmith, eds., *The Case against the Global Economy: And for a Turn to the Local* (San Francisco: Sierra Club, 1996).

82   Larsson, *Race to the Top*, 136. Also see Philippe Legrain, "Cultural Globalization is Not Americanization," *Chronicle of Higher Education*, May 9, 2003, B7–B10.

83   Friedman, *The Lexus and the Olive Tree*, 295–97 claims to have coined the term "glocalization," but credit belongs to Roland Robertson, "Globalization: Time-Space and Homogeneity-Heterogeneity," in *Global Modernities*, ed. Mike Featherstone, Scott Lash, and Roland Robertson (Thousand Oaks, Calif.: Sage, 1995).

84   Andrew F. Walls, *The Missionary Movement in Christian History: Studies in the Transmission of Faith* (Maryknoll, N.Y.: Orbis, 1996); 7–29; Philip Jenkins, *The Next Christendom: The Coming of Global Christianity* (New York: Oxford University Press, 2002).

CHAPTER 12

1   Wendell Berry, "The Gift of Gravity," in *Collected Poems 1957–1982* (San Francisco: North Point, 1984), 257.

2   In this essay I treat postmodernity as the intensification of several of modernity's most telling cultural innovations. I realize that defining modernity/postmodernity has become a highly contentious issue, but do not view this essay as the proper forum to sort out the relevant concerns. My understanding of this debate has been most informed by Steven Best and Doug Kellner, *The Postmodern Turn* (New York: Guilford, 1997); David Harvey, *The Condition of Postmodernity* (Cambridge: Blackwell, 1990); Anthony Giddens, *The Consequences of Modernity* (Stanford: Stanford University Press, 1990); Zygmunt Bauman, *Liquid Modernity* (Cambridge: Polity, 2000); Albert Borgmann, *Crossing the Postmodern Divide* (Chicago: University of Chicago Press, 1992); and Adam

Seligman, *Modernity's Wager: Authority, the Self, and Transcendence* (Princeton: Princeton University Press, 2000).

3   Zygmunt Bauman, *Globalization: The Human Consequences* (New York: Columbia University Press, 1998), 25. Bauman describes how the movable, flexible nature of markets turns all of us into tourists or vagabonds who can carry out little more than a superficial and ephemeral connection with reality. "There ought to be a proviso 'until further notice' attached to any oath of loyalty and any commitment. It is but the volatility, the in-built temporality of all engagements, that truly counts; it counts more than the commitment itself, which is anyway not allowed to outlast the time necessary for consuming the object of desire (or, rather, the time sufficient for the desirability of that object to wane)" (81). It is precisely the superficiality of our relationships that leads to one of the paradoxes of globalization: the time that creates our greatest access to the far reaches of the world at the same time (owing to economic packaging and technological framing) makes difficult a genuine or deep encounter with others.

4   See Rowan Williams, "On Being Creatures," in *On Christian Theology* (Oxford: Blackwell, 2000), and my own *The Paradise of God: Renewing Religion in an Ecological Age* (New York: Oxford University Press, 2003), especially chap. 2, for a description of the implications that follow from our inability to see ourselves and the world as God's creation.

5   Karl Barth, *Dogmatics in Outline* (New York: Harper & Row, 1959), 20.

6   A great number of scientific organizations now exist that are devoted to making scientific research available to a wide public. A good place to begin is with the Intergovernmental Panel on Climate Change (www.ipcc.ch) and the Union of Concerned Scientists (www.ucsusa.org). Excellent, up-to-date resources on the wide range of environmental destruction are also available from the Worldwatch Institute (www.worldwatch.org).

7   For a wide range of essays describing the effects of globalization on local economies see *The Case against the Global Economy: And for a Turn to the Local*, ed. Jerry Mander and Edward Goldsmith (San Francisco: Sierra Club, 1996). As regards food more specifically, see the essays in *The Paradox of Plenty: Hunger in a Bountiful World*, ed. Douglas H. Boucher (Oakland: Food First, 1999).

8   For a description of the numerous harmful effects of industrial agriculture see Andrew Kimbrell, ed., *Fatal Harvest: The Tragedy of Industrial Agriculture* (Washington, D.C.: Island, 2002). An excellent short summary can be found in Frederick Kirschenmann's essay "The Current State of Agriculture: Does It Have a Future?" in *The Essential Agrarian Reader: The Future of Culture, Community, and the Land*, ed. Norman Wirzba, 101–20 (Lexington: University Press of Kentucky, 2003).

9   There is a growing literature on the "New Agrarianism" that includes
     The Art of the Commonplace: The Agrarian Essays of Wendell Berry, ed. Nor-
     man Wirzba (Washington, D.C.: Counterpoint, 2002); *The New Agrari-
     anism: Land, Culture, and the Community of Life*, ed. Eric T. Freyfogle
     (Washington, D.C.: Island, 2001); and *The Essential Agrarian Reader: The
     Future of Culture, Community, and the Land*, ed. Norman Wirzba (Lexing-
     ton: University Press of Kentucky, 2003). The leading agrarian writer
     of our time is Wendell Berry. Among his many works, readers should
     begin with *The Unsettling of America: Culture and Agriculture, The Gift of
     Good Land, Home Economics, What Are People For?* and *The Way of Ignorance*.

10   For a developed exegetical treatment of God's relation to creation see
     Terence E. Fretheim, *God and World in the Old Testament: A Relational The-
     ology of Creation* (Nashville: Abingdon, 2005).

11   In *The Omnivore's Dilemma: A Natural History of Four Meals* (New York: Pen-
     guin, 2006) Pollan gives eloquent testimony to the manifold ways in
     which industrial eating obscures the many biological and social rela-
     tionships that tie us to the earth and each other. Thoughtless, ignorant
     eating, in other words, renders a world without gravity and grace.

12   We should recall that the Hebrew word for grace (*hēn*) carries the con-
     notation of the life-giving womb. Acts 17:28 continues this maternal,
     womblike imagery as Paul endorses the words of the Greek poet Ara-
     tus: "For 'In him we live and move and have our being': as even some of
     your own poets have said, 'For we too are his offspring.'"

13   Nicholas Lash, *Believing Three Ways in the One God: A Reading of the Apostle's
     Creed* (Notre Dame, Ind.: University of Notre Dame Press, 1992), 104.

14   The reference is to Wendell Berry's Sabbath poem "To Sit and Look at
     Light-Filled Leaves" (from *A Timbered Choir: The Sabbath Poems 1979–1997*
     [Washington, D.C.: Counterpoint, 1998], 8), where Berry imagines cre-
     ation before the fall.

> To sit and look at light-filled leaves
> May let us see, or seem to see,
> Far backward as through clearer eyes
> To what unsighted hope believes:
> The blessed conviviality
> That sang Creation's seventh sunrise,
>
> Time when the Maker's radiant sight
> Made radiant every thing He saw,
> And every thing He saw was filled
> With perfect joy and life and light.
> His perfect pleasure was sole law:
> No pleasure had become self-willed.

For all His creatures were His pleasures
And their whole pleasure was to be
What He made them; they sought no gain
Or growth beyond their proper measures,
Nor longed for change or novelty.
The only new thing could be pain.

15 David Bentley Hart, *The Beauty of the Infinite: The Aesthetics of Christian Truth* (Grand Rapids: Eerdmans, 2003), 253. Given the primacy and importance of delight, it is highly indicative that the time of modernity is characterized by widespread boredom, and by the inability to find our world (most basically our food) delectable. For a helpful analysis on boredom as a distinguishing characteristic of modernity, see Michael Hanby's "The Culture of Death, The Ontology of Boredom, and the Resistance of Joy," *Communio* 31 (2004): 184–88.

16 I have developed this theme in *Living the Sabbath: Discovering the Rhythms of Rest and Delight* (Grand Rapids: Brazos, 2006).

17 Bruce V. Foltz, "Nature's Other Side: The Demise of Nature and the Phenomenology of Givenness," in *Rethinking Nature: Essays in Environmental Philosophy*, ed. Bruce V. Foltz and Robert Frodeman, 330–41 (Bloomington: Indiana University Press, 2004). This modern view is in striking contrast with the view of several early church fathers who maintained that creatures are a "pure passivity before free and inexplicable grace." Though Creator and creature are separate, creatures are what they are, are at all, only because of their openness to God. For a description of this theme, particularly as it is summarized and developed in the thought of Maximus Confessor, see Hans Urs von Balthasar, *Cosmic Liturgy: The Universe According to Maximus the Confessor* (San Francisco: Ignatius, 2003), esp. 137–54.

18 Bronislaw Szerszynski, *Nature, Technology and the Sacred* (Oxford: Blackwell, 2005).

19 Philip Sherard, *The Rape of Man and Nature* (Ipswich: Golgonooza, 1987), 92.

20 Dietrich Bonhoeffer, *Letters and Papers from Prison*, ed. Eberhard Bethge (New York: Macmillan, 1971), 369–70.

21 Quoted by Larry Rasmussen in *Earth Community Earth Ethics* (Maryknoll, N.Y.: Orbis, 1996), 303–4.

22 This passage from *A Week on the Concord and Merrimack Rivers* is quoted in David M. Robinson's excellent study *Natural Life: Thoreau's Worldly Transcendentalism* (Ithaca, N.Y.: Cornell University Press, 2004), 1.

23 Wendell Berry, "In Distrust of Movements," *In the Presence of Fear* (Great Barrington, Mass.: Orion Society, 2001), 38, 37.

24 Vaclav Smil, *Energies: An Illustrated Guide to the Biosphere and Civilization* (Cambridge, Mass.: MIT Press, 1999), x.

25 Wendell Berry, "Window Poems 19," in *Collected Poems*, 88.

26 Wendell Berry, "A Native Hill," in *Art of the Commonplace*, 23 (emphasis in original). See also my essay "Placing the Soul: An Agrarian Philosophical Principle," in *Essential Agrarian Reader*.

27 Wendell Berry, "Two Economies," in *Art of the Commonplace*, 233.

28 Thomas Traherne, *Centuries of Meditations* II, 62, in *Poems, Centuries, and Three Thanksgivings*, ed. Anne Ridler (Oxford: Oxford University Press, 1966), 242.

29 Wendell Berry, "The Mad Farmer, Flying the Flag of Rough Branch, Secedes from the Union," from *Entries: Poems* (Washington, D.C.: Counterpoint, 1997), 39–40.

30 Berry, "Mad Farmer," 39–40.

Contributors

Editor

James K. A. Smith is associate professor of philosophy at Calvin College in Grand Rapids, Michigan. As specialist in philosophical theology and contemporary French philosophy, Smith works at the intersection of philosophy, religion, politics, and science. He is the author of several books, including *Speech and Theology: Language and the Logic of Incarnation* (Routledge, 2002), *Introducing Radical Orthodoxy* (Baker Academic, 2004), *Jacques Derrida: Live Theory* (Continuum, 2005), and *Who's Afraid of Postmodernism? Taking Derrida, Lyotard, and Foucault to Church* (Baker Academic, 2006). He is also the editor of *The Hermeneutics of Charity: Interpretation, Selfhood, and Postmodern Faith* (Brazos Press, 2004) and *Radical Orthodoxy and the Reformed Tradition* (Baker Academic, 2005).

Contributors

Luke Bretherton is senior lecturer in theology and politics at King's College London. He has worked with a variety of faith-based NGOs, mission organizations, and churches in a wide range of cultural contexts both in the United Kingdom and elsewhere (notably East Africa, Central and Eastern Europe, and Russia). He is the author of *Hospitality as Holiness: Christian Witness amid Moral Diversity* (Ashgate, 2006), and coedited a volume entitled *Remembering Our Future: Explorations in Deep Church* (Paternoster, 2007). He is currently working on a book on Christianity and different aspects of contemporary politics as well as an Arts & Humanities Research Council funded project on Christianity, urban politics, and pursuit of the common good that focuses on broad-based community organizing as a case study.

Janel Curry is dean for research and scholarship and professor of geography at Calvin College. She holds a Ph.D. from the University of Minnesota. Dr. Curry has held numerous leadership positions in the area of rural geography, including being chair of the board of the Leopold Center for Sustainable Agriculture at Iowa State University and chair of the Rural Geography Specialty Group of the Association of American Geographers. Dr. Curry has published on the topic of community and natural resources in journals such as the *Annals of the Association of American Geographers*, *The Geographic Review*, *Agriculture and Human Values*, and *Society and Natural Resources*.

Michael S. Horton is professor of theology and apologetics at Westminster Seminary in California, where he specializes in systematic and historical theology. His work has appeared in journals such as the *International Journal of Systematic Theology*, *Westminster Theological Journal*, *Books & Culture*, and *Modern Reformation*. He is editor of several books, including *A Confessing Theology for Postmodern Times* and the author of over a dozen books, including most recently *Covenant and Salvation* (Westminster John Knox).

Mebs Kanji is assistant professor of political science at the University of Calgary. His research interests are in the areas of Canadian and comparative politics, focusing mainly on the study of values and value diversity, and their implications for social cohesion, political support, and democratic governance. He is coeditor of *Priming Public Opinion Research: A Sustained and Systematic Approach*, 2nd ed. (ITP Nelson, 2006).

Ronald A. Kuipers is assistant professor of the philosophy of religion at the Institute for Christian Studies in Toronto. He recently completed a Social Sciences and Humanities Research Council of Canada postdoctoral fellowship at the University of Toronto's department of political science. His research focuses on those areas where issues in the philosophy of religion intersect with contemporary social and political thought on matters of judgment, criticism, and secularization. He is the author of *Critical Faith: Toward a Renewed Understanding of Religious Life and Its Public Accountability*, and has published numerous articles in journals and anthologies.

John Milbank is professor of religion, politics, and ethics at the University of Nottingham, England, having previously taught at Lancaster, Cambridge, and the University of Virginia. One of the leading figures associated with radical orthodoxy, Milbank is the author of *Theology and Social Theory* (2nd ed., Blackwell), *The Word Made Strange* (Blackwell), *Being Reconciled* (Routledge), and *The Suspended Middle: Henri de Lubac and the Debate Concerning the Supernatural* (Eerdmans). Along with Graham Ward and Catherine Pickstock, he is editor of the Radical Orthodoxy series published by Routledge.

J. David Richardson is Gerald B. and Daphna Cramer Professor of Global Affairs at Syracuse University. He is a research associate of the National Bureau of Economic Research, Cambridge, Massachusetts, and a senior fellow at the Institute for International Economics, Washington, D.C. From 1970 to 1991 he was on the economics faculty of the University of Wisconsin, Madison. He has also taught on a visiting basis at the University of Michigan, the University of Notre Dame, Wheaton College (Illinois), and the Foreign Service Institute of the U.S. Department of State. He specializes in empirical research on border policies under imperfect competition, on regional trade, and on trade and labor-market outcomes, with a focus on the United States. He has authored two books, coedited nine books, and written numerous other monographs, book chapters, and papers for professional journals.

Scott Waalkes is associate professor of international politics at Malone College, where he has taught since 1998. During the 2004–2005 academic year, he was on sabbatical as a Fulbright Scholar in the Middle Eastern nation of Bahrain. His B.A. is in political science from Calvin, and his M.A. and Ph.D. in foreign affairs from the University of Virginia. The author of several articles and numerous book reviews in international studies, he is currently writing a book on Christian responses to globalization.

Iain Wallace was born in the United Kingdom and educated at the Universities of Oxford and Bristol. Iain Wallace has been on the faculty of the department of geography, Carleton University, Ottawa, Canada, since 1970. His background is in economic geography, and recent research has focused on processes of globalization, particularly the relationship between economic growth and the natural environment. His publications include *A Geography of the Canadian Economy* (Oxford University Press, 2002) and *The Global Economic System* (Routledge, 1990), and articles and book chapters on the global agri-food system, the Canadian mineral industry, and Canadian environmentalism. He is a member of the Anglican Church of Canada and has published papers addressing the relationship between geographical and social theory and biblical theology, most recently in *Christian Scholar's Review* (2002).

Graham Ward is professor of contextual theology and ethics at the University of Manchester. His previous books include *Barth, Derrida, and the Language of Theology* (1995), *Theology and Contemporary Critical Theory* (1996), *The Postmodern God* (1997), *The Blackwell Companion ot the Postmodern God* (2001), *True Religion* (2002), *Cultural Transformation and Religious Practice* (2004) and *Christ and Culture* (2005). He is the former executive editor of *Literature and Theology*.

Norman Wirzba chairs the philosophy department at Georgetown College, Kentucky, teaching in the areas of the history of philosophy, environmental philosophy and ethics, and Christian theology. He is author of *The Paradise of God: Renewing Religion in an Ecological Age* (Oxford) and editor of *The Essential Agrarian Reader: The Future of Culture, Community, and the Land*, (with Bruce Ellis Benson) *The Phenomenology of Prayer* (Fordham University Press), and *Living the Sabbath: Discovering the Rhythms of Rest and Delight* (Brazos). He is also coeditor of *Transforming Philosophy and Religion: Love's Wisdom* (Indiana University Press).

Lambert Zuidervaart is professor of philosophy at the Institute for Christian Studies and a member of graduate faculties in philosophy and theology at the University of Toronto. Zuidervaart is currently conducting research into theories of truth and theories of globalization, with an emphasis on German philosophy from Kant through Habermas. He is the author of *Social Philosophy after Adorno* (Cambridge University Press, 2007); *Artistic Truth: Aesthetics, Discourse, and Imaginative Disclosure* (Cambridge University Press, 2004); and *Adorno's*

Aesthetic Theory (MIT Press, 1991), coauthor of *Dancing in the Dark: Youth, Popular Culture, and the Electronic Media* (Eerdmans, 1991), and coeditor of *The Arts, Community, and Cultural Democracy* (St. Martin's Press, 2000), *The Semblance of Subjectivity: Essays in Adorno's Aesthetic Theory* (MIT Press, 1997), and *Pledges of Jubilee: Essays on the Arts and Culture* (Eerdmans, 1995).

Index of Names

✳

Adams, John, 31
Addams, Jane, 171, 172
Adenauer, Konrad, 173, 177
Adorno, Theodor, 99–115,
  119, 279n17, 281n6, 281n7,
  282n24, 282n25, 282n26,
  283n28, 283n30, 283n32,
  283n33, 284n34
Agamben, Georgio, 143, 153,
  155, 156, 216, 293n65, 293n67
Alighieri, Dante, 24,
  148, 149, 291n30
Aquinas, Thomas, 24, 26,
  29, 33, 34, 247, 268n20,
  272n3, 272n10, 297n6
Arendt, Hannah, 153, 155–56, 158
Aristotle, 19, 26, 34, 149, 214, 216
Asad, Talal, 41–42, 259n2,
  265n38, 271n36
Augustine, 20, 21, 23, 29, 31,
  33, 34, 48, 51–57, 62, 148,
  151–52, 268n20, 270n27,
  272n3, 273n24, 274n39

Ballanche, Pierre-Simon, 32
Barth, Karl, 51, 157, 158, 162,
  242, 247, 273n19, 291n29
Bauman, Zygmunt, 210, 319n3
Baumeister, Thomas, 101
Benhabib, Seyla, 102
Bensel, Richard F., 172–73
Bentham, Jeremy, 149
Berger, Peter, 8, 9, 10, 11, 70,
  195, 260, 263, 264, 266, 286
Berry, Wendell, 252–58,
  320n9, 320n14
Blair, Tony, 209, 213
Blank, Rebecca M., 166
Bodin, Jean, 149, 311n23
Bonhoeffer, Dietrich, 250, 251
Braun, Bruce, 130
Bryan, William Jennings,
  171–72, 204, 304n42
Buchez, Pierre, 32
Bush, George W., 209,
  213, 262n15, 272n5

Subject Index

✳